C000229062

Nelson's VICTORY

Nelson's VICTORY

250 Years of War and Peace

BRIAN LAVERY

Seaforth
PUBLISHING

Copyright © Brian Lavery 2015

First published in Great Britain in 2015 by
Seaforth Publishing,
Pen & Sword Books Ltd,
47 Church Street,
Barnsley S70 2AS

www.seaforthpublishing.com

British Library Cataloguing in Publication Data
A catalogue record for this book is available from the British Library

ISBN 978 1 84832 232 5

All rights reserved. No part of this publication may be reproduced or transmitted in any form or by any means, electronic or mechanical, including photocopying, recording, or any information storage and retrieval system, without prior permission in writing of both the copyright owner and the above publisher.

The right of Brian Lavery to be identified as the author of this work has been asserted by him in accordance with the Copyright, Designs and Patents Act 1988.

Typeset and designed by Roger Daniels

Printed by Printworks Global Ltd, London & Hong Kong

CONTENTS

INTRODUCTION & ACKNOWLEDGEMENTS

HMS *Victory* was launched, or rather floated out, from a dry-dock at Chatham on 7 May 1765. Now preserved at Portsmouth, she is perhaps the most famous ship in the world, and certainly the most famous vessel still extant. Nelson's career is in a sense parallel to that of the *Victory*; both started their seafaring life at Chatham in the third quarter of the eighteenth century, and his cult continues long after his death, still in parallel with the *Victory*.

Many books have been written about HMS *Victory*, mostly focussing on the two years when she was Nelson's flagship, or on the single afternoon of the Battle of Trafalgar, though a notable exception was Kenneth Fenwick's work of 1959 that sought to tell the full story of the ship since she first took to the water 250 years ago. A new audience and new research since Fenwick's time offers scope for a fresh appreciation of the great ship. So this present work contains some surprises: that the ship was almost wrecked on her launch, that diplomacy conducted on board her played a crucial role in causing Napoleon's invasion of Russia in 1912, and it is said that in 1914 Kaiser Wilhelm set the First World War in motion on a desk made from her timbers. The book tells the story of Horatio Nelson, who was born a few weeks before his most famous ship was ordered, and whose career paralleled hers in many ways. It does not ignore the Battle of Trafalgar, and indeed it offers some new material on the battle and the campaign that led up to it. But it says much more about the other lives of the ship, which at different times was a flagship, a fighting ship, a prison hospital ship, a training ship for officers and boys, a floating courtroom, a signal school, a regional tourist attraction and a national icon. It looks at the ship through many eyes, including Queen Victoria, admirals, midshipmen and ordinary seamen, and Beatrix Potter who visited as a girl.

The career of the *Victory* reflected the changes in the navy and society throughout her long history. She was an expression of power in the long wars with France. Like Nelson himself, she had low points; she became a prison ship before being rescued and rebuilt and was often neglected while afloat in Portsmouth Harbour. She was an early training ship for naval boys and then became the Royal Navy's first signal school in the age of electricity and early radio, which was highly appropriate for the ship that sent the most famous naval signal of all time. She lay in Portsmouth Harbour as the navy changed from wood to iron and steel, from sail to steam and to long-range shell-firing guns. She literally collided with the modern age in 1903 when she was hit by the battleship *Neptune*. In 1922, she entered dry dock to become a pioneering preserved ship, an example to many other vessels around the world. She continued to serve as an inspiration during the Second World War, which she survived despite being hit by a German bomb.

The *Victory* is today very much a shrine to Lord Nelson but this book also deals with her designers, the dockyard workers who built her, and the thousands of men and boys who sailed, fought or trained onboard her. Though life in the ship was almost entirely masculine, there is evidence that women served on board her in the 1790s.

Though the *Victory* has always been very much a British icon, she has an international dimension. Though British oak was revered material for shipbuilding, much of her original timber came from the Baltic and in later years she was restored using teak from India and iroko from West Africa. At least seventy-five of the men who fought on board her at Trafalgar came from outside Great Britain, including some from the United States, West Indies, Africa, Netherlands, Sweden and even four Frenchmen. The *Victory* played a key role in setting up the alliance, including Russia, Prussia and Sweden, which led to the downfall of Napoleon's empire.

Many people are due acknowledgments for their help: in the longer term, my late friends David Lyon and Colin White; former colleagues in the National Maritime Museum including Roger Knight, Chris Ware, Pieter van de Merwe and Simon Stephens; colleagues during twenty years on the Victory Advisory Technical Committee, especially the successive chairmen Alan McGowan and Jonathan Coad, as well as George Lawrence, Peter Goodwin; Jeremy Michell and Lawrie Phillips, as well as successive captains of the *Victory*, and the current curator Andrew Baines. I would like to thank the staffs of the National Museum of the Royal Navy and the Royal Marines Museum, the London Library, the National Archives and the National Maritime Museum, and Jenny Wraight of the Naval Historical Branch. Special acknowledgements are also due to Lord De Saumarez of Guernsey, Christer Hägg for Swedish sources and Rachel Magowan for German contacts; also to Julian Mannering of Seaforth for co-ordinating the publication.

This book originated when Richard Holdsworth and Alex Patterson of Chatham Historic dockyard asked me to be guest curator for an exhibition to commemorate 250 years since the *Victory*'s launch, and I am grateful to them for the opportunity, and for the paths it led me into. But that is not the end of the story for the *Victory* is likely to remain as the centre of attraction at Portsmouth Dockyard far into the future. With her new management and the beginning of a long-term repair, there are still many issues to be resolved but her history has not come to an end.

VICTORY

1 WAR FOR THE WORLD

A Meeting of the Board

Their Lordships of the Admiralty gathered in the Boardroom as usual in the morning of 13 December 1758, after travelling through the bustling and often lawless streets of London. It was not a particularly cold morning for the time of year, the temperature did not drop below 40° Fahrenheit (4° Celsius) and the weather was fair, but their lordships probably welcomed the heat coming from the marble fireplace, perhaps lit by the 'necessary woman' or housekeeper, Mrs Clack. The lords took their seats round a long table. At one end of the room stood a grand cabinet with bookcases and a globe in the centre. Above that was a wind indicator, made in 1749 by the marine artist and ship's carpenter John Cleveley.[1] Currently, it showed a breeze from the south-west and reminding their lordships that their great fleet of nearly 400 ships was totally dependent on natural forces for its movement. Above the fireplace were rolled maps covering all the seas where the Royal Navy operated, while the winter sunlight entered through a row of windows on the other side, highlighting an intricate carving of nautical instruments by Grinling Gibbons. In the 1740s their Lordships had ordered a huge model of a first-rate ship of the line for the Boardroom, 'japanned and varnished', fully rigged with guns and elaborate decorations. It is not clear if it was still there in 1758, but if it was it might remind them of the glories of sea power as well as its hazards – for the ship on which it was based, the *Victory* of 1737, had gone down with all hands, more than 1,100 lives, in 1744.[2]

The Admiralty Boardroom as drawn by Rowlandson and Pugin in 1808. The collaboration is not entirely successful in that Rowlandson's figures are not to the same scale as the room and furniture. The First Lord is nearest the viewer, the assistant secretary is reading out a paper at the other end of the table.

(© National Maritime Museum, Greenwich, London, PU1358)

Previous page: The *Victory*'s magnificent stern.

(Jonathan Eastland/Ajax).

Lord George Anson sat at the head of the table facing the globe and wind indicator. At the age of sixty-one, he was distinguished in appearance but corpulent in a way that was becoming unfashionable in the second half of the eighteenth century. He was not the kind of First Lord of the Admiralty who 'never went to sea', he had sailed more of the oceans of the world than almost anyone, including a famous four-year circumnavigation that had made him rich with the capture of a Spanish treasure galleon. He had also succeeded in a major battle, which was quite rare at the time. He knew all about the faults of the navy, including over-rigid ship design, brutal manning practices, bad relations with the army and corruption. He did not avoid favouritism, those who had performed well under him found themselves in positions of great authority, but he was a good judge of character and they served their country well. Though he tended to rely on others for political skills and oratory, Anson had a great presence and a vision for the navy that would create the force later deployed with great effect by Nelson. Anson was famously taciturn, he said little and rarely put pen to paper so we know very little about his thoughts.

He main assistant on the board was another admiral, the well-balanced and literate Edward Boscawen, but he was absent that morning, perhaps resting after receiving the thanks of the House of Commons for capturing the French base of Louisbourg at the mouth of the St Lawrence River. The only other members present were Dr George Hay, a clever lawyer of Scottish descent who was a friend of the actor Garrick and the satirist Hogarth and could speak well in the House of Commons; and Thomas Hunter, son of a governor of the colony of New York who was a hard-working and efficient administrator, 'a very sensible, able man' according to the prime minister. The fourth man sat at the opposite end of the table. He was the Secretary to the Admiralty, John Cleveland. Though he was not without his political interests, he held his office permanently and had been in the department since 1746. With numerous fees and perquisites, his regular income was much larger than any of the lords though, unlike a naval officer, he did not have the opportunity to become rich through prize money. Cleveland controlled much of the business of the department, but on the morning of the 13th his role was to advise the board and take minutes. Despite the obvious talents of his colleagues, Anson was the only one with the naval knowledge and vision to decide on the main business of the morning, to build new ships for the navy. He, above all people, knew the strengths and weaknesses of the different types, of the role of two- and three-decker ships of the line and the new-fangled frigates.

Lord George Anson painted by Sir Joshua Reynolds around 1761.

(© National Maritime Museum, Greenwich, London, BHC2516).

Trade, Navy and Empire

The British had already fought four years of war with France, or more if informal hostilities before the official declaration are taken into account. It was part of a global struggle between the two countries lasting more than a century. At this stage, the wars were largely about trade and empire, which demanded both a strong Royal Navy and an extensive merchant marine. Erasmus Phillips wrote in 1725:

> Trade is to the Body Politck as Blood is to human Body, it diffuses itself by the minutest Canals into every part of a Nation, and gives Life and Vigour to the whole. Without this, no Country can be happy within herself, or support herself without against the attacks

Robert Dodd's painting shows the Pool of London with shipping moored in the river Thames waiting to unload.

(© National Maritime Museum, Greenwich, London, BHC1879)

> of a powerful Neighbour. Trade it is that brings us all the Aids, the Conveniencies [sic], the Luxury of Life, 'tis she that encourages all Arts and Sciences, gives Hope to Invention, and Riches to Industry; Strength, Wisdom and Policy are in her Train; Plenty, Liberty, and Happiness are her perpetual Companions.[3]

Since roads were very poor and the canal age had hardly started in Britain, the great bulk of this trade went by water – up and down rivers, along the coast and overseas to Europe, India, the West Indies and North America.

This was intimately connected with a great navy. As Lord Haversham had put it fifty years before, 'your fleet and your trade have so near a relation, and such a mutual influence upon each other they cannot well be separated; your trade is the mother and nurse of your seamen; your seamen are the life of your fleet; and the fleet is the security and protection of your trade, and both together are the wealth, strength, security and glory of Britain.'[4] The French philosopher Voltaire was equally clear on the importance of trade and sea power in different forms: '...trade, which has made richer the citizens of England, has helped to make them free, and this freedom has, in turn, enlarged trade.... It is trade which has gradually created the navy, thanks to which the English are masters of the seas.'[5]

Underlying all this, though rarely stated in clear terms, was the essential idea of mercantilism – that trade was a zero-sum game, in which one's own commerce could only expand at the expense of someone else's. A century ago, the English had become very jealous of the Dutch success in trade and merchant shipping and countered it by fighting three wars with them, while imposing the Navigation Acts (enforced from 1651 onwards) which decreed that *British* goods should be carried in *British* ships. This, too, helped to foster the navy, which did very little to train its own seamen. Instead, it recruited them from the merchant service, either as volunteers or through the press gang. A warship needed about ten times the crew of a merchant ship to man its guns, so a large merchant shipping industry was essential to naval success, as well as creating a need for naval power to protect it.

Much of the trade was short-range. Vast quantities of coal were brought down from the north-eastern fields to heat London and the other southern cities through the winter. Timber, hemp and tar from the Baltic were essential for both naval and merchant shipbuilding, while manufactured goods and wool were exported to northern Europe. Colonies were a large element in successful trade, as they produced goods that could not be grown at home but could be sold at great profit, both in Britain and in other European countries which did not have their own supplies.

The East India Company had started as a commercial organisation in the east, but now it vied with its French counterpart on the sub-continent for control of the native rulers, and hence of the lucrative trade in spices, silks and pepper. It operated a fleet of large merchant ships, the only ones which came close to the navy's ships of the line in size, and it remained profitable though its control of the trade was undermined by those who robbed and cheated it and by private traders known as interlopers – indeed, one of them had been Thomas 'Diamond' Pitt, the grandfather of the great war leader and parliamentary orator who was now Secretary of State.

In 1756, just as the war was breaking out, Britain imported a record £1.8 million worth of sugar from the West Indies and re-exported a large proportion of it at great profit. The commercial importance of the trade was taken for granted by Malachy Postlethwayt who wrote in 1745 that it was 'of such essential and allowed Concernment to the Wealth and Naval Power of *Great Britain,* that it would be as impertinent to take up your Time in expiating on that Subject as in declaiming the common Benefits of Air and Sun-shine in general.' It depended heavily on the slave trade from Africa and Postlethwayt's pamphlet was entitled *The African Trade, the Great Pillar and Support of the British Plantation Trade in America*. He wrote that '*White Men* cannot be obtained near so cheap, or the Labour of a sufficient Number be had... as we have of the *Africans*.' Therefore, he wrote euphemistically, 'are we not indebted to those invaluable People, the *Africans,* for our *Sugars, Tobaccoes, Rice, Rum*, and all other *Plantation Produce?*' Of course, he ignored the horrors of the transatlantic slave trade. Olaudah Equiano, one of its victims, wrote:

> [The ship] was so crowded that each had scarcely room to turn himself...so that the air soon became unfit for respiration, from the variety of loathsome smells, and brought on a sickness among the slaves. This wretched situation was...aggravated by the galling of the chains, which now became unsupportable...The shrieks of the women, and the groans of the dying, rendered...a scene of horror almost inconceivable.[6]

The British colonies in North America occupied the whole seaboard from the boundaries of Spanish Florida to Nova Scotia and the St Lawrence River and had a population of well over a million. The southern colonies also deployed slave labour, mostly brought in by American ships. Their most important product was tobacco, of which Virginia and Maryland alone exported eighty-five million lbs by 1750. Much of that went to the rapidly growing city of Glasgow, whose shipping, like that of Liverpool, was relatively free from the raids of French privateers. Most of the tobacco was sent across the narrow central belt of Scotland for re-exportation to northern Europe. The northern American colonies, on the other hand, were largely self-sufficient and often more troublesome than the south, especially New England. They did, however, export large quantities of timber for ship's masts, while the waters off Newfoundland and Nova Scotia provided a seemingly endless supply of cod for the home, West Indian and European markets.

Since each European nation only allowed its highly-profitable colonies to trade with the mother country and it was widely assumed that trade could not be expanded, war between the maritime nations was highly likely, if not inevitable. The Spanish had waned since their great days of the sixteenth century, though their empire still offered the dream of riches to British adventurers. The Dutch had declined partly because their geographical position allowed them to be invaded by the French or blockaded by the British. France was now the great rival, and not just over trade and colonies. It was a Roman Catholic nation, which the majority of English, Scots and Welsh believed meant they were natural prey to tyranny and absolutism. This was confirmed by the character of the French monarchy, in which King Louis XV could levy taxes and write laws without the need for a parliament. The earlier wars between Britain and France, between 1689 and 1714, had largely been dynastic and were formally about the succession to the English and Spanish thrones. Colonies began to play an increasing role in the conflict and, after a long peace, Britain found herself at war with France as well as Spain in 1744. The French had a great army, the British had a great navy and most of the issues were unresolved when a compromise peace was reached in 1748.

A Bad Start

When the war resumed formally in 1756, the island of Britain was more united than it had ever been. Scotland had formed a union with England half a century before and the lowlanders in the west were making great profits from trade with the empire. It was only ten years since the last revolt by the Jacobite highlanders had been brutally put down, but William Pitt, the Secretary of State, found a way to integrate the clans into the British war effort while solving the army's manpower problem. He recruited from a 'hardy and intrepid race of men' into the highland regiments of the British army with great success. On the island of Ireland, the largely Roman Catholic population was alienated and sullen but did not revolt – indeed it supplied large numbers of men for both the army and navy.

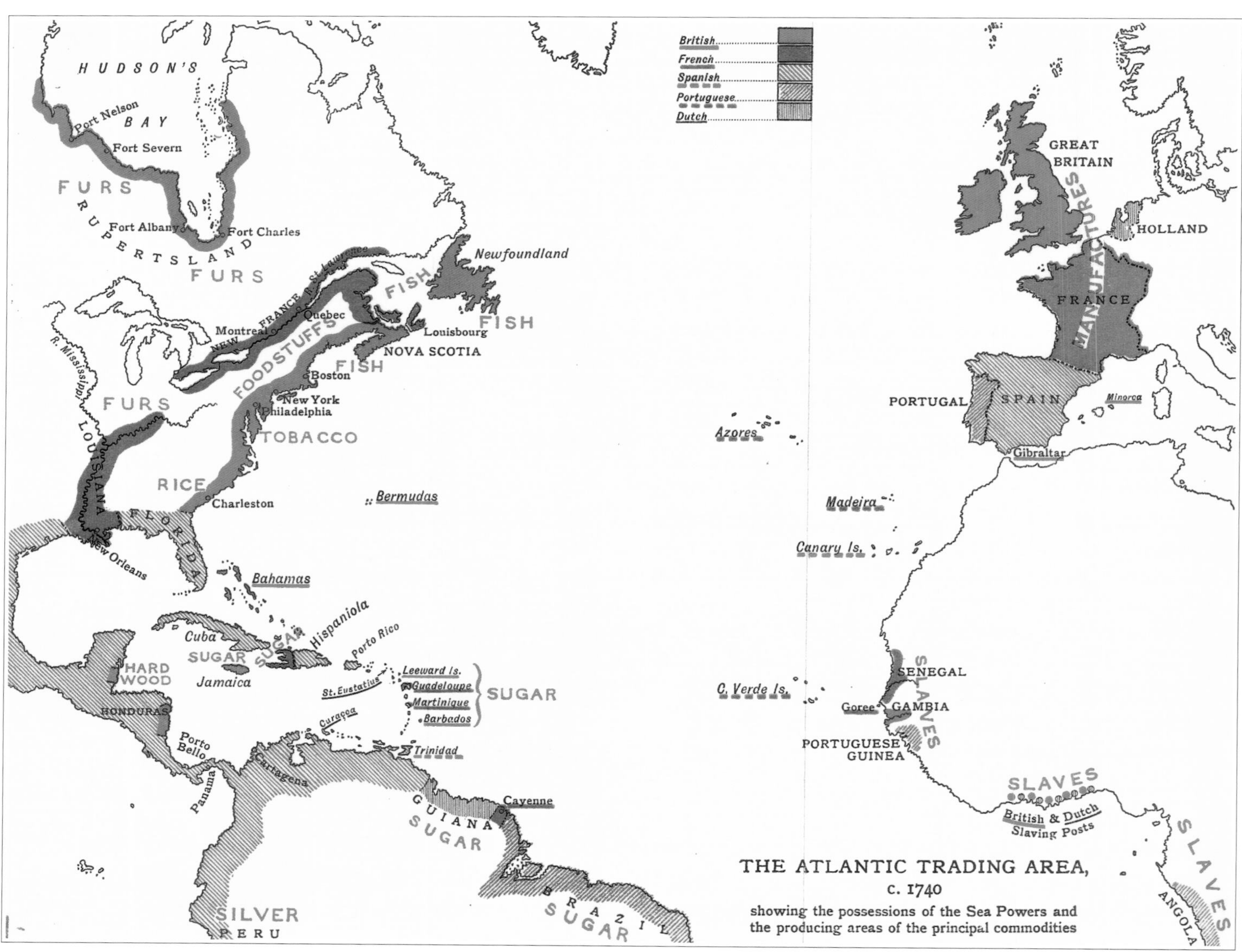

The Atlantic in the mid-eighteenth century, showing the trading areas and national rivalries.

(Taken from James A. Williamson, A Short History of British Expansion, *1922)*

Admiral Byng is shot on the quarterdeck of his flagship *Monarch*. His only privilege was to drop his handkerchief to order his own death.

(© National Maritime Museum, Greenwich, London, BHC0380)

Despite the strength of the Royal Navy, the growing conflict had not started well. In North America, the French were trying to hem in the British colonies by an ambitious scheme to link their own sparsely-populated colonies in Canada and Louisiana along the great rivers. In 1754, Colonel George Washington had attempted to forestall this with a force of Virginians, but was captured. In 1755, Admiral Boscawen was sent out to stop French reinforcements reaching the Americas, though war had not been declared. He captured two ships, enough to undermine Britain's moral case without doing any real damage to the enemy. In India, the French ally Siraj-al-Daula took Calcutta and imprisoned his captives in the infamous 'Black Hole' where hundreds of them died. Britain's European ally, Frederick the Great of Prussia, was defeated twice during the summer of 1757. But for the navy the worst humiliation of all was in the Mediterranean.

The island of Minorca, captured in 1708, provided an excellent harbour for British activities in the region. In 1756 the French invaded and besieged General Blakeney's forces in Fort St Phillip. Admiral George Byng was sent out to relieve them, but his fleet was ill-equipped and poorly-manned because priority was given to forces for the Atlantic and home defence. Byng was not a great admiral and he fought a drawn battle with a roughly equal French fleet in May. He made the mistake of withdrawing to Gibraltar, which was unfairly interpreted as cowardice at home. A court martial found him not guilty of that charge but guilty of failing to do his utmost against the enemy. The badly-drafted law allowed no alternative to the death penalty, though the court recommended mercy. The government was afraid of rioting, for as the novelist Henry Fielding put it, 'none of our political writers...take notice of any more than three estates, namely Kings, Lords and Commons... passing by in silence that very large and powerful body which form the fourth estate in the community...the Mob.' Byng was executed by firing squad in Portsmouth Harbour in January 1757 and the French philosopher Voltaire commented, 'in this country it is thought well to kill an admiral from time to time to encourage the others.' The affair cast many shadows over the war effort and on the discipline of the officers of the navy. It also showed that the system of naval tactics was inadequate, but strategically it was not as disastrous as it might have been. One of the main functions of the British presence in the Mediterranean was to support allies such as Austria-Hungary. This time the main ally was Prussia to the north so the Mediterranean was not so vital.

Meanwhile. the war situation was gradually improving elsewhere. In India, General Robert Clive re-took Calcutta and fought the decisive Battle of Plassey in June 1757. An attempt to capture the great French fortress at Louisbourg at the mouth of the St Lawrence River failed that year, but Boscawen was more successful in 1758. Meanwhile, Frederick the Great of Prussia had victories at Rossbach and Leuthen. Under the inspired war leadership of William Pitt the Elder, Britain was at last poised to impose its power around the world, but there was still a great deal to be done.

The Ship of the Line

The members of the Board of Admiralty were fully aware of all this as they drafted their order on the morning of 13 December 1758. They felt it necessary to explain the need for new ships, perhaps using the terms that would justify the expenditure to Parliament, for there was no real need to convince their subordinates in the Navy Board and dockyards.

> ...It appearing that many of the several classes from their age and condition cannot continue in service more than two or three years, whereby there will probably in the year 1761 be, exclusive of accident to which war subjects them, at least twelve ships of the aforesaid classes less than at present; and as ships of this magnitude may require one with the other two years to build...[7]

It was 'of the utmost importance to this kingdom to keep the navy on the present respectable state...' Therefore, the Navy Board, who were responsible for shipbuilding and finance, were desired and directed 'to cause five ships of the classes mentioned on the other side to be set up and built in His Majesty's yards... as soon as there shall be room for them...' The list was headed by a 100-gun ship to be built at Chatham, followed by a 90 in the same dockyard, 74s at Deptford and Plymouth and a 50-gun ship at Portsmouth, while more ships were to be built by contract in private shipyards. The order was signed as 'Your affectionate friends' by Anson, Hay and two other members of the board who had missed the main meeting, Gilbert Elliot and John Forbes. An Admiralty envoy, perhaps the head messenger Henry Doody, took it to the Navy Board in Seething Lane near the Tower of London, on the site of the building where Samuel Pepys had once worked and waspishly recorded the office politics in his diary. His successors had the duty of putting the Admiralty's order into execution.

All the vessels ordered from the dockyards on 13 December, except the fifty at Portsmouth, were ships of the line, the battleships of the day. It was not the job of these ships to protect commerce directly, for they were far too expensive to cover every point where shipping might be attacked. Instead, their task was to meet an enemy fleet of similar ships. If that could be defeated or contained, then the country would be free from the threat of invasion and smaller ships would be able to operate at will. Convoys of merchant ships could be protected against raiders, enemy commerce would be disrupted or destroyed and his colonies, especially small islands in the West Indies, could be captured. But all this depended on having a fleet of ships of the line that could neutralise an enemy one.

The concept of the ship of the line depended on the fact that there was no single weapon mounted in each ship that could dominate a battle, in the way that the galley's ram had done in classical times or the guided missile would do in the future. The 'great gun' was the only effective weapon over the seas (except when ships were close enough to board) for only it had range and penetrating power to damage an enemy ship. But there was no question of mounting a small number of very large guns in a major warship. There were no viable mechanical aids and the ball would be too heavy for a man to handle – the *Victory* herself would set the limits of this during her first commission. An effective warship needed a large number of guns, and these could only be mounted on the broadsides. Guns had been fitted to ships since medieval times, but it was only with the invention of the gunport around 1500 that large ones could be fitted low down in the ship. Henry VIII's ships, including the *Mary Rose,* had more and more added during their careers, which may well have contributed to her sinking in 1545. By that time, the large sailing ships were encountering problems with galleys, which could attack them in their most vulnerable areas in calm weather. This led to the fitting of guns firing all round for defence. The Elizabethans developed this by making the armament more offensive, using as many forward-firing guns as the form of a ship would allow, and turning the ship round to fire salvoes. But it was not entirely successful – the Spanish Armada of 1588 was not destroyed by gunfire as the

A detail from Thomas Whitcombe's painting of the Battle of the Saintes in 1782 shows the British 90-gun *Formidable* engaging the French *Ville de Paris,* in traditional fashion, with an exchange of broadsides.

(© National Maritime Museum, Greenwich, London, BHC0446)

English sailors had hoped, but by bad weather as it fled. Guns were ineffective at long range, and each would fire only a single shot before the ship had to retreat to reload.

In the following century, new developments in gunnery began to change the picture. Mass production of guns became closer with the use of iron instead of brass. Gunports were made wider so the guns could be aimed over a greater area. A device known as the train tackle was fitted at the rear of the carriage and hauled tight when the gun was inboard to retain it during reloading. More men were allocated to the gun crews in action. The breadth of ships tended to increase giving more space for gun operation. It became possible to build a ship with a large number of guns, which could stand and fight rather than retreat to reload.

During the English Civil War, which began in 1642, the navy supported Parliament against the King, but had to develop long, fast ships known as 'frigates' to deal with Royalist privateers and gun runners. It was only natural that most of their gun power was mounted on the broadside. From 1652 the English Navy was in conflict with the Dutch and larger vessels were needed. The long, narrow frigate hull was expanded and adapted to carry more guns and became something rather different, while older ships had more and more guns fitted, the great majority firing on one side or the other.

The early battles of the First Anglo-Dutch War (1652–54) were fought by individual squadrons but with limited success. It was only when the 'generals-at-sea', Robert Blake, Richard Deane and George Monck, began to impose army discipline on the fleet that it would be formed into a single line of battle so that one ship would not get in the way of another. This was tested at the Battle of the Gabbard in 1653, when a Dutch report said:

> It was (for the most part) with the ordnance, the ships of either side coming seldom within musket shot of each other, of the English, having the wind and more and greater guns, made use of these advantages, plying the Dutch only with their ordnance. And when the Dutch, finding the great disadvantage they were at, endeavoured to get the wind that they might come nearer, the English,

Battles of the Second Anglo-Dutch War, such as the Four Days Fight of June 1666 depicted by Abraham Storck, usually began with the ships in line but soon descended into melees. By the end of the century much more rigid discipline was imposed on fleets.

(© National Maritime Museum, Greenwich, London, BHC0286)

> by favour of the wind, still prevented them, so as they could do little hurt to the rebels...

English success was short lived, the Dutch learned to use the line of battle and built bigger ships. The numerous battles of the second and third Anglo-Dutch Wars (1664–67 and 1672–74) were hard-fought in the confined waters of the southern end of the North Sea. The Dutch rarely avoided battle, because they could only win the war by breaking the English blockade, and fleets of up to a hundred ships on each side fought it out.

The Line of Battle

The situation was different after France became the main enemy in 1689. Unlike the Dutch, the French did not have to join battle unless it suited them – they were much less dependent on seaborne trade, and their coastline was far longer and more difficult to blockade. There were only two full-scale sea battles in the War of the League of Augsburg (1689–97) and only one in the War of Spanish Succession (1702–14). Not only could the enemy avoid action, but, even if he fought, the result was usually indecisive as two fleets bombarded one another at medium range. At Malaga in 1704, neither side lost a ship during a day of battle. There was a different outcome during a brief war with Spain in 1718, when a Spanish fleet of eighteen ships fled on the approach of a slightly stronger British force. Admiral Byng (father of the unfortunate victim of Minorca) showed how it could be done by allowing his ships to attack the retreating Spanish line. Eleven of them were taken or destroyed, but Byng had made it look too easy and the Spanish were not considered dangerous opponents at this time so the lessons were lost.

Apart from that, admirals had become obsessed with obeying the *Permanent Fighting and Sailing Instructions* that had been issued around 1710 and were based on the experience of the previous century, though with later additions at the discretion of the commander-in-chief. Keeping the line was paramount, as Article 21 decreed, 'none of the Ships in the Fleet shall pursue any small Number of the Enemies Ships, unless the main Body be disabled, or run.'[8] Off Toulon in 1744, Admiral Mathews was not supported by his second-in-command Richard Lestock during an attack on a Franco-Spanish fleet. No ships were taken on either side. At the subsequent court martial, Lestock attacked Matthews on the grounds that he had not maintained a proper line of battle, and Mathews was dismissed from the service. A pro-Lestock *History of the Mediterranean Fleet* published soon afterwards asserted,

> A Line of Battle is the basis and foundation of all discipline in sea fights, and is universally practised by all nations that are masters of any power at sea; it has had the test of a long experience, and stood before the stroke of time, pure, and unaltered, handed down by our predecessors as the most prudential, and best concerted disposition that can possibly be made at sea.[9]

Some regarded this as an extreme view, and one of Mathews's supporters claimed that 'greater stress than ordinary is laid on order and discipline' in that work. Nevertheless, the younger Byng, who had sat on the Mathews court martial, did his best to maintain his line off Minorca in 1756, though the signal book did not allow him many options to correct the movement of his ships, and the result was indecisive, but fatal to him.

There were other battles with different results. Off Cape Finisterre in May 1747, Anson was in command of a fleet of seventeen ships of the line which chased a French convoy escorted by five ships of the line, and he captured eight warships including the classic 74-gun *Invincible*. Later in the year, Admiral Sir Edward Hawke repeated the feat in the same area, capturing six ships of the line. However, these were regarded as exceptions, in that the enemy was in retreat, covered by the case when 'the main Body be disabled, or run' in the words of the *Fighting Instructions*. But, generally, the trend was still conservative and in 1769 Falconer's *Marine Dictionary* stated:

> This disposition, which is the best calculated for the operations of naval war, is formed by drawing up the ships in a long file, or right line, prolonged from the keel of the hindmost to that of the foremost, and passing longitudinally through the keels of all the others, from the van to the rear, so that they are, in the sea phrase, in the wake of each other.[10]

The Battle of Negapatam off the coast of India in 1782, painted by Dominic Serres and showing British and French ships in line – the battle was inconclusive, though the British suffered heavier casualties.

(© National Maritime Museum, Greenwich, London, BHC0448)

The First-Rate

The head of the naval pyramid was the first-rate ship of the line. In the navy, the term 'rate' meant quantity, that is number of guns, rather than the quality of the ship. In 1618, James I's navy was divided into 'royal', 'great', 'middling' and 'small' ships and his son's fleet had six 'ranks', while the Commonwealth of 1649–60 had the same number of 'rates'. Originally, it was mainly a method of assessing the pay of certain officers. Some, such as lieutenants and midshipmen, were paid at a flat rate but their number varied according to the size of the ship. Others, including the captain and many warrant officers such as the master, carpenter and surgeon, had responsibilities that rose with the size of the ship and were paid according to its rate. It soon became recognised that ships of the fourth-rate and above were fit to stand in the line of battle against any ship that might be opposed to them. By the late 1690s, ships of 20 or 24 guns were in the sixth-rate, those from 30 to 48 were the fifth-rate, 50s and 60s were in the fourth-rate, the third-rate included ships of 64 to 80 guns and the second-rate included quite a large number of three-deckers of 90 guns. The term 'first-rate' became almost synonymous with a three-decker of 100 guns, and as yet no one had thought of building even bigger ships.

Peter Pett poses rather unrealistically beside the highly-decorated stern of his father's masterpiece, the *Sovereign of the Seas*.

(© National Maritime Museum, Greenwich, London, BHC2949)

The 100-gun ship started with Charles I's great *Sovereign of the Seas* in 1637 that pre-dated the idea of the line of battle and helped to shape the concept. At the time Trinity House, the main authority on navigation, protested that 'neither can the wit of man build a ship well conditioned and fit for service with three tier of ordnance'. But Charles was confident of his Divine Right to rule and pressed ahead. His main aim was prestige to overawe both his own subjects and his rivals Louis XIII of France and Kristian IV of Denmark; but the three-decker warship had several advantages, including more gun power, higher guns to fire down on an enemy and more space for use as a headquarters.

Phineas Pett made a model of her, which was seen in his house in Woolwich by Peter Munday in 1635–37:

> ...We saw the model or mould of the said ship, which was shown to his Majesty before he begun [sic] her. The said model was of admirable workmanship, curiously painted and gilt, with azure and gold, so contrived that every timber in her might be seen and left open and unplanked for that purpose...[11]

The poets, too, played their part and Thomas Cary wrote:

> Triton's auspicious Sound usher thy raigne
> O're the curl'd billowes, Royal **SOVERAINE**,
> Monarchal Ship, whose Fabrick doth outpride
> The **Pharos**, **Colosse**, Memphique **Pyramide**;
> And seems a moving Towre, when sprightly gales
> Quicken the Motion, and embreath the sailes.
> We y[et]t have heard of **SEAVEN**, now see ye **Eight**
> **Wonder** at home; of naval art the height.[12]

The *Sovereign of the Seas* cost the enormous sum of £65,586, with £6,691 for decorations alone, compared with about £6,000 for a standard 'great ship' of 40 guns. This did not aid Charles's cause. He was trying to raise the tax of ship money against popular opposition, and spending the money on such great ships, rather than small, fast ones for defence against pirates, did not make it any more palatable. In 1642, the English Civil War began and he was executed in 1649

More first-rates followed over the rest of the century, including the *Naseby* of 1655 (renamed the *Royal Charles* in 1660) and the *Richard* of 1658, re-named the *Royal James*. Not all had 100 guns and none matched the *Sovereign* until late in the century. In 1677 Samuel Pepys, as Member of Parliament and Secretary to the Admiralty, asked a suspicious House of Commons for money to build thirty new ships. He saw the value of three-deckers, which 'did the service against the Dutch' but was aware of their cost in money and timber – 'God knows where materials shall be had for so many First and Second Rates.' The bulk of them was to be made up of twenty two-deckers of 70 guns apiece, a class which had evolved over the previous thirty years. He asked for a single 100-gun ship, but also nine second rates of 90 guns, which were essentially cut-price first-rates. They could serve as flagships as needed but also as strongpoints in the line of battle. The single 100-gun first-rate, named the *Britannia*, was to be of 1,739 tons when built at Chatham by the latest member of the Pett family, Phineas II, and launched in 1682. The 1677 programme set many precedents for the future including standardised ship specifications and armament. It also established the second-rate as a standard group rather than a mixture of various older ships. It isolated the first-rate as a special type within the fleet, of great value and prestige.

The first half of the next century was less imaginative and followed the precedents rather too slavishly. The older first-rates were lost, scrapped or re-classified and by 1714, when the Hanoverian regime took power, the navy only had seven of them, all of 100 guns. It was now policy to 'rebuild' old ships when decayed (though less and less old timber was used in the process as the years went on) and to replace lost ships with others of the same type, all built to a regular establishment of dimensions. The design of ships, including first-rates, did not change much and the first-rate was still highly regarded as a fighting ship. According to Falconer's *Marine Dictionary* of 1769:

> ...The larger ships are in other respects highly preferable in a line of battle. They overlook those of an inferior rate, which are accordingly laid open to the fire of their musquetry [sic]. In a high sea they can more safely employ the artillery of their lower deck than a smaller ship; and if both are obliged to shut their lower deck ports, the advantage of the three-decked ships, with regard to their cannon, will yet be considerable; they have three tiers against two, and two against one.[13]

That was not a universal view. The naval architect Marmaduke Stalkartt wrote of 100-gun ships, '...ships so bulky in their dimensions, though they may be useful in particular cases, are far from being generally so. Their sails are so very heavy that it is with the utmost difficulty that they are managed if the wind blows high.'[14] They were also expensive. In 1789, a 100-gun ship cost £67,600 to build and fit for sea, while a 74, the standard type of ship of the line, cost £43,820. A 74 could be built on a slip in any of the Royal Dockyards or, by contract, in a private shipyard; a 100-gun ship had to be built in a precious dry-dock in a Royal yard, where it would take up space for several years, preventing other vessels coming in for urgent repair and cleaning. Three-deckers were generally poorer sailers than two-deckers, because their higher sides caught the wind and made it more difficult to sail to windward. That was not necessarily a problem for a fleet flagship, she only had to match the slowest sailing ships as she would be a centre of a formation, and smaller ships would carry out patrols and do the chasing. And in any case, the *Victory* would eventually prove that a well-designed three-decker could sail very well.

The 100-gun first-rate was not the only type of three-decker. Eighty-gun ships of three decks had been built since the 1690s and their use was stoutly defended by a group of senior officers, who argued in 1745 that they had 'observed on many occasions the advantage which 80-gun ships with three decks had over those with two and half...' But the sea officers did not agree and the three-decker 80 was allowed to die out after that. The 90-gun ship continued to develop and there were thirteen of them in the fleet in 1757, compared with five 100s. But Stalkaart wrote, 'If we were to examine a 90-gun ship, we should find her very irregular and disproportioned, for if a 74-gun ship can carry her guns upon two decks, the ship of 90 guns may as well be calculated to bear 100 as 90 guns.'[15] The 90, later rearmed as the 98, was still essentially a cut-price first-rate. The difference between 90 or 98 guns and 100 does not seem very great, but a first-rate, with 42-pounders on the lower deck and 24-pounders on the middle, could fire a broadside of 1,182 lbs. A 90, with only 32 and 18-pounders, could fire 907 lbs, so the 100-gun ship had a thirty percent superiority

The largest ships were symbols of national prestige and the loss of one was a national disaster. Many ships were lost during 150 years of wars, but a first-rate was special and an aggressive enemy like the Dutch might well target such prestige-ships. The first to go was the *Royal Prince,* a rebuild of James I's great ship of 1610, now carrying 92 guns. She ran aground during four days of battle in 1666 and was captured. The Dutch were unable to defend their prize and according to Sir Thomas Clifford who was a witness, '...they set her on fire, the sight of which was a sensible touch to every man's heart in our fleet...She was like a castle in the sea, and I believe the best ship that was ever built in the world to endure battering, but she is gone...'[16] An even more humiliating loss was the *Royal Charles*, ex-*Naseby,* towed away by the Dutch during the Medway Raid in 1667 and carried triumphantly to the Netherlands. And the new-built *Royal James* was isolated and burned at the Battle of Solebay in 1672. Pepys was particularly distressed this time because his patron, the First Earl of Sandwich, was among the casualties.

These three at least had the dignity of being lost to enemy action. The *Royal Sovereign,* King Charles's old *Sovereign of the Seas,* looked spectacular as she burned in the Medway in 1697, but the disaster was attributed to 'the action of a poor, helpless old wretch who, not seeing how to set his candle, it caught hold of some combustible matter which soon set all aflame.'[17] By the next century, the Royal Navy was stronger, the French were less aggressive and the rigid line of battle did not encourage the singling out of an individual ship, so losses of first-rates were due to accident. The *Victory* of 1737, whose model had decorated the Admiralty boardroom, was the flagship of Admiral Balchen in 1744 when she disappeared in bad weather off the Channel Islands in 1744, a loss which baffled historians for two and a half centuries. The design of the ship might have been partly to blame, she was criticised for her high stern with four galleries. The most celebrated loss of all came some years after the launch of the *Victory*. The *Royal George* capsized at Spithead in 1782, taking over a thousand men, women and children with her. The poet Cowper wrote his *Toll for the Brave* but his attribution of the disaster to a land breeze which 'shook the shrouds' was probably not correct; nor was the suggestion that her timbers had collapsed due to faulty repair work. Almost certainly it was the result of faulty seamanship, by having too much weight on one side during loading operations.

Despite the horrific violence involved in a naval battle and the overcrowded conditions on board, the romantic side of the ship of the line spread into literature and art. In 1843 John Ruskin wrote about the paintings of his friend J M W Turner and especially *The Fighting Temeraire*:

> ...A Ship of the Line is the most honourable thing that man, as a gregarious animal, has ever produced. By himself, unhelped, he can do better thing than ships of the line; he can make poems and pictures, and other such concentrations of what is best in him. But as a being living in flocks, hammering out, with alternate strokes and mutual agreement, what is necessary for him in those flocks, to get or produce a ship of the line is his first work.[18]

A first-rate, in particular, was a thing of beauty as well as power. As a boy, Thomas Byam Martin was rowed across Portsmouth Harbour in 1781:

> In going across the harbour we passed close under the stern of the old Royal George. It was the first time I ever floated in salt water; the first hundred-gun ship I ever saw. Ye gods! what a sight – what a sensation!... It is impossible to forget the breathless astonishment and delight with which my eyes were fixed upon the ship... Old John Allen... said..., 'I see, sir, you are already determined to be a sailor.'[19]

The building of a new first-rate, like the one ordered in December 1758, was a major event, though in practice it would be many years before the ship would repay the materials, timber and money spent on her.

The highly-decorated stern of the *Royal George* as seen on a model of the 1770s.

(© National Maritime Museum, Greenwich, London, D4082-7)

2 BUILDING THE *VICTORY*

Thomas Slade

Once it had been decided to build several new ships in December 1758, it was the job of the shipwrights to design them. In some cases they could simply pull out established plans from large drawers, copy them by pricking holes through vital points onto a sheet below, join them up and send the result on to the shipbuilding yard. Even first-rates could be treated this way, the *Britannia* was under construction at Portsmouth on the plans of the *Royal George*; but the new ship was to be the largest built for the navy so far and would be specially designed while using long-established practices. This was the task of the Surveyor of the Navy, Thomas Slade, a very experienced and capable shipwright.

Formally, the shipwrights were all part of one profession but a young man was apprenticed to an individual rather than to the dockyard or the navy as a whole, and his future career largely depended on his master's status. If he was bound to a master shipwright or his assistant, the boy had high expectations and would learn all about ship design. If not, he would become a manual workman, knowing how 'to Hew, or Dub, to Fay a Piece when it is Moulded to his place assigned, or the like', as a manual of 1664 put it[1],– though he was a highly skilled and quite privileged craftsman. The upper class of shipwrights were not always confined to design and management; according to Lord Sandwich, officers' apprentices should be 'put to their tools' instead of just being employed solely in the 'mould loft and drawing rooms'. He reasoned that '...the most eminent in the profession did so, and that a man can't be master of the profession without it.'[2]

Sir Thomas Slade (1703/4–1771), Surveyor of the Navy from 1755 and designer of the *Victory*.

(© National Maritime Museum, Greenwich, London, BHC3030)

The Admiralty and the Navy Board had had their differences in the recent past, and in 1746 the Navy Board had rebuked the superior body, claiming that the supervision of shipbuilding was 'a trust reposed in us by the Crown... from an opinion we are competent judges in such matters.'[3] But by now nearly all the members were Anson appointees, including the Controller of the Navy Sir Charles Saunders who had sailed with him on the circumnavigation of 1740–44. From the shipbuilding point of view the most important members were Thomas Slade and William Bateley, the joint surveyors of the navy. They had arrived suddenly at the office on 7 August 1755 not long after the old surveyor, Sir Joseph Allin, had been taken ill and become 'disordered in his senses.' They carried a warrant from the Admiralty authorising them to 'inspect the books and papers as joint Surveyors of the Navy till the patent shall pass for their appointments.' This normally took months, but Anson did not miss the opportunity to get his own men in office as war loomed and with British ship design clearly lagging behind. The new men quickly took up the work even before they were regularly appointed and within three weeks Slade had produced a design for a new type of 74-gun ship, a class which the old Navy Board had resisted but which soon proved to be the most successful type of two-decker.

Slade was as taciturn as Anson and left very few papers. He was born in Ipswich or Harwich in 1703 or 1704 and trained as a shipwright at Deptford Dockyard under the patronage of his uncle Benjamin, who rose to become Master Shipwright at Plymouth. Benjamin attracted the notice of Anson by making a very fine model of his ship *Centurion,* while Thomas took the lines off several French prize ships to assess their designs. When Benjamin died in 1750, his nephew transferred into the Master Shipwright's post and by 1753 he moved to Deptford. This brought him into direct contact with the central administration, for the 'Navy Board have frequently occasion to send for the Deptford Officers for information on matters respecting the several Branches of business in the Dock Yards, so the Principal Officers in this Yard have been usually considered as the most experienced ablest Officers in their several Branches.'[4] Like most Anson protégés, he was highly competent and John Henslow, his eventual successor, wrote, 'He was truly a great man in the line he trod, such a one I believe never went before him, and if I am not too partial, I may venture to say will hardly follow him.' Once in office as joint surveyor, he spent the late 1750s working on designs for the new 74-gun ships of the line and frigates, based on French layouts but not slavishly copying their design. He did not introduce any new practices in design, except perhaps a more efficient method of drawing the lines, but his designs were well executed and many of them were repeated years after his death.

Designing the Ship

In designing the new first rate the first task was to settle the dimensions and it seems that Slade was given an unusually free hand. Like all shipwrights he had to balance the various factors that would contribute to good sailing qualities, as described by a naval architect of the time:

> To give a ship... that form which shall make her weatherly, or, in other words, to keep a good wind and sail swiftly, she must have a great length and good depth of keel; her breadth not to great; her sides not kept parallel, or the extreme breadth not continued, too far aft; as this would be against velocity.... If a good depth in hold be given,... she will feel a great resistance sideways, or in her broadside, with little resistance ahead, she will, consequently, sail fast, and not fall much to leeward.[5]

There was nothing radical about the layout of the new ship – apart from the details it would have been familiar to Phineas Pett as he designed the *Sovereign of the Seas*. The essential features were the three gundecks running the length of the hull. The lower one provided the main dimension, the 'length on the gundeck', which was far from being the full length occupied by the vessel but gave an indication of the useable space inside.

Slade knew that the most recent 100-gun ship, the *Royal George*, had already seen nearly three years hard service since she was commissioned in May 1756. No formal sailing report from that period has survived, but one of 1762 suggests that she behaved 'very well' in most conditions of sailing; that she was capable of a high speed of eleven knots in ideal winds and sea, and that 'She will wrong all three-deck ships she has been in company with and will keep way with most two-deck ships.' Clearly something was right about her design. For the new ship, Slade stated, 'the principal dimensions... are the same as the *Royal George*, except an addition of eight feet to the length of the Gun Deck, which will enable her to fight Thirty Guns in a Tier on the Lower, Middle, and Upper Decks, and make her more comfortable as to the Capacity of her Body, and thereby support the whole with more ease, and at less Draught of Water.'[6] The extra eight feet was precisely the distance between each pair of gunports on the new ship. The breadth under the planking was to be 50ft 6in, slightly less than the *Royal George* as built. The third dimension stated was the depth-in-hold of 21ft 6ins, identical to the *Royal George*. This was the distance between the top of the keel and the gundeck. It was less important than the others, but it gave some indication of the depth of the hull underwater, though not precisely.

Having settled the dimensions, the next task of the designer was to draw out the plans of the ship, usually to a scale of four inches to the foot or 1:48. Until 1745, it had been common for the Navy Board to issue the dimensions of the new ship, often in considerable detail according to the current 'establishment' and let the master shipwright concerned, either in a Royal Dockyard or a private shipyard, draw out her lines. The only proviso was that a copy of the draught had to be sent to the Admiralty for approval. In 1745, Anson and the Admiralty had tried to enforce change on the ultra-conservative shipwrights by establishing not only the dimensions of each new ship, but the actual draught to which it should be built. However, that had proved a failure, the new ships did not 'steer so easy, nor sail so well, as was expected.' From 1755 the detailed design of each ship was done in the Navy Office in London, for now that Anson had his own men in place, he could trust them to do a good job. It seems likely that Slade supervised the design of the new 100-gun ship very closely, with the assistance of draughtsmen attached to Deptford Dockyard.

He started with the sheer plan or side view of the ship. The keel was drawn first, a straight line 176ft long which would constitute the lowest part and backbone of the vessel. The basic shape of the bow was formed by the stem post, a circle tangential to the keel – other options were available but this was the one most favoured by British designers. At the other end of the ship, the sternpost was straight in order to fit the rudder to it. It was at an angle of about six degrees from the vertical, whereas a French designer would have favoured a more upright post angled at about four degrees.

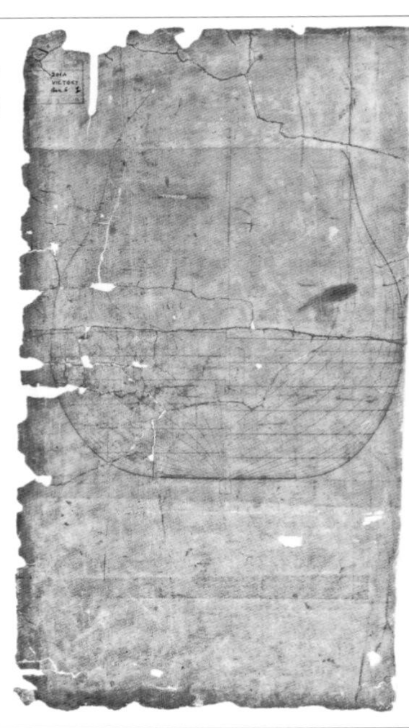

The only surviving original draught of the *Victory* is faded and damaged, so much of our information comes from later copies. However, it shows the sheer draught taking up most of the space to the top and right, the lines or body sections to the left of that and something of the waterlines below the sheer draught.

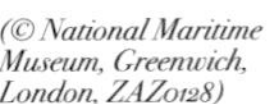

(© National Maritime Museum, Greenwich, London, ZAZ0128)

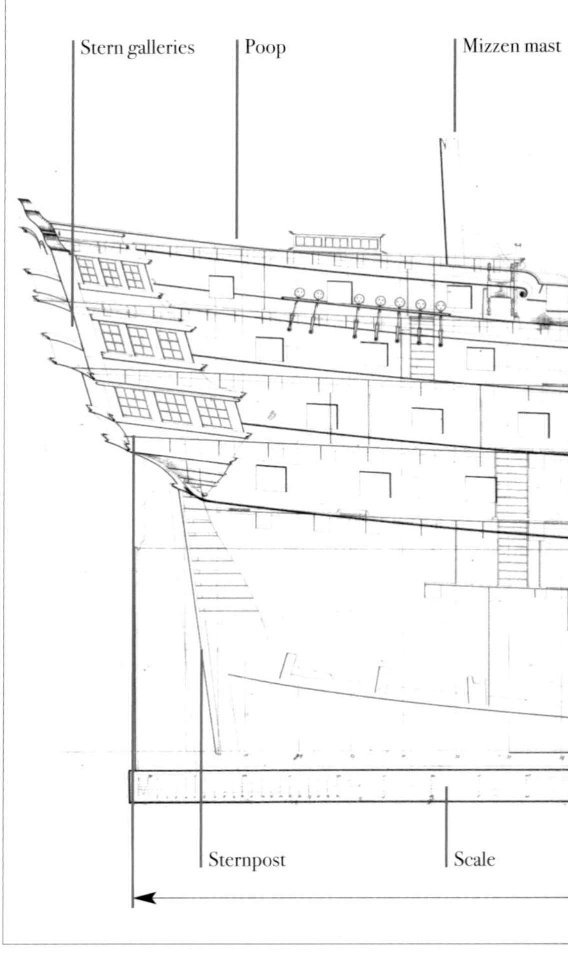

The Decks

The depth-in-hold had been decided early and that determined the height of the gundeck above the keel, in midships at least. Practical considerations controlled the layout of the decks. She was already defined as a three-decker, which meant that it had three complete decks of guns, not counting the orlop deck below the waterline which of course was unarmed, the quarter-deck and poop deck above the aftermost part of the ship and the forecastle above the bows. Each deck had a certain amount of sheer, that is it was curved when seen from the side with the lowest point near the centre of the ship to allow rainwater and spray to drain towards the pumps. The position of the lower or gun deck was the most important. It would carry the main armament of the ship, and if its gunports could not be opened due to rough weather or the heel of the ship, then she would be at a great disadvantage in action. This meant that the lower cills of the gunports had to be kept a certain distance above the waterline when the ship was on an even keel, but not too high as the weight of the guns

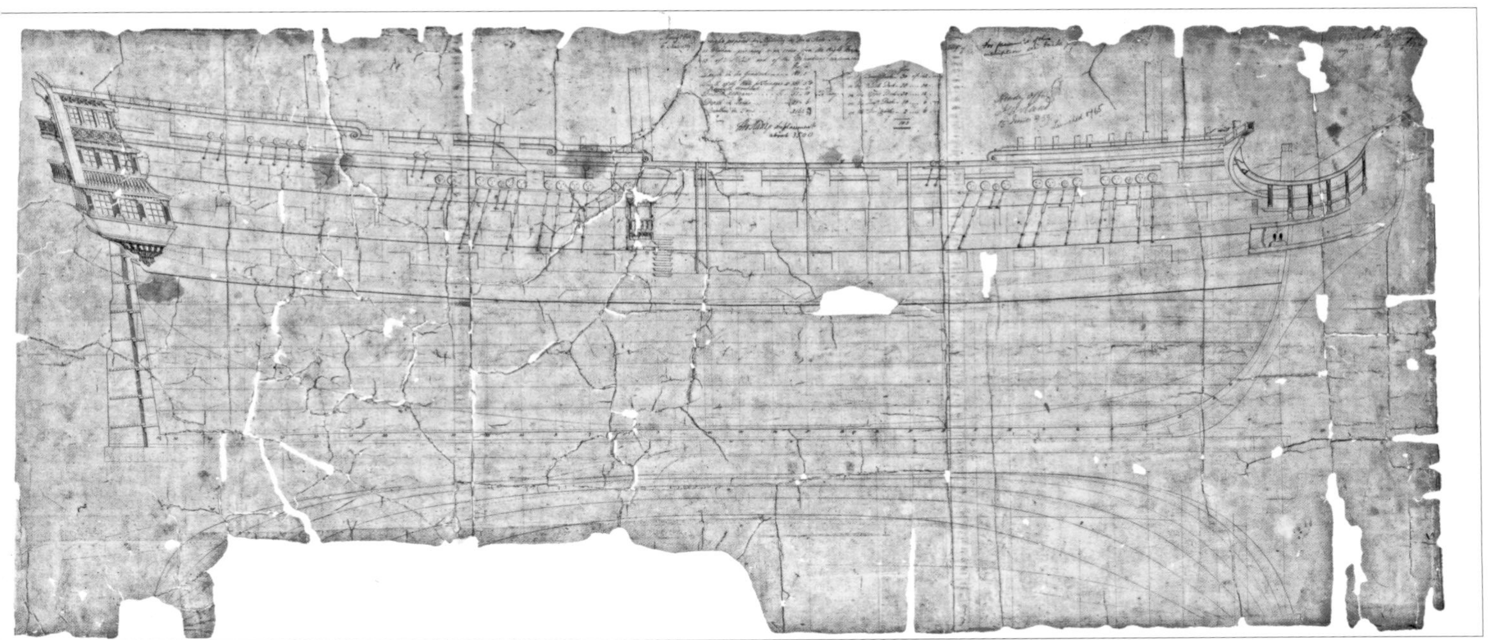

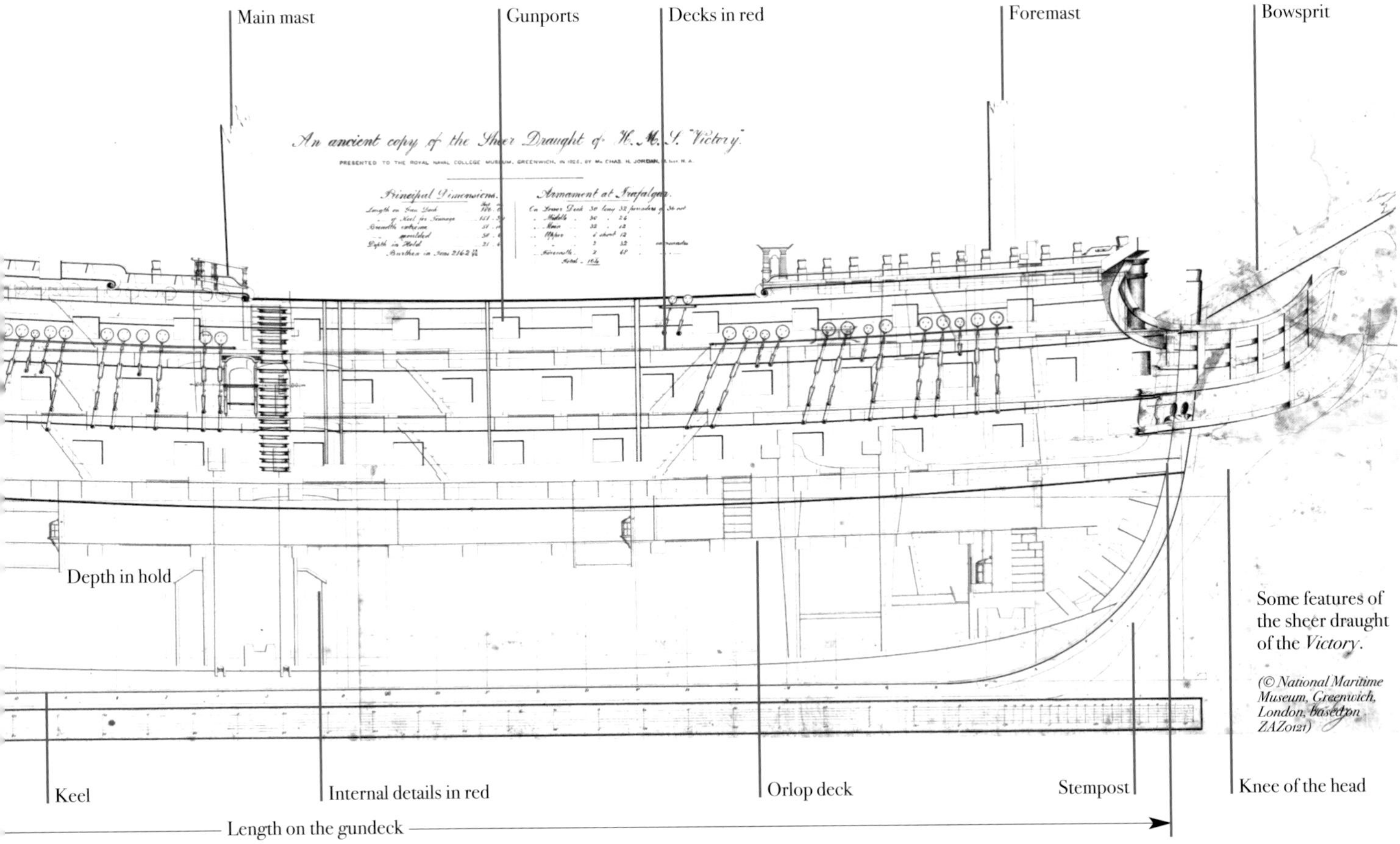

Main mast
Gunports
Decks in red
Foremast
Bowsprit
An ancient copy of the Sheer Draught of H.M.S. "Victory"
Principal Dimensions.
Armament at Trafalgar.
Depth in hold
Keel
Internal details in red
Orlop deck
Stempost
Knee of the head
Length on the gundeck

Some features of the sheer draught of the *Victory*.

(© National Maritime Museum, Greenwich, London, based on ZAZ0121)

would affect stability. Slade apparently hoped for 4ft 10in, but much depended on how the ship was ballasted in service. Naturally the height of the gunports would control the height of the lower deck, which was two feet below the line of port cills.

The other decks followed the line of the lower deck. Those above, the middle and upper deck, were parallel to it while the orlop deck below was flatter as it did not have to drain off the water. It was permissible to have a small gap between the lower and orlop decks, which meant that it was often necessary to crouch very low when passing along the orlop. This was not acceptable with the other decks, as they had to bear guns and allow enough room for the men to operate them. A certain minimum height between decks was needed, allowing for that fact that it would be constantly interrupted by the deck beams and other timbers which supported the planks of the deck above. In the case of the new first-rate this was 7ft 2in.

The distance between the gunports on each deck was determined by the needs of the structure rather than the guns and gunners. It was obviously necessary to stagger the ports of one deck with those above and below. The frames which avoided all the gunports and passed all the way from the keel to the topsides were among the most important parts of the structure, and were arranged in pairs so that the joins within the frame could overlap. Therefore, once the position of a lower deck port had been settled, the ones on the middle deck would be the width of a double frame forward or aft of that. The upper deck ports would be directly above the lower deck ones and those of the quarterdeck were above those of the middle deck – the poop carried no guns, while the forecastle did not need any ports as such because its guns were in the open. Slade had arrived at the eight feet added to the new ship from the *Royal George* dimensions, on the basis that a lower or middle deck port took up 3ft 4in and the two sets of frames between them took up 2ft 2in each, making a total of 7ft 8in between the ports on each deck. Slade completed the profile by drawing in the main

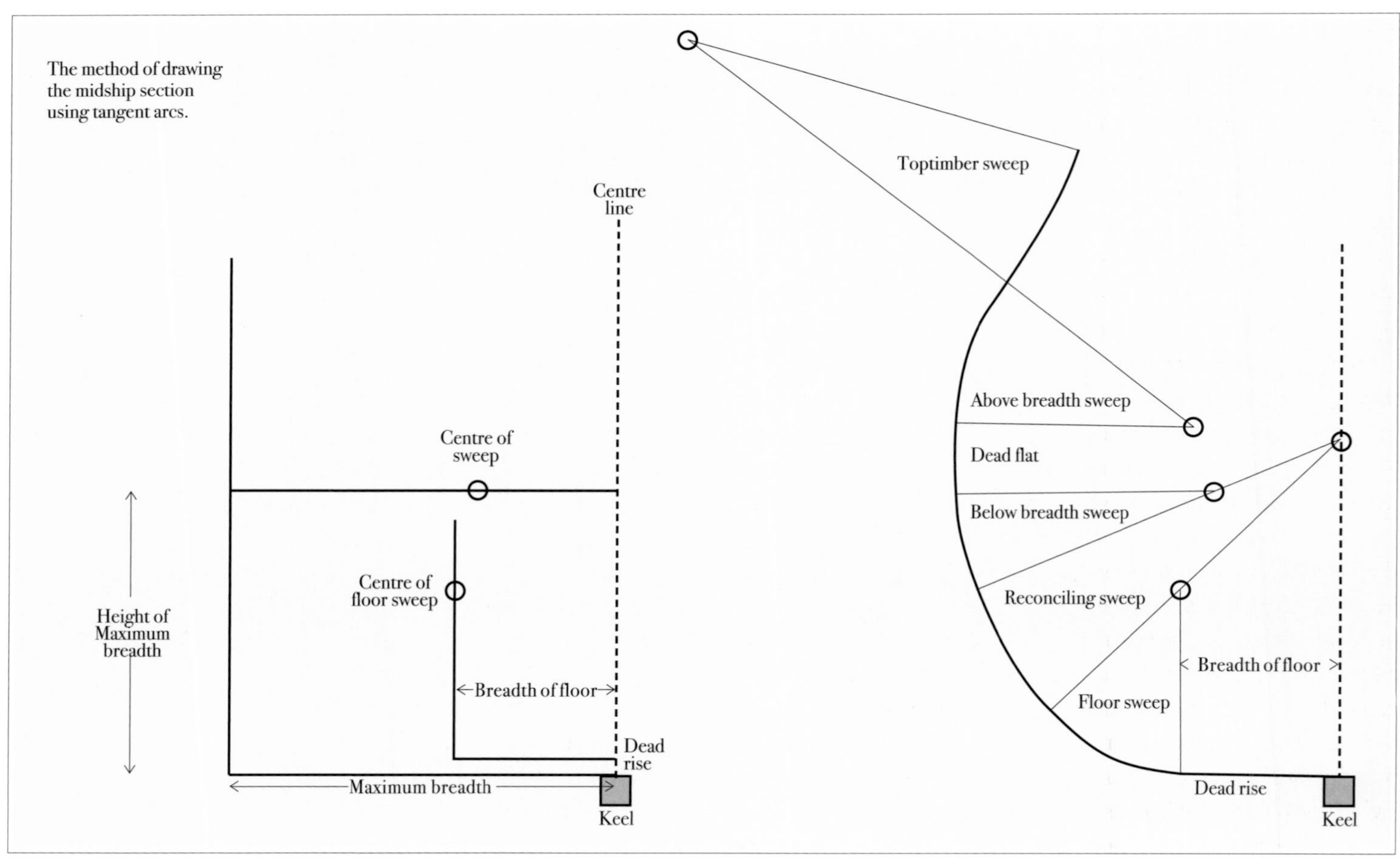

The method of drawing the midship section using tangent arcs.

elements of the external structure. Thicker planks known as wales had a greater sheer than the decks and were drawn on, as were the channels which would spread the shrouds and the outlines of the bow and stern decoration.

The Midship Section

Next the draughtsman would turn to the bow and stern views of the ship. The design had been based on the dimensions of the *Royal George*, though not the lines as is sometimes suggested. This becomes quite clear when comparing the plans of the two ships, starting as Slade would have done with the midship section. Like all the cross-sections of the ship it was based on simple shapes, straight lines and arcs of circles, which even poorly-educated shipwrights could understand and reproduce. Merchant ship designers tended to use an almost square section to get the maximum cargo, fast ships often had a nearly triangular section while many French ships had a sharp 'turn of the bilge' producing a hexagonal cross section when the upper works were included. But Slade, like most British warship designers, favoured a roughly circular midship section. He drew a rectangle as the basis. The breadth was already fixed and the height controlled by the depth in hold and the height of the decks. He settled on the maximum breadth of the midship section, in this case 50ft 6in.

The floor of the ship was very flat by normal standards, rising only about 6¾ inches, and 10ft 4½ inches wide. The rest of the shape was controlled by two arcs of circles, known as the 'floor sweep' and the 'breadth sweep'. The first was tangential to the floor and had a diameter of twelve feet. The breadth sweep passed through the maximum breadth with a diameter of 18ft 3in in midships. These two were joined by a circle of greater diameter, the reconciling sweep. Above the maximum breadth the sides were parallel for a short distance, known as the 'dead flat' 3ft and 6in high. After that the hull narrowed with its 'tumble-home'. It was believed this tended to increase stability by moving the upper guns closer to the centre line, and it had minor advantages such as creating a narrower deck which allowed the crew to move from one side of the ship to the other faster. The narrowing began with the above breadth sweep, and continued with the toptimber sweep, the only one which was convex and allowed the hull to become more vertical near the top of the sides.

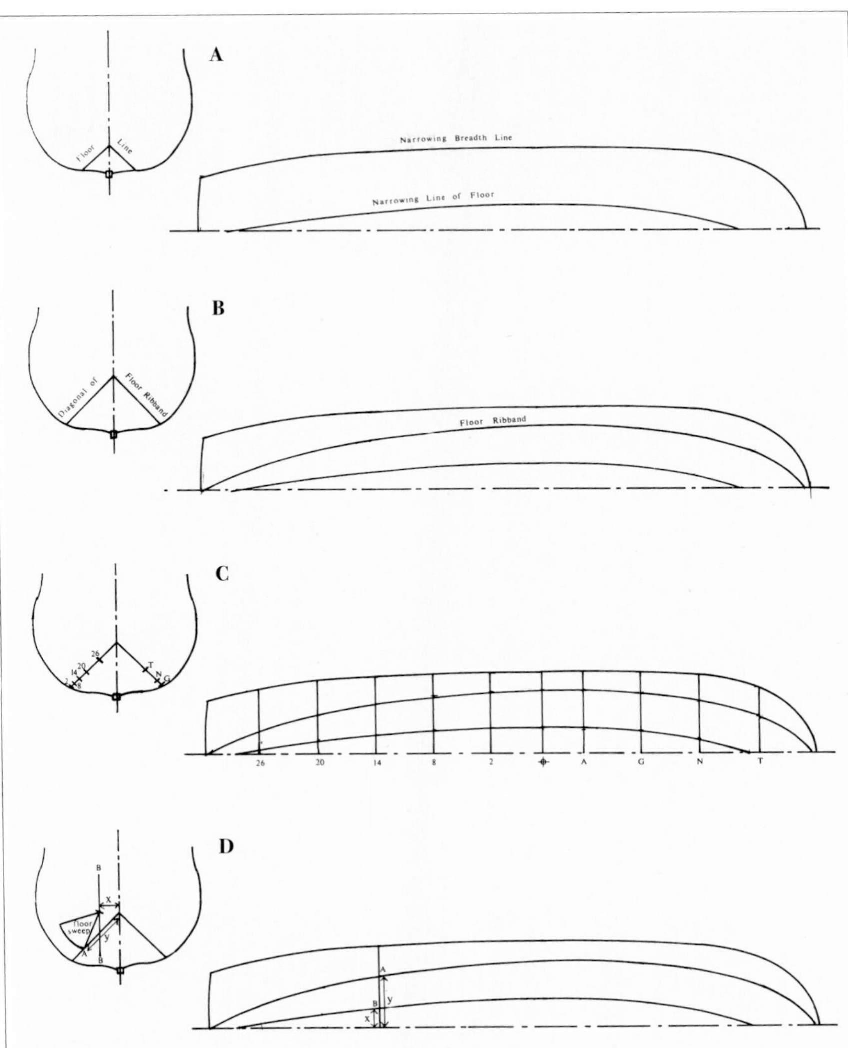

The development of the method of draughting the lower hull:
A. The older system, using the narrowing lines of floor and breadth, **B.** Diagonal of floor ribband added, **C.** Frame stations marked on the horizontal plan, and transferred to the diagonal of floor ribband on the body plan, **D.** Drawing the floor sweep for a sample frame, number fourteen. The point where it crosses the diagonal is Y on the horizontal plan and the distance of the centre of the floor sweep (B) from the centre line is X. The diameter of the floor sweep is constant and its centre is found by drawing a circle centred on line BB which passes through the point for that frame (A) on the diagonal.

(Taken from Brian Lavery, Ship of the Line, *vol II, London, 1984)*

The Lines

Having completed the profile and the midship section the designer now had to produce the rest of the hull shape. The overall aim was to create a 'fair' or streamlined hull in which water resistance was minimised, but at the same time it had to be able to support the weights. The gun layout, however, provided a problem in that the bow and stern naturally provided less buoyancy but carried more guns. A radical solution would have been

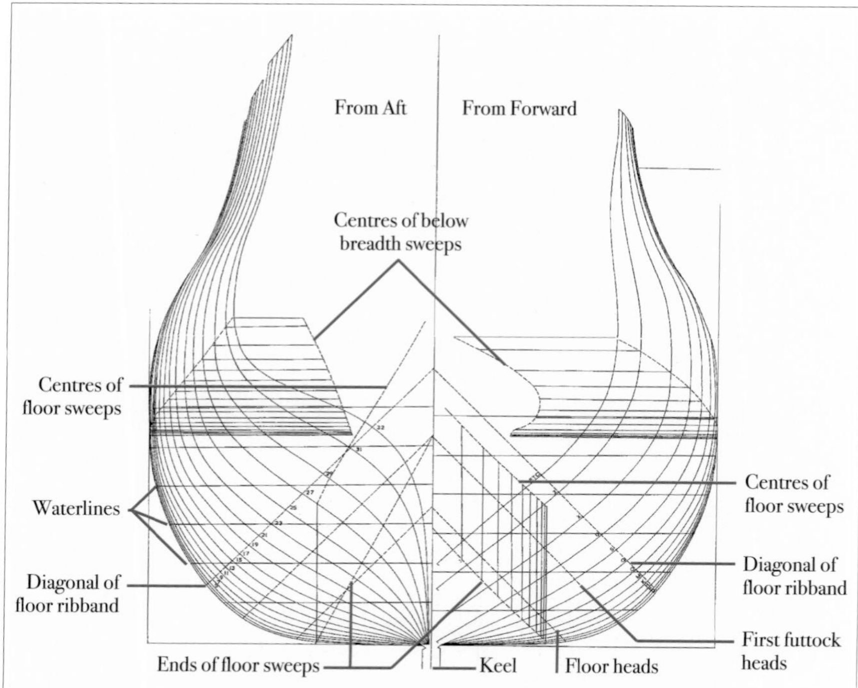

The main features of the body sections plan, with the view from aft to the left and from forward to the right. It shows how the diameters of the sweeps or arcs are reduced towards the bow and stern. This is copied from Slade's draught and the diagonal of floor sweeps is numbered in the original, suggesting it was important to his technique.

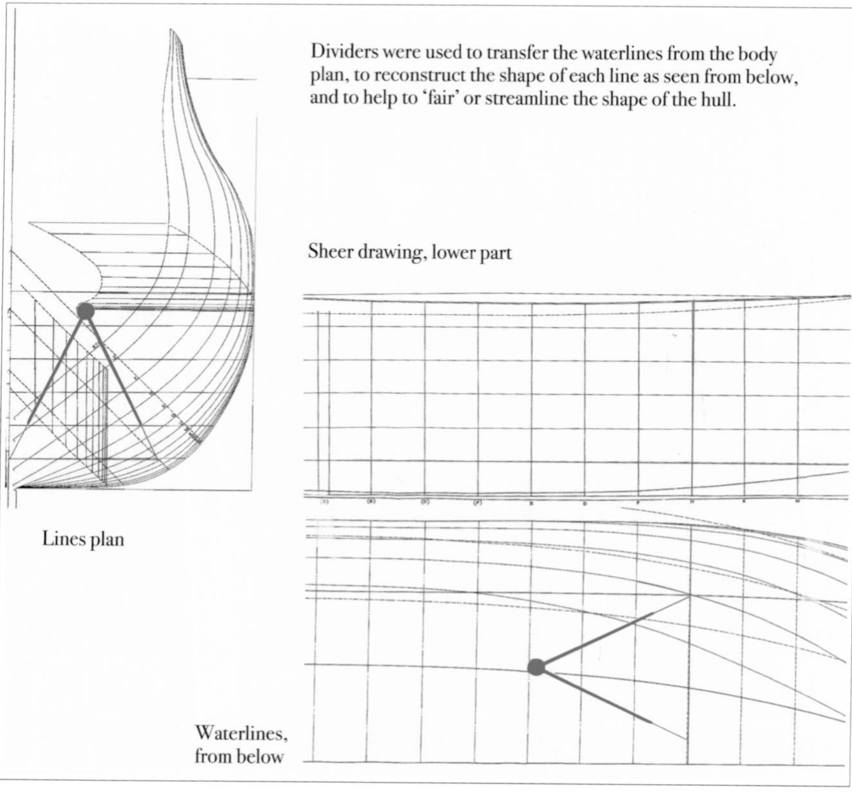

Dividers were used to transfer the waterlines from the body plan, to reconstruct the shape of each line as seen from below, and to help to 'fair' or streamline the shape of the hull.

to transfer most of them to midships, but no one suggested that – indeed, more would be added with the introduction of carronades in later years. Shipwrights simply accepted that if a hull was too long it would tend to 'hog' or sag at the ends. A three-decker, however, could be longer than a two-decker because of the extra strength given by the third deck.

At the bow the hull was almost round just above the waterline as seen from above, and soon reached something close to its maximum breadth, which allowed room for the guns. Below the waterline the hull was increasingly sharp in its lower parts. Aft, the underwater shape had to be even sharper to allow water to reach the rudder; but above water it still had to be wide, both to give space for the guns and to accommodate the officers. This could be difficult and Captain Kempenfelt, when serving in the *Victory* in 1779, commented on the failure of two 74-gun ships. '...the after body is too clean near the water edge, by which, when by the wind, the quarter is not supported... I am told it is the practice of the French and of our best builders to make the after body clean under water; but at the water's edge to give a fullness to support or resist the pressure of the sail.'[7]

The designer used a set of construction lines to modify the shape of the midship section towards the bow and stern. The common method was to draw out narrowing and rising lines of the floor (actually the same line seen in different planes) to mark out the end of the floor in successive frames, and hence the situation of the floor sweep; and the rising and narrowing lines of breadth, which did the same job for the breadth sweeps. These lines would rise and narrow towards the bow and stern, but away from midships the shape had to be joined to the keep by means of a straight line or curve – in which case the rising and narrowing lines of the floor became purely theoretical and merely guided the shape of the other lines. Possibly this caused Slade to use a line known as the 'diagonal of floor ribband', a real line which would make it easier to 'fair' or streamline the hull or remove local bumps which would reduce its sailing qualities. Most designers had a hollow in the bows, but Slade characteristically preferred a straight diagonal line, as seen in cross-section, to join the sweeps to the keel. Whatever method he used to draw out the lines, the designer would complete the 'fairing' process by drawing theoretical water lines on

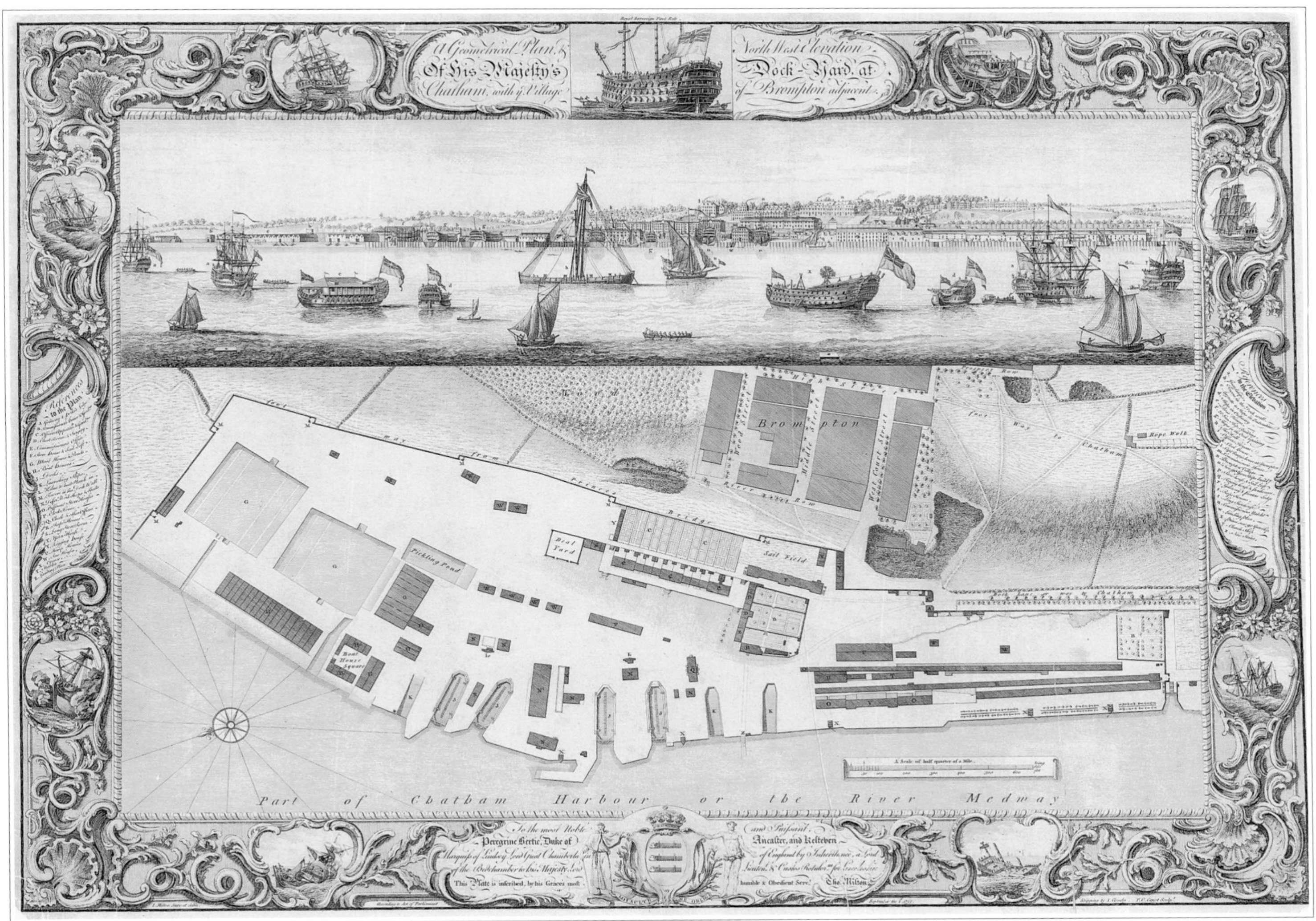

Chatham Dockyard in 1755 as shown in a print by Thomas Milton and Pierre Canot, with help from John Cleveley the Elder who later became carpenter of the *Victory*. The dock where the ship was built is near the centre of the picture, with docks and building slips along the waterfront. The long building to the right is the ropery, with mast and boat ponds to the left.

(© National Maritime Museum, Greenwich, London, PAH9721)

the plan. He selected six levels 3ft 6in apart on the sheer plan and body sections, transferring the width at that point to another view, the underside of the ship. There was no possibility that the ship would actually float at these levels, except the main one which was the 'load water line', the point at which a ship normally floated. Their main function was to test the shape of the hull and make sure it was smooth.

The draught 'proposed for building a first-rate at Chatham' was ready by 6 June 1759 and was sent to the Admiralty. On the 14th it was returned to the Navy Board with the message, 'We do hereby Signify to you our approval of the Said Draught, and returning it to you herewith, desire and direct you to Cause a ship of the first rate to be set up in Chatham Yard and Built by it.'

Chatham Dockyard

First-rates were invariably built in the Royal Dockyards rather than in private yards, and in dry-docks rather than building slips as it was considered dangerous to launch such a large ship in a narrow river, with the risk of hitting the opposite bank, or of the capsize of such a high-sided vessel. Chatham Dockyard had continued to develop in the first half of the eighteenth century even though its greatest days during the Dutch Wars were past. It got new storehouses, workshops, dry-docks, offices and officers' houses. According to Lord Sandwich the yard was to be 'kept singly to its proper use as a Building yard.' This was because it had 'great extent of yard' as its riverfront, and outside it had 'room to moor half the fleet of England.'[8] The programme for a Royal visit of 1778 gave some idea of the yard's facilities, apart from the ships in dry-docks and on slips that he was to see:

> When landed to proceed to the [Commissioner's] House, walk through his garden to the sail loft – hemp houses – upper forest – rope houses – down upon the anchor wharf – storehouses there – rigging house.... clock storehouse – blacksmith's shop... large mast house... small mast house... mast ponds – store boat houses – new wharf – working boat houses and lower mast house – cross between the lower forest and south end of mast ponds...[9]

Though it had its limitations as an operational naval base, Chatham was an excellent place for shipbuilding. 'The Site of this Yard is exceeding Convenient for Docks and Slips and here is sufficient flow of Water for Docking and Launching the greatest Ships.'[10] It had the longest river frontage of any of the Royal Dockyards, allowing four dry-docks which were mostly used for repair of the underwater hull, and three slips where new ships could be built.

Dry-docks at Chatham, from a model made in 1772–74. The one on the left is the Old Single Dock where the *Victory* was built. Behind it is the clock tower storehouse with sawpits under its arches and timber stored to the right. Behind these is the officers' terrace where the senior officials lived, with the master shipwright in the centre.

(© National Maritime Museum, Greenwich, London, L2712-007)

The records show that the new ship was 'begun' on 23 July 1759. Some have interpreted this to mean the ship was 'laid down' or the keel was laid on blocks, though the term was not used at the time. Very few examples of the detailed records kept by the dockyards – the 'Progress on the works at His Majesty's said yard the past week' – have survived, and those that have mostly relate to Portsmouth in the 1740s and 1770s. However they show, for example, that work began on the rebuilding of the 48-gun ship *Tilbury* began on 8 February 1743, but it was only on 1 March that the shipwrights 'laid the keel on the blocks.' It has also been inferred that there was some kind of ceremony attended by dignitaries. There is no evidence for this and, in fact, her predecessor in the Old Single Dock, the large 74-gun ship *Valiant*, was not floated out until 10 August, two weeks after the new 100-gun ship was begun. The term simply meant that the first workmen were employed in cutting out parts for the ship, for the Dockyard officials kept careful accounts of how the labour was used; and obviously the parts of the keel had to be made before they could be laid down. Presumably that happened soon after 10 August, and there is no evidence that any kind of ceremony took place, for this or any other ship of the time.

Timber

Timber supply was one of the greatest constraints on British sea power, and in 1771 Lord Sandwich wrote, 'timber and men are what is wanting to make our fleet invincible'.[11] Timber came in different types, which were carefully stacked separately in the dockyards – for keels, beams, futtocks, knees, plank and so on. The Royal forests occupied great areas of land but were largely depleted of suitable timber – only the New Forest and the Forest of Dean were still useful but they supplied Portsmouth and Plymouth while Chatham was reliant on private contractors such as Henry Mills, described as 'a considerable timber merchant' in 1771. Most of the wood came from East Anglia, apart from a small quantity from Sherwood Forest. Mills claimed, 'that in Sussex, Kent, Surrey, Berkshire, part of Hampshire, Essex, Suffolk and part of Norfolk it had been almost all cut down within these 30 years.'[12] Proximity to a navigable river greatly increased the value of timber. Gabriel Snodgrass of the East India Company claimed that 'there is yet plenty of large timber within 40 or 50 miles of water carriage, and in the interior parts of the kingdom, great quantities of large timber' but it was difficult to transport over the poor roads of the day.[13] The American colonies had great forests but their timber was mistrusted except for use in masts. The navy faced competition from house-builders, from ironworks which still used charcoal, from farmers who were hungry for arable land, and from merchant shipbuilders – though only the East India Company built ships which were large enough to need the bigger timbers of a ship of the line. Plank came via Danzig (later Gdansk) after being floated down the Vistula. More came from Hamburg or from Holland and was floated down the Rhine. 'Compass' timber, the rounded pieces used to make the frame of the ship, was largely native. These pieces and the L-shaped 'knees' were the most valuable and could not be grown intensively in forests, as the trees would grow straight up seeking air. Curved or 'compass' timber for the frames and knees of a ship of the line had to grow for perhaps 100 years and not every landowner was prepared to make such a long-term investment, even if it was his family's patriotic duty. Thomas Mitchell, late of Chatham Yard, stated that 'Hedge Rows... will always produce the finest Compass Timber and Knees...'[14] As the main building yard, Chatham had by far the largest stock of 'English Oak Timber and Knees' in October 1760, with 11,462 loads, each containing fifty cubic feet.

The Shipwrights

In October 1758, just before the new ship was ordered, Chatham Dockyard employed 1,751 men besides officers and clerks. There were plumbers and house-carpenters whose main role was to service the yard itself rather than the ships. There were unskilled men such as the 'scavelmen' who had to shovel the mud out of dry docks. There were sailmakers and riggers whose work began after the hull of the ship was completed. There were forty-three pairs of sawyers who cut up the timbers ready for use, and seventy-six caulkers assisted by thirty oakum boys. But the men who played the leading role in shipbuilding and repair, and the largest group in the dockyard, were the 725 shipwrights.[15]

The shipwrights were a boisterous group and fiercely protective of their privileges. In 1740, Commissioner Hughes at Portsmouth had heard 'three loud acclamations or huzzas' in the yard. He made enquiries and found that 'the shipwrights had... got intelligence that one William Ainell... had not regularly served his time to the trade, and for this reason... the shipwrights surrounded him, put a piece of quarter between his legs, took him up on their shoulders, carried him just without the gate, then sat him down, gave three shouts... and returned to their duty.' For a shipwright normally had to serve seven years apprenticeship and neither workers nor management wanted to dilute the labour force in any way. There had been an even greater disturbance at Chatham as recently as 1755. By tradition shipwrights were allowed to take home 'chips', pieces of timber which were too small for shipbuilding. The definition of chips tended to expand over the years, until the commissioner at Chatham decided that a piece which could be carried under a man's arm was lawful, one which had to be carried on the shoulder was not. Security was increased at the gate, but the 'men with chips on their shoulders' forced their way through. There were several days of rioting and marines were deployed to restore order. The supposed ringleaders were illegally pressed into the navy and taken round to Portsmouth where they were released and left to find their own way home.

Mary Lacy was disguised as a man when she began an apprenticeship in Portsmouth Dockyard in 1763. When the indenture was signed, '...my master went and bought me a saw, an ax and chizzel, which made me very proud to think I had some new tools to work with.' Similarly, at Chatham in 1778, John Allan spent three shillings on 'heeling an ax' for his apprentice George Carr and 5/6 on a handsaw, followed by two shillings for another handsaw, 1/6 for 'formers and gouges' and four pence for 'a plane iron.'[16] With no mechanical aids the work could be very hard, especially since there were no twist drills, as Mary Lacy found:

> The first work I was called upon was, to bore holes in the bottom of a ship called the Thunderer, which, as I was at first unacquainted with the method of doing it, proved hard work for me. This occasioned me to think I should not be able to serve out my time without being discovered.[17]

The apprentice's wages were paid to his master, and John Allan took a total of £271 on behalf of George Carr in three years and three months from 1780–83. In return he was responsible for his keep and about once a month he paid him two shillings or 2/6 pocket money. When

Mary Lacy's master became bankrupt, he '...now became so poor, that he was not able to buy me a pair of shoes.'[18]

Erecting the Frame

The building of the ship was closely supervised, and according to a slightly later account, 'On a ship of the Line in the Royal Dock Yards, there will be seldom less than Six Officers, besides the occasional Visits every Day of the Builder and his two Assistants.'[19] John Lock had served as his father Pierson's assistant when he was master shipwright at Portsmouth in the 1740s. He became master shipwright himself at Plymouth in 1752, before transferring to Chatham in August 1755. He was a bachelor but his large six-storey house in the centre of the officers' terrace was managed by Mrs Ann May, 'who has lived several years with me as housekeeper... friend and companion and often my careful nurse.' His will hinted that the relationship was even closer, for any child born to Mrs May within nine months of his death would have a share in his estate.[20] He did indeed die in April 1762 while the *Victory* was building and was succeeded by John Allin, who transferred from Portsmouth. He had already served for twenty-six years, ten of these as a master shipwright. He had been apprenticed to his father, served seven years as foreman afloat at Deptford, two years as master caulker at Chatham, assistant master shipwright at Woolwich, first assistant at Chatham, the master shipwright at Sheerness, Woolwich and then Portsmouth.

This detail of John Cleveley's painting of a shipyard on the Thames is dated 1762, around the time when he became carpenter of the *Victory*. It shows a two-decker with its frame nearly complete, and another ship with the stern structure in place and the floors crossed. It provides a rare, if rather distant, view of shipwrights at work.

(© Glasgow Museum, Scotland, 850E4566)

The work on the new first-rate was rarely mentioned in the records and we can safely assume that the building followed the standard procedure. The keel was a straight piece, rectangular in cross-section and made up of several parts joined in line by overlapping joints known as scarphs. The curved stem post, also made of several pieces joined together, was raised. A whole assembly was put together at the dockside to form the stern. The stempost, which was the basis of the lower part, was straight and almost vertical. Above it were several horizontal timbers known as 'transoms', and on each side of them were the elegantly curved horizontal timbers known as 'fashion pieces'. The lyre-like structure was raised in a single piece. Meanwhile the floor timbers which formed the lower part of the hull were being cut out and put in place to give a ladder-like appearance to the hull as seen from above.

It was impossible to find a single piece of timber with the right grain to form the whole of one of the ship's frames, so it was made up of several parts known as 'futtocks'. These came in pairs on each side, with joins arranged so that they did not overlap. Thus one frame comprised the first futtock, third futtock and upper futtock. The adjacent one, which joined the end of the floor timber already laid across the keel, comprised the second futtock and toptimber. Each pair of frames was assembled on the dockside at the same time as its opposite number on the other side. A rope passed over the structure above the keel and tackles were attached to either side of it so that the frames on each side could be hoisted into place together. These were the full frames which ran all the way from the keel to the top of the side. They were linked by the upper and lower cills of the gunports, and above and below these were the filling frames. A long piece with several scarphs, the 'keelson', was placed above the structure to help lock the frames in place. Towards the bow and stern the central structure above the keel was raised higher and known as the 'rising deadwood'. There were no floor timbers in these areas, instead the heel of each timber joined the deadwood and they were set at an increasing angle forward or aft to put them at right angles to the planking. Right forward, the hawse were set parallel to the keel to face the oncoming water, while in the after part the transoms formed much of the shape. The frame of the ship was held in place by temporary pieces. Cross-spalls prevented the structure from collapsing inwards until the deck beams were fitted and ribbands held the different timbers apart – they could also be used to check the fairness of the hull and a shipwright could employ his adze on the futtocks to remove any local anomalies.

A ship in the early stages of construction at Deptford, with the sternpost in place, the stern structure raised, the floors crossed and a pair of assembled futtocks about to be raised into position. This is a detail of a print by Milton and Canot, part of the same series as the Chatham print above.

(© National Maritime Museum, Greenwich, London, PZ5606)

A Change in Fortune

The war situation improved through the year of 1759 as the hull of the *Victory* began to take shape. In February the French abandoned the siege of Madras in India, and two months later the British took Masulipatam. In the West Indies, the island of Guadeloupe was taken from the French in May. In August the French were defeated at the Battle of Minden in Germany and later in the month came the first major naval victory when Admiral Boscawen took three French ships of the line and destroyed three more off Lagos in Portugal. Meanwhile, Admiral Sir Charles Saunders was using his fleet to take General James Wolfe's army up to the main French stronghold of Quebec, which they captured on 18 September. For the Royal Navy, the crowning glory came on 20 November when Admiral Hawke chased a French fleet of twenty-one ships of the line into Quiberon Bay in south Brittany, where they destroyed the flagship *Soleil Royal*, took or sunk several more and forced others up the river Vilaine where they were stranded. It was the clearest naval victory for at least a century and the great actor-manager David Garrick produced the lines which became a naval anthem:

A model showing the *Victory* under construction, with scaffolding and staging erected, the frame complete and the main wale, painted black, in place.

(© National Maritime Museum, Greenwich, London, SLR0505)

Come, cheer up, my lads, 'tis to glory we steer,
To add something more to this wonderful year;
To honour we call you, as freemen not slaves,
For who are so free as the sons of the waves?
Heart of oak are our ships,
Heart of oak are our men:
We always are ready;
Steady, boys, steady;
We'll fight and we'll conquer again and again.

The letter-writer Horace Walpole claimed that 'Our bells are worn threadbare with ringing for victories.' But with the great French fleet defeated, the new first-rate building at Chatham was no longer needed urgently and within a year another factor would tend to slow down her construction.

King George II died on 25 October 1760 and was succeeded by his grandson who became George III. Just five days later, the new-first rate was named *Victory*. There was nothing surprising in the name itself. It was

The Battle of Quiberon Bay in 1759 as painted by Nicholas Pocock. Hawke's flagship the *Royal George* is engaging the enemy flagship *Soleil Royal*, mistakenly shown as a three-decker. After this triumph, the construction of the new first-rate was much less urgent.

(© National Maritime Museum, Greenwich, London, BHC0399)

common for the first great ship of a new reign to be named after the King, but there already was a *Royal George*, and as yet the twenty-two-year-old King had neither wife nor sons to give their names. The Admiralty was unlikely to reach back to previous sovereigns such as *Royal Charles, Royal Anne* or *Royal James* as they would be reminders of the deposed Stuarts. Another traditional first-rate name, *Britannia*, was already in use as was *Royal Sovereign* as the successor to the *Sovereign of the Seas*. It would be the next century before first rates were named after admirals such as St Vincent and Nelson, or parts of the United Kingdom such as Hibernia or Caledonia. The name *Victory* had been used for two smaller ships in the sixteenth and seventeenth centuries. It was promoted to first-rate status in 1691 when the *Royal James* was renamed – clearly it was no longer appropriate to have a ship named after the deposed King, while the new name drew attention to the victory over the French at Barfleur and La Hogue that year. The next *Victory*, launched in 1737, was technically a rebuild of that ship, though it is doubtful if any old timber was actually reused. She was tragically lost in 1744 so the name was available.

The timing is slightly more surprising than the actual name. The old king had died suddenly and the new one was still taking up the reins so it is not likely that he would have time to think about a ship name, not even that of the largest ever built for his navy. On the afternoon of the 25th, just hours after his grandfather died, George III referred to 'this bloody and expensive war' – though ministers including William Pitt persuaded him to tone that down to 'expensive but just and necessary war' in public. Nevertheless, the King planned to seek peace as soon as possible, while his current ministers thought otherwise. It is not unlikely that the name of the new ship was a subtle reminder of the victories that had already been won in 1759, and others that might follow if the war was pursued to a logical conclusion.

With the French fleet defeated and peace in prospect, there was no urgent need for a ship like the *ictory* and work on her slowed down. We do not know or sure what stage she was at when this happened, but erhaps this was fortunate in that it allowed a great deal f time for her timbers to season, which did not happen vith most of the ships completed during the war. Later, he private shipbuilder Barnard of Harwich admitted, in the last War he built a Seventy-gun ship and aunched her within the Year; but he acknowledged hat was too short a time...'[21]

lanking

According to the French shipwright Blaise Ollivier who isited England in 1737, 'The English employ about hree or four years in building a three deck ship... The English shipwrights frame their ships first and leave hem in that state while they work slowly on the deck-beams, the wales, and the ceiling etc. They take extreme care not to install any timber which is not purged of its sap...' – though the last point was to be neglected in the ate 1750s as ships were rushed forward to fight in the war. Once the frame was reasonably complete, and perhaps allowed to stand in season for a year or more, he builders could move on to other stages. The external planking of the ship began with the lower wales, thicker pieces of plank fitted just below the level of the lower gundeck ports, and sometimes slightly interrupted by them. The other wales might be added above that, while the planking below the lower wale reduced gradually by means of the black strakes. The rest of the planking of the bottom was a uniform thickness of four and a half inches to give a smooth surface. The lowest strake, the 'garboard', had its edge fitted into a recess in the upper edge of the keel known as the rabbet. The surface area tended to reduce towards bow and stern as some of the planks, known as 'stealers', came to an end before reaching the stem or sternpost.

Internally, the thickness of the planking varied more as there was no reason to keep it smooth. In the hold, pieces known as 'thick stuff' covered the joins of the futtocks, with slightly lighter pieces called 'footwaling' on either side. There were more thick planks known as 'clamps' under the beams of each deck to support them. The rest of the planking between the gunports was known as 'spirketting'. Each deck was supported by heavy beams, usually made in three pieces and scarphed, running across the ship. Lighter pieces known as 'carlines' ran fore and aft between the beams, with even smaller timbers known as 'ledges' between them, parallel to the beams. This ensured that there was always support for the trucks or wheels of the gun carriages, beyond the deck planking which was four inches thick. The ship was kept rigid by means of vital pieces called 'knees'. Hanging knees were set vertically to support the beam from below, with one arm of the L fixed to the beam. Standards were fixed above, while lodging knees were set at the level of the deck itself, in the angle between the beam and the sides of the ship. Down the centre of each deck ran a series of essential features including mast partners, capstans, hatchways, ladderways and pumps. Back in the hold, the whole structure was further strengthened by thick curved pieces known as 'riders', fitted over the thick stuff, clamp and so on. Deck hooks were large curved pieces at the forward end of each deck, serving to support the hull structure as well as the deck itself. As the planking of each part of the ship was completed it was likely to be caulked. A small space was left between

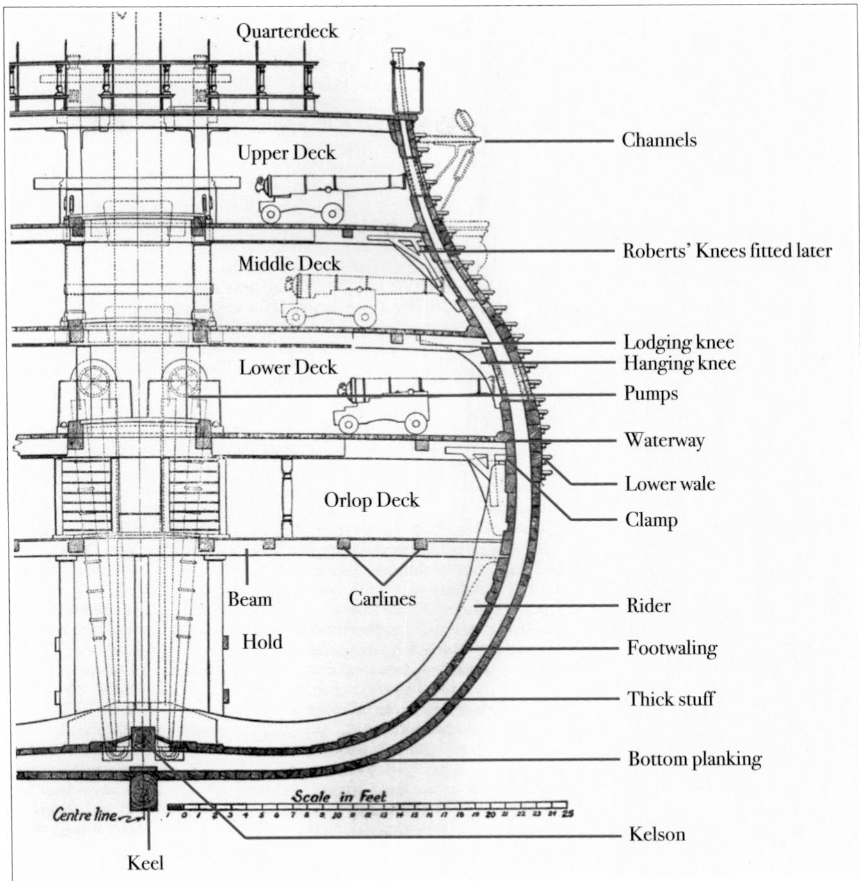

Midship section of the *Victory*, showing details of decks, planking etc. This was done after her second great repair in 1801–1803, so shows added features such as Roberts' knees with iron braces, but the general principles are the same.

(Taken from Arthur Bugler, HMS Victory: Building Restoration and Repair, *II vols, London, 1966).*

each strake of this planking and it was filled using oakum or stands of rope, then tarred over. Seventy-six caulkers and thirty oakum boys were employed on this task at Chatham in 1764.

Peacetime

The war ended with the Treaty of Paris in 1763. Britain gained Canada, leaving only a few French fishing rights in North America. The West Indian islands of Tobago, Dominica and St Vincent were taken over, though some complained that the sugar-rich Guadeloupe should have been retained instead of Canada. In India, the French had to recognise the supremacy of the British and Minorca was given back by Spain while Florida was added to the British colonies. In many ways it was the most complete victory of the century, though the main ally, Prussia, had been abandoned without achieving her war aims while the North American colonists no longer feared the French presence, but found other issues to occupy them.

In peacetime the main priority of the dockyards was the repair of ships coming home after many years of hard wartime service. In September 1764 the Chatham officers reported of the *Victory*:

> ...Her works have been unavoidably greatly retarded at times by taking off the shipwrights and other artificers to give proper dispatch to ships ordered to be fitted or under repair. In my humble opinion she will not be finished before the latter end of April next, at which time I hope she will be ready to launch provided the joiners and carvers can keep pace with the shipwrights.[22]

There had been a tendency to restrict the amount of decoration carried on ships ever since the early years of the eighteenth century, but the *Victory* was an exception to that trend. Her figurehead was an amazing construction, far more elaborate than those fitted to the first-rates *Royal George* and *Britannia* in recent years. Even the description of the decorations ran into 1,700 words and the head was charged with political symbolism. It was surmounted by a bust of George III

A model of the *Victory* as completed, showing the open stern galleries. It is mounted on a launching cradle and the model is normally displayed on a building slip, though actually the ship was built in a dry-dock and did not need a cradle.

(© National Maritime Museum, Greenwich, London, BHC0514)

ith a shield in front bearing the union flag with erubs' heads representing the four winds. Behind ere figures of Britannia to starboard and Victory to ort 'trampling down, envy, discord and faction... ehind that were Fame blowing a trumpet and Peace olding a branch of palms and denoting the happy onsequences resulting from victory.' There was a ritish lion behind, 'trampling on very rich trophies of ar.' The whole assembly was supported by figures in e costumes of Europe, Asia, America and Africa, with nall figures representing navigation and mathematics n one side, and on the other a cornucopia representing eace and plenty. The language of the description went eyond the imagination of the average shipwright or Javy Board official, and it seems likely that it was ıpired by the Earl of Egmont, First Lord of the dmiralty since September 1763, who certainly had the ange of antiquarian interests needed, and who was ccused rather unfairly by Horace Walpole of making pompous additions to the dockyards'. If there was a olitical message, it was that the peace of 1763, supported by the King, was successful and happy, bringing bout 'the happy consequences arising from victory ringing about a peace...' But it is difficult to see who ould be moved by such a message. Only a few naval fficials would ever read the description, and very few part from sailors would get close enough to the real hing to see the details, and even fewer would appreciate heir meaning. It is remarkable that such an elaborate arving could be fitted when the navy was suffering severe post-war economies and it must have had high-evel support. Even so the Navy Board recoiled at the price of £190 for the head alone and reduced it by £10; the 'very rich model... done in clay' was reduced from £20 to £15. However the other carvings were paid for in full – a trail board aft of the head for £7.11.0, a taffrail at the stern with 'a very rich bust of His Majesty' with Neptune and Britannia on either side for £55.8.0; and quarter pieces forming the edges of the stern, one with a woman 'pouring forth the riches of the universe' and Mars the god of war for £57.12.0. There were carvings representing the seasons of the year for £44, a cove under the upper stern balcony cut with the royal monogram and various heraldic symbols for £18, counter pieces with eagles for £14 and various other pieces to a total of £8.1.0.

The Launch

The men worked through the winter of 1764–65 and shipwright John Russell ruptured himself carrying a piece of footwaling on board.[23] On 28 April the Master Shipwright wrote to the Navy Board that the ship would be ready to launch at the next spring tide – high water caused by the fortnightly cycle was needed to launch a ship or float one out of dock. The Admiralty agreed and preparations went ahead. The Chatham hulk, normally used for fitting masts to ships, was moored opposite the dock entrance. A stout cable was attached to it, passing through two triple-blocks to give extra purchase, and a large team of men was allocated to haul the ship out when the tide was high enough.

But Hartly Larkin had a sleepless night. He was the 'foreman afloat' of the yard, responsible for the workers on ships in the harbour. He could not put the idea out of his mind, that 'His Majesty's Ship *Victory*, which was to be hove out of the dock the next day, should be jammed between the gate riders against the apron wharf.' In that case, 'the ship should be hove 60 or 70 feet astern and on blocks then be jammed in the gateway with nothing to receive the body, it could have been of the utmost consequence'. As soon as it was daylight, he was in the yard and 'tried the breadth of the dock at two certain heights and likewise the ship at two fixed waterlines and compared the one with the other and found that the ship at the upper breadth broader than the dock by 6 inches, and at the lower breadth broader than the dock by 9½.' He alerted Allin, the master shipwright, who was already suffering from 'violent and frequent attacks of a bilious disorder in his bowels' which caused his retirement two years later.[24] He sent an assistant to check the figures then showed signs of panic when they were confirmed. 'What must be done, the ship cannot go out today.' Someone, and Larkin does not say it was him, answered, 'if you will please to let as many shipwrights as can be employed on the dock and gates she may be got out.' The shipwrights hacked away at the parts of the open gate, before the tide rose inside the dock and the ship began to float. They competed the work in time and the hull was ready to be hauled out into the river on schedule.[25]

On 7 May 1765 the *London Public Advertiser* reported, 'This day will be launched His Majesty's ship the *Victory*, estimated the largest and finest ship ever

A model of the *Victory*'s original figurehead showing its elaborate and perhaps symbolic decoration. The Perspex support is not part of the original.

(© National Maritime Museum, Greenwich, London, SLR2530)

This 1772 print shows a three-decker after floating out from a dry-dock at Chatham, possibly the 90-gun *Barfleur* which was launched in 1768. The sheer hulk which played a key part in the hauling out is shown to the left, while in the foreground a boat's crew is preparing to secure the ship to a square wooden buoy. The ship carries the usual array of launching flags.

(© National Maritime Museum, Greenwich, London, PAD1035)

built. Several of the Lords of the Admiralty, Commissioners of the Navy, and many persons of quality and distinction, are expected to be present, for whose reception great preparations are making through the town.' Such people might well have intended to be there, but it is unlikely that they actually came, for by the day of the launch the country was in yet another political crisis, over the appointment of regents in case the King was ill. The Board of Admiralty held a meeting that day, attended by all seven members. It is highly unlikely that one member of the House of Lords and six of the Commons would have left London at such a critical moment, and indeed that day the House of Commons debated the regency issue from two in the afternoon until ten at night. The Admiralty meeting, which was only concerned with routine business, was probably held in the morning to allow members to attend Parliament. London society tended to follow the routines of the legislature, so it is unlikely that many of the 'persons of quality' found their way into Kent for the launch. The Commissioners of the Navy, popularly known as the Navy Board, probably did as they had no meeting that day but seemed well informed about the status of the ship when they did meet a few days later.

We have no description of the *Victory*'s launch, there was no local paper at the time and presumably not enough 'persons of quality' to attract interest in London. The nearest we have is the launch of the 74-gun *Prince of Wales* in the Welsh port of Milford Haven a month later, though it is difficult to assess how different the atmosphere would have been from

Chatham – the *Prince of Wales* was a smaller ship, but a very big fish in the small pond of a remote shipbuilding town. In any case the *Gentleman's Magazine* reported: 'Ten thousand spectators covered the hills all round, which, with a great muster of sloops and other vessels, made a beautiful appearance.'

In 1767 Hartly Larkin petitioned the Navy Board for some reward for his service in saving the *Victory*, citing the case of his colleague, the master blacksmith at the yard who had been rewarded for inventing a new method of welding the links of mooring chains. The Navy Board decreed that 'No notice be taken of this application', perhaps because they wanted to forget an embarrassing incident, perhaps because they feared setting an expensive precedent – but they did not deny that Larkin's facts were correct. He remained in post until 1779 when he was granted superannuation, 'so as to admit of a more active man to act in his place.'[26]

In Ordinary

There was no immediate need for the *Victory* and she was to be laid up 'in ordinary' like most ships of the peacetime navy. On 13 May 1765, less than a week after the launch, the Navy Board ordered that:

> As His Majesty's Ship *Victory* should be kept well down in the water to preserve her form from straining, direct Chatham Officers to cause her to be laid at the 5, 6 or 7 moorings at Gillingham as shall be prepared for her, and keep her as low down as the depth of water will admit.[27]

Clearly they were concerned that during a long stay the ship would tend to 'hog', as even without the guns the bow and stern would have the extra weight of the forecastle, poop and quarterdeck with less buoyancy to support them, especially if the ship was floating high.

Chatham was considered more suitable for laying up smaller ships rather than first-rates, as the Medway was shallow in most places and dredging methods were primitive before the advent of steam. According to a report of 1774:

> The Moorings for Ships laid up here extend from a little below Rochester Bridge to the lower part of Gillingham Reach, an extent of above 4 Miles, within that space there is only five Moorings for Ships of 74 Guns and upwards where there is Water sufficient for them to lay at and swing on float at low water in Spring Tides if they are properly Ballasted, but there is for 20 such ships if they are kept at a light draught of Water but this is very prejudicial to them.

The ship was laid up 'in ordinary' which meant that she was paid for out of the ordinary budget of the navy rather than the allowance for 'men voted', with a formula which included a sum for the wear and tear of ships at sea. She was under the care of her standing officers, so called because they stayed with the ship whether she was on active service or not. All were warrant officers, for commissioned officers were only appointed for sea service. The most senior was the purser, though he was not expected to supervise the others and each worked

Mooring chains of the type which held the *Victory* for thirteen years in the Medway. Their locations in the estuary can be seen on the map in Chapter Three.

(Taken from Blanckley's Naval Expositor, *(1750), author's collection)*

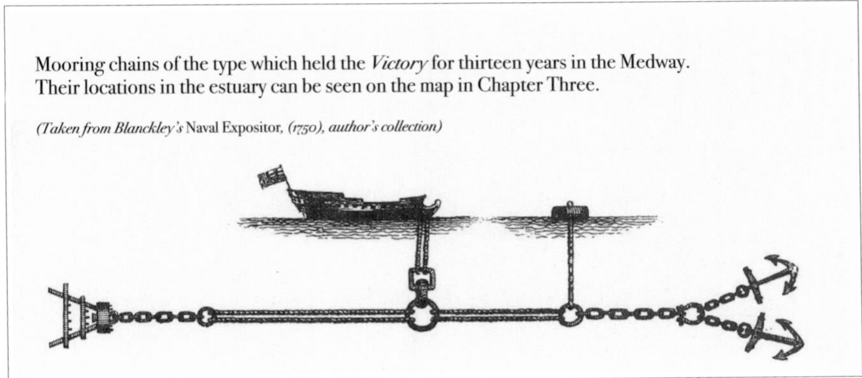

largely in his own department. The purser, William Davis, was a supply officer whose duty was 'to take charge of the provisions of a ship of war, and to see that they are carefully distributed to the officers and crew...'.[28] The Boatswain, Edward Hummary, had served sixteen years by 1765 and swore he was more than fifty-two years of age in order to qualify for superannuation.[29] The Gunner was Thomas Moulden, who stayed in post until he died ten years later. The cook was Stephen Oliver, until he was allowed to exchange with Richard Green of the unfinished 64-gun *Prudent* in 1767.[30]

Warrant officers were paid according to the rate of their ship and most would regard an appointment to a first-rate as the peak of their careers. John Cleveley of the *Victory* was rather different, he constantly longed for his home thirty miles away in Deptford where his wife Sarah lived with most of their children. Cleveley had his son, also John, on board as his servant or apprentice and both developed parallel careers as marine artists. John senior had made the wind indicator for the Admiralty Boardroom. He had worked on a plan and view of Chatham produced by Thomas Milton in 1755–56, part of a series showing the Royal Dockyards; but apart from that father and son found no inspiration in the muddy waters and flat landscape of the Medway, and most of the father's pictures are of Deptford. In 1769 he petitioned to be transferred back there and instead he was offered superannuation, which allowed him to follow his other career. His son was transferred to the yard at Deptford but apparently did not complete his apprenticeship. He did, however, have a deep understanding of ship architecture which stood him in good stead as a marine artist.

During 1765–66 around fifty able seamen were employed on board, probably preparing the ship's rigging. Most of it would be put in store, but the countless pieces of rope had to be prepared. Apart from that, the officers were concerned with routine maintenance and there was little variety in life, except when they were given leave, as the purser frequently was, or when the boatswain led a party to move a ship to and from Sheerness. At 7am on 3 February 1767 the peace was disturbed when the *True Friend*, a lighter employed by the Victualing Office, collided with the *Victory*'s bows in a fog. She 'carried away several pieces of the carved work from the head' at a cost of £5.5.0.[31] Women were forbidden to live on board the ships in ordinary and this was announced by 'printed orders that are hung up in the bulkhead of the steerage of every ship.' However, warrant officers tended to feel that it was one of their privileges to have their family with them, and in September 1767 the authorities found eight wives on board different ships. None were discovered in the *Victory*, either they obeyed the regulations or were better at hiding. The wives on the other ships were ordered ashore.[32]

Repairs

In the summer of 1767 it was found that the bottom of the *Victory* was 'touched by the worm'. This was shipworm or *teredo navalis*, one of the navy's greatest problems before coppering of bottoms became standard. It was native to tropical and sub-tropical waters, but ships sometimes brought it back and it found a home in the Royal Dockyards. It was rife at Sheerness further down the river, which was the main reason why large ships like the *Victory* were not laid up in the deeper water there. Two hundred and forty tonnes of ballast were taken out to inspect her bottom from inside. Externally, she was repaired as much as possible while still afloat, by heeling her to one side then the other, breaming her or burning off weed, and graving her or repairing the caulking.[33] This was not enough and she had her first major maintenance, a 'triennial trimming' in the Old Single Dock at Chatham from 7–21 March 1768.[34] The shipwrights found 'the bottom in several parts slightly touched by the worm, which have penetrated within the surface of the plank about half an inch, and about a quarter of an inch diameter, and some of them appear to be yet alive.' She was breamed again to remove the intruders.

By this time, Chatham Dockyard was mainly concerned with the aftermath of the war. The navy was reduced from 432 ships in November 1762 to 360 in 1771. Older ships, such as the three-decker 80s and the 50s, were scrapped, mostly by selling the hulls to contractors. The fleet had largely been rebuilt under Lord Anson and some of the ships had been put together too hurriedly and needed repair. As they returned from years of hard conflict, they were docked in turn and brought up to readiness for any future conflict. As Lord Sandwich wrote in 1771, '...considering the very severe services on which our fleets were employed during the last war and the great number of them that were consequently worn out in actual service at sea, it seems to me rather to be wondered that we have so many good ships still in our ports.'[35]

In May 1771 she was inpected during the Admiralty visitation of the Royal Dockyards led by the Earl of Sandwich and it was reported, 'The *Victory* appears in every respect in perfect good condition, except that by the Carpenter's report she makes 10 inches of water in 24 hours...' Their lordships were also concerned about the ballasting of the ship, but the dockyard had a difficult balancing act. 'The officers being asked if she ever took the ground, answered that she scarce ever touches the ground where she lies.' That meant that she did occasionally touch bottom and the reason was apparent. 'We found on enquiry that the depth of water in this port is scarcely adequate to the draught of the capital ships built according to the present establishment.' This meant that most of them could not be ballasted as low as the Navy Board had intended for the *Victory* in 1765 – 'The consequence of which is very apparent by their losing their sheer, which weakens them greatly...'

A few days later, on 18 May, the Chatham officers informed the Navy Board that 'this day His Majesty's Ship *Victory* was taken into the 2nd Dock.' She was returning to her original building place, for on 30 March that year, Commissioner Hanway of the yard had been ordered to 'letter and number the docks in future from 1–4, beginning with the South Dock...'[36] This time she needed more extensive work and it was soon revealed why she leaked so much – the caulkers 'discovered the oakum, about twenty feet in the keel seam on each side abaft and under the dovetail plates decayed, which we apprehend was the occasion of the leak complained of by the carpenter.' Large amounts of 'thick stuff' were ordered for planking and in July the yard officials reported that the work would 'exceed her triennial trimming' – that is more than a routine repair.'[37] The work was completed at a cost of £4,276 and the ship floated out on 10 October after five months in dock.

She was repaired again in 1775 and Lord Sandwich was pleased during his annual visitation, that the *Victory*, 'to our great satisfaction requires much less to be done to her than was originally apprehended and she will be finished in August, and her repairs estimated only at £3,000.'[38] She returned to her quiet life at her moorings, though not quite forgotten or ignored. She was something of a minor tourist attraction in the river, and in 1776 *The Kentish Traveller's Companion* noted, 'here was built the *Victory*, a first-rate, carrying 110 guns, and the largest ship in the navy. She now lays at moorings near Gillingham.' She was back on dock in February 1777, when it was found that ten strakes of sheathing near the keel had to be replaced. She was undocked in April and her rigging was fitted, perhaps to sail her back to the moorings at Gillingham. In May the officers were ordered 'to let the rigging of the *Victory* remain overhead and to spread it.'[39] This meant that she was ready to sail apart from her guns and stores, for the Admiralty and Navy Board were well aware that she might at last be needed for her intended role.

A view of Chatham Dockyard by Thomas Mitchell, who was assistant master shipwright in the 1770s and a talented marine artist. It was drawn from his house in the officers' terrace. The ship on the right is almost certainly the *Victory* undergoing repair in Number Two Dock in 1771, the first definite picture of the ship. The 60-gun *Medway* is to the left in Number One Dock. The masts over the *Victory*'s stern are on the sheer hulk and are not part of the ship.

(© British Library, London, AN140386001)

3 THE YOUNG NELSON

Nelson Goes to Sea

On 29 September 1758, less than three months before the Lords of the Admiralty met to order the building of the *Victory*, a Norfolk parson's wife gave birth to her sixth child – though two had already died in infancy as was quite common at the time. The baby, named Horace, had two surviving brothers and a sister, none of whom gained any distinction in life, and two more unremarkable brothers and two sisters would follow. The family was solidly middle class in that Reverend Edmund Nelson depended on his parochial income rather than landholding, and most of his children were apprenticed or married to tradesmen and merchants. Any social status came from his wife Catherine Nelson, the great-niece of Britain's first prime minister, Sir Robert Walpole, and sister of Maurice Suckling, a rising naval officer. Legend attributed various acts of bravery to the young Horace, but we only know for sure that he was educated at the Royal Grammar School in Norwich and Sir John Paston's School in North Walsham where, according to a schoolfellow, he was 'under the lash of Classic Jones...'[1] His mother died when he was ten, a particularly vulnerable age. Though he rarely mentioned her afterwards, much of his life can be seen as a search for a replacement.

Like all great men and women, Nelson was fortunate to grow up at a time when his talents were needed. The first stroke of luck was that in 1770 there was a crisis over what the British called the Falkland Islands. This raised the threat of war with Spain and required the

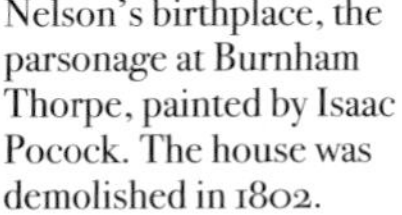

Nelson's birthplace, the parsonage at Burnham Thorpe, painted by Isaac Pocock. The house was demolished in 1802.

(© National Maritime Museum, Greenwich, London, BHC1772)

mobilisation of the navy; his uncle, Maurice Suckling, was appointed to command a ship after seven years on the beach. A captain had almost a free hand in appointing young men as trainee officers and at twelve, Nelson was just the right age to start. A career in the navy was obviously attractive to an adventurous young man, and it had its advantages for the father of a large family. It needed a certain amount of money to fit a boy out for the navy but after that he was paid and might even win some prize money for the capture of enemy ships – unlike the church or the law which required an expensive university education, or the army in which an officer had to buy his commission. At first Suckling was sceptical, 'what has poor Horace done, who is so weak, that he, above all the rest, should be sent to rough it at sea? But let him come and the first time we go into action a cannon-ball may knock his head off and provide for him at once.' But he was wrong about his first point, Nelson's constitution, though subject to many illnesses, was fundamentally sound; and far more important, he had dedication, courage and self-belief which would lead him on to great things, as he would soon demonstrate to Suckling. According to legend, Nelson arrived at Chatham to wander round the town until taken in hand by a friendly naval officer and directed towards Suckling's ship, the 64-gun *Raisonnable,* named after a French prize. The logs and muster books suggest a more prosaic reality, that he joined the ship at Blackstakes, some way down the river Medway, on 23 April 1771, probably after having sailed across the Thames Estuary from Norfolk. He may have looked weedy and bewildered among the strange gear and burly sailors as Victorian artists loved to portray him, but there is no way of knowing that. He was rated as a captain's servant, which did not mean that he tended to Suckling's personal needs – in fact he was a kind of nautical apprentice.

The first problem for Nelson's career was that the dispute with Spain was now resolved (though not finally, as events of more than two centuries later would show). The *Raisonnable* was not likely to go to sea as very few ships of the line were commissioned in peacetime, but Suckling was offered a different appointment, to the 74-gun *Triumph* which was to serve as a guardship. She was one of the best ships in the fleet, built on the dimensions and lines of the French *Invincible* but to British standards of construction. She was 'a ship which, for the space of more than twenty years, was considered the finest of her class then existing'.[2] She was almost as large as a 100-gun ship. When she was rigged early in 1771, it was found that Woolwich yard had issued some items of standard 74 rigging, which were far too short. Some of the *Victory*'s shrouds and backstays were taken out of store to equip her, to be replaced with new ones.[3]

Captain Maurice Suckling, painted in 1764, seven years before he took Nelson on as a volunteer.

(© National Maritime Museum, Greenwich, London, BHC3045)

According to Lord Sandwich's report of that year, the *Triumph* and two other 74s were 'in complete condition, and ready for service in any part of the World, being sheathed, and completely fitted and stored.'[4] Their guns were in place, unlike the ships in ordinary, and each had a crew of 350 men, needing only 250 more to put to sea; though as guardships they would normally remain in harbour unless there was another war scare or they were needed for a special occasion. Meanwhile, Captain Suckling took some responsibility for the twenty-one ships, including the *Victory*, which were laid up in ordinary in the river. He was happy enough to have a regular appointment, but it was not what he had planned for his nephew. He used his contacts to have Nelson signed on as an ordinary seaman in the *Mary Ann*, a small merchant ship trading with Jamaica. This was quite valid in terms of Nelson's

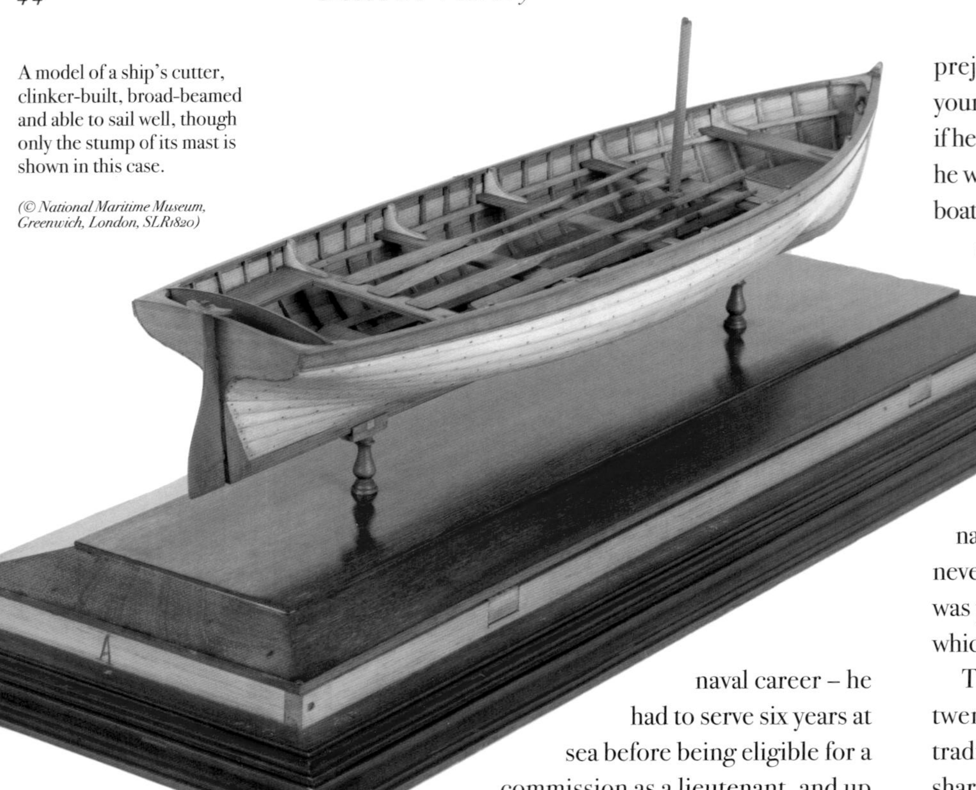

A model of a ship's cutter, clinker-built, broad-beamed and able to sail well, though only the stump of its mast is shown in this case.

(© National Maritime Museum, Greenwich, London, SLR1820)

naval career – he had to serve six years at sea before being eligible for a commission as a lieutenant, and up to half of that could be in merchant ships.

It also gave him an excellent opportunity for learning. We know little about the *Mary Ann*, but a typical merchant ship had a small crew, perhaps fifteen to twenty officers and men, a tenth of that borne by a warship of similar size. There was no possibility of hiding in a crowd or behind authority, of delegating to a petty officer or using heavy labour to solve problems. There was no room for a passenger and, very literally, everyone had to pull his weight. We can assume that the young Nelson had to haul on ropes, climb the rigging to take in sails, take a turn at steering the ship and perhaps learn some navigation across the ocean. By the time he returned, he was, in his own words, 'a practical Seaman'. He had taken on the merchant seaman's 'horror of the Royal Navy', largely caused by fear of the press gang, and adopted the saying of the lower deck 'Aft the more honour, forward the better man!'[5] – for the officers lived near the stern in a merchant or naval ship, and the seamen further forward.

Learning to Sail

After he rejoined to the *Triumph* in the Medway in July 1772, he found it was 'many weeks before I got in the least reconciled to a Man-of-War, so deep was the prejudice rooted'. Captain Suckling recognised the young man's spirit of adventure. He promised him that if he would put some effort into the theory of navigation he would be allowed to take charge of one of the ship's boats, which would give him a good deal of independent service. The ability to navigate was a defining skill of a sea officer, though in practice he would rarely do it in much detail, leaving that to the ship's master. There is no sign that the *Triumph* carried a schoolmaster, but the ship's master had the duty of training midshipmen and boys in the arts of navigation. Nelson apparently did his best, though he never took well to the classroom or book-learning. He was promoted from captain's servant to midshipman, which gave him more authority over the crew.

The cutter of a 74-gun ship was usually eighteen or twenty-five feet long in those days, clinker-built in traditional fashion with overlapping planks. It had a sharp bow and a wide beam of 7ft 4in or 6ft 2in. It was good for sailing, but could be rowed when the winds were light or contrary and was 'commonly employed in carrying light stores, provisions, passengers &c. to and from other ships.'[6] It had a crew of four or six according to size and was equipped with a fore and mizzen mast, both with fore and aft sails for going close to the wind. Nelson also took charge of a 'decked longboat.' The longboat was normally the largest of the ship's boats, though not in fact the longest. It was broad beamed and strongly built for heavy work and a decked version was probably larger than the normal 31ft issued to a 74-gun ship and, as Nelson says, it was 'attached to the Commanding officer's ship at Chatham.' In July 1771 Suckling asked to keep on the longboat which had been used by the 74-gun *Conquestador* when she was the guardship in the Medway, as it was 'much better adapted to the navigation of this river than the one I have.' This was agreed by the Navy Board.[7] It was big enough for its movements to be recorded in the ship's log, though the name of the person in charge is never mentioned. It was almost as big as a small merchant vessel, such as the hoys that transported goods and passengers in the Thames and Medway. Such a boat could be 'armed and equipped, for cruising short distances against merchant-ships of the enemy, or smugglers or for impressing seamen' – although two of these were wartime activities and there is no evidence that Nelson acted against smugglers at this stage in his career. Instead, he was probably employed 'to bring heavy stores and provisions on board, and also to go up small rivers to fetch water, wood, etc.' A standard longboat for a 74-gun ship had a single mast 30ft long with a 15ft bowsprit over the bows. The head of the mainsail was supported by a 9ft 9ins gaff and its foot was spread by a 23ft 4in boom, while the triangular foresail was supported by the bowsprit – we can assume that those of the *Triumph*'s longboat were slightly larger than that.

Nelson may have had to bring his boat alongside many of the twenty-or-so ships laid up in the Medway, for the longboat was often used to carry men from the *Triumph* to ships being fitted out, and he perhaps visited the *Victory* for the first time, though there is no mention of her in the log. At the very least, he must have sailed past her many times. The most common task of the longboat was bringing water casks on board the *Triumph*. A 74 carried around 200 tonnes of water when fully equipped and it was policy to keep them fully topped up in case the ship had to sail suddenly. A longboat might carry twelve butts, each containing 108 gallons. In an average period, the boat was sent watering every three or four days, but that was greatly increased after she came out of dock and the whole supply had to be replenished. The boat had different characteristics when sailing so heavily loaded and navigation needed more care with deeper draught. The boat was at its busiest from 23–26 November 1772. On the first day, it went to Sheerness with marines for the *Endeavour* storeship – Captain Cook's famous ship, now carrying supplies to the Falkland Islands. Next day, it took officers stores' ashore, then the 25th and 26th were spent watering.

The Medway wound eleven miles from Chatham to the Thames Estuary at Sheerness. Tides ranged from fourteen to twenty feet rise and fall, and sometimes there were strong currents, The first part, as far as Gillingham, had reasonably firm banks for most of the way and a channel which was deep enough for a longboat, if not a ship of the line. A sailor could find his way quite easily in peacetime by following the line of laid-up warships, though he would probably sail to windward of them as far as possible to avoid being becalmed in their shadows, and he would have to avoid being swept onto them by sudden gusts of wind or tide rips. The river below Gillingham seemed wide enough on the map but the navigable channel was narrow even for a boat. The area was dominated by low-lying islands, banks of mud or 'oaze' and creeks with tidal streams which might catch the unwary. For example, the one off Yantlet Creek which would tend to pull a boat into it in a falling tide. If Nelson used a pilot book such as Chandler's *Seaman's Guide and Seaman's Coaster's Companion* which ran into many editions during that century and the next, he would find advice on Long Reach, the seventh of ten stretches of river between Chatham and the Thames:

> LONG REACH is near 3 miles in length, and extends E. by S. ½S. and W. by N. ½N. The leading mark is, Minster-church a sail's breadth open of the beacon upon Ockham-ness. All the way from the north-point of Folly-reach (also called Dormitt's-ness) to Bishop's-ness, which is the east point of this reach, the marches are bold-to. A little below the ness begins Bishop's Oaze, which is steep-to, and dry at half-tide. The mark for it is, Hoo-church, and handspike's length open of Bishop's-ness; but this mark is not to be depended upon when Kitt's Hole is open with the beacon point. From West Hoo-creek, down to the beacon, is flat oaze, on the upper part of which is only 4 or 6 feet of water: the other part is dry. Between the upper end of this oaze and the north shore is a small channel, but of no other use than as an oister-layer. The thwart-mark for the oaze is Minster-church just open of the Beacon-point.[8]

Nelson's seamanship was not confined to the Medway and he later wrote, 'Thus by degrees I became a good pilot, for vessels of that description, from Chatham to the Tower of London, down the Swin, and the North Foreland; and confident of myself amongst rocks and sands, which has of many times been of great comfort to me.'[9] These were some of the main features of the Thames Estuary – the Swin was the main channel heading north-east out of the estuary.

The logbook makes no mention of the longboat going beyond Sheerness, so presumably Nelson was in charge of the ship's cutter when he sailed further afield. This too involved difficult navigation, plus the hazards of different types of vessel making passage or anchored in forty-eight miles of an increasingly narrow river. It was essential to have either the tide or the winds in one's favour, and preferably both. The banks were close together as the sailor reached the Hope, a two-and-a-half mile stretch running south-west, in which, according to the standard pilot book, 'the tide sets very strong over to the Kentish shore'.[10] Then the boat turned west into Gravesend Reach past the town of that name with many ships anchored off it waiting for favourable conditions. At Woolwich Reach, Nelson would pass a naval dockyard not unlike the one at Chatham, with rows of warships moored in the centre of the river. There was a rock lying just off the commercial shipyard at Blackwall, 'of which you must be very careful, as the tide sets strong upon it'. Sailing round the great loop north of Greenwich, the boat would pass through about twenty of the thirty-two points of the compass. On the south bank was the Royal Naval Hospital, one of the most dramatic buildings in the country, while the north shore was bleak, with a row of windmills and a gibbet where the bodies of executed pirates might hang. There was another sharp bend then another naval dockyard at Deptford, smaller and older than Chatham and Woolwich. Ships in ordinary were moored off the Red House, the naval victualing store, and the passage was narrow. By this time London would be in sight, its skyline dominated by the dome of St Paul's Cathedral and the spires of numerous churches. The Pool of London, the main

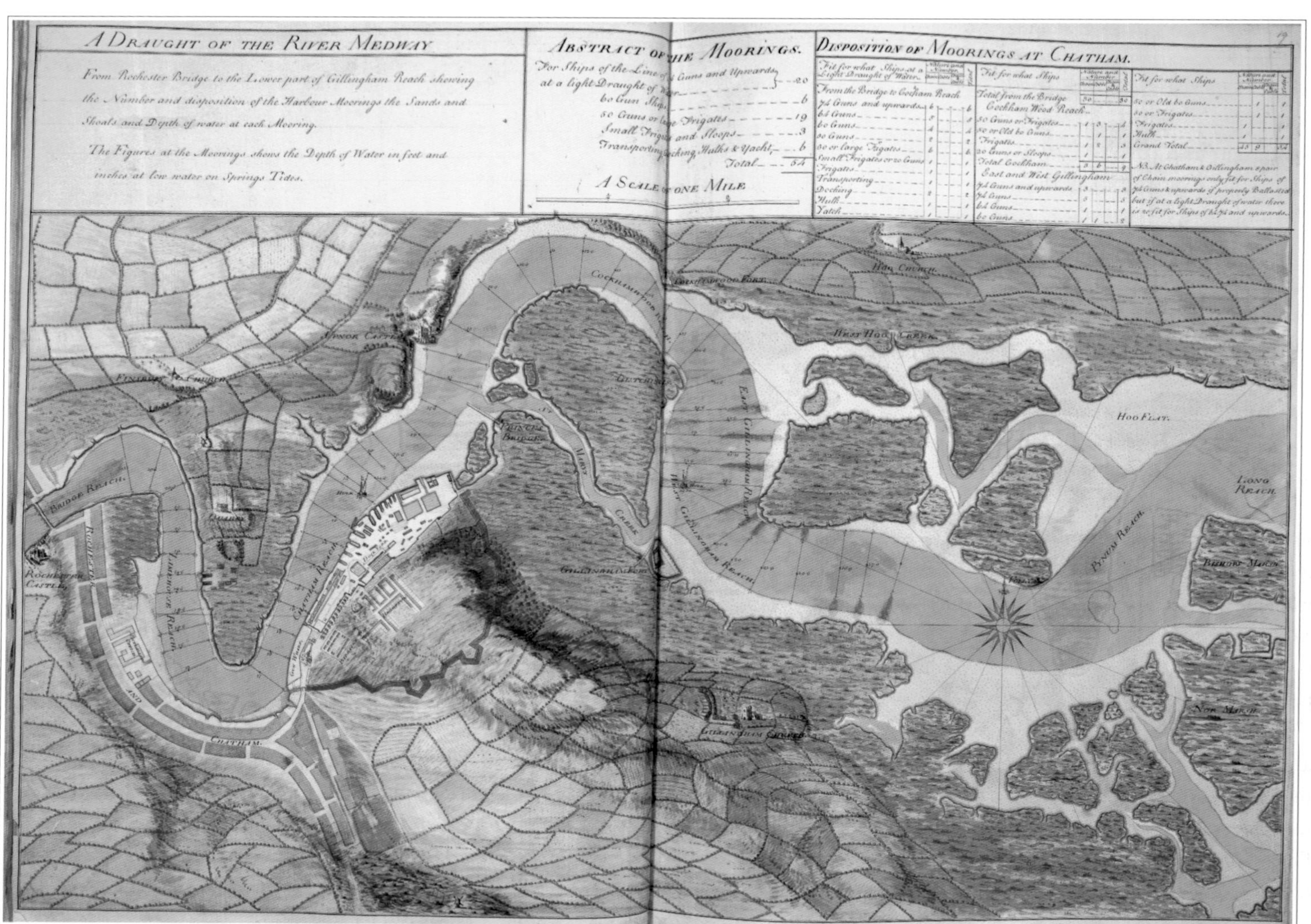

A map of the Medway Estuary in 1774. The towns of Rochester and Chatham are on the bend to the left, with the dockyard just above that. The sheer hulk is moored just off the dockyard and chains are stretched across the river as far as Gillingham for mooring the ships of the ordinary.

(© The British Library, London, Kings44)

harbour area of the city opposite the Tower of London, was likely to be overcrowded with shipping as the wharves were inadequate for the traffic. Nelson made no claims for knowledge beyond this point, for that would have taken him through the even greater hazard of old London Bridge, where tidal streams were so strong that about fifty people were lost in an average year. From the Tower, Suckling only had a short walk to the offices of the Navy Board in Seething Lane; if he had to go further upriver to the Admiralty he might hire a boatman and wherry to take him to Whitehall Stairs.

There were other tasks during Nelson's period on board. He arrived just as the *Triumph* was being rigged for service as a guardship then she was de-stored and unrigged to go into a dry-dock for routine repair between 24 January and 10 February 1773, while the men lived in the 60-gun *Dunkirk*. This gave some chance to learn the layout of the numerous ropes and the hundreds of different bends, hitches, slices, pendants, Turks heads, eyes and countless other types of ropework which were used in about forty miles of rigging. In view of Captain Suckling's obvious concern for his nephew's training, there can be little doubt that the young man was given every chance to discover the details of masts, sails and rigging during the process. Floggings were far less common in the peacetime navy manned by volunteers, but he was probably present on 26 September 1778 when Marine Thomas Mansell was punished.[11] Perhaps such events were part of the reason why merchant seamen had their 'horror of the Royal Navy'.

By stages, Nelson had learned the building blocks of seamanship – handling of ropes and sails as part of a team, navigation in deep waters and pilotage in shallow, and boat-handling under sail and oar. It would have been impossible to conduct a Nelsonic battle without a thorough understanding of exactly what a sailing warship could and could not do, in any conditions of wind and weather. He must have participated in gunnery exercises on board the *Triumph*, for example when the 'great guns and small arms' were exercised on 8 September 1772. Normally this was a dumb show, in which the guns were loaded then unloaded without firing, but the *Triumph* also fired salutes, for example for the French ambassador on 1 September 1772, or to commemorate the King's accession in 26 October. But apart from that, he had learned to sail before he learned to fight and his education was in progressive stages. This was partly a matter of luck as there was no war on at the time, but it also reflected Suckling's careful management. For most midshipmen, a good education was largely dependent on chance, a matter of having good instructors and interested officers, for there was no real training system. A young man might well be thrown into the action before he understood what was going on. For example, Frederick Hoffman had never seen a ship of the line before he joined the frigate *Blonde* at Portsmouth in October 1793, but after less than a month on board and only a few days at sea he was in action with French frigates.[12]

Broader Waters

But still Nelson was not content with the confined and homely waters of the Thames and Medway. He heard of an expedition fitting out for the Arctic under Captain Skeffington Lutwidge in the converted bomb-vessel *Carcass* and by his own account, 'nothing could prevent my using every interest to go...' No boys were to be taken, but Nelson had himself re-rated as captain's coxswain, in charge of Lutwidge's own boat. According to the muster book, Horace Nelson (as he was still known officially) transferred to the *Carcass* on 6 May 1773. Ironically, the *Triumph* had been ordered to put to sea on 17 April and was preparing for it. On 2 June the longboat was hoisted on board, for the ship was about to sail to Spithead – but Nelson had already gone and he would miss the inspiring sight of a Royal review of the fleet, a demonstration of the British sea power which he would later come to symbolise.

In the *Carcass*, Nelson took charge of a four-oared cutter manned by twelve men and his Medway experience stood him in good stead. 'I prided myself in fancying I could navigate her better than any other boat in the ship.'[13] On his return in October, he applied for a voyage to India as 'nothing less than such a distant voyage could in the least satisfy my desire of maritime knowledge.' He saw a great deal of the East, which he would never visit again, but his health suffered not for the last time.

Nelson lost touch with the Medway after that, partly because Suckling took up the civil post of Controller of the Navy, in April 1775. As a senior member of the

Navy Board, he had no direct role in the appointment of officers, but he was now close to the central administration and had a good deal of influence. There is no doubt that he found suitable positions for his nephew, taking advantage of the war with the American colonists that began with British defeat at Lexington and Concord that very month. In September 1776 Nelson was made acting-lieutenant in the 64-gun *Worcester*, his only service in a ship of the line at sea in his early career. On 9 April 1777 he passed the oral examination for lieutenant. His certificate stated in standard form that 'he can splice, knot, reef a sail, &c., and is qualified to do the duty of Able Seaman and Midshipman.' It listed his service in six different naval ships totalling six years and three months, slightly over the minimum of six years required; and, unlike many candidates, there was no false sea-time in this. The only misleading statement was that 'he appears to be more

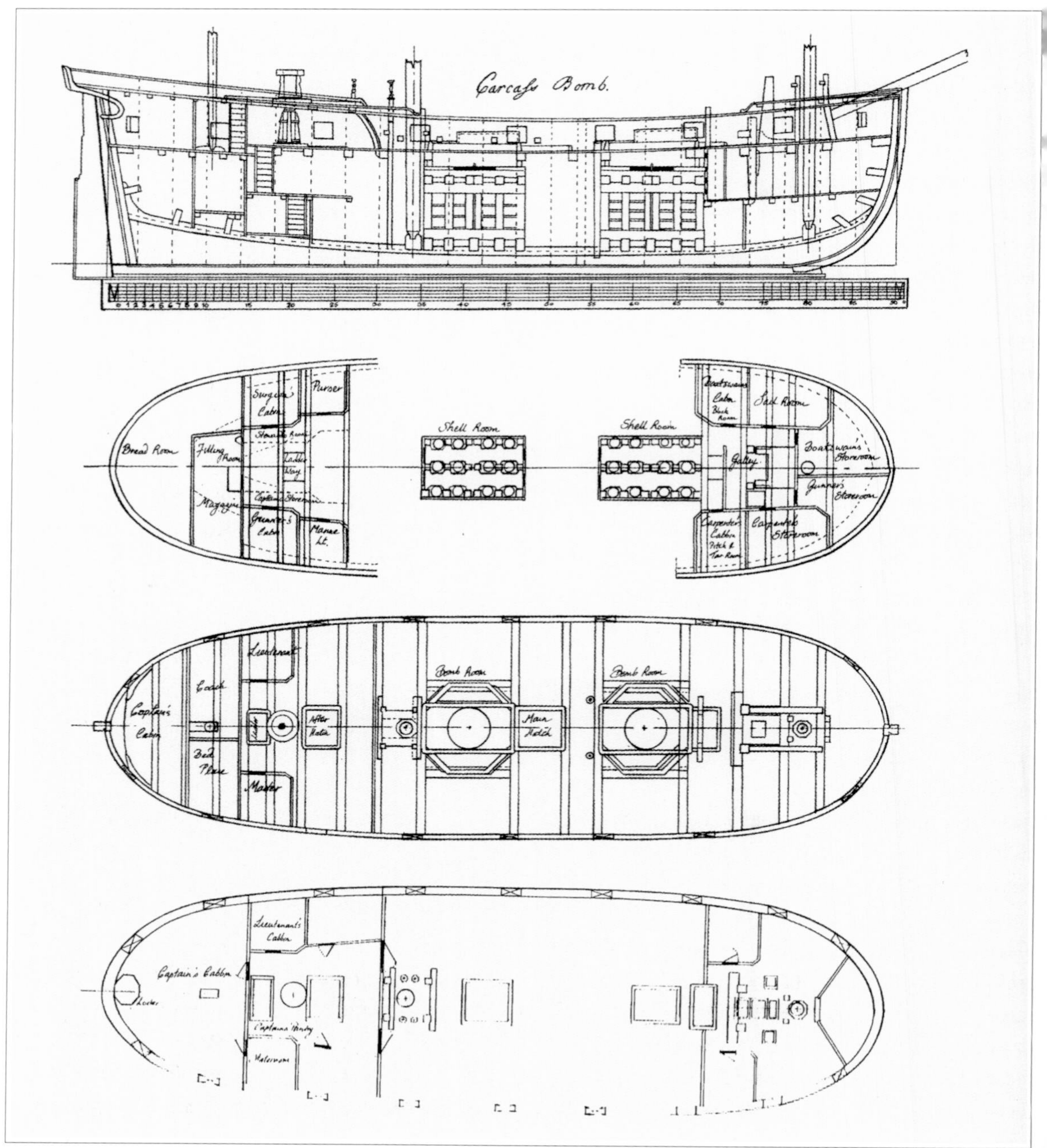

Details of the bomb vessel *Carcass* before its conversion for exploration, showing the stowage for shells below decks and the mountings for two mortars.

(© National Maritime Museum, Greenwich, London and Goodwin)

than twenty years of age' as required by regulation; in fact, he was not yet 18.

He quickly joined the frigate *Lowestoffe* as lieutenant and he met a new mentor, Captain William Locker – which was fortunate, as Suckling died a year later. Locker was more of a teacher than a career planner and Nelson learned how to fight as well as sail. He later wrote, 'I have been your scholar; it is you who taught me to board a Frenchman by your conduct when in the Experiment; it is you who always told me "Lay a Frenchman close and you will beat him"'.[14] Nelson went to the West Indies in the *Lowestoffe* and Locker put him in charge of a schooner named the *Little Lucy* after the captain's daughter. 'In this vessel I made myself a complete pilot for all the passages through the Keys (islands) situated on the north side of Hispaniola.' Back in the frigate, he was proud of an incident when, as the first lieutenant failed to board a prize ship because the sea was too rough, and the ship's master offered to go instead, Nelson claimed priority and succeeded. He wrote, '...it is my disposition, that difficulties and dangers do but increase my desire of attempting them.' He had only been with Locker for fifteen months but he wrote to him regularly until his death in 1800. In July 1778 Nelson became third lieutenant of the new 50-gun *Bristol* and soon gained the trust of Captain Robinson, who was not put off by his youth and put him in charge of a watch, saying, 'he felt as easy when I was upon deck, as any Officer in the ship.' But Nelson wrote, 'nothing particular happened whilst I was in this Ship...' However, that did not last long, in December, at the age of twenty, he was promoted to the rank of commander and put in command of the brig *Badger* of 137 tons and fourteen 4-pounder guns – equivalent to the fire power of a pair of guns on the middle deck of the *Victory*. He was sent to protect the settlers of Honduras from American depredations and on 11 June he was promoted yet again.

'The Merest Boy of a Captain'

Now, he had reached the rank of full or post-captain, rather than captain by courtesy, such as a commander or a lieutenant in command of a small ship. There was no formal assessment system, so an officer had to attract the attention of those in authority. He could reach the rank of post-captain by having good connections, especially with the Admiralty in London or a commander-in-chief overseas. He might distinguish himself in battle, or he could rise through sheer ability. In Nelson's case, it was the first and last of these that caused his advancement, as he had not taken part in any outstanding action. It was the last promotion by selection in a naval career, after that an officer would rise by seniority alone through the various grades of admiral, to become an admiral of the fleet if he lived long enough. Early promotion was essential for an ambitious officer and Nelson had one of the earliest of all time, a captain at the age of 20 when he was barely old enough to be a lieutenant, according to the formal regulations.

His new ship was the *Hinchinbrook*, a 28-gun frigate, formerly the French *Astrée* captured in 1778. Again, Nelson was involved in land activity, this time commanding the batteries of the naval base at Port Royal, Jamaica, against a possible attack. In 1780 he took command of the naval side of an expedition against San Juan in Nicaragua, which might have opened up a new route to the Pacific – but his health collapsed again and he was sent home to recover at Bath.

In August 1781 Nelson fitted out the small frigate *Albemarle* at Woolwich and passed down the Thames through long-familiar waters to the Nore in October. After a summer in the North Sea 'to try my constitution' as he put it, he sailed for Spithead in March 1782 to encounter the *Victory* again, now preparing to hoist the flag of Admiral Lord Howe in command of the Channel Fleet. As he waited for a convoy to assemble he met some old friends and watched something of life in a great fleet – courts martial were held on captains and admirals hoisted their flags. Many young officers would have envied his relatively independent command, but Nelson was tired of the *Albemarle* and unhappy about taking a convoy to Quebec, where he expected to spend the winter. However, it was not as bad as he had feared and indeed he wrote to his father about 'Fair Canada' which helped restore him to health, but he longed for a transfer to the West Indies, the 'grand theatre of Actions' where the British and French fleets were now confronting one another. He sailed south to New York, still in British hands, and found Rear-Admiral Lord Hood in charge of a squadron on the way south. He went on board the flagship where he met

Prince William Henry, third son of King George III, serving as a midshipman on board the 90-gun *Barfleur*. When he arrived in his barge, the Prince saw him as 'the merest boy of a captain that I ever beheld' and commented on his old-fashioned dress and pigtail – Nelson was never a follower of naval fashion, and after serving in an obscure station he was presumably even further out of date compared with a prince in a flagship. Hood introduced him to Nelson and like many he was soon impressed with his personality. 'There was something irresistibly pleasing in his address and conversation; and an enthusiasm, when speaking on professional subjects, that showed he was no common being.'[15] Nelson now wanted command of a ship of the line and Hood promised him that he was a candidate for one. He got on well with the admiral. 'He treats me as if I was his son, and will, I am convinced, give me anything I can ask of him.' They discussed naval tactics and Hood asserted that Nelson 'Could give him as much information as any officer in the fleet' – slightly surprising as Nelson had not been in a major battle. However, he was still in the *Albemarle* in the West Indies in February 1783 as the war drew to a close. 'We are all in the dark in this part of the world, whether it is Peace or War.' On 13 February he landed to drive the French out of Turk's Island but it proved to be his last action. Peace had already been agreed and Hood's squadron was ordered home. Nelson was back in Portsmouth by the end of June with orders to pay off the ship after 'tossing about in various climates.'

This painting of Nelson by Francis Rigaud was started in 1777 when he was a lieutenant, but completed in 1780 after his return from the West Indies as a captain. The fort in the background is San Juan in Nicaragua, which he helped capture before being taken ill.

(© National Maritime Museum, Greenwich, London, BHC2901)

There is no reason to believe that it was part of Suckling's plan, but Nelson had not just learned all the techniques and virtues of a naval officer – he had avoided most of the faults. As he had served mostly in small ships, he never became *just another officer* but always had to take his full share of responsibility. Because of his rapid rise, he spent very little time in wardrooms with his fellow lieutenants. Almost every account of wardroom life shows some tension between the occupants, for perhaps a dozen men – lieutenants, marine officers, masters, surgeons, pursers and perhaps chaplains, might be stuck together in a closed society for years at a time. It tended to produce rivalry, especially among the lieutenants who were competing for promotion, and a negative view of naval life that Nelson never acquired in his early years. He would find plenty of reasons for discontent in his later life, but always on a much higher plane than the petty disputes of a wardroom. He had gained experience in convoy escort and amphibious warfare, but none of fleet battle, which many regarded as the main function of a naval officer. And because he had served in fringe campaigns away from the main battlefleet, he was never broken in to the discipline of a large and unwieldy organisation, so, when the time came, he could approach fleet battle with an open mind.

While Nelson was rising rapidly through the ranks his future flagship, the *Victory*, was involved in a different kind of war, of frustration, indecisive action and internal rivalry. *Victory* would be at the centre of some of the bitterest rivalries in the history of the Royal Navy, and would carry some of the most distinguished as well as the least successful flag officers.

4 TO SEA AT LAST

The War for America

When the delegates of thirteen American colonies famously proclaimed on 4 July 1776 that 'these United Colonies are, and of Right ought to be, Free and Independent States' and that they were 'absolved from all allegiance to the British Crown...', it was largely the result of George III's misguided attempt to impose taxes on them to pay for their defence. It was also the culmination of a long series of incidents, many of them involving naval ships and marines, which had increased tension and led to open conflict. But still the hull of the *Victory* lay unused in the River Medway, for this was not her kind of war. The Americans had no battlefleet and their naval effort largely consisted of commerce raiders such as John Paul Jones, who attacked shipping in British waters and created panic in 1778–79. Meanwhile, the British tried to reconquer their North American territories. Admiral Samuel Graves asked for more of the old 50-gun ships to 'serve in the Rivers on this Continent; they are handy Ships, and from their easy Draught of Water can go in and out of Harbours...'[1] The Earl of Sandwich, now First Lord of the Admiralty, was convinced that Admiral Howe, with around ninety ships off North America, had enough strength to make it 'very difficult for the Americans to receive their supplies, carry on their trade, and fit out privateers to annoy the trade of Great Britain'.[2] However, the British ships were diverted into service as troop transports. On land, the British were heavily defeated by American forces at Saratoga Falls in October 1777.

Sandwich could see that the conflict was about to take a very different turn, with both France and Spain preparing to take revenge for their defeat in the last war. Ships of the line had to be got ready to meet this threat, including, above all, the *Victory* – in January 1777, Admiral Keppel was already making plans to hoist his flag in the ship if he should be called, and, in May, Sandwich promised to 'take care that the *Victory* shall be commissioned and be getting ready' for Keppel as soon as he had completed a holiday in Europe.[3]

By February 1778, Sandwich knew that the French were putting their fleet into commission, including the great three-decker *Bretagne*. He wrote, 'If they have commissioned a ship of 110 guns, surely it is time to commission the *Victory* and every line of battle ship that can be got fit for service'.[4] On 10 March the order went out to Captain Sir John Lindsay appointing him 'Captain of His Majesty's Ship *Victory* at Chatham, which we have ordered to be fitted and stored at that Place for Channel Service....'[5] At the age of forty, Lindsay was the son of a laird and one of a growing band of Scots who were rising to prominence in the navy. A collection of naval biographies which was not always uncritical of its subjects described him as 'Not less distinguished for his nautical abilities, than for his polite accomplishments.'[6] He had carried out some of the trials of Harrison's chronometers, but perhaps his greatest claim to later fame was that he fathered Dido Elizabeth Belle with a black slave he had found on board a Spanish prize in the West Indies. She was adopted by Lindsay's uncle the Earl of Mansfield, the Lord Chancellor, and played a complex role in the anti-slavery movement in Britain. Lindsay arrived on board *Victory* on 12 March and read out his orders to put the ship into commission. It was not intended that he should serve as the *Victory*'s captain for long, just fit her out and deliver her to Portsmouth where she

Captain Sir John Lindsay, first commanding officer of the *Victory* and father of Dido Elizabeth Belle

(Wikimedia)

would be taken over by Admiral Keppel with his own staff and crew, and Lindsay would transfer to a slightly smaller ship.

Meanwhile, on 16 March, the Admiralty threw peacetime financial prudence to the winds and ordered the Navy Board that as 'every thing in your power may be done to get the King's ships in readiness, you are to cause such an additional number of workmen to be entered in the several yards, as can be employed for that purpose.' But this did not include docking the *Victory*, as the facilities were needed urgently for fast frigates. The *Victory* had not been docked since March the previous year. A fast ship should be cleaned every four months or so, but slower speed was acceptable in a flagship which should not outrun the ships under her command.

Admiral Augusus Keppel, painted by the leading portrait painter of the day, Sir Joshua Reynolds, in 1779.

(© National Maritime Museum, Greenwich, London, BHC2822)

Admiral Keppel

Admiral Augustus Keppel was a man of great distinction. He had survived Anson's circumnavigation at the cost of most of his hair and teeth to scurvy. His early rise was almost as meteoric as Nelson's – he too was a captain by the age of twenty. He lost his ship, the *Maidstone*, off the west coast of France in 1747 but was exonerated of blame. In 1749, at the age of twenty-four, he led a peacetime squadron in the Mediterranean. In 1759 he commanded a ship of the line with distinction in the great victory at Quiberon Bay and showed humanity in rescuing French survivors. In 1761 he took charge of the naval part of a highly successful and lucrative expedition to capture Belle Isle off the French coast. He was popular with officers and men as well as the public, and highly competent in the basic skills. '...there is not better seaman than Keppel, few so good, and not a better officer', wrote Admiral Boscawen.[7] With Howe already employed in America, Keppel was the only admiral with enough seniority and experience to command the main fleet but, from the government's point of view, he had a serious defect. It was perfectly normal for a successful captain or admiral to take up a seat in Parliament, but mostly for the influence and social prestige it brought. Keppel, however, had been highly active for the last fifteen years as a supporter of the Rockingham Whigs, the most radical group of the day. They opposed the government policy on America and Keppel had refused to serve against the colonists. Now, as war with the old enemy France loomed and Britain might be threatened with invasion, it was his clear patriotic duty to take up arms. By the middle of March, Sandwich had alerted him 'that I might probably in a few days be ordered out to take the command of the fleet now fitting out.'[8] It was only natural that the commander-in-chief of the Channel Fleet, the most important in the navy in the circumstances, should have the biggest and best flagship – 'this important ship', as Keppel called it.

Keppel had a very clear idea about how the *Victory* should be armed. In the past, a first-rate had carried 42-pounder guns on the lower deck, but on 10 March Keppel wrote from his home in Audley Square, London, that 'A gun carrying a ball of 32lb weight seems, to my poor judgement, preferable on many accounts.' He reasoned that the smaller ball was easier for a man to handle and 'it may, on board ship, be fired much oftener than a larger gun.' The smaller barrel would allow it to be traversed fore and aft more than the large gun, and it would save weight and be 'a considerable ease to a ship at sea.' A 42-pounder of the time weighed sixty-five cwt or 3,302 kilos, a 32-pounder weighted fifty-five cwt so 300 cwt or fifteen tonnes were saved by the change. The carriages and tackle of the 32-pounder were also slightly lighter. This was presumably a success and the reduction in weight might have contributed to the *Victory*'s sailing qualities. It set a precedent, though it was 1790 before the Admiralty ordered all 42-pounders on first rates to be replaced, and at least two ships were still carrying them after that.[9]

Keppel also had views on how the fleet should be organised. Having sat on the Byng court martial and reluctantly condemned him to death, he was aware that Byng had only one admiral under him and had divided his fleet into two squadrons, with himself in the centre of one of them. When the fleet had to reverse direction, he found himself near the rear and lost control of the action. Keppel therefore demanded at least two admirals under him so that he could lead the centre section, and he was given Sir Hugh Palliser, a supporter of the government and a Lord of the Admiralty, though junior to Keppel on *The Navy List*; and Sir Robert Harland. Keppel visited the *Victory* in the Medway on 6 April before proceeding to his main fleet at Portsmouth. He had plenty of other ideas – the incessant firing of salutes should be replaced by cheering to save on gunpowder, and the names should no longer be painted on the sterns of ships. It was useful for identifying ships laid up in ordinary, but 'it will lead neutral vessels that speak with the King's ships to the knowledge of their exact force.'[10] This was agreed, and on 18 April, the authorities at Chatham acknowledged an order 'to cause the *Victory*'s and *Formidable*'s names to be rubbed out of their sterns.'[11]

Fitting Out

Meanwhile, Captain Lindsay carried on with getting the ship ready. His most immediate problem was the shortage of skilled men, both to fit the ship out and to man her at sea. Volunteers could be found, largely by offering 'bounties' of 30/- (£1.50) per man. The press gang was already out in force to find seamen on shore, or to take them out of the numerous merchant ships entering the Thames, but it was not enough as dozens of ships of the line were fitted out in preparation for a new world war. The government was still very sensitive about public opinion and was reluctant to impose two measures which would speed up the manning – an embargo on shipping leaving port, and a 'press from protections'. The first would stop all merchant ships leaving port until the navy was fully manned but, of

A seaman with his hammock, marked up with its place on deck when stowed in the rails round the sides of the ship, and containing his mattress and other bedding. Taken from the album produced by Gabriel Bray in the frigate *Pallas* in 1775.

(© National Maritime Museum, Greenwich, London, L5332)

course, it would be highly disruptive to commerce. The second meant ignoring the protections or certificates issued to seamen on essential services – to impose it would destroy trust in the Admiralty, and it would disrupt the very services the protections were intended to cover. Sandwich believed that such measures could only be adopted if war was imminent, and that was not yet. In the meantime, Lindsay had to do his best with what he could find. He only had forty-eight of his ship's company of 850 on board on 14 March, rising to eighty-four on 11 April. A detachment of eighty-seven marines arrived, while drafts of pressed men and volunteers from the receiving ship *Conquestador* just outside the Medway, were sent on board. This raised the total number to nearly 400.

Several hundred tons of ballast was laboriously taken out so that the ship would float at her proper level once all the rigging, guns and stores were in. The upper masts were fitted and rigged. Early in April, Lindsay was allowed a party of naval pensioners from Greenwich Hospital to take the ship down the estuary to Blackstakes, where her fitting would complete. There was a hitch as the dockyard yacht *Chatham* failed to arrive carrying 100 men, so the dockyard lent a party in their place, adding a total of 165 'supernumeraries for victuals' to the 400 of the regular crew.[12] It was enough and the *Victory*'s sails were filled at midday on 13 April when she left Chatham and anchored at Blackstakes at two that afternoon. The King took a personal interest in his greatest ship and wrote to Sandwich that the account of the movement, 'has given infinite satisfaction to me.'[13] But the hull was not as complete as it might have been; on 16 April the officials of Chatham Dockyard reported that it was 'absolutely necessary to employ a number of shipwrights and caulkers onboard the *Victory* at Blackstakes, and that they will not complete the different works in less than eight or nine days.'[14] They were given permission to have the men work on Sunday, rather than ferrying them back and forth on the day of rest. Every ship carried a number of boats for various duties – moving anchors, carrying stores, transporting the captain and officers or taking the crew to another ship or ashore for very limited amounts of 'liberty' or leave. The cutters were designed for good sailing, while the captain's barge and the pinnace for the officers would row well. The ship should have been issued with a large longboat for heavy work but unfortunately they was none for a first-rate in stock at Chatham, so she was issued with one for an 80-gun ship instead. The marine detachment was increased to a captain, two subalterns, four sergeants, five corporals, two drummers and 130 privates.[15]

The main task at Blackstakes was to get in the guns and ammunition, for it was considered too dangerous to handle gunpowder in the vicinity of Chatham and the water was often too shallow for a great ship carrying its full weight of metal. The crew was employed scraping the decks until 6am on 20 May when a small cargo boat, a hoy, came alongside with the first of the upper and lower deck guns, weighting up to two and a half tonnes each. These were hoisted from the yardarms one by one then hauled in through the gunports to be mounted on their wooden carriages. The middle deck guns were fully fitted by the 22nd, while shot was lowered on board and stowed near the mainmast.

The *Victory* saw the King much more closely at the end of the month, with a Royal visit to the Medway. She was issued with a Royal Standard especially for the occasion and, according to the log of 27 April:

> At 8 came on board His Majesty again, attended by Lord Sandwich, Marquis of Lothian, Admiral Campbell, Commissioner Proby. His Majesty held a levee were present all the Navy Officers from the Nore to here. The Commissioned Officers being introduced by Lord Sandwich to His Majesty.

Lord Sandwich took the opportunity to show the ship to the his Royal master. 'We passed much time on board the *Victory*, and I cannot express how much the King was pleased with her appearance.'[16]

Gunpowder was brought on board on 1 May and stowed carefully in the magazines below decks. The breechings, which would restrain the guns in rough weather or battle, were finally fitted and the topsails and staysails were 'bent' or attached ready for sailing.

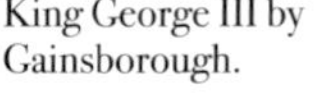

King George III by Gainsborough.

(© Royal Collection)

An allegorical print of the role of the Marine Society in providing boys for the navy. On the far right, boys are taken from their destitute families, while others are rescued from the streets to be brought before a benevolent Britannia. Then they are equipped with clothing and hats for sea service.

(© National Maritime Museum, Greenwich, London, D1790)

On 6 May the ship received a draft of 185 men 'turned over' from the old 50-gun *Antelope*, but eleven of them had to be sent to hospital straight away with ulcerated legs and were not expected to recover, while eleven more would probably be 'condemned as unserviceable' when the surgeon examined them.[17] A draft of poor-boys recruited by the Marine Society was probably more welcome, as officers' servants if nothing else.

To Portsmouth

The *Victory* filled her sails early in the morning of 8 May and began to move down the river. The wind was favourable and she did not have to anchor at the Nore, but when it shifted she had to go north towards the Essex coast. She caught the tide and Lindsay used his skills as a seaman to take her south through the intricate passages between the sandbanks. On the 7th he had written to the Admiralty that 'I have not lost a man since I left Gillingham', but that was not to last. Seaman John Smith fell overboard in the afternoon of the 9th and was drowned, as few seamen could swim in those days. *Victory* anchored off North Foreland in Kent to await a favourable wind. Three vessels had been ordered to go with her as tenders but she 'greatly outsailed them' so she was given the fast cutter *Peggy* with a pilot to take their place. She sailed again early next morning, saluting the ships anchored in the Downs off the east coast of Kent. When she arrived at Spithead near Portsmouth on the 12th, Lindsay had 'the pleasure to acquaint their Lordships, that the ship both works and sails well, so that I do not doubt of her answering every expectation that can be formed of her.[18]

Keppel had been awaiting his flagship for some time, while having to make do with the 90-gun *Prince George*. He was pleased when the ship arrived and he and his staff came on board on the 14th to view her. On Friday

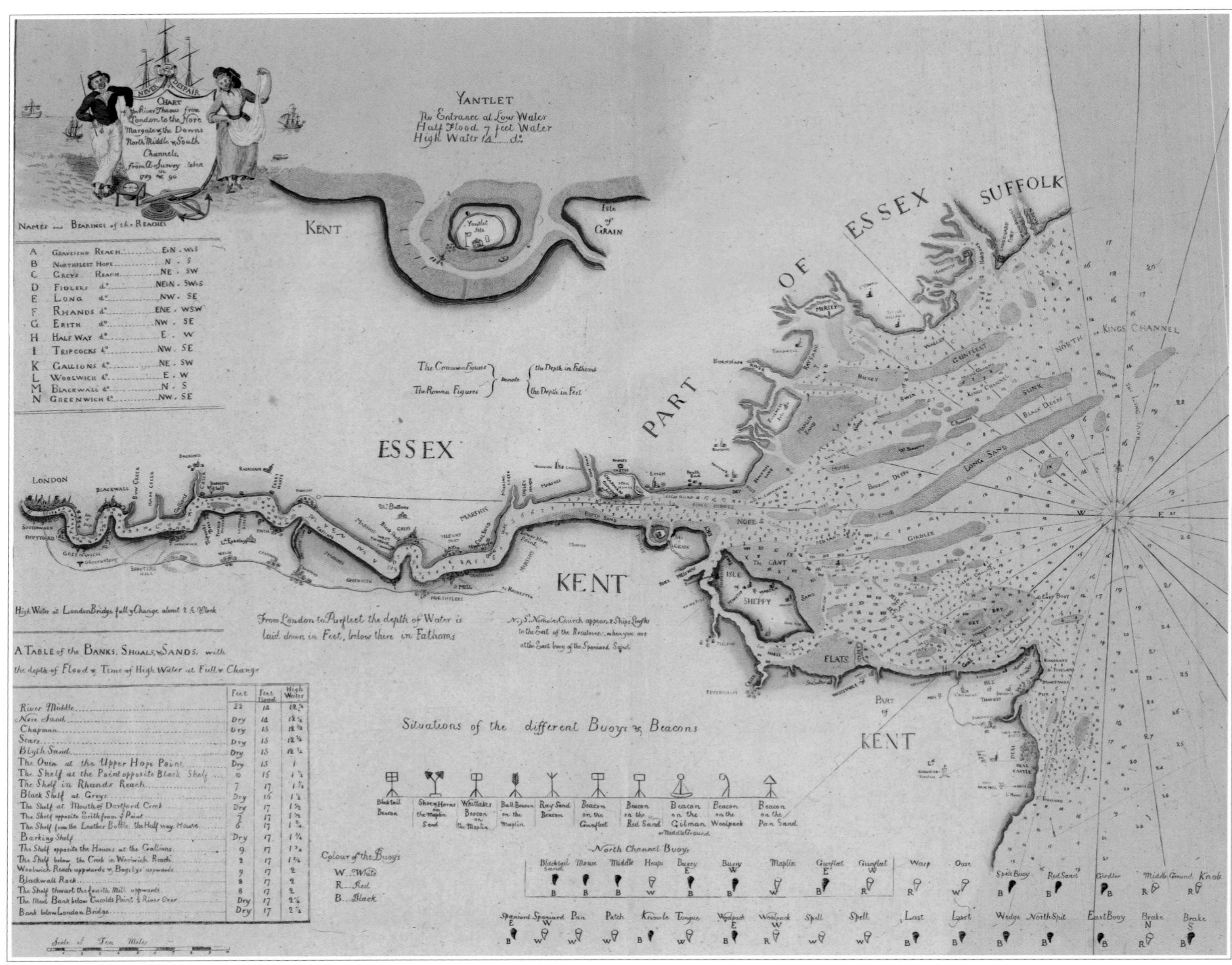

The Thames Estuary on a chart of 1790 by Richard Stanier. It shows the numerous sandbanks in the estuary in yellow, with seamarks shown below. The anchorage of the Downs is to the bottom right.

(© National Maritime Museum, Greenwich, London, B7431)

15 May, according to the final entry in Lindsay's log, 'the People making ready for getting into His Majesty's ship *Prince George* by Orders.' Keppel came on board permanently the next day and his flag was hoisted at the mainmast to show his rank of admiral of the blue. Apparently, his views on salutes were accepted, for the logs of the ships in harbour do not mention any firing of guns as he hoisted his flag, though they had been fired many times during recent Royal visits. The new Captain, Jonathan Faulknor, was a long-term Keppel follower who had lost his father in Balchen's *Victory*. Keppel also brought Rear-Admiral John Campbell as the captain of the fleet, or chief of staff. He was a friend of the admiral since they had served together on Anson's voyage. Campbell was a great pioneer of navigation, he helped develop a system of finding the longitude by lunar measurements which was a rival to the chronometer, and he inspired the improvement of Hadley's octant to become the sextant, now made in brass instead of wood and measuring over a wider arc.

Those who stayed behind from the *Victory*'s old crew included many of the key warrant officers and their servants (or apprentices) – though Lindsay insisted on keeping his master-at-arms, the head of the ship's police and Keppel brought his own purser, Thomas More, who would help him with the administration. Soon the

Victory's gunner became 'so low spirited and dejected' that he had to be replaced – for as Keppel put it, 'a gunner is too material an officer to be indifferent about.'

The ship had a nominal complement of 894 officers and men as a flagship, but never had more than 739 actually mustered during this period, reducing to 721 by 16 June. Nevertheless, the ship was crowded as, on 6 May, Keppel brought on board his retinue – his Flag Lieutenant George Rogers and thirty-one men including clerks and servants. Campbell also brought his clerk and eleven servants. But the condition of the ships was still not perfect. Keppel was pleased about 'the zeal that animated Sir John Lindsay and his officers to bring so expeditiously the *Victory* to Spithead', but he was now in 'a ship that is in her present state, materially unfit for sea service.' Every man on board had to be 'doubly worked, bad as the weather has been' and Keppel turned down a request from the port admiral to provide crews and boats for press gangs as it would 'cause such delay following of it' and 'confusion without end' when his priority was to get the ships fitted. The ship had been laden with shingle ballast at Chatham, but now it was common to put a layer of iron bars or kentledge below that. Each bar weighed up to 320 lbs and had to be hoisted into place, but that was not the hardest work. The barrels already in each part of the hold had to be removed and the shingle ballast shifted so that the iron could be laid. The work kept the crew occupied with heavy labour for nearly a week.

Some faults were all too obvious. Faulknor complained that the main capstan was too close to the aft bulkhead meaning that shorter bars had to be used and it was 'rendered of very little service.' The barrel of the steering wheel was too large and had to be replaced, 'as it would be by no means safe to proceed to sea with that she now has on board.' The glass windows in the admiral's cabin did not fit round the guns as they should, and he also wanted glass ports for the middle deck guns in the area of the lieutenants' cabins. The Navy Board agreed to move the capstan forward one 'room' (or the space between two deck beams) and to carry out the other modifications, though it drew the line at glass for the lieutenants' cabins. Keppel also objected that many of the rigging blocks were made of wood, rather than a wooden shell with brass coaks and iron pins. The Navy Board replied that there were none in stock as it would be 'a very great loss to the public to lay them by' but the *Victory* could have them when the old ones were worn out. On the other hand, it was agreed that the ship's sides should be painted with white lead mixed with oil of pine, as had been done with Keppel's previous ship the *Prince George*.[19]

By the 29th, Keppel was hoping for a wind to take the *Victory* down to St Helens near the eastern end of the Isle of Wight, where the fleet was assembling. The next day, he reported that she was under sail down the Solent. Although he was still not happy about the numbers of ships allotted to him, he refrained from saying too much to Sandwich 'or I shall be led to my political ideas.' By 1 June, he expected to be at sea on the next tide with 'twenty English ships of war… certainly a formidable force.' Finally, on the 2nd he reported 'the *Victory* is at length in the Channel and wind at the SE of it.' She was finally sailing on active service.

Flagship of the Channel Fleet

It was a fine fleet which sailed round Bembridge Point on the eastern end of the Isle of Wight on 13 June, even if its progress was slow and it often had to anchor due to light winds. It was well-balanced, with three squadrons of six to eight two-deckers, each led by a three-decker flagship carrying an admiral, with Keppel in the *Victory* in the centre of the line. The other ships were mostly the new style of 74 developed during the Seven Years War, good sailers with a powerful armament. There were four of the smaller 64-gun ships with only 24-pounders on the lower deck. There was an 80-gun ship, the *Foudroyant,* but it was not an old and unstable three-decker, but a French-built two-decker, captured in 1758 and refitted at Plymouth. This was a modern fleet. It had a distinguished set of captains, and more than half of the senior officers would eventually be commemorated in the *Dictionary of National Biography* – though in some cases for their political as much as their naval activities, which would prove a weakness in itself.

That was not the only weakness. Keppel lamented the lack of frigates for reconnaissance – he had only three, plus one fireship and a few cutters. Most of his crews were untrained in naval ways as their ships had just been commissioned, but they were sailing out to meet an enemy force which, as far as they knew, was fully ready for battle. The winds were very light and progress was slow, but when the ship was about twenty-five miles south-east of the Lizard in Cornwall Keppel began the training, by exercising the men at the great guns and small arms. The next day, the fleet formed its line of battle for the first time with the *Victory* in the centre and Harland's *Queen* and Palliser's *Ocean* in the middle of their own squadrons – though even such a simple manoeuvre had to be perfected, and three of the ships had to be called back to their stations. But once in position off the mouth of the Channel, opportunities for fleet exercise were limited. As he was short of frigates, Keppel often had to detach two or three of his ships of the line to investigate strange sails on the horizon.

Soon Keppel was beginning to show guarded respect for his flagship's sailing qualities. Although the 74s *Valiant* and *Elizabeth* sailed best, as could be expected from two-deckers, 'the *Victory* meets with no disgrace as yet, which is a great deal for a ship of her size, near fifteen months off the ground with tons of mussels on her bottom'. The next day he described some of the slower ships, commenting. '...the *Victory* although as long since cleaning as any, is not reckoned among the bad sailers'.[20] This was more than faint praise, she could clearly keep up with most of the two-deckers despite her foul bottom.

Britain was not formally at war with France yet and Keppel had a dilemma in dealing with French frigates which were following his fleet. On 17 June the frigate *Milford* came alongside the French *Licorne* and a 74-gun ship fired one of her guns to persuade the French captain to come under the stern of the *Victory* so that Keppel could talk to him in the morning. But the *Licorne* tried to escape at daylight until a shot was fired across her bow. Captain Lord Longford of the 64-gun *America* was talking to her when she discharged a full broadside – normally suicidal for a frigate as her light guns could not penetrate the sides of a ship of the line while her own structure could not resist the shot of 24 or 32 pounders. Indeed, the *Licorne*'s broadside only wounded three men in the *America,* and she instantly hauled down her colours to surrender. The British ships refrained from firing back and the *Licorne* was brought to the *Victory*. Meanwhile, another French frigate was detained, and on both ships Keppel's officers found papers showing that the fleet at Brest had thirty-two sail of the line compared with his own twenty. His orders were '...if the French fleet... shall be manifestly superior to yours... you are... to return with the squadron under your command to St Helens for a re-inforcement [sic].' Keppel therefore took his fleet back to the Solent, arriving on 27 June after two weeks at sea. It was not what Nelson would have done twenty years later, but he had a well-trained, battle-hardened fleet and was against an enemy whose navy had been severely disrupted by revolution. Some of Keppel's crews were barely trained to operate their own ships and collectively they would need much practice in fleet manoeuvres to make an effective fighting force. The French also had their weaknesses but they were at perhaps their highest point in the century. They had learned a good deal from their defeats in the last war, they had built new ships and had formed an efficient corps of seaman gunners to carry out key tasks in action.

In Action off Ushant

More ships of the line were coming forward to join the fleet, partly manned from an incoming convoy of East Indiamen. Keppel only had twenty-four of the line when he sailed again on the 9th, but he was joined by more over the next few days until he had thirty. The French fleet of thirty-two of the line had already sailed. It was urgent to beat them, as the Spanish were expected to declare war soon and the combined fleets would outnumber the British. The British and French fleets were in sight of one another as the haze cleared away on the afternoon of 23 July and the stage was set for an epic battle between two forces of equal strength. But the French admiral, d'Orvilliers, soon realised that Keppel had been reinforced since his encounter with the frigates, and nothing happened that day except that both fleets formed line of battle. During the night the wind changed to give the French the weather gage, so that they had the wind behind them and could control the tactics of the battle. For the next four days Keppel tried to sail his ships to windward to get closer to the enemy, but they evaded him. The weather was much more changeable on the 27th and Keppel used his skills to get nearer. After much manoeuvring, the two lines passed one another at a relative speed of six to eight knots and varying ranges, an old-fashioned style of 'passing battle'. British gunfire was aimed at the enemy hulls but did little damage at distance; the French were aiming at the rigging and several of the British ships had their mobility impaired. One of them was the 90-gun *Formidable,* flagship of Sir Hugh Palliser, which also suffered from the explosion of a gun. He was also unable to answer Keppel's signal to bring his division into line for a new attack. Night fell and Keppel stationed his ships ready to resume battle in the morning. D'Orvilliers stationed three of his fastest ships with lights in the positions the flagships would have occupied in a line of battle, and set sail back to Brest. When the sun rose, Keppel's lookouts could only see the French fleet disappearing into the distance. The *Victory* had suffered eleven killed and twenty-four wounded, the highest of any ship except the *Formidable*. The French could claim to have inflicted more damage on the enemy but had retreated from the scene of the action so Keppel claimed a victory.

There was no alternative but to return to Portsmouth to have the damaged ships repaired. There was another cruise in August when Keppel issued orders from the *Victory* that his captains were to keep as close as possible at all times, as it would be 'of the utmost consequence, upon falling suddenly and unexpectedly in with the enemy's fleet in great force...'[21]

The fleets were laid up that winter and the *Victory* remained at Portsmouth while the admirals went home on leave. Palliser read an article in an opposition newspaper claiming that his failure to support Keppel had allowed a great victory to slip away. He went to Keppel's house and demanded support, which was refused. Now he blamed Keppel for the failure and rashly demanded court martial on him, which the Admiralty unwisely agreed to. It assembled on board the *Britannia* on 7 January 1779 but a special act had been passed to allow it to take place on shore because of Keppel's health. This made it even more politically charged than it might have been, with Keppel supporters crowding the galleries. Several of the charges carried the compulsory death penalty so it carried an echo of the Byng court martial more than two decades earlier, with the essential difference that this time public opinion was wildly in favour of the defendant. Keppel was acquitted and the court proclaimed, '...the charge is malicious and ill-founded... Admiral Keppel... behaved as became a judicious, brave and experienced officer...' In Portsmouth, guns were fired in celebration, in London, the mob, reportedly including people of some distinction, looted Palliser's house and even attacked the Admiralty. Palliser then demanded a court martial on himself to clear his reputation. He was found not guilty of all charges but the court commented that he should have done more to keep Keppel informed of the condition of his ship.

A French view of the Battle of Ushant, painted by Theodore Gudin. The British did not commission paintings of such a disappointing action.

(Wikimedia)

The dispute spread to the lower decks of both Keppel's and Palliser's flagships and at the end of March Sir Thomas Pye, the commander-in-chief at Portsmouth who had presided over the trial, reported 'that should the *Formidable*'s and *Victory*'s ships' companies meet it would be fatal to many of them as there is such an inveteracy towards each other...' He recommended delaying the docking of the *Formidable* until the *Victory* was clear of the yard.[22] In fact, the ship was in dry-dock with the spring tides of 1–2 April, to have her bottom cleaned for the first time since March 1777, so that her full sailing qualities might finally be developed.

The battle off Ushant caused much rethinking of naval tactics which led eventually to Nelson's victories. It caused the Scottish landsman and naval tactician John Clerk of Eldin to comment:

> It is remarkable, that, when single ships have encountered another, or when two, or even three, have been engaged of a side, British seaman... have never failed to exhibit instances of skilful seamanship, intrepidity, and perseverance; yet when ten, twenty, or thirty great ships have been assembled, and formed in a line of battle, it is equally remarkable, that, in no one instance, has ever a proper exertion been made, or even a ship lost or won on either side.

He began to devise a new system of tactics including breaking the enemy line, though it has always been controversial how much this actually affected the officers at sea.

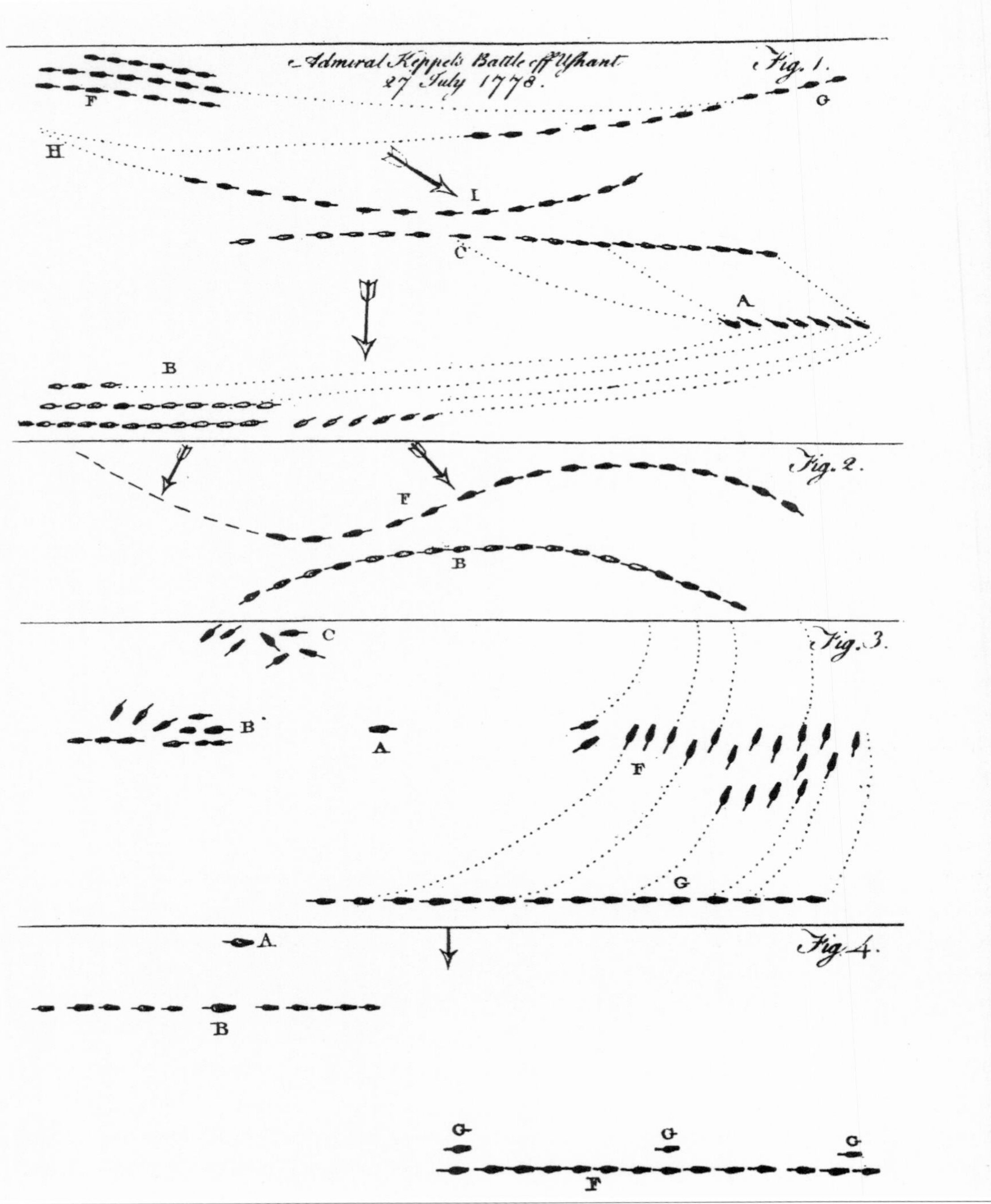

Clerk of Eldin's view of the Battle of Ushant. Figure 1 shows the two fleets forming up, with the British marked B below, then engaging in a passing battle. This continues in figure 2 with the French (marked F) having the weather gage. In figure 3 both sides are now in some disorder with Keppel's fleet in two groups marked B and C, with Palliser's *Formidable* at A; the French form a new line. In figure 4 the two fleets are in line overnight but the French leave three frigates (marked G) bearing lights while the rest of the fleet escapes.

(Taken from Clerk of Eldin, Essay on Naval Tactics, *1790)*

5 YEARS OF FRUSTRATION

Hardy and Geary

The other effect of the battle off Ushant and the courts martial was that Keppel and his associates declined to serve again, while Palliser and his few friends were too unpopular to be employed. The Admiralty was forced to retrieve Sir Charles Hardy from Greenwich Hospital to command the Channel Fleet. He was old for his sixty-four years and very amiable, but incompetent. To Benjamin Thompson (later Count Rumford), who was on board the *Victory* to experiment with artillery, he was 'not a fit person to command a great fleet at this time',[1] though he later moderated this. Captain Kempenfelt wrote that Hardy was 'a man who never thinks beforehand, and therefore is always under the confusion of a surprise when anything happens'. He had 'not the least idea of what an officer should be, so that he destroys his own authority and those in command next under him' – and he did not alter his opinion.[2]

Rear-Admiral Richard Kempenfelt not long before his death in 1782, painted by Tilly Kettle.

(© National Maritime Museum, Greenwich, London, BHC2818)

Hardy was given a first-class officer in his Captain of the Fleet, Richard Kempenfelt. In the aftermath of the Keppel and Palliser courts martial, he soon observed that an 'undisciplined, audacious spirit showed itself upon several occasions in the *Victory* when we first went on board her'.[3] Kempenfelt had his ideas on ship discipline and organisation. He supported the system of 'divisions' by which the crew was put in groups under the supervision of lieutenants and midshipmen for welfare and discipline. '...if six, seven, or eight hundred men are left in a mass together, and the officers assigned no particular charge over any part of them, who only give orders from the quarterdeck or gangways – such a crew must remain a disorderly mob...'[4] But it is not clear if he had any chance to apply his ideas during his time in the *Victory* for, as first-captain as he called it, he was not responsible for the running of the ship. Indeed, he complained constantly, Hardy 'gives his directions to the captain of the ship [or] to the lieutenants, without ever passing through me.'[5]

Kempenfelt did however use his time in the *Victory* to develop another of his ideas. The failure at Ushant, on top of Minorca and several other debacles, had shown the inadequacies of the traditional signalling system. This was highlighted in the *Victory* when Hardy put up what he thought was the signal for line of battle ahead and was surprised when the ships backed their sails and began to hoist out boats – in fact, he had signalled them to send in their weekly returns, for the books did not make a clear distinction between operational and administrative signals. Kempenfelt was mortified by this, though his advice had probably been ignored as always.[6] But in his cabin he was working on a much more effective signalling system and sending his ideas on to Charles Middleton, the Controller of

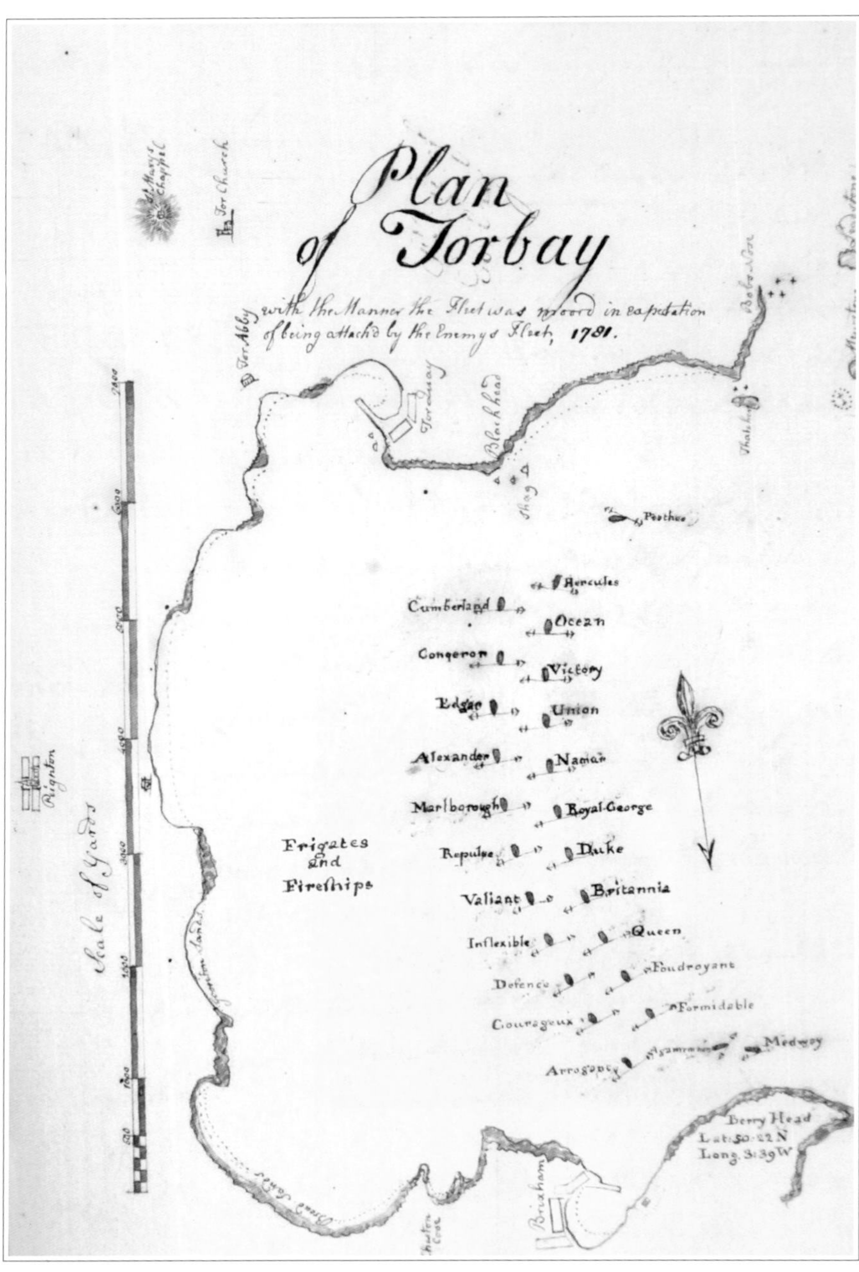

Pakenham's plan of the fleet at anchor in Torbay with the *Royal George* in the centre of the first line and the *Victory* near the northern end. The second-line ships are arranged to fire though the gaps in the first line.

(© National Maritime Museum, Greenwich, London, PAK/2)

the Navy. His experience on the Palliser court martial showed him that the French had a much superior technique with specialised signal flags and he began to devise his own, believing 'signals should be simple, clear, and easily discernible.' He produced a numerical code in which standard messages could be transmitted by a combination of flags, or they could be used to spell out words where that was inadequate.

On Monday 21 July, while off Land's End, Admiral Hardy called his captains on board the *Victory* to tell them that they were now effectively at war with Spain. His own force of around thirty-five ships was heavily outnumbered by the combined fleet of up to sixty-six, and the enemy had definite plans for an invasion of southern England. Strategy was indecisive, but the British fleet mostly cruised west of the entrance to the English Channel to protect trade and hopefully to meet the enemy if he tried to enter, or to invade Ireland. In fact, the combined fleet of sixty-three ships evaded him and was sighted off Plymouth in the middle of August, causing panic on shore. Hardy was being driven eastwards by the winds, but the French and Spanish were not ready for a landing. On the 29th Hardy sighted the enemy and formed line but it was not 'judged prudent to hazard a battle against so great a superiority', After several days of manoeuvring, the fleets parted. Every possible ship was pressed into service and Hardy took the fleet to Spithead where he could replenish quickly, rather than the outer anchorage of St Helens which the politicians would have preferred. He gave orders 'to complete provisions to two months, and to keep the ships in constant readiness for action and for sea, in case the enemy should come up Channel.'[7] Sandwich came down in person to visit Hardy, but already the combined fleet had returned home and abandoned the invasion plan for that year.

Victory was in dock in Portsmouth in March 1780, and her hull was coppered for the first time, giving an increase in speed and removing the necessity to be cleaned regularly so that she would sail well for two years, rather than four months, since the last docking. On 16 May Admiral Hardy returned to duty and hoisted his flag on board the *Victory*. He was on shore in Portsmouth the next day when he suffered a seizure and died. On the 22nd his barge's crew from the *Victory* carried his coffin from the Fountain Inn through the streets to the Landport Gate where it was put on a hearse, while troops lined the streets and the *Victory* and other ships fired 20 minute guns in salute. Next day Admiral Francis Geary hoisted his flag at the main topmast head of the *Victory*, 'to the great surprise of everybody' according to Captain Lord Longford of the 74-gun *Alexander*. He was seventy years old and had not been to sea for twenty years, but there were still very few candidates for the post, as many officers refused to serve after the Keppel affair.

Geary had no interest in experiments with signals. On 3 July a convoy was mistaken for an enemy force. Geary saw Kempenfelt bring his signal book on deck. He went up to him and 'with the greatest good-humour, and squeezing him by the hand... said quaintly, "Now, my dear friend, do pray let the signals alone today: tomorrow you shall order as many as you please."'[8] There were more fruitless cruises during the summer when Geary stayed off Brest for a month to prevent the junction of the French and Spanish fleets; then went south to the Bay of Biscay to cover the second relief of Gibraltar. The enemy had lost his drive and no invasion threatened that year, but there was dismay when sixty-one ships of a convoy for the east and west Indies were captured while the fleet was at Spithead, for one-in-seven men were down with scurvy. In August Geary struck his flag 'from his advanced age and ill state of health.' Admiral Barrington refused the command and departed, which Longford felt was 'to the great regret of every honest man in the service'. Admiral George Darby took Geary's place, the next in a line of old and undistinguished commanders. In this case, he was reliable and popular but lacking in experience at this level of command. On 10 September he shifted his flag from the *Royal George* to the *Victory* but soon shifted it again, leaving the *Victory* to Rear-Admiral Drake.[9]

On 9 September Kempenfelt, now promoted to rear-admiral, hoisted his blue flag at the mizzen mast of the *Victory* under the overall command of Darby. The fleet was in Torbay, anchored in two lines with the three-deckers in the outermost one and the *Victory* third from the northern end. It was moored 'in expectation of being attacked by the enemy's fleet' but Captain Lord Longford had his doubts about Darby's plan. '...it is better to be at sea than in this bay, where a resolute and superior enemy might come and anchor without us, and might with the first leading wind attack and destroy the fleet.'[10]

Lord Howe

By this time, the British had been defeated at Yorktown in Virginia and any hope of re-conquering the American colonies was lost. The government fell at the end of March 1782 and Keppel took office as First Lord of the Admiralty in succession to Sandwich – though the new minsters lacked administrative experience and were not backed up by a permanent civil service as in later years. This sent waves throughout the highly politicised fleet and Darby resigned, to be replaced by Richard Lord Howe, who had held the main naval command in America in the early years of the war, in co-operation with his brother William, who commanded the army. He had no success there, largely because of political constraints, and he returned home to take a strong anti-government position over the Keppel-Palliser affair. Now, with a new government, he was available for service. He had none of the obvious faults of his predecessors – he was relatively young at fifty-six, very experienced and had no animosity towards the government. He thought deeply about naval tactics and independently he came to the same conclusions as Kempenfelt – that new orders and signalling systems were urgently needed. In the North American command, he had issued an entirely new signal book, including tactics for chasing and attacking the enemy's rear, and he continued to refine these.[11]

Howe was also deeply concerned with the condition of the seamen and on 4 May, on board the *Victory*, he reissued his *Instructions and Standing Orders for the General Government and Discipline of the Ships of War* – the first admiral to try to control his captains in so much detail, which made him unpopular with both officers and the lower deck. The orders were for the whole fleet rather than just the *Victory*, and indeed they were based on ones he had already issued at New York in 1776, but they give some idea of how he intended his flagship to be run. Howe agreed with Kempenfelt on

Lord Howe, who flew his flag from *Victory* in 1782.

(© National Maritime Museum, Greenwich, London, BHC2790)

the need for supervision and ordered that the men be put into divisions under lieutenants and squads under midshipmen, who were to muster their men every morning and evening and make sure that each had 'a sufficient provision of dry, warm clothing', though it was paid for out of the seaman's own funds. Marines were to work with the seamen when at sea apart from sentries. They should not be forced to go aloft, though they were not to be 'restrained from rendering themselves expert in a seaman's duty.' In harbour, they were to be divided into three guards, with sentries in uniform to challenge all boats and report 'All's well' every ten minutes or quarter of an hour.

The seamen were also to be divided into three watches at sea, rather than the more normal two. This would allow more rest, especially for the petty officers who would 'execute their duty with greater punctuality and exactness whilst it is their turn to be on watch.' That might leave the ship short-handed during manoeuvres unless more men were called up, but 'the Admiral will have attention to give timely notice whenever he is about to tack, or make any other alteration that may require more assistance.' New seamen were to be trained in harbour in fair weather, 'to accustom the raw men to go aloft', manipulating sails as necessary. Howe was concerned with 'free circulation of air' below decks, and ordered that the hammocks be got-up in dry weather, or at least lashed-up in bad. Every boat leaving the ship was under the command of an officer who was to keep his men together on shore to prevent desertion or theft. On board the ship, a midshipman was to inspect below decks every hour during the night to look out for smoking or unauthorised lights. A constant lookout was to be kept from the mastheads when at sea, with the man relieved early if he was the first to spot an object, or kept on for extra duty if he failed. A midshipman of the watch 'or other discreet person' was to look out for signals. The crew was to be exercised at the great guns and small arms every day at sea in fair weather. The captain was allowed to fire the muskets as much as he liked, but he was 'never to use powder in the great guns, without an order or signal from the Admiral.' The ship was to be kept 'in a constant state of readiness for action' and at 'quarters' or action stations, men were to carry the powder to the guns, 'instead of boys, who are not of trust to be relied on for this important duty.' If battle was joined, each captain was to fire his guns as quickly 'as can be prudently attempted, on the first junction with the enemy.'[12]

In May, Howe took a fleet to the North Sea where the Dutch fleet was assembling off the Texel in the entrance to the Zuyder Zee, threatening an invasion of the English east coast. In June he sailed westward to protect a convoy from Jamaica and encountered the Franco-Spanish fleet off the Scilly Isles. Howe was determined to keep his fleet in order against superior numbers and, according to Captain Lord Longford in the *Alexander*, 'Lord Howe in the *Victory* kept to windward out of the line in order to see the situation of the fleet, which he could not have done in the line, and which was extremely necessary on account of the heavy sailing ships.'[13] But most of Howe's newly-coppered ships could outsail the enemy and he gained the windward position between Scilly and Land's End, causing the French and Spanish to retreat again.

Triumph and Tragedy

Meanwhile, in April 1782, after a succession of indecisive actions in the western Atlantic and Caribbean, Admiral Rodney at last took the decisive step of 'breaking the line' and won a major victory in battle against an enemy with his fleet still in good order. The British possessions in the West Indies were now relatively safe. Fighting continued in India, but otherwise the main focus of conflict was now on Gibraltar. The Rock had been conquered by the British in 1704 and was granted to them by the Treaty of Utrecht in 1713, but it remained a sore point with the Spanish. The main motivation for them to declare war was a French promise to keep on fighting until it and Minorca were restored to them. Minorca was taken in 1782 while Gibraltar had been under siege by Spanish and French forces since the summer of 1779. The garrison under Lieutenant-General George Elliot looked increasingly heroic amidst failure elsewhere. The besiegers had already tried bombardment by land, fireships, gunboat raids, blockade and naval assault, though with little co-ordination between them. The rock had been relieved by Admiral Rodney's fleet on the way to the West Indies in January 1780, when six Spanish ships were captured, and by Darby in April 1781; but it was still beleaguered and another attack was expected, as the defenders watched the French building powerful floating batteries across the bay in Algeciras. Howe's job was to relieve Gibraltar for a third time.

There was tragedy much nearer home. The fleet was anchored at Spithead on 29 August when the famous *Royal George* began to heel over, then capsized completely with the loss of perhaps a thousand men and visiting women and children. Admiral Kempenfelt, one of the great hopes for the navy's future, was on board his flagship at the time and was drowned. It was probably the result of bad seamanship, rather than faulty maintenance, as was asserted at the time, or a 'land-breeze' which 'shook the shrouds' as was stated in Cowper's poem.[14] By 9 September, Howe was considering plans to raise the hull, including one by Thomas Spalding involving 'a machine constructed on the principles of a diving bell, but with the addition of some considerable improvements.' Meanwhile, it was noted that the hull had shifted to a more upright position for no apparent reason; but there was no time to pursue the matter any further.

The Relief of Gibraltar

Howe was delayed at Spithead as a convoy of 183 ships heading for the east and west Indies and Portugal as well as Gibraltar was slowly assembled. He finally sailed on 11 September with thirty-four of the line, six frigates and two fireships. They made ninety-one miles on the 15th, but after that they rarely made more than fifty miles a day as gales alternated with calms – on the worst day, the 21st, they only made six miles in hazy weather. The convoy was dispersed on the 16th when the wind 'flew round suddenly to the NW and blew strong' but it was 'pretty well collected' by the end of the day. Again, on the 24th, there were no more than thirty sail in sight, but that rose to 135 the next day. Howe planned his tactics on the way out, putting his ships in six columns instead of the normal three. He considered the possibility of mounting a night attack and called his captains on board the *Victory*. They were asked one by one, in reverse order of seniority, and each was in favour until Captain John Jervis of the *Foudroyant*. He believed it would cause confusion and would 'deprive

The *Royal George* sinking. Crew and visitors can be seen in the water and clambering along the side. Gosport and Portsmouth can be seen in the background. The horror of the event is accentuated by the calm weather and the closeness of the land.

(© National Maritime Museum, Greenwich, London, PAH9500)

The Relief of Gibraltar, with the *Victory* in the centre of the painting with the fleet and transport ships to the left and right.

(© National Maritime Museum, Greenwich, London, BHC0453)

the British fleet of the advantage of making use of his Lordship's admirable code of day signals, while those for the night were very imperfect.'[15]

At last, on 8 October, Howe arrived off Cape St Vincent expecting battle any minute. He sent a frigate ahead to find out if Gibraltar was still holding out. She returned two days later with excellent news – not only was the Rock still in British hands but a major attack had been defeated. On 13 September, two days after Howe sailed from Spithead, the floating batteries that had long been observed under construction were sailed across the bay and began their attack, watched by royalty and about 80,000 spectators on the Spanish side. Despite extra timbering and pumping systems to deal with fire, they were no match for the red-hot shot fired from the shore and all ten of them were set alight, to the delight of the watching defenders. After 'entertaining all Europe for some months past with their preparations', as Lord Longford put it, the assault had failed utterly. But Elliot and his men were running short of powder and of certain types of food so the relief force was still necessary.

There was another storm on the night of the 10th and 11th as the fleet approached Gibraltar, but Howe kept the warships and convoy together. As the Rock came closer, they saw fifty ships of the line at anchor in Algeciras Bay but they found that one French ship of the line had been driven ashore in Spanish territory while others had collided with one another and the *San Miguel* had fallen into British hands. Howe formed his fleet into two lines with the *Victory* leading one of them, which was unusual in those days. The enemy did not attempt to come out to meet them. Howe had given careful instructions for the ships of the convoy that were to enter Gibraltar harbour, on how to avoid the tricky currents of the area, but apparently only four of them paid attention and were able to sail in, while the others were swept past. The enemy fleet of about fifty sail began to come out on the 14th and Howe's ships remained at action stations all night to meet them. The enemy had the weather gage and Howe was still hampered by about twenty ships of the convoy, but the wind changed and next day the last ships of the convoy were got safely into the bay while the warships were in danger from 'the violence and variation of the wind.' On the 18th, four ships of the line and several frigates reached Rosia Bay south of the main harbour and unloaded troops. The next day, Howe formed his fleet into three lines to sail back through the straits.

Once outside the Mediterranean, Howe hoped that the enemy would run past him in the night to give him the weather gage and put him between them and their base but, as morning dawned on the 20th, off Cape Spartel just outside the Mediterranean on the coast of Africa, Lord Longford 'saw the enemy's fleet about five leagues [fifteen miles] directly to windward, bearing down'. Howe formed his fleet in line of battle to await them but at first they seemed reluctant, despite their superior numbers. It was after sunset before they approached within a mile, opening fire at extreme range – Longford noted, 'they hauled up and began a very great fire, most of their shot falling short.' The British decided not to waste ammunition by replying, which perhaps caused the Allies to think they had done some damage. Sixty-one men were killed in all, none in the *Victory*, and 108 wounded. Longford remarked, 'there was nothing to be dreaded in the superiority of their numbers... I had not a very high opinion of the manoeuvres of the Combined Fleet or what they would be able to effect' – anticipating Nelson's view of the enemy's capabilities.[16]

It was to be the *Victory*'s last action for some time; back at Portsmouth at the end of the year, she was judged to need a 'middling repair' before further service. Hostilities ended in 1783 with British recognition of American independence on fairly generous terms, and peace treaties with France, Spain and the Netherlands.

Back in Ordinary

Reduced again to the ordinary at the end of the war, the *Victory* was laid up at Number-eight Mooring on the west shore at Portsmouth – a 'swinging' mooring in that the ship was only fixed by the bows and would swing with the wind and the tide. Only older ships were moored bow and stern, but in that situation they were in danger if there was a strong cross-wind. In September 1783 the officers of Portsmouth Dockyard wrote that 'The *Victory* lies at the 8th west shore which is the only mooring she can lay at in this harbour from her length, and should she be placed at the 5th, 7th or 8th east shore it would entirely stop the moving of ships up and down the harbour' – presumably when she was swinging with the tide. She had a relatively large crew for a ship in ordinary, of six officers, ten servants and thirty-five seamen. Their duties included 'to clean the ships, to attend the stoves, awnings, windsails and ports, to wet the decks and sides &c in the proper seasons of the year.' The main object was to ensure that the ship was properly aired internally to prevent long-term decay.[17]

The dockyard officials seemed very confident about the condition of the *Victory* for the next few years and she did not feature in the estimates for ships needing repair. However, she was still fastened with iron below

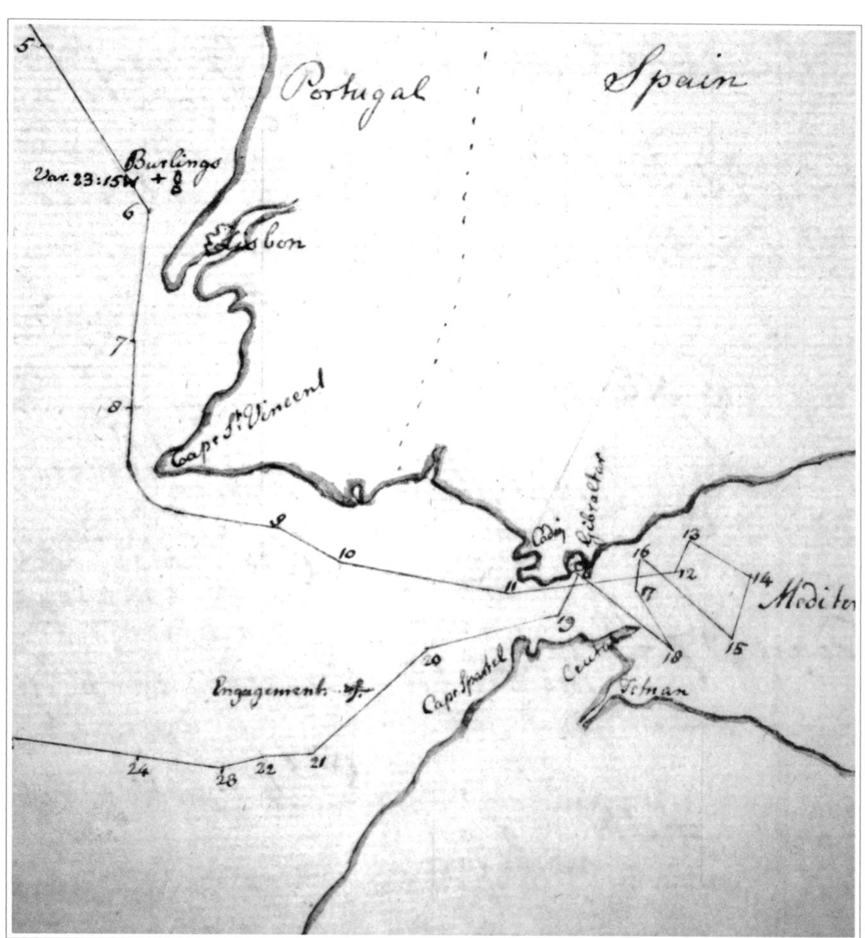

Pakenham's plan of the British fleet's movements off Gibraltar in October 1782. It shows the arrival after rounding Cape St Vincent, tacking in unfavourable winds in both directions just inside the Mediterranean and the site of the engagement on the 20th.

(© National Maritime Museum, Greenwich, London, PAK/2)

the waterline – it had been discovered that iron and copper interacted with one another to cause both to decay. A temporary solution was to isolate the copper from the iron as much as possible by using tar and sheets of paper, but that would only last for two or three years. There was a long-term programme to drive out every iron bolt below the waterline in every ship in the navy and use copper alloy instead, but so far it had not reached the *Victory*. In September 1787 she was ordered to be fitted out for sea on a threat of war following an attempted revolution in the Netherlands. The dockyard officers found that her foremast was badly decayed and recommended substituting the mainmast of the 74-gun *Hector* which was currently under repair. Otherwise, it only cost £790 to put her in condition for sea, compared with £6,364 for the 90-gun *Barfleur*, and £1,826 for the 74-gun *Bellona*. However, the crisis was over before she put to sea, and early in November the dockyard officers reported that they had taken off some of her copper and found that the caulking underneath was still 'very sound and good.' They wanted to replace the iron bolts as part of the general programme, but found that the blocks which held the ship up in the dry-dock were too low for the work. She was floated out incomplete, while the *Hector* was put in her place. As to the *Victory*, she had not been repaired in thirteen or fourteen years apart from a temporary one in 1783 and the officers recommended, 'when she is redocked, to take out some strakes to examine the state of her frame and have a proper survey on her before we go on with bolting her with copper.' Already the size of the repair was growing and by the end of the month it was estimated that the repair of the hull, masts and yards during the coming year would need £10,064 with £1,880 for coppering and £2,876 for copper bolts.

There were delays as the *Hector* clogged up the only suitable dry dock for longer than expected and the *Victory* was not put in until 24 December, with the 74-gun *Colossus* taking over her mooring. By the end of April, it was planned to replace fashion pieces which formed the main structure of the stern, and by June there was mention of two pieces of apron, the stemson and some of the transoms needing attention. It was not unusual for more defects to be found once a hull was opened and on 12 August the dockyard reported, 'that in unbolting and taking off the several parts to make good her defects, we have discovered her frame to be in a much worse state than we could have supposed...' Hundreds of pieces of timber were listed as being decayed or rotten, including the keel, thirty-two lower futtocks, eighty-two second and 124 third futtocks, along with numerous pieces of clamp, spirketting, beams and many other features. She would need 'a great instead of a small repair' and an extra £29,620 was needed in addition to the money granted last year. Later, the mainmast and bowsprit were also found to be defective. The work was finally completed in April 1788, at a total expense of £37,523, more than half her original cost.

Russian Interest

A compliment to the *Victory*'s sailing qualities came from a faraway quarter during the 1780s. To further an alliance with Catherine the Great of Russia, D Masal'skiy was allowed to enrol as a shipwright apprentice at Portsmouth in May 1780.[18] He got hold of the dimensions of the *Victory*, probably the 'offsets' or measurements taken at many points on the lower hull, as the basic dimensions of length, breadth and depth were common knowledge and would be of little use in constructing a ship. They could have been taken off the *Victory* during her dockings in April 1779 or March 1780. In Russia, Constructors A S Kastanov and I James used them to build four ships of the *Ches'ma* class. Surviving plans of the *Rostislav* of 1784 are indeed very similar to the *Victory* below the waterline, though the construction lines for floor and breadth sweeps are slightly different, suggesting that they were indeed

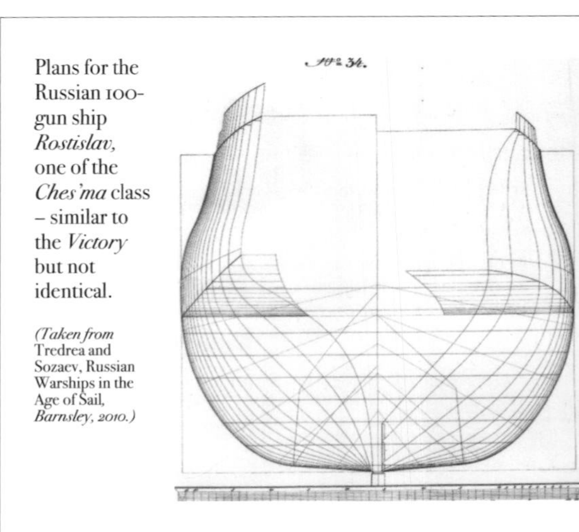

Plans for the Russian 100-gun ship *Rostislav*, one of the *Ches'ma* class – similar to the *Victory* but not identical.

(Taken from Tredrea and Sozaev, Russian Warships in the Age of Sail, *Barnsley, 2010.)*

made from offsets rather than actual plans. In 1784 another Russian apprentice, Vasilii Vlasov, was able to obtain a copy of the plans of the *Victory* at great expense. These were used for four more ships by Jonathan Coleman, built between 1785 and 1790.[19]

Nelson in the West Indies

After paying off the *Albemarle* in 1783, Nelson spent time in France with his friend Captain James Macnamara, but he failed to learn much of the language. Seagoing appointments were rare in peacetime, but in March 1784 he was appointed to the 28-gun *Boreas*. He hoped to go back to Indian waters, but instead he was sent to the West Indies. He carried Lady Hughes, wife of the commander-in-chief and 'a fine talkative woman' who clearly did not fit into the masculine, disciplined life of the ship. He also had a large complement of midshipmen, whom he took good care to train, doing 'the duty from rigging the topgallant mast to stowing the ballast.' Once in the islands, he found companionship with his fellow captain and long-term friend Cuthbert Collingwood, but he was soon in dispute over seniority with the commissioner of Antigua Dockyard, Captain John Moutray. It was a very different matter with Moutray's young wife Mary, and Nelson and Collingwood competed for her affections – 'What a treasure of a woman', wrote Nelson. His crew was difficult, there was a duel between two of the midshipmen and a large number of floggings of seamen. Nelson kept his ship active, 'always on the wind, and when it happened that any of the other ships were in company, he was always forming the line, exercising, chasing, etc.' And he soon found a cause to arouse his interest.

Under the Navigation Acts (enforced since 1651), the ships of the new United States had no right to trade with the British colonies in the West Indies, though in practice the islands could barely survive without imports of American food and other goods. Nelson observed that Hughes was 'led by the advice of the Islanders to admit the Yankees to a trade, or at least to wink at it.' It is a great irony that the man who originated the phrase 'turning a blind eye' was almost the only one who was not able to do so in these circumstances. He stopped and searched American ships and confiscated their contents. He spent a good deal of time in court and at one stage he was unable to leave his ship in English Harbour, Antigua, for fear of being served a writ. He became very unpopular with most of the islanders, except for John Herbert, president of Nevis. Nelson came to know his niece, Frances Nisbet, and her young son. His assessment of her in his letters was far less passionate than that of Mary Moutray and other women he had courted unsuccessfully, but he married her on March 1787 on Nevis.

In the meantime, another figure had re-entered his life. Prince William Henry, later Duke of Clarence and eventually King William IV, was in command of the frigate *Pegasus* at the age of 21. He was under the orders of Nelson, for Admiral Hughes went home in August 1786. The prince was not an easy captain to serve under, he tended to impose military-style discipline on his officers and seamen and soon had disputes with his

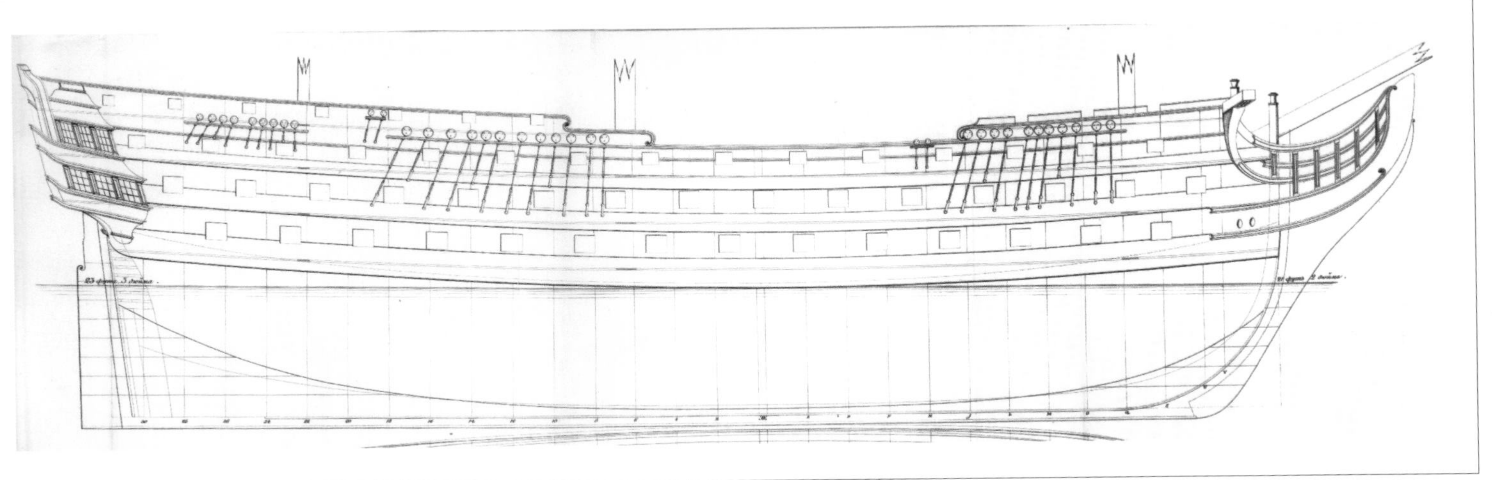

A miniature of Frances Nelson by Daniel Orme, probably executed in 1798 after a relatively happy period in her marriage.

(© Royal Museums Greenwich, London, MNT0047)

midshipmen and petty officers, including the master-at-arms who was essential to ship's discipline. The biggest dispute was with his First-Lieutenant, Isaac Schomberg, a highly competent officer who had been appointed to look after the prince – but William demanded a court martial on him and Nelson unwisely agreed, for he had a rosy view of the *Pegasus* – 'one of the finest ordered frigates I have seen.' He covered for William's administrative errors and was later informed that the Admiralty was 'much disappointed and dissatisfied at the little attention you have shewn to the rules and practice of the service as well as... the *General Printed Instructions*'. When he returned home in July 1787, he was a senior captain and a married man with a stepson, but he had yet to find out how much his career prospects had suffered.

The Armaments

As Nelson's star was falling, the *Victory*'s was rising again. She was ready for service in 1790 when there was another dispute with Spain, over Nookta Sound near Vancouver. According to the young Lieutenant Byam Martin, 'the din of war ran through the country like wildfire, and we candidates for promotion as a most auspicious event.' The fleet was mobilised again and the press gang was employed, though the *Victory* was manned largely by the bounty paid to volunteers – 227 able seamen, fifty-eight ordinary and 102 landsmen were paid a total of £899, with sixty-one more being recruited later. Despite her recent repair, she needed £11,525 more to put her into service. The fleet was commanded by Lord Howe, who hoisted his flag in the *Victory*, but only until the new 100-gun *Queen Charlotte* was ready. After that, Lord Hood took over the *Victory* as commander of the rear division of the fleet. Howe had been developing new signalling systems for years and this was a chance to try them out. His orders for new flags strained the resources of Portsmouth Dockyard, which had to employ teams of tailors to sew them.[20] Nevertheless, he was no believer in delegation – only flagships had full sets of flags, plus the frigates that were stationed outside the line to repeat orders. Howe had a fleet of thirty-one ships of the line and, according to Byam Martin, 'After making a show off Ushant, and cruising for some time, the fleet arrived off the Lizard... the moment the admiral received his dispatches the fleet crowded all sail for Ushant... but after manoeuvring awhile off the French coast we had the mortification to return to Spithead on the 1st of September without a bird in hand, or even a shot being fired.' The fleet was paid off but as late as January 1791 the *Victory* and several other ships had not been taken back to their berths in the harbour due to bad weather and the other ships taking up the moorings.

She was fitted out again in 1791, this time flying Hood's flag as commander-in-chief, for an affair known as the 'Russian Armament '– a dispute over Catherine the Great's ambitions in the Black Sea. Hood was a far more popular admiral than Howe and had already won the esteem of Nelson in the West Indies. Though he was sixty-six years old and had had indifferent health

Detail of a naive painting of the fleet offshore, showing the *Victory*, probably anchored off Weymouth or Torbay, and flying the flag of an admiral of the blue.

(© Compton Verney House Trust)

in the last few years, he was still highly energetic. As a naval commander, he had carried out one of the neatest actions of the last war when he anchored his ships in a chevron formation to beat off a larger French fleet and save the island of St Kitts. He took part in Rodney's victory off the Saintes in 1782, but was furious and outspoken about this chief's failure to pursue the beaten enemy. He too had strong ideas on signals and his secretary, John McArthur, helped him to develop them. In his opinion, Hood had 'the sternness of the old school... tempered by a tenderness and urbanity, that prevents its ever being oppressive, or tyrannical.' To Nelson, he was 'equally great in all situations which an admiral can be placed in.'

Midshipman Jeffrey Raigersfield was appointed to the *Victory* after service in ships of the line and frigates:

> ...I was sent on board the flag ship of the Commander-in-Chief. This was again a new life to me, for it may be said with propriety, that a first-rate man-of-war, when flag ship, is in all respects a court afloat; but when she bears the flag of the Commander-in-Chief, she is completely so. Although the duties on board of a flag ship are much the same, yet a vast difference is visible in the general tone of things...[21]

There was huge public interest in the great fleet of thirty-six ships of the line that assembled at Spithead, moored in two lines with the *Victory* between them in the centre. Three Baltic pilots were taken on board the *Victory* in case operations were needed in that sea.[22] According to Martin, 'The large fleet at Spithead drew people from all parts of the kingdom, and dinners and balls were quite the order of the day.' The Prime Minister, William Pitt the Younger, dined on board the *Victory* with Hood and Henry Dundas, the powerful and astute Treasurer of the Navy. Although they encountered wet and windy weather, Hood believed that the prime minister was never 'in better health and spirits.' He gave his guests 'the best turtle they ever ate, and as good wine as they ever drank; and at seven they left me, very highly delighted with the events of the day.' For those who could not make it to Portsmouth, Robert Barker set up a panorama in Leicester Square, London, with a circular picture measuring more than 10,000 square feet, with a diameter of ninety feet. But the fleet did not go to sea, Parliament was divided while Catherine remained firm and got her way. Hood wrote to his brother of unanimity throughout the fleet and 'there has not been a dispute between any two boat crews since I came here' – a contrast to the days of Keppel when the *Victory* and *Formidable* had to be docked separately.[23]

The *Victory* was still in good repair after this mobilisation, though it was estimated it would take £1,749 to prepare her hull for the sea again from the ordinary, plus £57 for masts and yards, and £2,626 for 'furniture and stores' – in January 1792 she was listed

Admiral Samuel Hood, painted by James Northcote.

(© National Maritime Museum, Greenwich, London, BHC2774)

among thirty ships which had been fitted out in 1790 and 1791 which would need all of their rigging blocks to be 'overhauled, refitted and made good before they can be completed for sea service.' She might have gained a different kind of fame in September 1792 when the Navy Board ordered that 'a court martial is to be held on board the *Victory*, for trying the mutineers belonging to the *Bounty* and rush-bottom chairs, tables and flags were to be provided for the occasion' – but, in fact, the trial of Midshipman Peter Heywood and five others was held on board the 90-gun *Duke*. In December that year defects were found in her foremast, while in January 1793 the Navy Board ordered that she be equipped with stern and top lanterns like those of the *Queen Charlotte*.

The *Victory* painted by Robert Dodd, flying Hood's vice-admiral's flag, red at the fore, probably showing the ship during the mobilisation of 1791. The red ensign is pre-1801, without the St Patrick's cross, and the ship has only the lower wales and upper sides painted black, a typical style for the time. This is the earliest known clear view of the ship under sail.

(© National Maritime Museum, Greenwich, London, BHC3694)

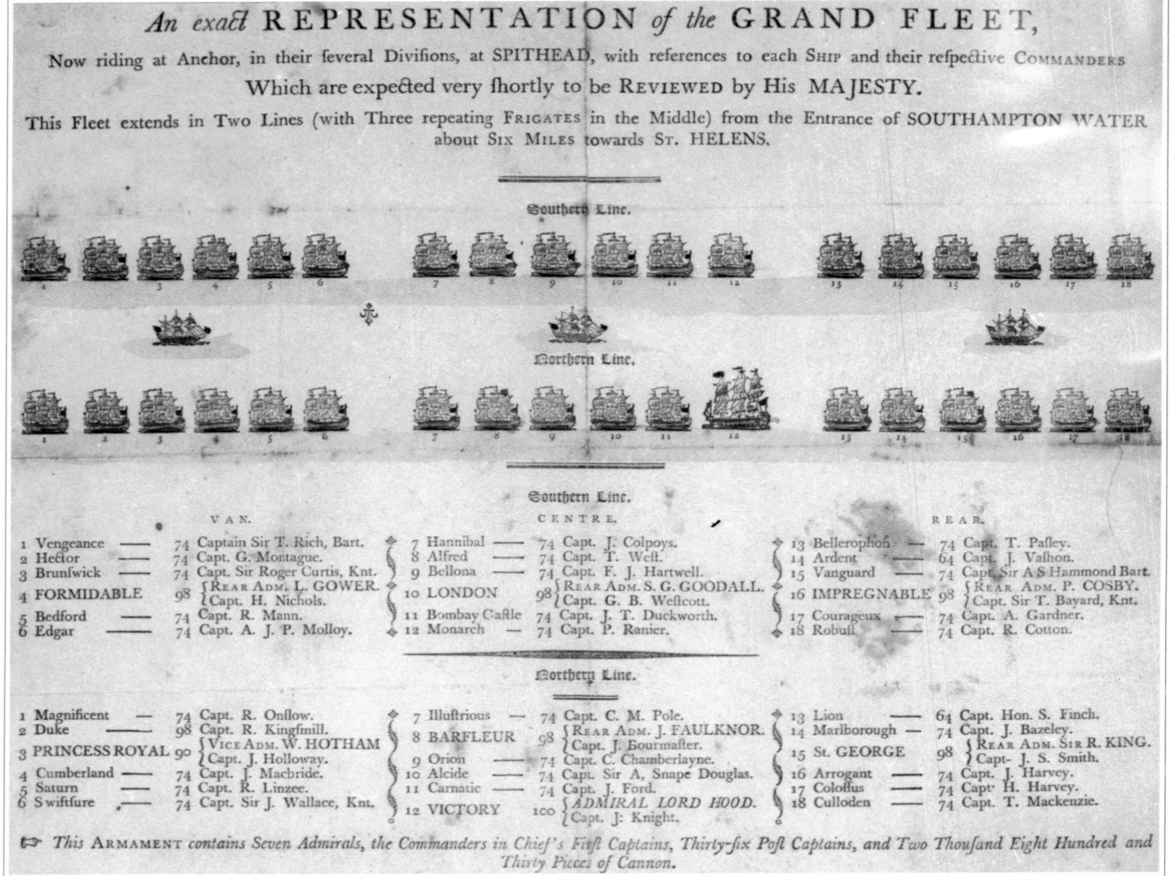

An exact REPRESENTATION *of the* GRAND FLEET,

Now riding at Anchor, in their ſeveral Diviſions, at SPITHEAD, with references to each SHIP and their reſpective COMMANDERS
Which are expected very ſhortly to be REVIEWED by His MAJESTY.
This Fleet extends in Two Lines (with Three repeating FRIGATES in the Middle) from the Entrance of SOUTHAMPTON WATER about SIX MILES towards ST. HELENS.

Southern Line.

	VAN.				CENTRE.				REAR.		
1	Vengeance	74	Captain Sir T. Rich, Bart.	7	Hannibal	74	Capt. J. Colpoys.	13	Bellerophon	74	Capt. T. Paſley.
2	Hector	74	Capt. G. Montague.	8	Alfred	74	Capt. T. Weſt.	14	Ardent	64	Capt. J. Vaſhon.
3	Brunſwick	74	Capt. Sir Roger Curtis, Knt.	9	Bellona	74	Capt. F. J. Hartwell.	15	Vanguard	74	Capt. Sir A S Hammond Bart.
4	FORMIDABLE	98	REAR ADM. L. GOWER. Capt. H. Nichols.	10	LONDON	98	REAR ADM. S. G. GOODALL. Capt. G. B. Weſtcott.	16	IMPREGNABLE	98	REAR ADM. P. COSBY. Capt. Sir T. Bayard, Knt.
5	Bedford	74	Capt. R. Mann.	11	Bombay Caſtle	74	Capt. J. T. Duckworth.	17	Courageux	74	Capt. A. Gardner.
6	Edgar	74	Capt. A. J. P. Molloy.	12	Monarch	74	Capt. P. Ranier.	18	Robuſt	74	Capt. R. Cotton.

Northern Line.

1	Magnificent	74	Capt. R. Onſlow.	7	Illuſtrious	74	Capt. C. M. Pole.	13	Lion	64	Capt. Hon. S. Finch.
2	Duke	98	Capt. R. Kingſmill.	8	BARFLEUR	98	REAR ADM. J. FAULKNOR. Capt. J. Bourmaſter.	14	Marlborough	74	Capt. J. Bazeley.
3	PRINCESS ROYAL	90	VICE ADM. W. HOTHAM Capt. J. Holloway.	9	Orion	74	Capt. C. Chamberlayne.	15	St. GEORGE	98	REAR ADM. SIR R. KING. Capt. J. S. Smith.
4	Cumberland	74	Capt. J. Macbride.	10	Alcide	74	Capt. Sir A, Snape Douglas.	16	Arrogant	74	Capt. J. Harvey.
5	Saturn	74	Capt. R. Linzee.	11	Carnatic	74	Capt. J. Ford.	17	Coloſſus	74	Capt. H. Harvey.
6	Swiftſure	74	Capt. Sir J. Wallace, Knt.	12	VICTORY	100	*ADMIRAL LORD HOOD.* Capt. J: Knight.	18	Culloden	74	Capt. T. Mackenzie.

☞ *This* ARMAMENT *contains Seven Admirals, the Commanders in Chief's Firſt Captains, Thirty-ſix Poſt Captains, and Two Thouſand Eight Hundred and Thirty Pieces of Cannon.*

Hood's fleet assembled in the Solent for a review by the King. The *Victory* is at number twelve, leading the centre division in the nearest line. Three repeating frigates can be seen between the lines.

(© National Maritime Museum, Greenwich, London, PAF4673)

There were none in stock at Portsmouth so the officers took them from the *Queen Charlotte* instead.[24]

Nelson on the Beach

During all this, Captain Horatio Nelson was left in his father's home at Burnham Thorpe, dodging American shipowners who tried to sue him – he wrote, 'I have been plagu'd by the seizures made whilst in the West Indies'. Money was short on his half-pay but he absorbed himself in country pursuits, obtaining a hunting licence and building a pond in the shape of a warship. There is no evidence about his relations with his wife, but no children were conceived though neither was infertile and both had children with other partners. He was questioned about irregularities in the West Indies, while friendship with one of the King's sons did not guarantee Royal favour – often the reverse in view of the tortured family relations of the Hanoverians. At one stage he asked for the command of a guardship, but it is not likely that such static service would have suited his temperament. He was mortified not to be called to service during the mobilisations and in 1792 he wrote to the Duke of Clarence, 'in the Spanish Armament, when almost the whole service were called forth, I asked Lord Hood to interest himself with Lord Chatham that I might be appointed to a ship. His Lordship having declined doing it, has prevented my troubling him again for his interest or influence.' However, he deleted a more striking passage from the final draft – Hood had 'made a speech never to be effaced from my memory, viz. that the King was impressed with an unfavourable opinion of me' – devastating to a loyal officer like Nelson.[25]

Meanwhile, the old enemy, France, was taking on a new and more frightening form, after revolution broke out in 1789. Hood had promised Nelson a ship 'should a disturbance take place' and by 1793 it was clear that his services, however embarrassing they might be in peacetime, would be needed in the war that now threatened.

6 MEDITERRANEAN FLAGSHIP

The Sun Shines on Nelson

When the French Revolution began with the storming of the Bastille on 14 July 1789, much of British public opinion was in favour of it, as tending towards a constitutional monarchy like they enjoyed themselves. This began to turn to horror as the government passed into more extreme hands, and European opinion was shocked when King Louis XIV was executed by guillotine in January 1793, to be followed by his queen Marie Antoinette later in the year. British opinion remained divided over the revolution, with Tom Paine and the radicals demanding a more democratic system while Edmund Burke wrote forcefully about the dangers of radical change. The government of William Pitt the Younger knew which side it was on and began to mobilise the fleet to join a conservative alliance that already included Austria, Prussia, Sardinia and Spain. Britain declared war on 1 February 1793. The French were already victorious on land as their ragged but enthusiastic armies defeated the more formal forces of reaction. At sea the position was very different. They still had a very powerful fleet and a great deal of self-confidence after holding the British off in the last war, but many of the officers were aristocrats who were executed, imprisoned or went into exile. Naval command needed far more technical skill than army leadership, and hastily promoted petty officers, merchant ship captains and politically-motivated landsmen did not fill the gap, either individually or as a group.

One person who was delighted with the new war was Horatio Nelson. Finally released from his domestic boredom at Burnham Thorpe, he was appointed to the twelve-year old 64-gun ship *Agamemnon,* his first ship of the line. Some would have despised such a command, it was written not long afterwards, '...our naval officers either pray or swear against being appointed to serve on board them' – for a 64, with only 24-pounders on its lower deck, was likely to find itself up against a 74 or even a three decker in a line of battle. But Nelson saw it differently and wrote to his wife after a meeting with the First Lord, 'After clouds comes sunshine. The Admiralty so smile upon me, that really I am as much surprised as when they frowned.' He went back to his old stomping ground of Chatham to fit out the ship, which he regarded as 'without exception, the finest 64 in the service, and has the character of sailing most remarkably well.'[1]

The Mediterranean Fleet

Nelson did not know it yet, but he was to serve in the Mediterranean Fleet now fitting out at Spithead, to be commanded by his erstwhile friend and patron Lord Hood. *Victory* was to be the flagship, perhaps because Hood had formed an attachment to it during his previous service, or possibly because it was now considered the most fitting ship for such a command. *Victory* had been overtaken as the largest ship in the navy by that time, by the new *Royal George* launched in 1788 and the *Queen Charlotte* of 1789. That ship was to serve as flagship of the Channel Fleet, the most important one, under Lord Howe while the *Royal George* was to fly the flag of Vice-Admiral Sir Alexander Hood, the brother of Lord Hood, in the same fleet. This left the *Victory* for the next most important role, as flagship of the Mediterranean Fleet.

Captain Knight described the laborious tasks of fitting out in some detail. Early in the process, on the last day of 1792, 'PM, received on board gunner's and boatswain's stores.' There was no time to celebrate the new year and next morning, 'Employed getting the standing rigging out of the storehouse and bringing it alongside. Came on board 100 men from the *Duke* and the marines from headquarters.' In the afternoon, 'Received on board two months provisions for 200 men of all species, received on board coals and gunner's stores, employed clearing the lighter of the rigging and rigging the foremast. Riggers on board wolding the main mast.' On the 3rd

they rigged the mainmast and threaded the deadeyes that supported the shrouds, borrowing men from the *Hector* and *Alfred* to help. By the 7th they were 'swifting out the main rigging and rattling the fore ditto.' They began to receive anchors and the 9th was spent coiling their cables on the orlop deck and stowing the ground tier of casks in the hold. The ship was ready to move out of harbour to Spithead on the 16th and 'came to with the best bower in 16 fathoms.'[2] The ship exercised her guns while at Spithead. She fired off 200 lbs of powder in 'scaling, priming the 32- and 24-pounders'. Two hundred pounds more were expended firing salutes for the arrival of Sir Hyde Parker and the King's birthday. On 18 January the 12-pounders were exercised in firing five rounds at a mark, but mostly the gun drill was without firing, as usual, a pattern that continued during the commission.[3]

Midshipman Jeffrey Raigersfield had already experienced bullying in the frigate *Pearl* and the 74-gun *Courageaux*. He described this to Captain Knight of the *Victory*, who had been his captain in the *Triumph*, and was offered a place in the flagship. But the oppression followed him, at first the other midshipmen would not admit him to their mess. He reported this to the first lieutenant and captain, who assembled the officers and midshipmen on the quarterdeck, to ask them collectively and individually, 'Whether or not any of them knew any thing [sic] in my conduct inconsistent with the character of a gentleman.' There was silence, except that one master's mate mentioned an unsubstantiated rumour that he owed money to inns ashore. The midshipmen had to admit him to the starboard mess but he was still ostracised. However he found a niche, which Nelson would have approved of:

Captain John Knight. Although his command of the *Victory* in 1793–96 was not considered successful by Jervis, he later earned a reputation as a surveyor and chart-maker.

(© National Maritime Museum, Greenwich, London, L4379)

The *Victory* painted by Monamy Swaine in 1793. She still carries Hood's flag on the foremast and Eddystone Lighthouse off Plymouth can be seen in the background. The ship's name is painted on the stern.

(© National Maritime Museum, Greenwich, London, BHC3696)

> Being fond of boat duty, I was always well dressed by eight o'clock in the morning in uniform and ready,

> while others, whose turn it was to go in boats, were not so, and I frequently presented myself and took their turn. This disinterested conduct soon brought me under the notice of the lieutenants, and as I was found to be so good a boatman, and often came off to Spithead, when blowing very hard, and got safe on board when no other boat of the fleet would even leave the shore.

Lord Hood came on board on 7 May and the crews saluted him with three cheers, which was cheaper than gun salutes. Raigersfield described his arrival on board. 'The fleet was ready for sea, and orders had been given to prepare for the reception of the Commander-in-Chief: the day was fixed for his coming on board, and all officers were expected to be in full dress to receive him. He came alongside and upon deck, the band playing "See, the conquering hero comes!"' The young midshipman was delighted when his old acquaintance with the admiral was renewed. 'As he passed on the quarter deck into the cabin, it so happened that I was the only midshipman or person he took any notice of.' This restored his prestige in the gunroom, for a time at least.[4]

Hood's Captain of the Fleet was John Inglefield. William Hotham, nephew of the second-in-command of the fleet, was appointed seventh lieutenant of the *Victory* in January 1794 and found him to be, 'a remarkably handsome man, very good-natured and kind in his manners, but without the polish of a man accustomed to much good society.' He never quite recovered from the loss of the 74-gun *Centaur* in 1782. The Flag Captain was John Knight, a 'remarkably quick and active officer, but who 'was not too popular in the service, and was supposed to pay too much attention to domestic affairs during his service, and to have considered the ship he commanded more a house in which he was residing with his family [rather] than a ship of the British Fleet.'[5]

Hood's orders included the three main tasks of a British commander-in-chief in the Mediterranean. He was to protect trade, assembling convoys and using his frigates to escort them. He was to link up with actual or potential allies, which in this case seemed comparatively easy with the almost universal hostility to the French revolutionaries, and that the ambassadors to Spain, Portugal, Naples and Sardinia had instructions to negotiate 'a concert between [His Majesty]... as to the most effectual means to be taken against the common enemy'. Thirdly, he was to neutralise the French fleet at Toulon, either by blockading it or 'attempting some decisive blow against the naval power of France.'[6]

The Admiralty had resolved to send up the fleet in sections escorting convoys, and the *Victory* left Spithead on 23 May with a group of six more ships of the line and eleven smaller warships, protecting a convoy of East Indiamen. A few days later they passed close to Cape St Vincent in the south-west corner of Portugal, where Raigersfield could see 'the good fat friars sitting outside their convent... enjoying the agreeable freshness of the North-West wind, which soon wafted us by them, and to Gibraltar...'[7] Meanwhile, Nelson's *Agamemnon* was one of the ships sent into Cadiz for supplies, as Spain was an ally for once. He observed the condition of their navy as being one of '...very fine ships, but shockingly manned... I am certain if our six barge crews, who are picked men, had got on board one of their first rates, they would have taken her.'[8] This was something to note for the future. His relationship with the commander-in-chief was improving, but still wary. 'I paid Lord Hood a visit a few days back, and found him very civil: I dare say we shall be good friends again.'[9]

The fleet spent a week at Gibraltar then nineteen ships of the line sailed for Toulon where they arrived on 20 July. Raigersfield was one of the officers under Lieutenant Edward Cooke of the *Victory* in a French prize that was sent into the port with a flag of truce to arrange the exchange of prisoners. But, 'as we came under the high land that forms the western part of the entrance into the deep bay of Toulon roads, a shot was fired at us to bring us to, which we did, and shortly after a couple of gun boats.... came and took possession of us.' They were held at Fort de Malgue for several days until they were sent back with a packet of papers, but with no real agreement on the exchange.

Toulon

By the beginning of August,Hood was 'thinking the Toulon fleet will not come out for the present' and he decided to 'show the flag off Genoa'. On the 23rd he

A young man is introduced to the midshipman's berth, originally drawn by Captain Marryat and prepared for publication by George Cruikshank. The print contains much detail, including the 'oldsters' or older masters' mates etc. to the left; an unhappy midshipman cleaning shoes and another playing pranks outside the cabin, with noisy entertainment inside, and a black servant. In the foreground, a seaman uses a boatswain's whistle to control the movement of a cask being brought out of the hold while another searches for one in the depths.

(© National Maritime Museum, Greenwich, London, PU4722)

received commissioners from Marseilles who wanted to restore the monarchy in their province. Soon afterwards he was joined by a delegation of royalists from Toulon, who offered to deliver the great port up to the Allies. Hood was reluctant at first, he had no force of ground troops to defend the place, but he made a momentous decision, which would indeed be a 'decisive blow against the naval power of France'. 'I came to the resolution of landing 1,500 men, and take possession of the forts which command the ships in the Road.' He was aware of the risks, that 'in all enterprises of war danger more or less is to be expected and must be submitted to...' but it was worth it. He was 'impressed with the great importance of taking possession of Toulon, the great fort of Malgue and others on the main, in shortening the war, I fully relied that in case my endeavour should not succeed, I should be justified in running some risque, being conscious I acted to the best of my judgement as a faithful servant to my king and country.'[10] On the 28th he issued a proclamation from the *Victory*. He would 'take possession of Toulon and hold it in trust only for Louis XVII until peace shall be re-established in France...'[11] Lieutenant Cooke of the *Victory* was sent on shore again and apparently offered to pay the French crews in silver rather than paper. Troops from the various British ships, serving as marines, were rowed over to the 74-gun *Robust* and the master of the *Victory* watched them land at 11am. However ,Toulon was far from secure, most of the ships of the line in the harbour supported the republic, but the appearance of the Spanish fleet strengthened the allied hand. The *Victory* herself sailed into Toulon roads at 11 am on the 29th and anchored in seven fathoms of water. On the 30th she shifted her berth to a position half a mile east of Fort Eguelette, with her anchor in ten fathoms, as the position on shore was consolidated. The main post, Fort La Malgue, was given up by the royalists while

Toulon in Allied possession with forts Balaguier and L'Eguilette in the background. The three-decker in the centre foreground is possibly the *Victory*.

(© National Maritime Museum, Greenwich, London, PAH2315)

those defending the town were also taken over. But the whole port had a perimeter of fifteen miles, which would be much harder to defend, especially as Hood had no coherent land force.

Marseilles had been lost to republican forces but Toulon was a prize indeed if it could be held. According to Captain Edward Brenton, who was a poor historian but good recorder of nautical topography, it was 'the great and only naval arsenal of France in the Mediterranean... a place that has been called one of the finest ports of maritime equipment in the world.' It had the only dry-docks in the Mediterranean, as they were difficult to use in the tideless sea, but Toulon had a supply of convict labour for pumping and other works:

> Besides the inner harbour, which encloses the arsenal [ie dockyard], they have an outer harbour and a road. The inner harbour is a work of art [ie engineering] formed by two jetties... embracing a space large enough to hold thirty ships of the line.... As many frigates, and a proportion of smaller craft, besides their mast pond. The arsenal is on the west side, and the ships in ordinary, or fitting, lie with their sterns or bowsprits or their sterns over the wharf; the storehouses are within fifteen yards of them; the rope-house, sail loft, bake-house, mast-house, ordnance, and other buildings are capacious and good: the model [mould?]-loft is worthy of the attention of strangers.

The town itself, north of the dockyard, was 'fortified with great art, both on the land and sea approaches', but it was overlooked by hills which made the position difficult. Nelson was exultant (though he would see little of Toulon as the *Agamemnon* was mostly employed carrying messages for Hood) remarking, 'what an event this has been for Lord Hood: such a one as history cannot produce its equal; that the strongest place in Europe, and twenty-two sail of the line, &c., should be given up without firing a shot.'[12]

One day Midshipman Raigersfield showed some of the tactlessness that perhaps made him so unpopular with his messmates.

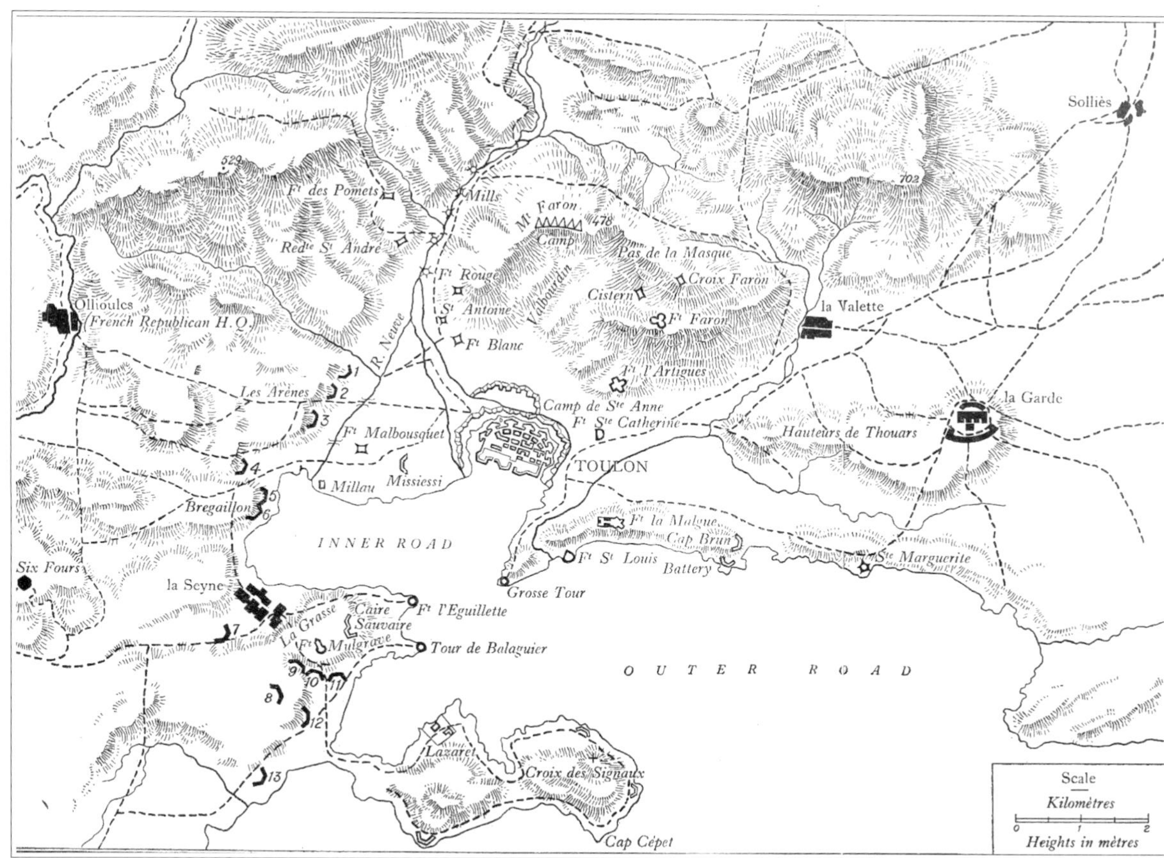

A map of the Toulon campaign showing the town, dockyard and main forts.

(Taken from J. Holland Rose, Lord Hood and the Defence of Toulon, *Cambridge, 1922, author's collection)*

> ...Being upon the quarter-deck with several other midshipmen, I thoughtlessly observed it seemed strange to me no preparations had been made for evacuating the place, not that it was now apparent it would be necessary, but in case it should so turn out, as neither the forts nor whatever else in our possession had been mined, or got ready for blowing up... Little did I think at that time that the accidental remarks of a young gentleman in his profession would find their way to the Commander-in Chief's ears, but they did however, and my promotion was retarded.[13]

In fact, it was only by a few days, but the young midshipman did not understand Hood's dilemma. In theory, the alliance against the French revolution was powerful, but the members all had different aims and capabilities. The Spanish greatly resented the British possession of Gibraltar and feared that they wanted another base in the Mediterranean. The French royalists wanted the fleet and base at Toulon kept intact so that they could be handed over to their king as soon as he was restored. The administration in London did not understand the delicacy of the situation and urged Hood to sail the French ships away, or prepare to destroy them and the dockyard as a last resort. On the spot, Hood had a very difficult balancing act.

The End at Toulon

Hood sought allies and especially land forces to secure his possession. Troops were sent from Sardinia and Piedmont and proved effective, those of Spain were less so, while the King of Naples vacillated. Hood's difficulties were compounded by the long distance from London – it took three weeks to get a message there, and even longer to get a reply. At first he was too optimistic, being 'confident we can hold what we have got'. Lord Mulgrave, who arrived early in September to take command of the British land forces, was even more sanguine and wrote to Pitt of 'the confidence I feel of the safety of this place'. Though he had taken measures to burn the dockyard in the event of a retreat, these were 'vague and I think improbable suppositions.'

This allowed the government to send troops to the West Indies rather than Toulon, while they had contradictory policies on sending men from Gibraltar. But by the time these decisions were being made, the situation had deteriorated. Hood deployed seamen ashore, including some from the *Victory*, but their style of gunnery was not suitable for land warfare, and in addition it meant depleting his crews.

Things got far worse on 16 September, when a young captain – soon to be promoted major – arrived to take command of the French artillery. Napoleon Bonaparte, with his supreme tactical skill already in evidence, soon recognised that the key to the situation was the peninsula of La Grasse, which controlled the entrance to the inner road and therefore the town and dockyard. Despite his junior rank, his unique leadership qualities inspired the troops and the attack was conducted with new vigour. He mustered all the guns he could find to fire on the fleet and on the vital position. By the 26th, Hood was reporting, 'We are kept in perpetual alarms and at very hard duty.' On 7 October he promoted Cooke of the *Victory* to the rank of commander and appointed him lieutenant-governor ashore, while manning gunboats with midshipmen and seamen. By 11 November, Hood was reporting from the town of Toulon, 'Seven thousand men now occupy these outposts. That number will not ensure their safety, if they be vigorously attacked; and in this place I must beg leave to repeat that should we be able to maintain all these posts, it may not prevent the dockyard and arsenal from being bombarded.'

On the morning of 17 December, Fort Mulgrave, on the Grasse peninsula, was attacked and taken, with Bonaparte leading the final assault. Eight men of the *Victory*'s crew were reported missing, besides four wounded, including Lieutenant Goddard in charge of the party – though unlike the *Britannia* and *Windsor Castle* she had no fatal casualties. The position was now untenable and Hood made plans for evacuation. The royalists of Toulon had no illusions about what to expect as the republicans advanced, and many took to boats to join Hood's ships. Captain Knight wrote in his log, 'All employed receiving French refugee men, women and children.' The admiral reported, 'that every inhabitant was brought off as manifested inclination to come.' The *Victory* alone carried 705 soldiers and 370 'refugee men, women and children at 2/3rds allowance.' Purser John McArthur made a brave attempt to list their names in the muster book, but he only issued 40 beds to them.[14] Apart from the distress of losing their homes and goods, conditions must have been barely tolerable in a ship designed for a crew of 850 in already cramped conditions, on a week-long voyage towards the island of Elba. But according to Lieutenant Colonel John Moore, who had joined too late with a substantial military force, they made the best of it:

> Every part of the ship... was crowded with French people, men and women; they are the principal families of Toulon, who made their escape on board the night of the evacuation. I heard a fiddle and dancing in the ward-room, and was not a little surprised when I was told it was the French dancing out the old year; few of them have anything but the clothes on their backs, and the prospect before them is gloomy, yet they contrive to make themselves happy... Her quarter-deck forms a curious medley. There were French ladies and gentlemen, officers of the navy and army, commissaries &c.[15]

But Moore said nothing about the condition of the poorer refugees and the soldiers crammed below decks.

Meanwhile Captain Sir Sidney Smith was charged with destroying the ships and dockyard, but it proved harder than imagined. On the 19th, as the *Victory* left Toulon roads for the last time, Captain Knight 'observed a great fire, supposed to be the ships and Arsenal.' It was initially claimed that twenty-seven ships, including seventeen of the line, had been destroyed; but it later emerged that only nine of the line and three others had been put beyond repair.[16] Three ships of the line were captured. The 74-gun *Pompee* proved to be a very fine ship but the *Scipion* was lost soon afterwards. The huge *Commerce de Marseilles* of 120 guns helped to inspire a move towards bigger ships that left the *Victory* behind, though she never served as an active warship in the Royal Navy due to her structural weakness.

To Corsica

The withdrawal was a major setback for Hood and the fleet, but already there was a new target where they might curtail French power and set up a major British

Ships blowing up and burning during the evacuation of Toulon – but in fact the damage was not nearly as serious as this dramatic view suggests.

(© National Maritime Museum, Greenwich, London, PY3230)

base in the region. On 20 November, a small boat had arrived off Toulon from Corsica. The Spanish Admiral Langara was horrified to hear that the islanders had thrown off the French yoke, but Hood was more sympathetic to the rebels for he 'always understood that a very great part of the inhabitants of Corsica refused to acknowledge themselves subjects of France.' He knew something of the recent history of the island. It had been under Genoese rule for centuries, until 1755 when Pasquale Paoli led the people in setting up a democratic government, twenty years before the American Revolution. Unable to control the island, the Genoese sold it to France and she used her much greater military resources to crush the democrats at the Battle of Ponte Novu in 1768. Among those who fought on the defeated side was Carlo Bonaparte, who now had to make the agonising decision about whether to accept French rule or go into exile, probably in Britain. He chose the former and as a result his son Napoleon was a French subject when he was born in the following year. The young man was back in the island in 1791, trying unsuccessfully to maintain the rule of the French revolutionaries there

Paoli did go into exile in Britain where he became a member of the circle of Doctor Johnson and James Boswell. He was a remarkable man, of great intelligence and charm. He was back in Corsica with the revolution, but was soon put off by its extremism and the execution of King Louis XVI. He led a revolt and soon only three fortified towns in the north of the island – Calvi, San Fiorenza and Bastia, were still in French hands. Hood sent Captain Edward Cooke, formerly of the *Victory,* to the island to make contact. Paoli requested British help and announced 'the desire of me and my people to put ourselves under the government and protection of His Britannic Majesty and his nation without reserve.' Hood was well aware of the importance of the island to France, while to Britain it would offer 'several ports, and that of San Fiorenza a very good one for the reception of His Majesty's fleet in that part of the Mediterranean.' He had already sent several ships before the main fleet of sixty ships, including transports, left Hyeres Bay off Toulon on 24 January after receiving Cooke's report and Paoli's offer. In this campaign, the roles would be reversed, Nelson would be in the thick of the action while the *Victory* was on the sidelines.

On the way, as Hood reported, 'towards daylight it blew very strong, and before ten o'clock quite a storm, which made it prudent for me to bear up for Porto Ferrra [on Elba]'. It got so bad that the pilot declined charge of the ship and they were driven to the leeward of the island where Hood 'passed three very disagreeable nights having had two main topsails blown to rags, and the topsail yard reduced totally.'[17] Although he did not conceal his dislike of Hood and the navy, Lieutenant-Colonel John Moore had to admire his coolness and seamanship on the last of these nights. He and his army colleagues were sleeping in the outer cabin of the admiral's quarters, opposite the open door of Hood's cabin. At 1am they were woken by Captain Inglefield, who told them to dress quickly as he feared the ship would run aground. Moore could see that Hood was 'not the least discomposed' by the news. The admiral dressed 'with the greatest deliberation' and Moore was reassured enough to go back to sleep. On deck, according to Lieutenant Hotham, Captains Inglefield and Knight and the master were 'all at variance as to what was to be done' until 'the calm presence of mind and the professional knowledge of our venerable Commander-in-Chief' came into play. Hood directed 'the main sheet to be a little eased off, the bowline checked, and the ship to be kept clean full' so that she 'passed by very close and with a heavy press of sail.'[18] The ship arrived at Porto Ferraio on the 29th, the refugees were landed and the ships were repaired during the next week.

They sailed on 6 February and next day they began disembarking troops under Lieutenant-General Dundas near the tower of Mortella, on the west side of San Fiorenza Bay. Hood noted that 'the walls of the tower were of a prodigious thickness, and the parapet, where there were two 18-pounder guns, was lined with bass junk five feet from the walls and filled up with sand. The cannonade from the heights above did not make much impression over the following two days while the frigate *Fortitude* was damaged by red-hot shot. The *Victory* was never close to the action and on the 11th a strong westerly gale forced her to take shelter under Cape Corse. She was back on the 17th to witness the tower being stormed by soldiers and seamen. Then the tower at Fornalli was attacked and Gilbert Elliot, the

prospective British governor of the island, watched as the sailors moved cannon into position over rough terrain. 'They fastened great straps round the rocks, and then fastened to the straps the largest and most powerful purchase or pulleys and tackle that are used on board a man-of-war. The cannon was placed on a sledge at one end of the tackle, the men walked downhill with the other end of the tackle. The surprise of our friends, the Corsicans, and our enemies, the French, was equal on this occasion.'[19] Circular fortifications like this had been out of favour among military engineers since the days of Henry VIII, but this affair made a strong impression on those involved. Meanwhile, the town of

The Mortella Tower off St Fiorenze in Corsica. It and the one at Fornells caused their attackers a great deal of trouble, which eventually led the British government to build chains of 'Martello' towers on the south and east coasts of England, and in other places throughout the world.

(© National Maritime Museum, Greenwich, London, Naval Chronicle)

Seamen landing guns from ship's boats on the coast of Corsica, then hauling them up a slope while soldiers look on.

(© National Maritime Museum, Greenwich, London, PAH2355)

San Fiorenza fell as the soldiers defending it retreated eastwards over the hills towards Bastia.

Bastia

There was no legal mechanism for placing army formations under the command of the navy, or vice versa, so in combined operations everything depended on good relations between the land and sea commanders. This did not happen in Corsica, where Dundas and Moore resented Hood's arrogance. There was a further complication in that there were several army regiments serving in the place of marines in Hood's ships, borne as part of the complement, and many of these had been landed to take part in the assaults round San Fiorenza. Soon Dundas and Hood clashed about what to do next. The admiral wanted to attack Bastia right away before the French had a chance to augment their fortifications. Dundas considered this to be 'a visionary and rash attempt' and wanted to await reinforcements. Hood was sceptical – 'I do not see there is a prospect of any coming', he noted. Councils of War on 16 and 20 March only reinforced prejudices, the naval officers voted to attack and the army to wait. Hood decided to press on with the resources at his command despite 'manifold obstructions, that were industriously thrown in my way.' The situation did not improve after Dundas was superseded by the even more cautious Brigadier-General D'Aubant.

Nelson had been off Bastia in the *Agamemnon* since 7 February with several frigates under his command, and he landed several times in the area. He observed the defences on 19 February:

> On the town-wall next the sea, about twenty embrasures; to the southward of the town, two guns are mounted on a work newly thrown up, and an officer's guard encamped there; they are also throwing up a small work commanding a large road to the southward of the town, which leads towards the mountains.'

And, as he noted three days later: 'I find the enemy every hour are strengthening their works.'[20]

Hood joined him with the *Victory* on the 23rd and stayed for two weeks, hoping that a show of force would bring a surrender. After replenishing at San Fiorenza he returned on 4 April to anchor south of the town ready to invest it, with Nelson taking charge of the seamen on shore and Lieutenant-Colonel Vilettes, an officer more in sympathy with Hood's aims, in command of the soldiers landed from the fleet. D'Aubant grudgingly lent two officers and twenty-five artillerymen, but Hood had wanted double that number. On the 11th, one of the *Victory*'s boats carried a message to the French commander under a flag of truce, but was told in no uncertain terms, 'I have hot-shot for your ships, and bayonets for your troops.' Hood had arranged his ships in a crescent off the town, the siege began and it was bombarded by land and sea.

On 15 May, a boat heading for Bastia with gunpowder was captured, and was found to be carrying the mayor's brother. He was brought on board the *Victory* where he was treated with 'great attention and kindness' by the officers. He expressed his alarm at the possible danger to his family if the town was stormed. John McArthur, Hood's secretary, cunningly offered him a place on the quarterdeck to watch an attack next morning and told him, 'nothing could avert the impending horrors, but a flag of truce with proposals from the town.' The prisoner offered to send a letter stating that there was no hope of relief, but instead Hood agreed to send in the coxswain of the captured boat, ostensibly to get some necessities for the prisoner, but actually to spread news of the impending attack.[21] By this time, a stroke of luck meant some army reinforcements had arrived from Gibraltar and were ready to join the fight. On the 19th, Hood 'received a message that the garrison was desirous of capitulating on honourable terms' and he sent a note to the shore. 'This brought on board the *Victory* three officers, who informed me that Gentili, the commandant, would assemble the officers of the several corps and the municipality if a truce took place, which I agreed to, a little before sunset.' On the 23rd, the French troops were embarked to be taken to France, while the British took possession of the town, the capital of Corsica.

Now Hood had to deal with another issue, returning the fleet to its more usual role. The French had repaired much of the damage done at Toulon and on 5 June a fleet of seven ships of the line, led by the 120-gun *Sans-Culotte*, sailed from the port. Hood sailed to intercept them with thirteen of the line, though Colonel Moore

The *Victory* off Bastia during the campaign against the town

(© National Maritime Museum, Greenwich, London, PAD5982)

complained inaccurately that 'Lord Hood, on the report of eight sail of the line having got out of Toulon, thinks proper to assemble and cruise with seventeen.'[22] The two fleets were in sight of each other by the 10th but Admiral Martin took his ship into the Golfe de St Juan between Antibes and Nice, where he anchored in a tight formation reminiscent of Hood's own masterly defence at St Kitts twelve years earlier. Hood was desperate to fight a fleet battle as the crowning glory of a naval officer's career. He made plans for his ships to attack with the *Britannia* and *St George* taking on the *Sans-Culotte*, the *Victory* and *Princess Royal* the 80-gun *Bonnet-Rouge* and so on – but the position was too strong and he had to retreat back to Corsica.

Calvi

Meanwhile, at a 'general consult' of the Corsican people on 14 June, Gilbert Elliot was proclaimed as viceroy of the island on behalf of King George III. Only Calvi was left in French possession. The town was on a prominent hill on the west side of a large bay and was well fortified, with outlying posts at Monteciesco in the hills south-west of the town, and the Fountain and San Francesco Batteries and Fort Mozello closer in. Nelson arrived in the area on 18 June and began to reconnoitre – the only landing place he could find was Porto Agro to the west of the town, though it was 'very bad; the rocks break in this weather very far from the shore, and the mountain we have to drag the guns up is so long and steep…'[23] The seamen worked to clear roads among the rocks and then began to haul guns up, but Nelson's 250 men were barely enough to haul a 24-pounder. He wrote to his wife eight days after landing, 'Dragging cannon up steep mountains, and carrying shot, has been our constant employment.'[24]

Hood arrived in the *Victory* after the stalemate at Golfe de St Juan to spend much time cruising offshore, for, as Moore put it bitterly, 'Lord Hood continues to hover round us eager to have his name in the capitulation.' The new army commander, General the Hon Charles Stuart, was well-respected by army and navy alike but Hood was suspicious that he was influenced by Moore. He lent men from the *Victory* to help with hauling the guns and 290, about a third of the complement, were on shore at one time or another. However, he continued to worry about what would happen if the French came out of Toulon and he would have to withdraw them. Guns were eventually set up at Notre Dame de la Serra on the top of the hill and on the right flank the Royal Louis battery, manned by French royalist sailors, opened fire on the hill fort of Monteciesco on 4 July. On the left, guns were lowered down the hill on the other side and the Grand Battery was set up in front of Fort Mozello. On the 12th there

A view from Notre Dame de la Serra looking down over the fortified hill town of Calvi, drawn by an officer on the spot during the siege of 1794. The *Victory* is offshore, number nine in the picture. Nelson lost the sight of his eye attacking Fort Mozello, seen in the left centre of the picture.

(© National Archives, Kew, Surrey, MPK 12/1)

was a heavy exchange of gunfire and Nelson was hit by gravel thrown up by a shot. He wrote, 'I was wounded in the head by stones from the merlon of our battery. My right eye is cut entirely down; but the surgeons flatter me I shall not entirely lose the sight of that eye; at present I can distinguish light from dark, but no object.' He had lost the sight of the eye permanently, though not the eye itself.

Hood continued to supervise, and he did not always approve of Nelson's style:

> My Dear Nelson,
> I thank you for your letter, and desire to have a daily account of how things go on. I would not by any means have you come on board; and do most earnestly entreat you will give no opinion, unless asked, what is right or not right to be done; whatever that may be, keep it to yourself, and be totally silent to every one, except in forwarding proposed operations...

The attack pressed on with Hood urging negotiation with the defenders, which the soldiers refused. Nelson eased the supply problem by finding a way to land stores and ammunition at Vaccaja, on the right side of the hills. There was a truce at the end of July and the French surrendered on 10 August, to be evacuated. Moore complained that Hood and the fleet had 'forsaken us' and there were not enough men to dismantle the batteries and remove stores.

After more time blockading Toulon, Hood was worn out and in November he left the station in the *Victory*. She arrived in Portsmouth on 5 December and Hood struck his flag ten days later. Moore had complained, 'It is singular under such circumstances Lord Hood should take the *Victory* home, when he might be conveyed equally well in a frigate.'[25] However, it did allow the *Victory* to be repaired after two years of hard service. She was taken into dock at Portsmouth on 5 January 1795. The yard 'made-good defects' in the ship, which must have been considerable as the repair cost more than £13,000 and took three months. Hood fully expected to return as soon as he had rested for the winter, but his frankness was too much for the administration and he had seen his last sea service, at the age of seventy.

Thus the *Victory* was absent when Nelson saw his first fleet action. The command devolved on Sir William Hotham with his flag in the *Britannia*. He was an undistinguished and rather unlucky admiral who had been in temporary command at New York when the British army was defeated at Saratoga in 1777, and in charge of the inadequate escort when a rich convoy was captured by the French in 1780. On 12 March he found a French fleet of equal numbers but far inferior crews, and began a chase. Only Nelson in the *Agamemnon* showed any enterprise, he chased one damaged French ship being towed by another and turned the ship to fire his guns on them occasionally. As a result, the *Ça Ira* and *Censeur* were captured, but Nelson was far from satisfied when the pursuit was abandoned. He stormed on board the flagship in an insubordinate rage and Hotham replied, 'We must be contented, we have done very well.' Nelson wrote to his wife, 'Now, had we taken ten sail, and had allowed the eleventh to escape, when it had been possible to have got at her, I could never have called it well done.' It was a credo for the rest of his life, but for the moment Hotham's conduct was considered satisfactory and he was honoured for the minor victory.

7 ST VINCENT

Action off Frejus

Victory was back with the Mediterranean Fleet by July 1795. On the 6th, Nelson was off Genoa in the *Agamemnon* with a squadron of frigates when he sighted a French fleet of seventeen of the line. He hastened to San Fiorenza Bay pursued by them, to find Hotham's ships watering and repairing, and a contrary wind made it difficult for them to leave immediately. Hotham had decided to remain in the *Britannia* rather than the much faster *Victory,* perhaps because as Betsy Wynne, future wife of Captain Fremantle of the *Inconstant*, put it a year later, the *Victory*'s apartments were 'not half as good and comfortable' as the *Britannia*'s; or perhaps because he subscribed to the old-fashioned view that the admiral should be in a slow ship so that the fleet could maintain its station around him. It was a decision that would have its consequences.

Instead, Rear-Admiral Robert Mann transferred his flag to the *Victory* from the *Cumberland* on the morning of the 8th and the fleet of twenty-three ships of the line, including six three-deckers, sailed at noon. They found the French off Hyeres Island near Toulon late on the 12th but that night a gale split the topsails of six ships including the *Victory* and *Britannia*. At daylight, they were fitting new sails when the French fleet was seen five miles away. Hotham wasted hours forming his ships in line. Eventually, at 8am he ordered a general chase, and soon the sailing qualities of the ships were evident. The *Britannia* was notoriously slow and Hotham was out of the action. The *Victory* on the other hand was in the leading group making eight or nine knots, along with the 74s *Culloden* and *Cumberland*, with the *Blenheim, Defence*, *Captain* and *Agamemnon* not far behind. Nelson was expecting to be 'close alongside an 80-gun ship...'[1] Hotham's order came too late, the wind was beginning to die down and speed was reduced to four or five knots. Admiral Mann hailed the ships near him and told them he intended to engage the third ship from the enemy rear, cutting off two more and perhaps forcing the rest to turn round and engage. But the wind changed again and allowed the three rearmost French ships to fire on the *Victory*, which fired back at the *Alcide*. The French ship was soon disabled and out of control, but the *Victory* was also damaged aloft:

> All the braces, bowlines, and running rigging shot away; all the stays except the fore-stay, and a great many lower shrouds; the main top-gallant mast, fore-topsail and spritsail yards shot away, and all the masts and bowsprit much wounded.[2]

According to an account by 'an eyewitness, and a lieutenant on board the *Victory*', who was probably the irascible, disgruntled and unstable Edward Brenton, 'the *Victory*, which ship ought to have pushed on and been foremost on such a day, hailed several of the ships to pass ahead of her; and she positively backed her main topsail to allow others to get in advance of her.'[3] But this did not take account of the damage to the ship, and the hint that Admiral Mann showed cowardice does not bear examination – Nelson wrote soon afterwards that he was 'a good man... in every sense of the word' without any obvious signs of sarcasm.[4] In any case, the *Alcide* caught fire and was destroyed while Hotham, according to Nelson, 'thought it right to call us out of action', the wind being directly into the Gulf of Frejus, where the enemy anchored after dark. His letter to his wife was only slightly more temperate than last time. 'Had Lord Hood been here', he wrote, 'he would never have called us out of action but Hotham leaves nothing to chance.' By September he was complaining again. 'I am almost afraid from the inactivity of our Admiral that the campaign in this country will end in a very different manner to what might be expected. It is almost in vain my shutting one door when the Admiral allows half a dozen to be open...'[5]

Jervis in Command

Hotham's health could not stand the strain of such a

command and in November a new commander-in-chief was appointed, much more to Nelson's taste. Admiral Sir John Jervis, the son of an eminent barrister, had once tried to run away to sea to avoid being put into his father's profession. Eventually, his family accepted his wishes and he joined his first ship in 1749. He commanded a sloop when Wolfe took Quebec in 1759, and there was an early indication of his attitude to discipline when the crew of the *Albany* refused to raise the anchor. Jervis ordered a boat's crew to cut the cable and the voyage proceeded. In 1778 he took command of the 80-gun *Foudroyant*, captured from the French twenty years before but still the largest, and some said the finest, two-decker in the service. He served in her throughout the long, frustrating campaigns of the Channel Fleet led from the *Victory*, supporting Keppel

Sir John Jervis, who became Earl of St Vincent after the battle of 1797.

(© National Maritime Museum, Greenwich, London, PU4448)

at his court martial, advising Howe not to attack at night and taking part in all three reliefs of Gibraltar. As a Member of Parliament, he was liberal in his politics even if he did not express himself well – he supported parliamentary reform and opposed the move towards war with France in 1793. But once war had started, Jervis put all his formidable energy into conducting it, as he did with all his commands. He was appointed to lead an expedition against the French colonies in the West Indies, in the hope of removing a huge source of revenue. It was a well-conducted naval operation, but the troops suffered heavily from disease on shore. On 3 December, he arrived in San Fiorenza Bay in the frigate *Lively*. Jervis had no respect for Captain Knight and wrote, 'it is a little unfortunate that this reptile Capt[ain] Knight should by accident have come to me again.'[6] But this was not the only change. The *Victory*'s log recorded, 'came on board Captain George Grey and superseded Captain Knight... Came on board Lieutenants James Ruse and Waller and superseded Lieutenants Hinton, Connor and Skyrme. Also Mr Weir superseded Mr Pettigrew, surgeon.' The admiral himself came on board in the early evening. But it is not true that, as his biographer claimed, the smoke of the salute was still clearing when the signal to unmoor was hoisted.[7] The ship did not raise her anchor for several days.[8]

Despite his comparatively progressive politics, Jervis had no patience with any kind of dissent or slackness. He ruled the fleet from the *Victory* with a rod of iron, though in many ways his measures were directed more at the officers than the lower deck, and he was careful to deny them any undue privileges – 'in the distribution of lemons, no consideration is to be had to the officers in preference to the men, but they are to be equally apportioned to the number of persons victualled.' He ordered that the ranges, the more sophisticated part of the galley stove used for officers' meals, should not be lighted until 11am each morning and put out as soon as the captain's dinner was served in the evening. The stove, which could only boil food and was used for the crew's meals, was 'sufficient for breakfast' even for the officers. And when he observed 'a flippancy in the behaviour of officers when coming upon the *Victory*'s quarterdeck', he demanded that 'the officers of the *Victory* will set the example by taking off their hats on such occasions and not touching them with an air of negligence.'[9]

Jervis was not keen on the illicit presence of women on board his ships, but what he objected to most was their use of water.

> 'A number of women have been clandestinely brought from England in several ships... the respective captains are required by the admiral to admonish these

ladies upon the waste of water and other disorders committed by them and be made known to all that on the first proof of water being obtained for washing from the scuttle-butt or otherwise, under false pretences in any ship, every woman in the fleet who has not been admitted under the authority of the admiral or the commander in chief will be sent to San Fiorenza to be shipped for England'.[10]

Jervis also enforced discipline on the fleet as a unit. In April 1796 he was concerned that, 'the ships of the squadron do not preserve the prescribed distances from each other in the order of sailing, with the precision necessary, for making a sudden impression upon the enemy...', which suggests he was thinking in terms of a formal battle. This was related to the general discipline of the fleet, for later that month he ordered that all officers should be present during tacking and wearing, and a sharp lookout should be kept to prevent collisions. He kept an eagle eye on manoeuvres of individual ships, and in August 1796 the captain of the *Barfleur* was reproved in orders for his 'expenditure of topsail yards', which was caused by 'the lifts not being boused sufficiently taut when the reefs were in'.[11]

Jervis had a cruel sense of humour. Early one morning he was unable to sleep and called the lieutenant of the watch into his cabin. The officer reported that the weather was fine, the sky was cloudless and the ships of the fleet were all in their stations, but Jervis wanted to go up on deck. The lieutenant did not want him interfering with washing the decks and other early morning preparations and tried to persuade him to get more sleep. Jervis knew that the officer was a good seaman but semi-literate and ordered him to read to him. He protested that the captain and first lieutenant would be expecting him on deck but Jervis persisted, then giggled silently under his bedclothes as the lieutenant stumbled through Locke's *Essays*.[12]

Jervis could be affable when the occasion demanded it. Betsy Wynne visited the flagship in July 1796:

We dressed to go to the *Victory*. The admiral was on deck to receive us with the greatest civility and kindness; nothing stiff or formal about him, and we were not at all embarrassed, as I feared we should be. He desired that we should pay the tribute which was due to him on entering his cabin. This was to kiss him, which the ladies did very willingly... the old gentleman is very partial to kisses.[13]

They sang a duet after dinner but they could not stay late, they were told that Jervis went to bed at 8.30pm so that he could rise at 2am the following morning.

Nelson was one officer who attracted his praise, for his 'zeal, activity and enterprise [that] cannot be surpassed' and Jervis could only lament that he did not have enough ships to put him in charge of a 'squadron equal to his merit.'[14] The main role of the fleet was now the blockade of Toulon and in the middle of June Jervis reported from the *Victory*, 'Nothing very material has happened during the two months I have been in this position: the enemy bears the blockade of Toulon with Christian patience.'[15]

Withdrawal from the Mediterranean

Already, the situation in the Mediterranean was becoming more difficult. The French revolutionaries had suppressed the revolts and beaten their enemies on the northern front. Napoleon Bonaparte, rapidly promoted to general, began a campaign in northern Italy with his ill-equipped but highly-motivated army, winning four battles in April alone. Piedmont and Sardinia were neutralised, while Bologna, which included the port of Genoa, surrendered in June, and at the end of the month the other great port of the area, Livorno, was occupied. To the south, the Kingdom of Naples was forced into a peace treaty, leaving no British bases on the mainland. Meanwhile, things were going wrong in Corsica. The interpretation of British protection varied between the two sides, while Paoli's enlightened ideas of liberty meant little in a land dominated by banditry and blood feuds. Since the British had no large army, it was impossible to rule the island without popular support, which was crumbling away when the French army landed. Nelson was given the job of evacuating stores including 1,200 barrels of powder from Bastia in September and October, concluding, 'its situation certainly was most desirable for us, but the generality of its inhabitants are so greedy of wealth, and so greedy of each other, that it would require the patience of Job, and the riches of Croesus to satisfy them.'[16] At San Fiorenza, Jervis looked on from the *Victory* as the

Mortella tower was 'reduced to a heap of fragments, somewhat resembling the ruins of Palmyra...' but Captain Pakenham prepared a model of it.[17]

If that was not enough, by August 1796 Jervis was writing of 'the lowering aspect of Spain, with the advanced state of the equipment of the French fleet in Toulon.'[18] She was forced into the Treaty of San Idelfonso with France and on 5 October she declared war on Britain. Jervis could see that his fleet was increasingly isolated. The only remaining base was a small island off the coast of Italy and Nelson wrote to his friend Locker, 'I remember when we quitted Toulon we endeavoured to reconcile ourselves to Corsica; now we are content with Elba'[19] But even that was not to last, for it was planned to withdraw to Gibraltar.

During all this, the *Victory*'s purser, Richard Thomas, had to keep the fleet supplied in adverse circumstances. There was concern for the crew's health and the need for fresh vegetables to prevent scurvy was understood. On 5 July, Thomas paid, 'to greens and

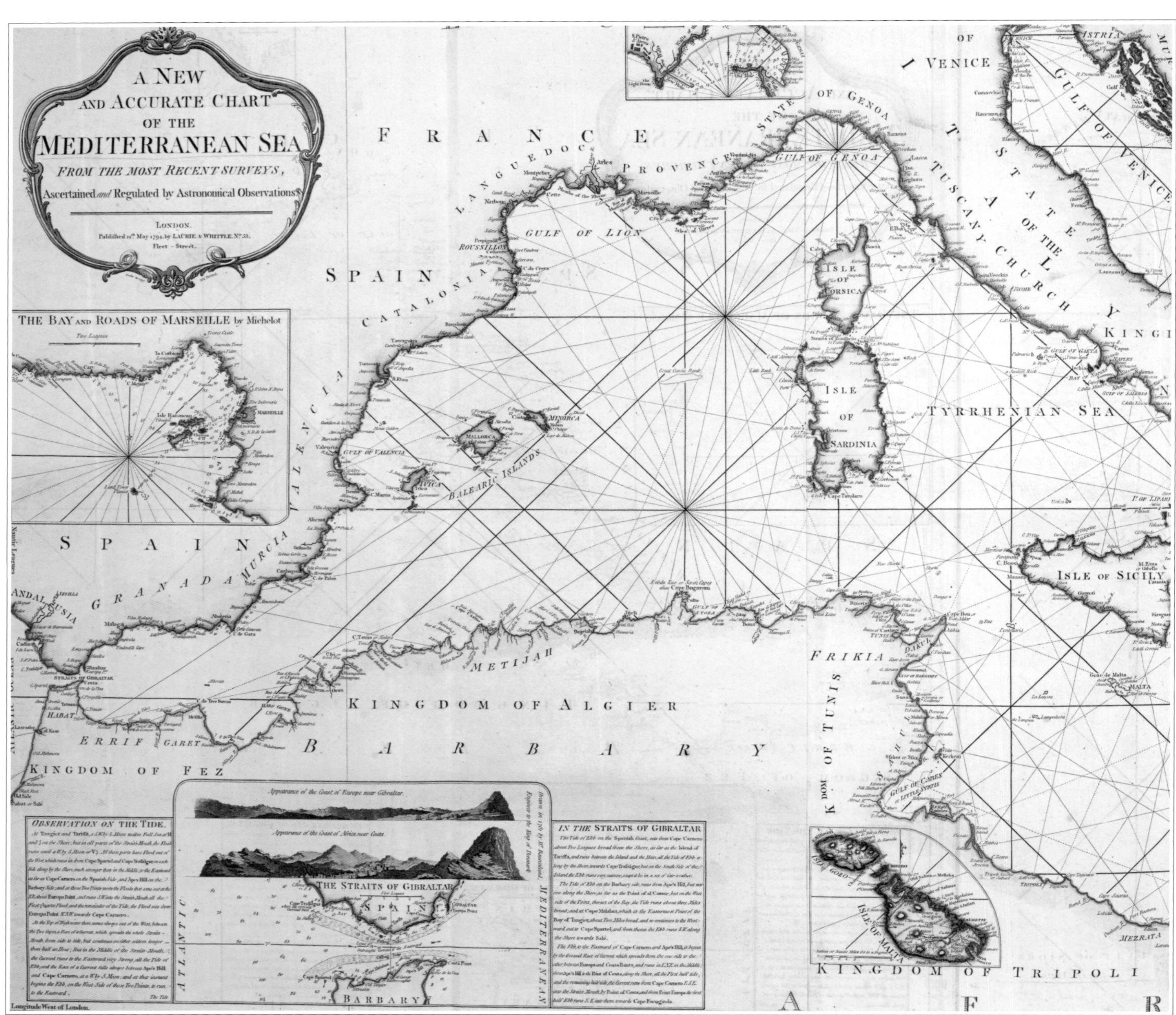

The Mediterranean in the 1790s. With Spain hostile and Corsica uncontrollable, Jervis considered it necessary to withdraw to Gibraltar.

(© The British Library, London, 146 cl (26))

onions for the ship's company's broth at San Fiorenza', and this was followed by 'greens' at Leghorn (Livorno) on 5 September and 6 August. By 23 September, the crew were reduced to short allowance of bread and later Captain Grey ordered it should 'in future be served out in the following manner, viz one-half bread and one-half flour'. On 26 September, the bread room was cleared out and it was found that three-and-a-half bags had been stolen and there were '50 bags of dust, but none full.' Two days later, the ship was put on '2/3rds allowance of all species of provisions except wines and spirits' – Jervis admitted it was 'rather a hard measure after such a cruise'. Even the bread that was available was full of weevils and the master of the *Victory* recorded, 'it was downright heart-breaking to see it, and hear the complaints.'[20] Supplies arrived in small quantities while the fleet was off Toulon, for example, twelve live oxen from the *Alliance* on 1 October, twenty-three pipes of wine from the *Speranza Risorta* on the 2nd and 5,370 hogsheads of flour on the 5th. More stores were taken on when the *Victory* anchored with the fleet in San Fiorenza Bay for the last time in October – fifty pipes of wine, six small bullocks, sixteen barrels of raisins from the *Ann* transport and 150 bags of bread. But on the 22nd they 'broached and used the remaining twenty-three bags of flour, the net weight of which was 3,019lbs [and] the remaining bag of rice was also broached and used; [which] netted 116 lbs.' However, the next day they received 'five casks rice and one cask supposed to be oatmeal.' At the end of November the situation was eased by the arrival of a fleet of victuallers from home and Jervis issued a general memorandum promising the payment of short-allowance money and praising the crews' 'general good conduct and becoming resignation to the necessity of this measure'. On 1 December they were ordered to 'commence whole allowance of all species of provisions tomorrow morning.'[21]

The government at home was divided about the withdrawal from Corsica and the Mediterranean and Dundas, the Secretary for War, wrote that it was craven to 'begin the war by running out of the Mediterranean.' Nelson was distressed at this policy. He had seen how weak the Spanish were early in the war at Cadiz and Toulon. At Hyeres Bay he had noted, 'no ships could behave better than ours, none worse than the French.' Even before Jervis took command he had believed 'this Mediterranean Fleet is as fine a one as ever graced the Ocean.'[22] Now, under strong leadership and discipline, 'they at home do not know what this fleet is capable of performing; anything and everything.'[23] But in the meantime he was ordered to evacuate the last remaining base at Elba with the frigate *La Minerve*. He arrived there on 27 December to find that the army commander had received no orders and refused to move, so a month was wasted in indecision.

Meanwhile Jervis's fleet reached Gibraltar on 1 December, after 'the most tempestuous weather I ever experienced in the Mediterranean, with the wind on our teeth until the last three or four days...'[24] Purser Thomas took the chance to buy some different goods – 200 lantern horns, six double padlocks, a bread serve, flour shovels and 'six quire foolscap, ½ hundred pens, two black lead pencils, four plain journals and four quire large course writing paper for wine and mess books.'[25] But facilities for a great fleet were poor there, the harbour was exposed to winds from the south and to Spanish attack across the bay at Algeciras, there were few provisions available and little water. The 74-gun ship *Courageaux* was blown out of the bay and wrecked on the African coast with the loss of 464 men. Some of the 129 survivors came on board the *Victory*. Jervis sailed for the Tagus where he hoped to find support from Britain's last ally in the west, Portugal, but the misfortune continued as the *Bombay Castle* ran aground in the entrance. At anchor off Lisbon, Jervis was cautious about contact with the natives and issued orders 'to avoid dissensions and quarrels with the Portuguese, which always terminates in assassination'.

Indeed, he was even more concerned about 'straggling and consequent desertions' of his men, so strict orders were issued about the responsibilities of officers in boats.[26] Jervis sailed on 1 February, but the 90-gun *St George* grounded on the way out, reducing his fleet to eight ships of the line, until a reinforcement of six more under Sir William Parker joined on the 6th.

The Battle of St Vincent

There was information that the Spanish fleet was out, for they were protecting a convoy of four merchant ships carrying mercury, a substance that was essential in the treatment of gold. Nelson only rejoined the fleet at 6pm on the 13th, so he had little time to settle back in the 74-gun *Captain* which he had commanded since June when he was not detached in a frigate. There was plenty of warning of the approach of the enemy. At 2.20am on St Valentine's Day a Portuguese frigate informed them that the Spanish fleet was fifteen miles to windward. Half an hour later the frigate *Raven* reported hearing 20 guns from the same direction. More sail was set as the ship came out of her night-time condition at 6am, then 'at ½ past 6, discovered a number of strange ships to windward, supposed to be the Spanish fleet.' Jervis was on the quarterdeck of the *Victory* as the notoriously cautious Captain Calder reported the sighting of the enemy:

> 'There are eight sail-of-the-line, Sir John.'
> 'Very well, Sir.'
> At 9am the ships were counted.
> 'There are twenty sail-of-the-line, Sir John.'
> 'Very well, Sir.'

At 10am the captured frigate *Bonne Citoyenne* reported yet more ships.

> 'There are twenty-five sail-of-the-line, Sir John.'
> 'Very well, Sir.'
> 'There are twenty-seven sail, Sir John.'

Calder remarked on the disparity between the two forces and Jervis replied, 'Enough, Sir, no more of that: the die is cast; and if there are fifty sail, I will go through them.' Captain Benjamin Hallowell, Canadian-born and 'of gigantic frame and vast personal strength' was a passenger on the *Victory* after his own ship had sunk. He was bold enough to pat his admiral on the back and exclaim, 'That's right, Sir John; that's right; by God we shall give them a damned good licking.'[27]

The Spanish fleet was in two sections and Jervis's ships were in a position to sail between them – dangerous if the enemy was able to counterattack, but devastating if he was not. At 11am the enemy force to starboard was seen to form some kind of a line of battle, though it was never very regular. The British ships prepared, running out their guns , hoisting colours and forming their own line 'as most convenient' with the *Victory* near the centre, seventh out of fifteen ships.

The line was led by the aggressive and dynamic Captain Thomas Troubridge in the *Culloden*, an officer who was sometimes considered as promising as Nelson. Nelson's *Captain* was third from the end, for as commodore he commanded the rear section of the fleet. At 11.12 the *Victory* hoisted the signal 'to engage the enemy'. Since the Spanish were to windward and not keen on battle, the British ships had to sail close to the

wind and then tack to reach them. Jervis expected the ships to do this one after another on reaching a certain point, so that the line was maintained, and around midday the *Culloden* began the process. At this rate it would take some time to bring the whole fleet into action, and the Spanish might well escape. Meanwhile, Vice-Admiral Joaquin Moreno launched a counterattack in his flagship, the 112-gun *Principe de Asturias*. He headed straight for the *Victory* and was within 'pistol-shot', almost ready to engage, when Jervis's ship backed her main topsail to bring her broadside to bear. Moreno seemed to lose his nerve, he turned round without trimming his sails and fired a broadside that was too high and did little damage. The *Victory*'s guns were better aimed and the *Principe de Asturias* was now presenting her stern, her most vulnerable area, to them.

At the Battle of St Vincent, the *Victory* rakes the Spanish three-decker *Principe de Asturias*, driving her off with considerable damage. Painted by Robert Cleveley, son of the ship's former carpenter.

(© National Maritime Museum, Greenwich, London, BHC0485)

Two devastating broadsides were fired into the Spaniard and she quickly retreated with several other ships.

Though he must have been pre-occupied with fighting off the great Spanish three-decker, at 12.45 the master of the *Victory* observed the *Captain* making a surprising manoeuvre. Nelson had seen the problem and 'perceiving the Spanish Fleet to bear up before the wind, evidently with an intention of forming their line, going large – joining their separated division – or of flying from us; to prevent either of their schemes from taking effect, I ordered the ship to be wore, and passing between the *Diadem* and *Excellent*, at ten minutes past one o'clock, I was in close action with the van... of the Spanish fleet.'[28] In a momentous move, he had anticipated Jervis's orders and broken out of the line of the battle to get at the enemy – for, unlike Jervis, he had seen the Spanish at Toulon when they were allies, and at home in Cadiz in 1793 when he had observed that the ships were 'shockingly manned' and that six barge crews could have taken one of their first-rates.

What followed was even more dramatic and daring. The tactic of boarding had declined over the years as ships fought at some distance from one another using cannon, but Nelson was prepared to use any means to get at the enemy. The *Captain* was dismasted and lost her steering wheel but she was alongside the 80-gun *San Nicolas* and Nelson led his men on board her through a window in the stern gallery, while Captain Berry boarded by another route. The shock tactics worked and Nelson went on to board the even larger 114-gun *San Josef*, and take it. Later he wrote with barely disguised false modesty, 'There is a saying in the Fleet too flattering for me to omit telling – viz, 'Nelson's Patent Bridge for boarding First-Rates.'[29] The battle off Cape St Vincent could well have been another disappointing affair in which one or at most two straggling ships were captured, but Nelson had transformed it into something much greater.

The *Victory* sailed on into the thick of the action and at the height of the battle Jervis stood on her poop to get a clearer view through the smoke, when a marine close to him was hit by a cannonball. Brains and blood were spattered over the admiral and even into his mouth, but he replied coolly to Captain Grey of the marines, 'I am not at all hurt, but do, George, try if you can get me an orange.'[30] Two more ships were captured by the time the battle ended.

That evening in the great cabin of the *Victory*, 'while taking over the events of the day, Captain Calder hinted that the spontaneous manoeuvre which carried Nelson and Collingwood into the brunt of the battle, was an unauthorised departure from the prescribed mode of attack! "It certainly was so," replied Sir John Jervis, "and if you ever commit such a breach of your orders, I will forgive you also."'[31] Nelson was rowed on board the *Victory* at dusk that evening, 'when the admiral received me on the quarter-deck, and having embraced me, said he could not sufficiently thank me...'[32]

The damaged fleet limped back to the Tagus with prizes in tow. The seamen had to improvise and according to the *Victory*'s log for the 15th, 'Unbent the topsails and bent others. Seamen knotting the rigging and setting it up.... the main staysail being cut in sundry pieces when furled, found it not worthy of repairing; used the remains to repair other damaged sails, having no old canvas on board. Cut up two painted hammock cloths to repair the other that had been cut with much shot.'[33]

The result was a clear and much-needed victory when British arms were doing badly elsewhere. Jervis was raised to the peerage and took the title of Earl of St Vincent from the site of the battle, on the suggestion of the King. Initial reports did not do justice to Nelson's role, until a book by Colonel John Drinkwater was published. Nelson was now a national hero for the first time. He was promoted to rear-admiral and his wife cautioned him to leave the boarding to captains.

Victory Replaced

Having repaired his ships at the Tagus, St Vincent established a tight blockade of Cadiz – from the inshore squadron Nelson wrote, 'We are looking at the ladies walking on the walls and Mall of Cadiz.' It became clear that the *Victory*'s repairs at Portsmouth had not been enough for the ageing hull. In September 1796 Captain Grey wrote, '...the ship is very weak abaft; the transoms between the lower and middle decks work exceedingly.' A month later St Vincent commented, 'every line-of-battle ship in the fleet will be found sound, except the *Victory*.'[34] And after the battle from which he took his title, St Vincent claimed, 'the step of a man from the poop ladder to the quarterdeck made her whole stern frame shake…' She had been in a collision which had carried away her starboard quarter gallery, though even the inquisitive brain of the admiral was not able to determine what had caused it.

By 1 March Spencer was sending out ships to reinforce the Mediterranean Fleet and he informed St Vincent that the *Ville de Paris*, named after the flagship captured at the Battle of the Saintes which sank soon afterwards, would be 'a good substitute for the *Victory*'. She carried 110 guns and was larger than the *Victory*, but most important, she was new. St Vincent decided to transfer to her, if only to speed up her working up 'as by that means be sooner in a state for service than she otherwise would'. He considered the possibility of giving *Victory* to Nelson as his flagship, but the young admiral preferred a 74 – the *Victory* was fast-sailing for her class but would never be as nimble as a two-decker. But for the moment, St Vincent planned to keep the *Victory* as she was better than the *Britannia*, sister of the ill-fated *Royal George*, and 'an impediment to the movements of the squadron.' However, Captain Sotheby had 'neither nerves nor experience for so great a charge.' St Vincent shifted his flag on 30 March and thanked Spencer for 'this noble ship, which feels like a rock after the trembling, leaky *Victory*…'[35] It was 28 June before Captain Sotheby left, to be replaced by William Cumming as captain of the *Victory*.

The sailors of the Channel Fleet had mutinied in

This print of Nelson boarding *San Nicolas* shows the ferocity of his attack, and his bravery in leading it – he can be seen to the right of the group making the attack, with his sword drawn and pointing forward.

(© National Maritime Museum, Greenwich, London, PY7917)

Nelson wounded at Tenerife, painted by Richard Westall for Clarke and MacArthur's biography, and therefore not an eye-witness view.

(© National Maritime Museum, Greenwich, London, BHC0498)

April and most of their demands were met, including the first increase in pay for nearly a 150 years. This was reflected on board the *Victory* on the 20th when Purser Thomas noted, 'An addition was this day made to the pay of petty officers, seamen etc, serving in the Navy...' It was also ordered that the supply of food and drink was to be increased by abolishing ancient practices – '16 ounces to the pound and 8 pints to the gallon to be given in all species of provisions.'[36] But already the seamen of the North Sea Fleet were in revolt at the Nore and were attempting to blockade the port of London in support of a more extreme set of demands. The revolt was eventually put down with a number of executions, and St Vincent was determined that it should not spread to his own fleet. An execution on board the *St George* on 2 July was carried out in conventional manner in that each ship in the fleet sent 'two boats with an officer in each and two marines or soldiers properly armed', who would go on board the ship 'to assist in carrying out the sentence of the court martial into execution', that is hauling on the rope by which a man was hanged. Six days later St Vincent went further to enforce discipline. Though the boats were to be sent as usual, 'the sentence is to be carried into execution by the crew of the *St George* alone and no part of the boats crews of other ships as is usual on similar occasions is to assist in this painful service, in order to mark the high sense the commander in chief entertains of the loyalty, fidelity and subordination of the rest of the fleet...'[37]

The *Victory* left the fleet off Cadiz on 30 August, missing even stricter orders from the commander-in-chief, including the use of marines to intimidate the sailors. She replenished at Lisbon and sailed from there on 8 September with the four Spanish prizes and two more three-deckers. At the end of the month she anchored in Torbay and at 1.30pm on 7 November she was back in her birthplace as she 'came to the moorings abreast Princes Bridge, Chatham.'

Nelson's Fall and Rise

In July, Nelson, now a rear-admiral, led an expedition to capture a Spanish treasure ship anchored off Santa Cruz, Tenerife. Everything went wrong, and Nelson was hit by a musket ball in the arm, which was amputated without anaesthetic as usual. It was traumatic, both mentally and physically. The effect of the loss of sight in his eye had only dawned on him slowly, but this time there was no mistaking the impact. He wrote to Jervis (who had not yet taken up his new title), 'I am become a burden to my friends and useless to my country... When I leave your command, I become dead to the World; I go hence, and am no more to be seen.'[38] He and his wife bought a house in Norfolk and she nursed him back to health, perhaps the happiest time in their marriage. As he recovered, he enjoyed fame for the first time. In December he placed paper in church offering 'thanks to Almighty God for his perfect recovery from a severe wound.' He was able to return to service.

His new flagship, the 74-gun *Vanguard* was fitted out at Chatham in 1797–98 with the *Victory* not far away – though Nelson left most of the work to his Flag Captain, Edward Berry, and only visited when she was floated out of dock on 17 December 1797. Nelson took a good deal of interest in the *Vanguard*'s officers,

The Battle of the Nile, showing Captain Foley's *Goliath* rounding the head of the French line. Nelson's *Vanguard* is six ships behind, with the blue flag on the mizzen mast.

(© National Maritime Museum, Greenwich, London, D8312D)

ncluding midshipmen, but left the manning to Berry. That started with a draft of sixty men from the *Victory*, now fitting out at Chatham for a very different role, and from the unlucky *St George* that had grounded off Lisbon and had been forced to stage St Vincent's show execution. Nelson did not join the *Vanguard* until she had sailed round to St Helens, where he hoisted his flag on 29 March 1798.[39]

There was a new task in the Mediterranean and Earls Spencer and St Vincent were agreed that Nelson was the man to carry it out. Bonaparte had abandoned the plan to invade England as 'a very daring operation and very difficult to put into effect'. He suggested another scheme, to invade Egypt. Besides the resources of that country, it would be a step on the way to India, the most prized part of the British overseas empire. He began to fit out a great fleet of transports in the ports of Italy and move troops towards them, while the warships in Toulon got ready to escort them. Of course, Spencer and St Vincent did not know what he intended – such a force could be going almost anywhere, to attack Portugal, to land in Ireland or even England, to support forces in the West Indies or India – but such movements could not be hidden, even without a fleet in the Mediterranean. Ships had to be sent to find out more, and Nelson was to lead them. He was given a squadron of three 74s and three frigates, but off Toulon on 20 May they were struck by a gale. The frigates were separated and the *Vanguard* was severely damaged. She had to be rescued by Captain Ball's *Alexander* off the coast of Sardinia and have her rigging temporarily repaired. Nelson pressed on with his mission, when almost anyone else would have gone to Gibraltar or Lisbon for fuller repairs. He never found his frigates again, partly because they assumed he would withdraw, and he had no specialised reconnaissance forces for the rest of the campaign. But off Toulon on 7 June, he was reinforced by ten more ships of the line, so now he had a real fighting force; but Napoleon had already sailed and taken Malta. Nelson went south and found that his opponent had already left the island. He deduced correctly from the wind that he must be going east, and Egypt must be the target. He passed the outliers of the French fleet but decided not to investigate them. Arriving at Alexandria, he found the locals had no knowledge of any French plan and impatiently he sailed away. That was a pity, for the French arrived next day and began their invasion.

Nelson replenished his ship at Syracuse and soon heard definite reports of the French attack. He sailed back to Egypt where he found thirteen ships of the line moored in a chevron formation in Aboukir Bay, perhaps inspired by Hood's defence of St Kitts in the last war. But it was far less competently done. There were major gaps in the line and, in any case, Mediterranean winds were far less constant that the trade winds of the Atlantic. Nelson gave the order to attack though night was falling, but it was Captain Foley who led the line. Using a French chart and his knowledge of seamanship, he spotted the space between the leading French ship and the shore and passed through it to attack the *Guerrier* on her unprepared side. Six more ships followed him, until Nelson arrived in the *Vanguard* and led the rest to the outer side to 'double' the enemy. He suffered a head wound and was taken below while the French flagship, the great 120-gun *L'Orient*, caught fire and blew up. By next morning his fleet had captured or destroyed twelve out of fourteen enemy ships of the line, an expression of the Nelsonian principle of total victory. The whole situation in the Mediterranean was altered overnight, British seapower was in command again and the way was opened for a new alliance against the revolution.

It was an epic campaign, but beside his head wound Nelson had suffered stress that is almost incomprehensible in the modern world – making strategic decisions without any reference to higher authority and undergoing the roller coaster ride of almost losing his ship, missing the French fleet, then finding it and winning one of the most decisive battles of all time. He took his wounded ships to Naples where he found comfort with the British ambassador's wife, Lady Emma Hamilton, and soon became involved in Neapolitan life and politics. He urged an army attack on the French in Rome, which soon failed, and he had to evacuate the royal family to Sicily as a revolution took place in Naples. The monarchy was restored but Nelson was implicated in savage reprisals against the revolutionaries, which sullied his reputation. He had become dangerously unbalanced and arrogant, as his behaviour at a dinner party showed:

> Pray, Sir, have you ever heard of the Battle of the Nile?... that, sir, was the most extraordinary ever fought, and it is unique, sir, for three reasons; first, for having been fought at night; secondly, for its being fought at anchor; and thirdly been gained by an admiral with one arm

A miniature of Emma Hamilton.

(© National Maritime Museum, Greenwich, London, MNT0042)

In 1800 he and Sir William Hamilton were recalled and proceeded overland to England, where a hero's welcome awaited Nelson.

Victory in Decline

While Nelson's star was falling and rising, the *Victory* was now more than thirty years old and it seemed that her active life was over after taking part in several disappointing actions and one single triumph, one in which she did not play the leading role. The Navy Board ordered the officers of Portsmouth Dockyard to survey her and on 11 October they reported finding 'several f her hanging knees sprung on the lower, middle and uarter decks, and 2/3 of all the knees in the ship equire unbolting and re-faying, as the ship has strained ery much; the copper is much broke at the water's dge, she has received some shot below the load water nark, lower masts are wounded and fished, the arboard knight's head is badly wounded and must be hifted.' They were 'humbly of the opinion' that the hip should be taken into a dock and that the repairs vould employ six companies of shipwrights for eight veeks. But, ominously, that only covered the 'defects lready discovered', they had not examined her under he timbers or much below the waterline and there was o guarantee that the whole hull would not be found o be rotten. Even so, it was not a particularly damning eport compared with some other ships, but the *Victory*'s age probably told against her.

Captain Cumming reported on her sailing qualities on 25 November 1797. This was perfectly normal and ndeed it was done on a standard printed from, but for ome reason it is the only one from the *Victory* to urvive. In the circumstances it was more of a vale-dictory, though there was still something to be learned rom her success. Cumming wrote that, 'in sailing with other ships she holds her wind very well with them, and forereaches upon most, or all ships of three decks we have been in company with...' He went on to say, 'with he wind large she sails well, as she does with the wind veering forward to being close hauled and forereaches upon most ships' – in other words she sailed well on all points of sailing. According to Cummings, she would 'run from ten or eleven knots', that is with the wind behind, which compared well with all but the fastest frigates. Close-hauled in a head sea, she could make three to four knots.

By early 1798 it had been decided to reduce the *Victory* to a hospital ship for prisoners of war. There were dozens of ships holding captives in the waters around all the naval dockyards, as described in a later report:

> The Medway is covered with men-of-war, dismantled and lying in ordinary. Their fresh and brilliant painting contrasts with the hideous aspect of the old and smoky hulks, which seem the remains of vessels blackened by a recent fire. It is in these floating tombs that are buried alive prisoners of war – Danes, Swedes, Frenchmen, Americans, no matter. They are lodged on the lower deck, on the upper deck, and even on the orlop deck.[40]

As a hospital ship the *Victory* would not get the full treatment. The sick men were unlikely to escape so she

An E W Cooke illustration of a prison ship. As well as bars on its gunports, a fully-fledged prison ship would often have obtrusive deckhouses and projections from its sides which would make it less suitable to return to active service.

(© Nation Maritime Museum, Greenwich, London, PW3148)

would not be fitted with grills over her gunports, as happened to the *Camperdown, Gelykheid* and *Sandwich* at Chatham around this time. Instead she would have forty-six marines as guards, though they too had their faults – in May 1798 Private James Walsh deserted. Apart from that, the complement of ninety included Lieutenant John Rickman in command and the usual standing officers. John McArthur was still purser though for much of the time he employed Richard Thomas as substitute. William Rivers had been gunner since 1790 and would see many more years of service with the ship. William Briggs was boatswain, Edward Casey was carpenter and Charles Carroll was cook. The medical staff was headed by Surgeon Richard Kent and his two mates, Matron Rebecca Hinde, Nurse Mary Dale and a washerwoman, Mary Smith. The rest of the complement consisted of naval ratings, mostly unskilled landsmen. The ship was moored in Gillingham

The *Victory* after her great repair, with the new and much plainer closed stern, without the open galleries. The middle and upper wales are now painted black, but the 'Nelson chequer' appearance is not yet completed by painting the gunports black.

(© National Maritime Museum, Greenwich, London, SLR0513)

Reach near where she had already spent thirteen years.[41]

More ships for 'prisoners in health' were needed by February 1798, especially after Admiral Duncan's victory at Camperdown on 11 October 1797 brought a large number of Dutchmen to the Medway. The Transport Board, which managed such ships, needed one more at Chatham and suggested the *Victory* which had 'only a few sick Dutch prisoners on board' might be suitable for the role. The Admiralty did not demur and ordered the Navy Board to implement the changes. This would begin a further step in her decline, for she would have grills fitted on the gunports and scuttles or holes would be cut in her sides for ventilation, and she would almost certainly be fitted with projections and deckhouses which would ruin her appearance and make her less fit for action. It was the Navy Board which objected – the changes would 'materially injure her for future service' if she was needed later, and in any case the Dutch prize *Vryheid* was available. The Admiralty agreed to have her converted, with the *Victory* continuing as hospital ship.[42]

Revival

It was decided that the *Victory* should be repaired, and on 19 January 1799 the Chatham officers nominated the 90-gun *Blenheim* of 1760 'to receive the sick prisoners now on board the *Victory*'.[43] But the *Blenheim* was not modified until a dock was ready for long-term work on the *Victory*, which did not occur until August, and on 14 September the *Victory* was paid-off as a prison hospital ship.[44] In the meantime a series of accidents increased the need for a three-decker like the *Victory*. On 19 October 1799 the 98-gun *Impregnable* ran aground on Chichester Shoals due to the negligence of the master and was wrecked. All the crew were saved, but the loss of the 100-gun *Queen Charlotte* six months later off the Italian coast was far more horrific, as described by Lieutenant Parsons:

> I still see the falling of my poor friend Lieutenant Erskine into the blazing furnace, reflecting a strong light on his agitated countenance, as he turned it full upon me, filled with indescribable horror – the piercing and agonised shriek... is forever ringing in my ears – the darting of the forked flames, from yard to yard and mast to mast,... The numberless sinking and struggling sailors – their despairing imprecations when beaten off from the already-overcrowded boats.[45]

In March 1801 William Pitt the Younger resigned as prime minister after seventeen years over the King's refusal to support Catholic emancipation in Ireland. A new government was formed under Henry Addington, a doctor and the first middle-class prime minister. The

Earl of St Vincent became First Lord of the Admiralty and began to apply his quarterdeck methods to the navy as a whole, including its civilian sector. The country was weary after eight years of war, the longest conflict in modern times, with food riots and a looming financial crisis. The Addington government went for peace at almost any price, giving up conquests in the West Indies, Cape of Good Hope, Minorca, Egypt and Malta, without any guarantee that the French would leave the Netherlands and northern Italy. The Peace of Amiens came into full effect at the end of March 1802.

St Vincent was convinced that this was permanent and began a programme of reform in the dockyards, which caused great disruption and staff shortages. Chatham Dockyard was short of 176 shipwrights on 1 April, twenty caulkers out of eighty-one and twenty riggers out of seventy. The officers complained that 'the work of this port will require every exertion in the shipwright's department, being so very short of hands.' The carpenters of the forty-four ships in ordinary in the Medway were to be employed on yard work to get the ships ready.[46] However, the work on the *Victory* proceeded despite the shortages and it may have been given priority.

There were grand plans to make the *Victory* a bigger ship to keep up with current trends by adding a section in midships, but these did not materialise. On 6 November 1800, Sir John Henslow, Surveyor of the Navy, wrote to St Vincent, 'since the receipt of your Lordship's answer respecting the lengthening the *Victory,* all thoughts thereof is given up, and it is intended that no alteration should take in her present repair than giving her an additional port forward upon the gun deck, for chase guns occasionally, for which there is ample room.' Already there was concern about her decorations and sketches for her carved work were sent from Chatham that month – it was an important issue since the Admiralty had decided in 1796 to 'explode carved works', to reduce drastically the amount of money spent on carvings, and the 1765 figurehead would not be repeated. But the surviving records are almost silent on the work on the hull, which must have been extensive, but was regarded as routine. A small clue came in February 1802 when Chatham Yard asked for the delivery of auger bits especially for the *Victory*, perhaps because the holes to be drilled in her timbers were larger than the normal run.[47] The story of the carvings continued, in March the Brompton-to-London coach carried a box containing 'three sketches proposed for a head and two for a stern for His Majesty's Ship *Victory,* with the carver's estimate for performing the same'. The Navy Board chose design number two for the head at a cost of £50, number one for the taffrail at £36 and number one for the quarter pieces at £38 per side, while number two for the stern was 'not to be attended to.'[48]

By March 1802 the ship was 'in a forward state' and plans were being made for after her launch. Certain parts were often left out of ships in ordinary to allow better air circulation and Chatham asked if the full deck planking was to be fitted. They were told to continue the quarterdeck planking forward of the mainmast, but not to fit the gangways along the sides of the waist. By June the possibility of a new war could not be ignored and the Navy Board ordered that her breadth and top riders should be bolted as they were 'foreseeing great delay would arise if the ship should be at any time ordered to be fitted for sea'.[49] By September the ship was almost ready for caulking, but there was a shortage of workmen able to do this. The Chatham officers resisted an attempt to hire fifty of them out to a merchant shipbuilder, though 'the *Victory* is in such a state as very shortly to require every exertion we can make in that department'. They were anxious because 'if the said ship is not caulked before the winter weather sets in, we fear she will receive a serious injury.' They also planned to make a suit of sails for Channel service, which was probably precautionary in case the ship was needed.[50] Anchors were to be made for the ship, though Chatham pointed out that were several unallocated ones in store which only needed small repairs.[51] By 4 March 1803 she was almost ready to float out and the officers asked if she was to be fitted for the ordinary – but she was soon ordered to be fitted as a seagoing flagship as war approached. On 19 March she was expected to be ready to receive men as part of her crew by 25 April, which was advanced to the 12th as work proceeded faster. Chatham agreed to use their 'utmost exertions' to get her ready, including taking men from other urgent work to copper her. They asked if the bulkheads of the admiral's cabin were to be fitted as before. On 9 April she was floated out of Number Four dock on a spring tide.

8 NELSON IN THE MEDITERRANEAN

The Hot Press

In October 1802, from his new home in Merton, south of London, Nelson wrote to the prime minister that 'my mind is ever at work for the honour and safety of our country' and referred to 'these rumours of wars' which were 'flying about.'[1] For the Treaty of Amiens did not stop French expansion, under the First Consul Napoleon Bonaparte she bought Louisiana from Spain, annexed Piedmont and continued to build up naval forces. Nevertheless, it was a surprise on 8 March 1803 when the King sent a message to Parliament, at the behest of the government, '...as very considerable military preparations are carrying on in the ports of France and Holland, he has judged it expedient to adopt additional measures for protection for the security of his dominions...'

St Vincent reacted, or perhaps over-reacted, with ruthless determination and threw himself into the mobilisation of the navy with his characteristic energy. Though war had not been declared, the impressment of seamen was hotter than ever before, and in Portsmouth and Plymouth marines were used to find seamen, who were mostly unsuspecting. Warships in commission put press gangs ashore, or sent boats over to passing merchantmen to press their crews. This was a 'press from protections', the certificates which were supposed to protect particular men from the gang were ignored, as Seaman John Wetherell found in a merchant ship off Shields: 'We...clearly saw two frigates and several boats making towards us. Shortly after one of the boats fired at us. We hove to, they came on board, gave orders to send everybody aft. A grim looking fellow took up the ships articles. Turning to Nicholson he remarked, "Where is your carpenter?" "There Sir, at the helm". "Relieve him and put his things in the boat." "Why sir, he is protected." "That is the reason we want him in our carpenters crew. Coxswain, bundle his things into the boat."'[3] Wetherell soon became part of a press gang rather than one of its victims and took part in a 'man plunder', as he termed it, at Harwich. 'The market house was to be their prison, where a lieutenant was stationed with a guard of marines, and before daylight next morning their prison was full of all denominations, from the parish priest to the farmer in his frock and wooden shoes.'[3] Later that year Admiral Lord Keith had to apologise to the Mayor of Margate

Nelson's home at Merton, south of London, from where he was recalled to lead the fleet in 1803 and 1805.

(© National Maritime Museum, Greenwich, London, 8252-A)

for impressing ten men who were not liable; 'on such an occasion as a general impress, it is morally impossible to carry the orders of government into execution without incurring some risk of seizing upon individuals who are not liable to be impressed.'[4] Benjamin Hamilton claimed that he was an apprentice when he was impressed into the Woolwich tender on 1 May, and that the master took away his indentures.[5] He, like more than a hundred men from the same tender, found themselves on board the *Victory* in the Medway. For the ship, though old, was part of the plan for the mobilisation.

Victory Fitting Out

Captain Samuel Sutton arrived to take command of the *Victory* on 11 April, two days after she left the dock as an empty shell. He had commanded the frigate *Alcmene* at Copenhagen and taken over the *Amazon* when her captain was killed. After that he did some administrative work for Nelson and the prime minister wrote, 'Captain Sutton has relieved you, in a great degree, from the pressure of some of the most laborious parts of your duty.'[6] But now it was understood that Sutton would fit out the *Victory*, as Lindsay had done many years ago, then hand over command to Nelson's favourite captain, Thomas Masterman Hardy. Dockyard riggers and marines were employed to help rig the ship while a regular crew was gathered. There was a setback early in May when much of the shingle ballast had to be taken out to re-stow the iron below it. By the 8th the crew was painting the main deck, while the following day three boats, each under a commissioned officer, were sent out to impress men. A draft of 284 men was sent on board on 11 May from the 64-gun Dutch prize *Utrecht*, followed by more from the *Zealand*. She was ready to sail down the river by the 19th, but the master attendant and pilot refused to move her during four days of bad weather. She arrived at Long Reach on the 23rd and began to take on water and stores. It was probably around this time that the painter John Constable saw the ship:

> At Chatham I hired a boat to see the men of war, which are there in great numbers. I sketched the *Victory* in three views. She was the flower of the flock, a three-decker of 112 guns. She looked very beautiful, fresh out of dock and newly painted. When I saw her they were bending her sails; which circumstance, added to a fine evening, made a charming effect.[7]

The 29th and 30th were spent hoisting in the guns, of which the ship now carried precisely 100. The lower deck was armed with thirty 32-pounders each 9ft 6in long and weighing around 55 hundredweight, all made

Another of Captain Marryat's drawings of a midshipman's life, this time showing a press gang engaged in a lively fight in a tavern. Unlike the one of the midshipman's berth, this one was never redrawn by Cruikshank, nor published.

(© The British Museum, London, 1891,1117.30)

One of Constable's three drawings of the *Victory* in the Medway, showing seaman working on the yards. The drawings, long known about, were only discovered, however, in 2002.

(© Thomson Collection, Art Gallery of Ontario)

by Walker and Company of Rotherham. The middle deck had twenty-eight 24-pounders which were two inches shorter and weighted 49–50 hundredweight. The upper deck had thirty-two 9ft 12-pounders of thirty-four tonnes. The shorter 12-pounders on the quarterdeck were all made by Walker.[8] There was more bad weather on the 13th and 14th and the *Victory* had to fire a gun to ask for assistance, but at 3pm on the 14th she let go her mooring and proceeded to Spithead to join the fleet, anchoring there in the afternoon of the 16th.

Nelson in Command

Soon after the King's message to Parliament, Nelson knew that he had been chosen to lead the Mediterranean Fleet. In many ways, it was the best command in the navy and he wrote after more than a year of hard service 'I believe that no officer could be placed in a more enviable command than the one I have the honour of being placed in.'[9] Lord Keith, an old adversary, was not pleased and complained, 'I cannot help being hurt at a junior officer being sent to a command I so lately held, and I hope with credit'.[10] The Channel and North Sea Fleets often had higher priority as the main defence against invasion, but they were close to home and subject to interference from above. The East and West Indies and North American Squadrons offered more opportunity for prize money but had far fewer ships. As well as leading the force in battle, the commander-in-chief of the Mediterranean Fleet had to keep it supplied in a mostly hostile area, to find his own bases and to conduct diplomatic relations with numerous and very different governments, from the corrupt Catholic monarchy of Naples to the piratical Muslims of North Africa. At the end of 1800, St Vincent had claimed that Nelson, 'never can become an officer fit to be placed where I am', that is as commander-in-chief. He had presumably reversed that opinion by 1803 by appointing him to such a vital command.

Nelson wrote on 26th March, 'War or Peace? Every person has a different opinion. I fear perhaps the former, as I hope so much for the latter.' He already knew that the *Victory* was to be his ship but it was feared she would not be ready in time for him to take command. He wrote, 'If war, I go to the Mediterranean in Hardy's frigate: the *Victory* is to be my ship – Sam Sutton is to fit her out.'[11] Nelson had written in 1795, 'the Mediterranean command has ever so much business compared to any other than a man of business ought to be here.'[12] He found such a man in Captain George Murray and was determined to have him as his captain of the fleet or first captain of the *Victory*. Born a few months before Nelson, Murray had commanded the *Colossus* at St Vincent but she was soon damaged and out of the action. He took part in the Battle of the Nile under Nelson and the ship was sent home in December 1798 carrying Sir William Hamilton's archaeological treasures. She was wrecked on the Scilly Isles but Murray was absolved of blame. In 1801, in the *Edgar*, he led the fleet into action at Copenhagen with heavy casualties. Murray was reluctant to accept Nelson's offer, perhaps he had seen the relationship between Jervis and Calder a few years earlier. He claimed, 'the nature of the duties often led to disagreements between the admiral and the first captain, and that he should be very unwilling to risk a diminution of the regard and respect which he entertained to his lordship.' Nelson replied that 'even should anything go contrary to his wishes, he would waive the rank of *Admiral*, and explain and expostulate with him as his *friend* Murray'.[13] That seemed to work and Murray joined the staff.

On 16 April Nelson still hoped that 'the *Victory* will not make more than a Spithead voyage' – that peace would be settled before she put to sea.[14] He wanted a barge rather than a cutter for his 'ease' and asked for the cabin to be fitted out as in the *San Josef*, a 114-gun Spanish prize in which he had served briefly in 1800–1. With Sutton's efforts the *Victory* was ready sooner than expected, which caused new problems. On 12 May Nelson was hoping to sail in her rather than the cramped *Amphion*. 'For all my things, servants, wines, &c. are ordered to be sent to her, be she where she will – even my sheep, poultry, hay, corn, and every comfort are ordered to her.' But now it was suggested that she might be allocated to the North Sea Fleet, the main defence against invasion, under Admiral Keith. There had been ill feeling between these two since Keith had been appointed to the Mediterranean Command over Nelson's head, and he had to write to St Vincent begging him to prevent this. He seems to have partly succeeded, two days later he wrote to Sutton from the

Admiralty that a waggon would soon arrive with his goods and he should procure 'twelve good sheep, some hay, and fowls, and corn, it will do no harm, for I may yet go out in the *Victory*.' In any case, the *Victory* was not particularly suitable for the North Sea Fleet. Keith did not need her for a flagship as he established his headquarters ashore at Ramsgate, and smaller vessels were much more useful in these shallow waters where they might be faced with small but numerous gunboats and barges. But another issue had arisen, it was now suggested that she might join Admiral Cornwallis in the Channel Fleet – it too took priority over the Mediterranean as the force which kept the main French force blockaded in Brest. Nelson made his plans: 'If Admiral Cornwallis wants her – which is very improbable according to what I have heard – but if he does, I shall remove nothing from the frigate but my cot: and therefore, be gone in five minutes'[15]

War was declared on 18 May and Nelson received his orders the same day. It was assumed that he would sail in the *Amphion* and go to Malta to secure the island. After that, in the most important part of his instructions, he was to:

> Proceed off Toulon, with such part of the squadron under your command as you may judge to be adequate for the service, and take such a position as may, in your Lordship's opinion, be most proper for enabling you to take, sink, burn, or otherwise destroy, any ships or vessels belonging to France, or the citizens of that republic...

He was to watch the proceedings of the French at Genoa and Livorno, to consider the possibility of an attack on Egypt and to watch for an attack on Naples or Corfu. He was to be 'watchful of the conduct of the Court of Spain', for a Franco-Spanish alliance already seemed possible. He was to watch out for a French squadron returning from the West Indies which might enter the Mediterranean. At the same time he was 'to be careful not to infringe the neutrality of other powers...'[16]

Nelson had received his appointment from the Admiralty on 16 May, settled his affairs on the 17th and left for Portsmouth at 4 am on the 18th, arriving 'smothered with dust at exactly one o'clock.' He had boarded the *Victory* at 3.30pm and was saluted with thirteen guns, beginning a partnership that would resonate through history. He was 'anxious and hurried' about getting the ship to sea.[17] On the 19th, he told St Vincent that 'If the Devil stands at the door, the *Victory* shall sail tomorrow forenoon'. He was back on board at 10am on the 20th, with Captain Murray, secretary John Scott and Lieutenant Pearce who was to be his signal officer. He also brought William Chevallier, his valet, who had been given an 'excellent character' by Alexander Davison, his prize agent, and a retinue of four more servants. Despite his promise to St Vincent, it was actually the afternoon when the ship raised anchor and sailed out of Spithead with the frigate *Amphion*, in 'a heavy shower of rain...with a northerly wind.'

He arrived off Ushant, the war station of the Channel Fleet on the afternoon of the 22nd and wrote, 'We are inside Ushant, but where is Cornwallis? However, we shall block up Brest till he comes to liberate me.'[18] Next morning he wrote to Lady Hamilton:

> My Dearest Emma,
> We are now in sight of Ushant, and I shall see Admiral Cornwallis in an hour. I am not in a little fret, on the idea that he may keep the *Victory*, and turn us all into the *Amphion* it will make it truly uncomfortable; but I cannot help myself.

But next day there was still no contact. 'What a wind we are losing! If I cannot find the Admiral by six o'clock, we must all go in the *Amphion*, and leave the *Victory*, to my great mortification. So much for the wisdom of my superiors.'[19] There was still no sign of Cornwallis and at 5pm on the 23rd Nelson shifted his flag to the frigate, which sailed off and was out of sight by 11pm. While waiting, the *Victory* captured a brig heading from Port au Prince to Nantes carrying coffee, cotton and sugar. Twenty-one prisoners were taken off her and a prize crew of a midshipman and six men was put on board. The Channel Fleet arrived back on station at noon on the 25th, and Cornwallis wrote to his superiors, 'You will be pleased to acquaint their Lordships, I did not detain the *Victory* a moment, but desired Captain Sutton to follow the Vice-admiral with all possible dispatch.'[20]

Despite these orders, Sutton was tempted to make

more prize money for himself and his crew on the way by acting like a frigate, chasing and capturing French ships whose crews did not know that war had been declared – though the attentions of a three-decker must have done something to raise the alarm. On the 27th they took another brig returning to France from the West Indies. Then, at 6am the next morning, they spotted a French frigate heading towards them and fired a 32-pounder at her. She turned out to be the *Ambuscade*, captured from the Royal Navy at the end of 1798. She was also coming from the West Indies but was only partly armed and had a reduced crew of 178 men. She was captured without a fight and was restored to the Royal Navy. The enemy was so unprepared that even the prize crew of the *Ambuscade* was able to take another ship, the *Marie Therese*, and send her into Gibraltar, where two sloops came out and tried to claim a share in the capture leading to another naval tradition – a dispute over prize money.[21] Meanwhile, there was another prize for the *Victory* on the morning of the 30th, a schooner from Martinique to Bordeaux carrying coffee and sugar. Prize money for the *Ambuscade* was shared with the frigate *Caroline* which happened to be passing. It was eventually paid and amounted to 20,270 Spanish dollars, valued at 4s 1½d or about 20.5p, of which 1,255 dollars went to Nelson as flag officer, Captain Sutton did rather well with 2,533 or £522, the lieutenants and wardroom officers had 168 dollars each, the midshipmen and mates had 140, the petty officers 29, and the seamen and marines were left with less than six dollars – a typical share out for the times.[22]

The *Victory* passed the well-known landmark of Cape Finisterre on the 31st but winds were light and contrary – on the 6th they had to clew-up all the square sails and use the fore and aft staysails, jibs and mizzen to get as close to the wind as possible. At last, on the 9th they were off Cape St Vincent and soon they were in sight of Gibraltar, where they took on water and stores and sailed on the 15th. It was never easy to find Nelson in the Mediterranean and Sutton went first to Malta before heading for Toulon. He found the ship was not perfectly trimmed and thirty tonnes of iron ballast were moved forward to correct this. There were good sailing conditions on the 24th with 'moderate breezes and fine weather, all sail set'. On the 30th they met the frigate *Medusa*, then took a French ship with the local lateen rig. But it took another month of cruising before, late on the 29th, they met the *Maidstone* which guided them towards the fleet under Nelson.[23] By 1 August, Nelson and his staff were on board the *Victory* and he wrote to Emma, 'a few days will put us in order.' Captain Hardy was busy hanging up a portrait of Lady Hamilton and their daughter Horatia.[24] To the Admiralty he reported, 'by the latest information of the enemy's force at Toulon there are seven sail of the line, five or six frigates and six or seven corvettes...apparently perfectly ready for sea'.[25]

The Wardroom

Due to the fame of the events that were to follow, we have more information on the officers and men of the *Victory* than any other ship of the period, and a few glimpses of ordinary life on board. Her new captain, Thomas Masterman Hardy, was ten years younger than Nelson and a Dorset man. He was first-lieutenant of the frigate *Minerve* in December when Nelson sailed in her and captured the Spanish frigate *Sabina*. Hardy was in the prize ship when she drew a Spanish squadron away from the *Minerve*, and he was captured. He was soon exchanged and back in the *Minerve* in February 1797. On the way to rejoin Jervis's fleet, they were pursued by more Spaniards. A man fell overboard and Hardy went out in the jolly-boat to rescue him but was swept towards the enemy ships. Nelson said, 'By God, I'll not lose Hardy. Back the mizzen topsail!' This was risky but it caused the Spanish to hesitate and the *Minerve* escaped. He was with Nelson during the disastrous raid on Tenerife, and at the Battle of the Nile after which he was promoted to the *Vanguard*. He became Nelson's flag captain and surveyed the waters before the Battle of Copenhagen. Hardy was a very tall man, a good practical seaman, often 'up to his elbows in rigging and reefing.' According to Edward Codrington, 'he has not beauty or those accomplishments which attract sometimes on shore above all other qualities, but he is very superior in his situation.'[26] He was a strict disciplinarian and 380 men were flogged on board the *Victory* in just over two years, more than in any other ship. According to Lieutenant John Yule who served under him, he had 'little consideration for those in his care.'[27]

The first lieutenant of the *Victory*, responsible for

organising the crew and for much of the administration, was John Quillam. He came from a humble and possibly disreputable background on the Isle of Man. He was first recorded in the Royal Navy in 1791 and rose through the ranks, being commissioned in 1798. He served with his fellow Manxman Peter Heywood who had been reprieved from hanging after the *Bounty* mutiny. Quillam was in Nelson's fleet, in the frigate *Amazon*, at Copenhagen when her captain was killed and that may have attracted the admiral's notice. Certainly he was well known to Captain Sutton who took over the *Amazon* after that. Quillam had no powerful connections so his expectations for promotion were low. Unlike more ambitious officers, he was able to concentrate on running the ship rather than looking forward to higher things. Technically, he was not the most senior lieutenant in the ship, but Nelson had a habit of choosing a particular officer for the role, rather than following the rules of seniority.

The most senior lieutenant was John Pasco, a man who was also from a humble background, the son of a caulker in Plymouth dockyard who was later dismissed during the St Vincent reforms. Young John was a servant in the midshipmen's berth in the *Pegasus* under Prince William Henry and became a lieutenant in 1795 after more than ten years' service, being recommended by the Prince, now the Duke of Clarence. Nelson had him serve as signal lieutenant, a highly responsible post in a flagship but one which did not carry the prerogatives of the first lieutenant. Nelson was inundated with applications for the eight lieutenants' posts in the *Victory* and had to turn down another by the Duke of Clarence – 'she is full, I have twenty on my list.'[28] Among the lucky ones was John Yule who was twenty-five and had served in the *Alexander* at the Battle of the Nile, then followed Nelson from ship to ship until being appointed to the *Victory* – he was one of five from his former flagship *St George*. George Miller Bligh was no relation to the captain of the *Bounty* but the son of an admiral – Nelson wrote that he was 'a very good young man.'[29]

The master was a key figure in any ship, responsible for navigation in the broadest sense of the term, including supervising difficult manoeuvres. He was a wardroom officer, equal in status to the lieutenants, but with fewer promotion prospects. Thomas Atkinson had probably come from the merchant marine like most

Captain Thomas Hardy, painted by Domenico Pellegrini in 1809.

(© National Maritime Museum, Greenwich, London, BHC2352)

masters. He was attracted by the bounty of £5 in 1793 and became master of a sloop two years later. Rising up through the rates, he was in the 74-gun *Theseus* during Nelson's disastrous raid on Tenerife in 1797 and the ship served under him again in the Nile campaign. He followed him in the *St George* during the Copenhagen expedition. Nelson thought he was 'one of the best masters I have seen in the Royal Navy' and had him appointed to the *Victory* – though by August 1805 he had still not passed the examination for master of a first rate, and Nelson took up his case.[30] During the last war he had collected or drawn many charts of the Mediterranean, including detailed ones of Toulon, Hyeres Bay nearby; the Maddelena Islands, and Cagliari in Sardinia; and Barcelona.[31] It was an experience which

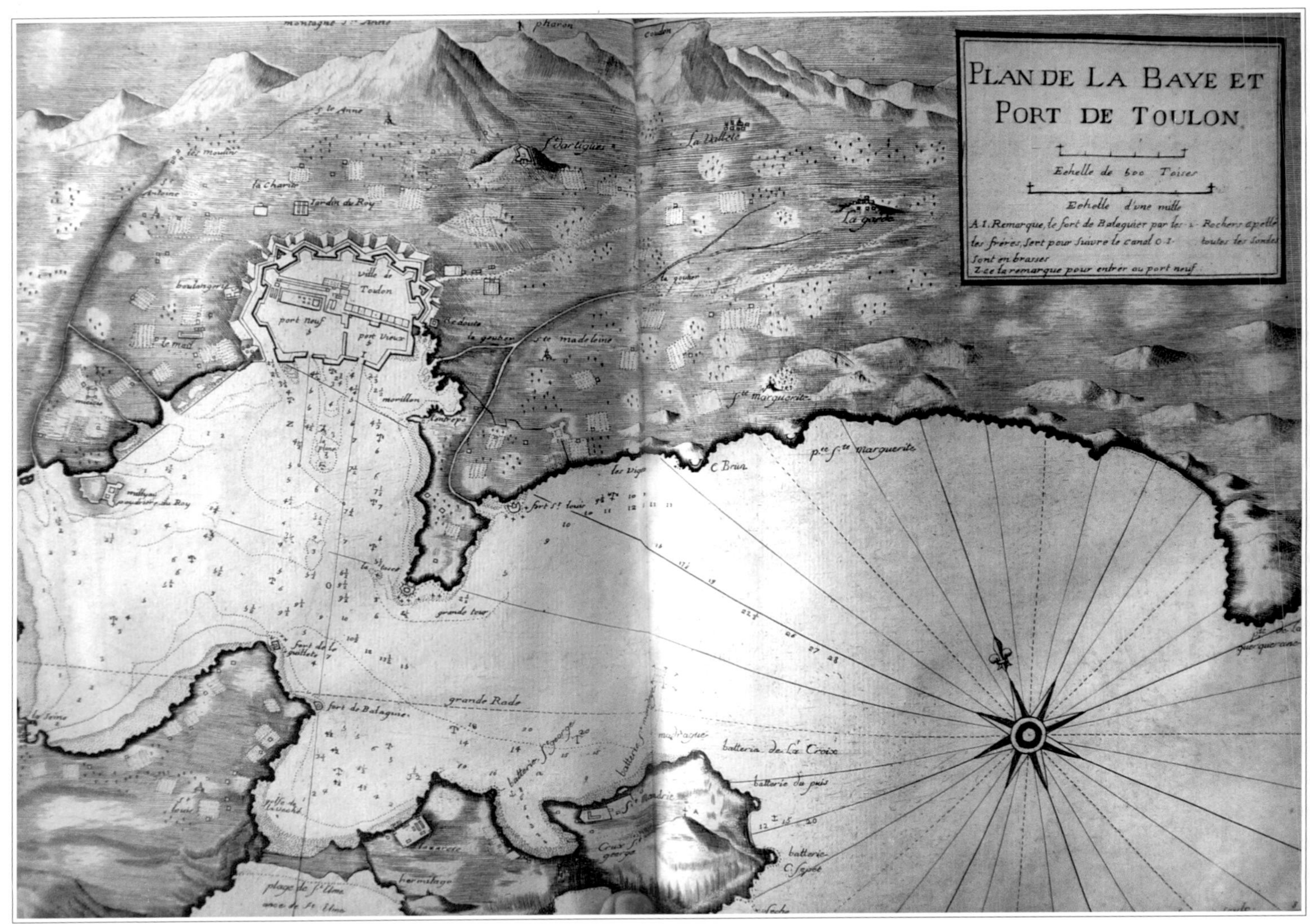

Charts collected by Thomas Atkinson, master of the *Victory*, including one of Toulon.

(Taken from Naval Historical Branch Recuiel de Plusiers Plans des Ports de La Mediterranee, *Thomas Atkinson's copy)*

would stand him in good stead over the next two years and he would continue the practice with a survey of Palmas in Sardinia in 1803.[32]

Initially, the surgeon was George Magrath, a native of Tyrone in Ireland and described by Nelson as 'by far the most able medical man I have ever seen'. He treated the admiral's own complaints with 'excellent remedies'. He was skilled 'not only in the discharge of his duties as surgeon of the *Victory*...but also in several particular surgical cases which he has performed with infinite judgement and skill.'[33] Nelson worried that such men might be lost to the army which offered better conditions.

John McArthur had remained in post as purser of the *Victory* throughout the peace, though he was suspected of gross profiteering in the Toulon affair and had many other interests, including publishing and acting as Nelson's prize agent. He had no wish to go to sea again and as soon as it became clear that the *Victory* was going to be put into commission, he tried to exchange into another ship. The Admiralty ruled against him going to 'an inferior rate' and plans to exchange into the new *Queen Charlotte* which had been ordered at Deptford fell through.[34] At the start of the war the Admiralty 'determined that he should go to sea, or give her [the *Victory*] up.' He was dropped and complained that he had been 'most cruelly treated' and driven out of the service. The *Victory* sailed without a purser, which left a serious gap in the administration of the ship and the fleet which would cause problems.

It was also ruled that 'no purser of a ship in which the admiral was should be his secretary' and Nelson turned to John Scott, who was recommended by his banker William Marsh. Nelson wrote, 'he is a very excellent young good man; and I am very fortunate in having such a one.'[35] John Scott would deal with the internal affairs of the fleet, while Nelson chose the confusingly similarly-named Reverend Alexander John Scott to be his 'foreign secretary' as well as the chaplain of the *Victory*. That was a post which was not always filled in an age which was quite casual about religion, but Nelson was deeply religious and keen to appoint one. He wrote in September 1803, 'I am sure that ship where divine service is regularly performed is by far more regular and decent in their conduct than where it is not.'[36] Scott was a remarkable man, 'one of the most learned men of the age and a great observer of men and manners' according to Nelson.[37] He was born in Rotherhithe on the Thames to a naval family and graduated from Cambridge in 1790 at the age of 22. He became chaplain of the 74-gun *Berwick* three years later, partly because of his debts, and served under Admiral Sir Hyde Parker who would become Nelson's commander at Copenhagen. He was an expert linguist who was already fluent in several languages before he learned Danish on the way across the North Sea. He was in the *Berwick* when she was struck by lightning in 1801, which increased his odd manner and 'very remarkable' appearance – he was 'pale, thin and tall in person, very romantic and enthusiastic'. He got to know Nelson better in London during the peace and was offered the post by him as soon as war broke out, getting into a 'scrape' with the Bishop of London by missing his visitation.[38] Scott naturally approved of Nelson's religion – 'He was a thorough clergyman's son – I should think he never went to bed or got up, without kneeling down to say his prayers.'[39] Nelson for his part was appreciative of his Sunday sermons, 'either thanking him for its being a good one, or remarking that it was not so well adapted as usual to the crew.'[40] But religious observance was only a small part of his duties, he translated reports, letters, proclamations and newspapers for Nelson and acted as his main intelligence officer, going ashore at Barcelona, Sicily and Sardinia to make contacts and find out all he could about enemy movements.

The marines had their own organisation under Captain William Adair from County Antrim in northern Ireland. He was from a well-established marine family with a father and brother in the Corps, and was first commissioned at the age of six.[41] He carried out fleet duties including the inspection of recruits from the Mediterranean and had four subalterns, William Crocket, James Peake, Lewis Reeves and John Bunce, all commissioned officers and members of the wardroom mess.

This was the wardroom of the *Victory*. There is no

Alexander John Scott, by Siegfried Bendixen in 1806. The background picture shows a ship being struck by lightning, which happened to Scott in the *Berwick* in 1801.

(© National Maritime Museum, Greenwich, London, BHC3016)

physical description of it but it was not unlike the one described by the chaplain of the 74-gun *Gloucester* in 1812, if a little larger:

> It is usually in a line-of-battle ship, about 35 feet in length, and 16 or 18 feet wide. Within the walls, which are of painted canvas, are the cabins of six officers; the centre of the room is occupied by the mess-table; and the extremity, under the stern windows, by a projection called the rudder head. The opposite end is so arranged as to do the office of a side-board; with the door of the entrance on one side of it; and a space to sling a quarter cask of wine, on the other.[42]

This was the communal space for nine lieutenants, a captain of marines, master, surgeon, purser, chaplain and marine subalterns on board the *Victory* in 1804. It seems to have been harmonious. With such leadership there was no need for the 'searching scrutiny into, and continual abuse of, the conduct of those in command' which was 'the perpetual theme at the ward-room table' according to Admiral Hotham.[43] Officers often mention particular friendships among themselves, for example Surgeon Beatty wrote that Lieutenant Ram (who arrived later) was 'one of his dearest friends' and there is no report of the discord that prevailed in many wardrooms – but perhaps that was just a rosy glow as memoirs were written in the aftermath of Nelson and Trafalgar.

The Other Officers

The standing officers usually came with the ship rather than being appointed on the recommendation of the captain or admiral. The carpenter was William Bunce. Nelson praised him several times, concluding that he was 'a very able and experienced officer, of great abilities and quick resources' with 'long and faithful servitude'.[44] Mel Jones the boatswain was 'an invaluable man'.[45] Gunner William Rivers had been with the ship since 1790, through the Mediterranean campaign, the Battle of St Vincent and the period of obscurity at Chatham. Early in his naval career, he had been a candidate for a commission as a master's mate in the *Triumph*, but in 1780 he opted for a warrant instead, offering more secure employment but poorer promotion prospects. He was better educated than the average gunner and kept detailed notebooks on the science of gunnery. The standing officers did not have access to the wardroom but had permanent and substantial cabins. They may have socialised together, but often spent much time with their numerous mates and apprentices.

Rivers's son William was also serving in the ship as a midshipman, a trainee officer who, in theory at least, had already served three years as first-class volunteer or in the merchant marine before his promotion. In fact, Rivers had been on board for most of his life since the age of six. Sharing the same mess, low down on the orlop deck of the ship, George Scott was a protégé of Lord Keith, the 'son of a worthy minister in our county', presumably Kincardineshire in Scotland. His patron asked 'if you can give him a lift and he deserves it.' – neatly illustrating the balance between patronage and competence which made the navy what it was.[46] It was similar for Robert Cutts Barton, the son of a naval captain. He had been to sea with his father, who asked Nelson unashamedly for 'patronage on his behalf with a hope that should he be found to merit it when an opportunity of promotion might happen your lordship would give him that step to which he is so ardently working forward.'[47] Benjamin Baynton's father only knew Nelson from 'the accidental circumstance of my living next door to him'. His education had mainly been his father's own work but he believed that the boy had 'one of the most ingenious minds I ever witnessed.' But he missed the sailing of the *Victory* with his son's chest and allowance, which he believed, 'was not to exceed five and twenty pounds a year, unless more be usual for a volunteer on board a flagship'.[48] The boy was enrolled as a landsman to start with but became a volunteer first class after five days.[49] If the wardroom was harmonious, the midshipmen's berth was less so, according to Peter Crawford who believed he had been 'an object of calumny and persecution' and 'stigmatised as a coward and neglect of my duty', which caused him to ask to be sent home and leave the navy after ten years' service without a commission.[50]

The Crew

Among the crew was Benjamin Thomson, who had been baptised in April 1781 in Tweedmouth just outside Berwick, and was an experienced seaman by the time he was pressed into the navy, perhaps taken from the *Hawke* packet-boat by the *Woolwich* tender in the Thames. He found himself on board the *Victory* on 6 May, where he was number 395 on the ship's muster – for a new book had been opened when she re-commissioned. He adopted his mother's maiden name of Stevenson, perhaps because he intended to desert at some time, or had already deserted under his own name. On 12 May he was issued with a shirt, two 'frocks' or loose shirts and a bed from the purser's stock at a cost of £1/6/11 [£1.35p], to be deducted from his wages.[51] Presumably he was used to the sea life in merchant shipping, but he was very unhappy on board the *Victory* and wrote to his brother asking him to get him 'clear of this wicked wooding worold [sic]' with its 'wicked state of life' or he would 'wish myself in my grave'. He worried constantly about what had happened o his possessions when he was impressed, and specially his watch which had his name engraved on he side, and his initials inside a heart.[52] But he was learly a good seaman, he was soon rated as petty fficer.

Edward Smith was also pressed and unhappy. He ad been the master of a West India ship and had to upport 'an aged mother, a pregnant wife and four small hildren, whose existence entirely depended on my xertions.'[53] His abilities and experience were soon ecognised and he was promoted to midshipman on o May but he was discharged at the end of July.[54]

The seamen were supervised by petty officers. The nost senior one, appointed by warrant from the Navy Board, was the Master-At-Arms Benjamin Chapman, he head of the ship's police. He was assisted by two hip's corporals who patrolled the mess decks to nforce the regulations. There were four boatswain's mates – John Cormick, John Welstead, John Hunniford and James Wright. They were expert seamen who supervised the men and their daily work but the post was often difficult to fill as it carried the duty of flogging, perhaps of one's friends. The individual parts of the ship, such as the masts, quarterdeck and forecastle, were supervised by their 'captains', though they were not recognised as fully-fledged petty officers. There were six quartermasters to supervise the steering, including the unhappy pressed man Benjamin Stevenson, and they were assisted by six mates. The gunner had mates, plus a quarter-gunner for each four guns, plus two yeomen of the powder room, who were responsible for the care of gunpowder. There were five yeomen of the sheets whose main function was to make sure that the ropes were free during manoeuvres. The Coxswain, Robert Brickleys, was in charge of the captain's barge and some of the men were appointed

Some of the officers and crew of the *Victory*. Among those shown are: 5. Scott the Secretary, 12. Captain Adair, 16. Sergeant Secker, 20. Chaplain Scott, 22. Surgeon Beattie, 23. Nelson, 24. Hardy and 31. Lt. Quillam.

(© National Maritime Museum, Greenwich, London, PY8032)

A bosun's mate with a 'rope's end' for beating the crew. From Chaplain Edward Mangin's journal of 1812.

(© National Maritime Museum, Greenwich, London, D 7689C)

by warrant because of their skills, such as William Smith the Sailmaker.[55]

The petty officers, seamen and marines lived on the lower and middle gundecks, the only fully sheltered decks above the waterline. Conditions were cramped, though perhaps less so than in a two-decker, which had only one deck to accommodate its men. They slung hammocks from the beams above, with fourteen inches allotted per man. They formed messes which ate at tables between the guns – though in 1798 the *Victory* had 136 messes, so not all of them could be accommodated there. Below the petty officers there were three main classes, the able seamen who were able to 'hand reef and steer', the ordinary seamen who had served at least two years at sea and the landsmen, adults with little or no sea experience.

In addition to the seamen there were fifty-four ship's boys, all, in theory, volunteers. A draft of twenty-seven was sent by the Marine Society, which trained and equipped poor or destitute boys for sea service. The older ones were volunteers-second-class and began training about the rigging, usually on the mizzen mast which was smaller than the others. Normally, they were over fifteen but Cornelius Carroll was only twelve – presumably he was related to the ship's cook Charles

Flogging round the fleet, with the victim tied to a triangle in the right-hand boat, guarded by a marine. It is towed by the boat in front and a drummer plays in the bow.

(© National Maritime Museum, Greenwich, London) [incomplete attrib]

Carroll and had spent much of his life on board ship. The younger ones, rated volunteers-third-class, acted as servants to the officers. One of the younger Marine Society boys was William South, a foundling with no known family, who was taken up by Hannah Jameson, a friend of Lady Hamilton. He was 'a good boy...and very clever, understands writing, arithmetic – waits at table and is quick and active'. In the *Victory* he became servant to the first lieutenant.[56]

The complement of the ship was unusually stable for various reasons. There were no battles which removed men by death or caused the promotion of others to fill the gaps – indeed Nelson wrote to the First Lord in October 1804, 'no captain will die or go home (if they can help it) that they assure me...'[57] He apologised to Vice-Admiral Bligh for the failure to advance his son, 'I wish I could promote him, but I see no prospect: the Admiralty fill all vacancies except death, and nobody will die.'[58] The health of the fleet was good and few died or became unfit, though in August 1804 four men were invalided from diseased viscera, ulcers and scrofula.[59] Men and boys were sent home for various other reasons, for example John Molton, who was found to be an apprentice whose labour, in effect, belonged to his master.[60] There were a few desertions, and early in 1804 William Gordon, William Brown, Richard Collins and John Marshall were caught and tried by court martial for attempting to run while ashore on Sardinia. Brown, Collins and Hamilton claimed that they had never intended to desert. They had become intoxicated after buying some wine, and then had missed the ships when they sailed the next day. They had given themselves up to the Sardinian governor as soon as they understood the situation. This did not prevail against Captain Hardy's relentless prosecution. The court martial of ten officers on board the *Kent* found them guilty and sentenced Brown to 200 lashes and Collins and Marshall to 150 each, 'on their bare backs with a cat of nine tails, on board of, or alongside, such of his Majesty's ships or vessels, at such time or times, and [in] such proportion, as the commander-in-chief... shall think first to direct.' This was flogging round the fleet, and the dreadful sentence was carried out on 30 January, with fifty lashes each alongside the *Victory, Superb, Tonnant* and *Canopus*.[61]

Changes

There were occasional changes among the officers. Some left on promotion, in October 1803 Midshipman John Ferguson was made lieutenant to replace an officer invalided from the *Superb*.[62] Midshipman William Faddy had served under Nelson in the *Vanguard* at the Nile when his father, the captain of marines, was killed. He was given an acting commission in the *Triumph* in March 1804. A month later, when Lieutenant John Lackey of the *Victory* was invalided, the Honourable Granville Waldegrave was promoted in his place. Nelson had had a long correspondence with his father, Lord Radstock, who had been third-in-command at St Vincent, and his son told him of his delight, 'this event will give you as much pleasure as it did me and your joy and satisfaction will be greatly increased when you hear that I am appointed to this ship' [ie. *Victory*].[63] When Thomas Pearce was unable to produce documents showing that he had served the required six years, Nelson was able to vouch for him from his 'certain knowledge' and he was commissioned.[64]

Other officers joined the ship from time to time. William Ram was a midshipman at the age of twenty-one when he joined in 1805, but Nelson arranged his commission. He was still gloomy and regarded himself as 'the most discontented fellow alive, nothing will please me, for ever on the fret.' He was keen on drawing but found that, 'this is a shocking ship for studying, for we are always in a noise being admiral you know we have a great deal of communication and there is a constant rotation of boats from one day's end to another.'[65]

Nelson was constantly short of men, lacking as many as 900 for the whole fleet at one point. Malta failed to produce the expected crop of seaman, though it became a recruiting station for marines from all over the Mediterranean – for St Vincent was determined to avoid relying on the army as in the last war. Captain Adair of the *Victory* was appointed as inspecting officer of these recruits. In May 1804 the Admiralty sent out 'fifty stout boys' as replacements but when they were spread throughout the fleet that was a drop in the ocean.[66]

Though she had excellent officers, the *Victory* was not a happy ship if the number of floggings are an indication. Boredom on a long blockade, lack of shore entertainment and prize money and absence of action were combined with Captain Hardy's fierce discipline.

Though twelve lashes was formally the maximum that a captain could award without a court martial, Hardy often inflicted thirty-six or forty-eight for single offences, for example on William Inwood, an American boatswain's mate, for insolence in December 1803. On August 1804, nineteen men were given a total 564 lashes, including four marines who had forty-eight each, in an extraordinarily long session of flogging.[67]

Blockade and Bases

Nelson's main role was to contain the French fleet in Toulon. British strategy under the Addington government was purely defensive, to await an invasion by Napoleon and defeat it, and Nelson's job was to prevent the Toulon Fleet from contributing to this after breaking out of the Mediterranean. He shared the common view that 'the French will attempt an invasion, I have no doubt nor ever had…'[68] He saw his role with characteristic aggression – 'to keep the French fleet in check and if they put to sea to annihilate them.'[69] He did this by a kind of cat and mouse game, by trying to lure them out rather than keeping them bottled up. In that sense, his plan was 'diametrically opposite' to that of Cornwallis, but it must be borne in mind that an escape from Brest would be a far more immediate threat than one from Toulon.[70] He was criticised by Captain John Whitby of the *Belleisle*, 'first, then, he does not cruise upon his rendezvous; second, I have consequently repeatedly known him from a week to three weeks, even a month, unfound by the ships sent to reconnoitre…thirdly, he is occasionally obliged to take the whole squadron in to water, a great distance from Toulon.' Once out, the French fleet could go almost anywhere and Nelson wrote with some exaggeration in October 1803, 'the French fleet have as many destinations as there are countries'[71]

The blockade of Toulon was not the only task of the fleet, and in January 1804 Nelson wrote:

> I have six frigates and sloops to watch the French Army in the heel of Italy to save the Morea which the Turks are in much fear about. Sir Alexander Ball [in Malta] calls loudly upon me for protection to their trade and provisions. I have four for that service. I am obliged to keep a sloop or two between Bonifacio and Sardinia to prevent the landing of 8,000 men from Corsica…

A few days later he wrote:

> *Narcissus* looked into Toulon [on] the 5th, there were nine sail of the line ready, I have left *Narcissus* and *Active* to watch them. Keats is gone to Algiers to see what is to be done with that Dey [sic] and knowing the exact state of the French fleet I thought I would not do better in the midst of the Keats mission to make my appearance in the Bay of Algiers.[72]

Nelson was keen to keep the fleet together, especially in winter when it was 'almost impossible in the continued gales of wind at this season for any ship to be certain of joining in any given time'.[73] When replenishing, he left frigates off Toulon to look out for enemy movements. One of the most difficult problems was the lack of secure and friendly bases. The Italian ports were either occupied by the French or under threat from them, including his old favourite of Naples. Spain was neutral and increasingly unfriendly. Minorca had been captured in the last war and given up in the peace. Gibraltar had a very poor harbour, barely the resources to feed its own population and, moreover, it was 700 miles away from Toulon. Malta was retained despite the Treaty of Amiens and had an excellent harbour protected by some of the most impressive fortifications in the world, but it too was far from Toulon. Nelson was almost obsessively against it and the governor, his friend Alexander Ball, complained, 'Lord Nelson declared that the Port of Malta was of little use; and he really seems to seek every occasion to justify this erroneous assertion. He now publically says he would as soon send a ship to St Helens [off Portsmouth] as to Malta.'[74]

This left only 'the barren shores of Sardinia', as Captain Whitby put it. The island was technically neutral and it would not be difficult for the French to invade it from Corsica, so Nelson needed all his diplomatic skills, as well as the assistance of Alexander Scott. The favourite anchorage was among the Maddalena Islands to the north of Sardinia which he visited six times. He used Agincourt Sound, named after the ship in which Captain Ryves had surveyed the anchorage, producing a chart which was, 'the most correct thing I have met with'.[75] He used Pula Roads to the south five times, and the Gulf of Palmas, surveyed by Thomas

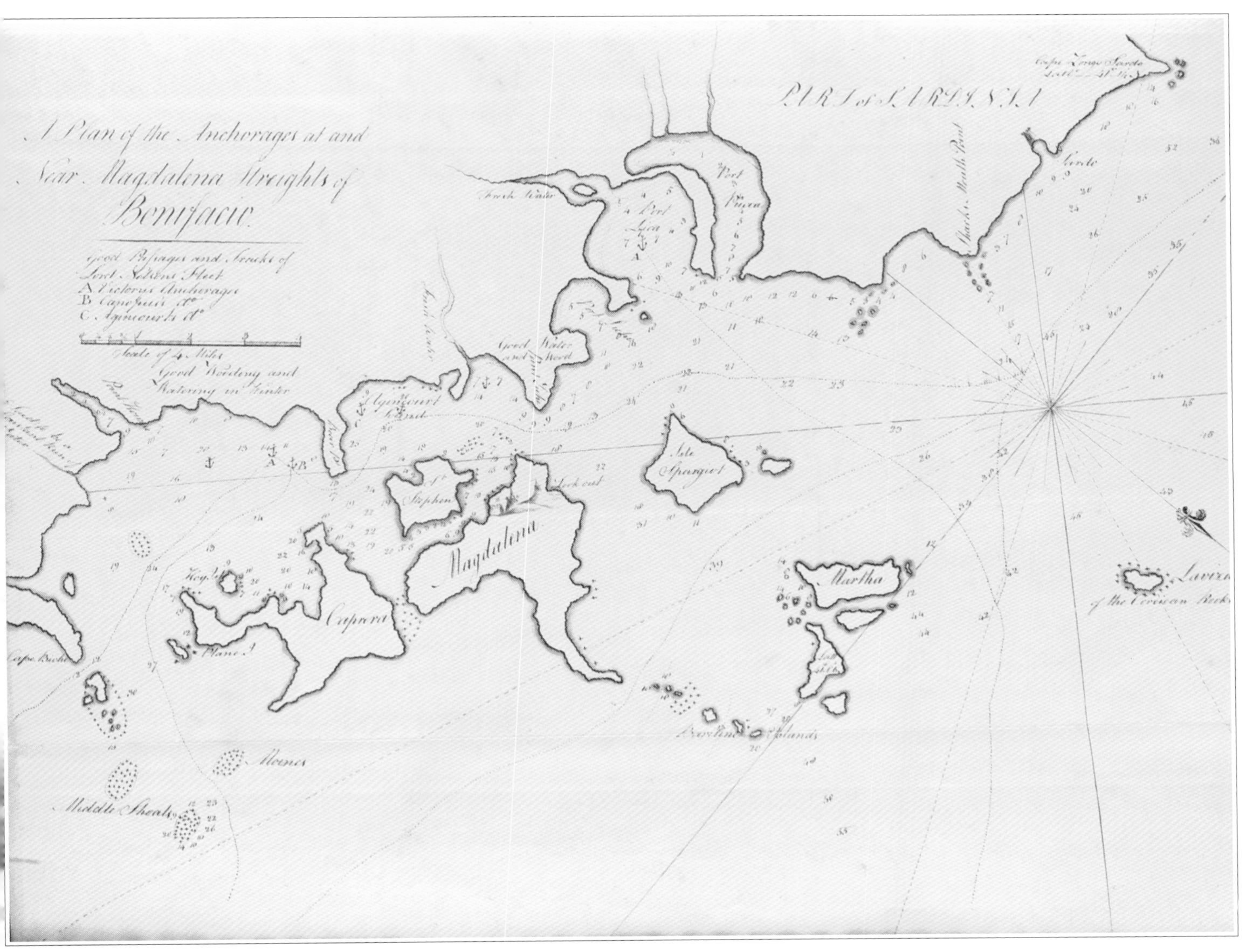

The Maddalena Islands, Sardinia, used by Nelson as an anchorage in 1803–1805. North is towards the bottom right of the chart.

(© National Maritime Museum, Greenwich, London, Chart F2125)

Atkinson, three times. One motive for the Sardinians allowing the British presence was a certain amount of protection from Barbary corsairs, though this was a difficult balancing act and Nelson wrote to the governor in November 1803, 'I am sorry it is not in my power to prevent the Barbary corsairs from landing in Sardinia as we are at peace with them, but if they had attempted a landing at this place during my stay I should have felt myself bound in honour to have afforded you every assistance in repelling them.'[76]

The *Victory* still had no purser, and in August 1803 Nelson recommended that Richard Bromley of the *Belleisle* be given the job. However, a purser was half supply officer and half businessman and had to offer a bond of up to £1,200 as security for the goods under his charge so, unlike other officers, it was difficult to make the appointment locally. James Cosgrove, the ship's steward, was the purser's assistant but was 'by no means equal to the discharge of that duty.'[77] The Admiralty informed Nelson that Walter Burke had already been appointed to the post and was about to sail out. He was from Limerick and a relative of the late conservative philosopher and politician Edmund Burke, and had been a purser for thirty years. But he did not appear on board and improvisation was necessary. In December 1803, they had to use the services of Bromley and 'a very handsome supply of dollars from Captain Hardy' to purchase bullocks, sheep and onions at

Nelson's cabin as reconstructed on board the *Victory* at Portsmouth Historic Dockyard.

(Jonathan Eastland/Ajax)

A reconstruction of one of the *Victory*'s great 68-pounder carronades. The Carron Company of Falkirk, which made the originals, was consulted about the replica in the 1920s.

(Author's collection)

Maddalena. Burke was still not there by March 1804 and Nelson fulminated against him. He considered 'Mr Burke's conduct not only reprehensible, but that he ought not to have any employment in the service' after being almost a year late to take the post up.[78] The Admiralty replied that he had been ordered to sail out in the *Hindustan* last October but made no excuse for him. When he finally arrived on 18 April 1804, he was the oldest man in the ship at about 64. It is not clear what kind of reception he had, but he seems to have been efficient in the post. The supply problem also eased with the appointment of agents in the various ports. There were many minor problems including a shortage of coal for galley stoves in May 1804, apparently because the master of the *Harmony* transport which brought it out had delegated the loading to his mate, who did not know that each basket emptied into the hold was supposed to be heaped.[79]

The *Victory* was unusual in that she carried few carronades. These were short-barrelled weapons, developed in the Carron Iron Works near Falkirk in Scotland, and firing a shot of around four times what would be fired by a 'long-gun' of similar weight, albeit over shorter ranges. Most 74s carried ten 32-pounder carronades on the quarterdeck and two on the forecastle, alongside long-guns fitted where they might damage the rigging.[80] In August 1804 the *Victory* transferred two from the *Kent*, and they made up for their lack of numbers with their weight. They were 68-pounders, whereas very few ships of the navy had carried anything more than 32-pounders ever since Keppel had ruled out 42-pounders for the *Victory* because the ball was too heavy to use in action. The problem would be even greater for a 68-pounder, but it turned out that the *Victory*'s gunners had an answer to this.

Changes continued among the officers. In December 1804, George Magrath left to run the naval hospital at Gibraltar. He was replaced as the *Victory*'s surgeon by William Beatty, the son of a revenue official in Ireland. He qualified as a surgeon's mate in 1791 at the age of eighteen and became a full surgeon on the frigate *Pomona* in 1795, when he was court martialled for a dispute with his captain over two men placed on the sick list – though he was ultimately exonerated. He served in the Mediterranean for much of that war and became rich with the capture of Spanish bullion. When war resumed in 1803, he was appointed to the 74-gun *Spencer* and, after a mishap in the rocks off Ferrol, the ship joined Nelson's Mediterranean Fleet in August 1804, where he may have made the acquaintance of the admiral.

Initially, the physician of the fleet, in charge of the general health of all the ships, was Doctor Snipe, who spent most of his time away from the fleet establishing a naval hospital on Malta. He was replaced by Dr Leonard Gillespie on 2 January 1805. Born in Armagh in Ireland, Gillespie was apprenticed to a local doctor then studied in Dublin. He started as a surgeon's mate in 1777 and served in America and the West Indies. In peacetime he made periodic visits to Paris and served as surgeon of the tiny sloop *Racehorse,* an experience he did not enjoy – he wrote of his 'narrow confinement within a sloop's wretched gunroom.'[81] He raised his status above that of a mere surgeon by qualifying as doctor of medicine at St Andrews in 1795 and published a book on the health of seamen in the West Indies. He applied for further naval service in 1804 and was appointed to the Mediterranean. With the Malta hospital up and running, he was able to spend his time with the fleet, mostly with Nelson on board the flagship. He was 'an able professional man, and of admirable and humane disposition' according to one of his colleagues.[82] In a very different department, Mel Jones left as boatswain and was succeeded by Henry William Willmet, who appeared at the end of March 1805

Life on Blockade

For Nelson at least, life was dominated by the need to be ready to meet the French fleet at any moment and he wrote to Alexander Davison in March 1804, 'day by day, my dear friend, I am expecting the French fleet to put to sea – every day, every hour and moment: and you may rely that if it is within the power of man to get at them, it shall be done; and, I am sure, all my brethren look to that day as the finish of our laborious cruise.' Nelson worked hard at his paperwork and it was recorded, 'Day after day might be seen the admiral in his cabin, closely employed with his secretary over their interminable papers. They occupied two leather arm-chairs, in the roomy pockets of which Scott, weary of translating, would occasionally stuff away a score or two of unopened letters.'[83] Despite his celebrity he had not lost the common touch. One evening in May 1804 off Toulon, a seaman was getting his hammock out of the rail when he swung round and knocked the admiral off his feet. He helped him up and apologised profusely, but Nelson answered, 'My man, it was not your fault, it was my own. I ought to have known better than to stand in our way.'[84]

Doctor Gillespie wrote an account of the pleasant life on board, a total contrast to his bitter recollections of life on board the *Racehorse* in the 1780s:

A mess deck between two guns. It shows the camaraderie and storytelling which were at the heart of a seaman's social life. The men have done their best to make it comfortable, with crockery at one end of the table. Their belongings are in bags hanging from the sides.

(© The British Museum, London, 1906,1016.19)

> Breakfast is announced in the Admiral's cabin, where Lord Nelson, Rear-Admiral Murray, the Captain of the Fleet, Captain Hardy, Commander of the *Victory*, the chaplain, secretary, one or two officers of the ship, and your humble servant assemble and breakfast on tea, hot rolls, toast, cold tongue, etc., after which, when finished, we repair upon deck to enjoy the majestic sight of the rising sun.[85]

There was something of a diversion from the usual

Another of Marryat's unpublished drawings, showing an essential part of the ship's daily routine, seamen washing the decks in the early morning under the supervision of a lieutenant.

(© The British Museum, London, 1891,1117.34)

monotony at the end of May when a small force of French ships of the line and smaller ships attempted to leave Toulon. Stevenson wrote to his brother:

> The 29th May we expected to come to action with the French fleet close in with Toulon, there being five sail of the line of us and 11 sail of the enemy that came within one gun shot and a half of us and then tacked ships and made all sail they could into the harbour and we chased them close into Toulon harbour. I don't think that they will ever venture so near us again, for they are much afraid of us.[86]

On 14 June eight sail of the line plus frigates and sloops 'cut a caper', as Nelson put it, at the entrance to Toulon but soon retreated in the face of the five British ships of the line.[87] Nelson was furious when French newspapers reported that he had retreated from the scene.

There was another diversion in September when a servant, James Archibald, fell overboard. Master's Mate James Flinn jumped in to save him and Nelson promoted him to lieutenant to the cheers of the midshipman. But he recognised the irony of the situation and, according to Scott, said 'with a good natured smile on his face, "Stop, young gentlemen! Mr Flinn has done a gallant thing today – and he has done many gallant things before – for which he has got his reward, but mind! I'll have no more making lieutenants for servants falling overboard."'[88]

Initially, Nelson had worried about scurvy in the fleet because Sicily, his usual source of lemons, was under French domination. In December 1803 he worried about the men sent ashore for wood and water who were 'subject [from the damp and marshy places where water is to be had] to disease.' Doctor Snipe ordered them to be issued with extra wine and spirits to prevent this.[89] But soon the ship's health began to improve, and in June 1804 the flagship had only nine men on the sick list – one each from fever, pulmonary inflammation, ulcers and wounds, and five more suffering from 'other complaints.' The situation was improving, four men had been put on the sick list the previous week compared with six who were sent back to duty. There were 274 sick men in the fleet of twenty-seven vessels. Only two had scurvy, both in the *Donegal*.[90] By August 1804, Nelson was tired and hoped for a few months rest at home. However, as he wrote in March 1805, 'I saw the certainty of the French fleets putting to sea and therefore no consideration could at such a crisis induce me to quit my post.'[91] But he soldiered on.

Despite her age, the *Victory* still had her sailing qualities. In October 1803 Nelson wrote, 'The weather off Toulon is not mended...but this ship is so easy in a sea that we scarce feel a gale'[92] In March 1804 Nelson's second-in-command, Admiral Bickerton, observed from the *Royal Sovereign*, '...we rolled rather heavily last night, at a time when I observed that the *Victory* to be quite steady.'[93] The rigging of the *Victory* remained sound in December 1803, unlike that of the other ships in the fleet.[94] Nelson claimed that the *Victory* 'left England without being caulked', presumably in her upper works as she would not have stayed afloat with no caulking below the waterline. This work had to be completed afloat by the crew, involving 'great exertion', and caulkers from six other ships were employed under the carpenter William Bunce.[95] But these were issues that could be dealt with by the crew, the hull was still in generally good condition after two years at sea.

9 THE TRIUMPH OF SEA POWER

The Fear of Invasion

After nearly two years of stalemate, Napoleon (who had crowned himself emperor in May 1804) could see that an invasion of Britain was not practicable unless their fleet could somehow be got out of the way. He had control of the Netherlands as a possible base for an invasion. He had built up a great fleet of invasion craft, which could mostly be rowed as well as sailed, so that they could evade the British frigates and sloops in a calm – but they were nearly all based in Boulogne, and could only exit at high tide. It would take three days to assemble them outside the port, giving the British plenty of warning. No one, even with modern weather forecasting, could guarantee three days of calm in the English Channel so control of the sea was essential, for at least a few days. Victory in battle was unlikely, so the only alternative was to lure the main British fleets out of the main theatre of action. The French and Spanish fleet in various Atlantic and Mediterranean ports would evade their blockaders and concentrate in the West Indies, making an irresistible force which would sail across the ocean and concentrate in the Channel. It would sweep aside the British frigates and sloops and clear the way for the Grande Armée to invade.

In Britain, St Vincent was quoted as saying, 'I do not say the Frenchman will not come; I only say he will not come by sea', but not everyone was so confident. As in the last war, companies of volunteers drilled in every town and village. This time, few of them felt the need to hint that they could be used against radicals as well as Frenchmen by putting the word 'loyal' in their titles, for now the country was more united than at any time since the Seven Years War. The middle-class radicals had long since been disillusioned by the French Revolution, and the coronation of Napoleon only confirmed their worst fears. The working-class movement was only beginning to emerge and was largely restrained by laws against trade unions. The Scottish Highlands had long since been integrated into the United Kingdom, and there was no major revolt in Ireland. The Addington government had no offensive strategy against the French, and there was none until William Pitt returned to power in May 1804. One result was the capture of Spanish treasure ships in October that year, leading to a declaration of war by Spain in December. But Nelson did not fear the Spanish as Jervis had done – as early as 1793 he had noted that they had '...very fine ships, but shockingly manned'.[1] He was not likely to abandon the Mediterranean and the blockade of Toulon. The new First Lord of the Admiralty was Henry Dundas, created Lord Melville, a close ally of Pitt and a powerful and astute Scotsman who was often suspected of excessive corruption even by early nineteenth-century standards.

The French Come Out

The *Victory*'s life changed in the afternoon of 19 January 1805, when the frigates *Seahorse* and *Active* arrived off the Maddalena Islands with an urgent message. Nelson ordered the fleet to sea before he had heard their news – that the Toulon Squadron had sailed two days earlier. He expected a repetition of 1798, for he had intelligence from Naples that the ships were carrying troops, and the wind over the last two weeks suggested a passage to the east. He made a fast passage to Alexandria but found no sign of the French. Hardy sounded a rare note of criticism when he wrote, 'our good commander in chief's great zeal and activity pushed us in rather too fast.'[2] The return passage was much slower, and back in Sardinia, Nelson heard that the French had turned back almost as soon as they had left due to a storm. He wrote, 'Buonaparte [sic] himself cannot be more disappointed and grieved at the return of the French fleet crippled into Toulon than I am...'[3]

The fleet resumed its station and made a feint towards Barcelona hoping to make the French sail south of Majorca. There was a fire near the *Victory*'s powder magazine, as recounted by Nelson's servant William Chevallier:

> The whole of the terrified crew runned [sic] up the rigging at that dreadful moment, when every man thought it was his last hour, Lord Nelson was then as cool and composed as ever I saw him before. He orders every man below to put out the fire, and such is the confidence and respect that the sailors have for him that everyone obeyed and in twenty minutes the fire was got under.[4]

But he was concealing the anxiety which others saw in him during this period, including Beatty. He was 'seldom enjoying two hours of uninterrupted sleep; and on several occasions he did not quit the deck during the whole night. At these times he took no pains to protect himself from the effects of wet, or the night air; wearing only a thin greatcoat...'

They returned to Sardinia to cover any move to the east, then cruised off Sicily. The French, under Villeneuve, sailed on 30 March, but it was 19 April before Nelson received news from the frigate *Amazon* that they had been seen passing through the Straits of Gibraltar ten days beforehand. According to Captain Francis Austen of the *Canopus*:

> The *Amazon* made the telegraphic signal that the vessel examined was from Cadiz out 5 days which reports that the French squadron arrived off there 10 days ago and was joined by 5 Spanish two-deckers & 2 frigates, all of which stood to the westward with a fresh wind at east.[5]

Sir John Orde's fleet off Cadiz had withdrawn to the north and had not encountered them. Nelson headed for Gibraltar. It was a slow passage and he wrote, 'my fortune seems flown away. I cannot get a fair wind, or even a side wind– Dead foul!'[6] On 4 May they anchored off Tetuan in Morocco to take on stores, then crossed the strait to Gibraltar where some officers were allowed ashore. But Nelson, according to Scott, 'observing and weatherwise as he was, perceived an indication of a probable change of wind.'[7] He ordered a gun to be fired and the Blue Peter flag to be hoisted from the mainmast to recall the men who had gone ashore. They set sail

The *Victory* in the centre of the fleet off Stromboli in January 1805, during the chase to Egypt and painted by Nicolas Pocock. It shows the ship with open stern galleries, as do other Pocock pictures. Fleets did not normally sail in formation except during exercises or in the approach to battle.

(© National Maritime Museum, Greenwich, London, PW5885)

so suddenly that some of the midshipmen had to leave their laundry behind. Nelson was fully aware of the risk he was taking and confided in Chaplain Scott, 'if I fail, if they are not gone to the West Indies, I shall be blamed: to be burnt in effigy, or Westminster Abbey is my alternative.'[8]

On 12 May, the fourth Sunday after Easter, Alexander Scott 'performed the church service to the people. The fleet steers to the west with a good wind.' They were sixty miles out from Cape St Vincent, according to Midshipman Rivers, and, with his usual Sunday custom, Nelson:

> ...Visited the men at quarters, the fleet at that time rolling down the Trades with a powerful crowd of sail, studding sail low and aloft, going 12.6 [knots] by the log. His lord[ship] took his seat upon the pump dale on the lower deck and made a very pithy speech to the following effect, that he was very sure the enemy was not more than 100 miles ahead and he hoped to get alongside of them. 'You know we have 10 sail of the line and they have 18. Our 74s will mangle one each, the others must take two then there will be three left for us and have no doubt that you will give a good account of them', to which the men responded with a hearty cheer.[9]

Later in the passage, Captain Murray asked him, 'I

The chase across the Atlantic and back again with the French fleet, in blue, only shown for the return voyage.

(Taken from Julian S. Corbett, The Campaign of Trafalgar, *London, 1910)*

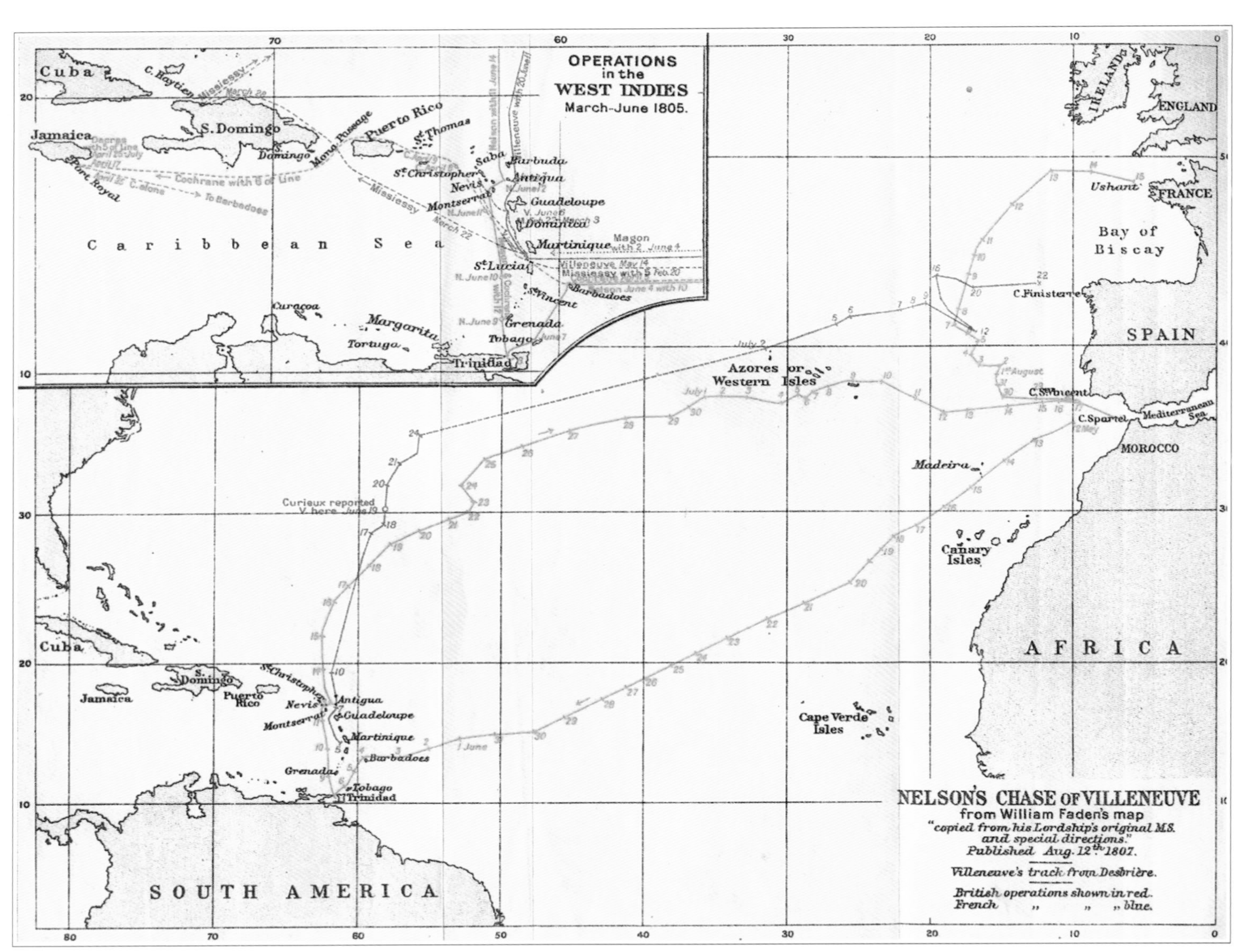

suppose, my Lord, that, by packing all this canvas on the ships, your lordship means to engage the enemy, in case you come up with them.' Nelson replied, 'dryly and shortly'. 'Yes, by God, I do.'[10]

The sailors probably enjoyed a fast sail in steady trade winds after years on blockade, but Scott had no sources of intelligence to collate, no letters to write and very little to do. He recorded:

> May 20. I know not what to write – it is the same old story.
> May 21. Nothing new – we must take it as it comes.[11]

Nelson used the voyage to develop his ideas on naval tactics, which were practical rather than theoretical, and there is no sign that he had read any of the numerous books on the subject published by the French in the last century or so. He may, however, have been influenced by Clerk of Eldin's *Essay on Naval Tactics*, written in the aftermath of the failure at Ushant in 1778. Hardy later wrote that Nelson had '...read Mr Clerk's works with great attention, and frequently expressed his approbation of them in the fullest manner.'[12] During the voyage he drafted a document beginning, 'The business of an English Commander-in-Chief being first to bring an enemy's fleet into battle, on the most advantageous terms to himself (I mean that of laying his ships close on board those of the enemy, as expeditiously as possible.)' If both fleets were willing to fight, 'little manoeuvring is necessary: the less the better; – a day is soon lost in that business.' He planned to gain the weather gage and then sail until his leading ship was near the centre of the enemy line. Then they would wear in succession and attack the leading enemy ships, 'passing, certainly, if opportunity offered, through their line.' Another plan was to decline the weather gage and then sail through the centre of the enemy line to cut him in two.[13] It was certainly a long way from the cautious manoeuvres which had been directed from the deck of the *Victory* in earlier wars, and the culmination of a series of attempts to escape the tyranny of the line of battle.

In the West Indies

On 4 June, the *Victory* and squadron anchored in Carlisle Bay, Barbados. It was the first time a British first-rate had crossed the Atlantic, for major squadrons off the West Indies or North America had been headed by second-rates of 90 or 98 guns in the past. It was a tribute to the quality of her 'great repair' at Chatham that Nelson had the confidence to make such a voyage, and to crowd on sail on the way to make a fast passage – he had gained ten days on the French. The Governor of St Lucia, General Robert Brereton, was convinced by a report that the French had been seen sailing south. Nelson was doubtful, but took on 2,000 troops and James Marguette a 'man of colour' as pilot. They headed for Trinidad expecting another Battle of the Nile in the Gulf of Paria. Instead, he found nothing and soon discovered that Villeneuve had been at Martinique, a hundred miles from Barbados, but by that time had had already sailed. Nelson cursed Brereton over the next few weeks, most vehemently to Emma. 'I have reason to hate the name of Gen. Brereton as long as I live and perhaps our country for ever...'[14]

Although it was possible that the enemy was going west to attack Jamaica, Nelson correctly surmised that he was heading back to Europe and set off to follow him, leaving Antigua on 12 June. He sent the sloop *Curieux*, under Captain Bettesworth, with a message to the Admiralty reporting his intentions and what he believed the French were doing. This set off a train of unintended consequences, which meant that one of the main decisions would be made away from Nelson and the *Victory*. On the 19th, Bettesworth sighted Villeneuve's fleet, heading further north than if it was returning to the Mediterranean. He made all speed for home and arrived at Plymouth on 7 July. He made haste to London by road and on the night of the 8th the First Lord of the Admiralty, Lord Barham, was awakened with the news. As an old sailor himself, he quickly appreciated its importance and assembled a squadron under Sir Robert Calder off Cape Finisterre to meet the French as they tried to reach the English Channel.

Calder's Action

Calder was still as cautious as when Jervis had mocked him after the Battle of St Vincent, and was not likely to need forgiveness for 'an unauthorised departure from the prescribed mode of attack' – but to be fair, there was little more he could have done when he met the French in intermittent fog on 22 July. He captured two ships, just as Hotham's fleet had done in 1795, but he

Carlisle Bay, the main naval anchorage off Barbados, by Captain Edward Brenton.

(© National Maritime Museum, Greenwich, London, PW8416)

would soon find that expectations had changed since then. More importantly, he caused the Franco-Spanish fleet to abandon the voyage to the Channel and put into Ferrol in north-west Spain. Napoleon's invasion plan soon began to unravel.

Meanwhile, Nelson knew nothing of this and continued across the Atlantic hoping for an encounter. On the 17th, Thomas Atkinson reported that some of the water casks were rotten and the ship only had a hundred tonnes instead of 145, so it had to be rationed for the rest of the voyage.[15] On the 18th, they boarded an American schooner bound for Antigua, with a log entry showing a fleet of twenty-two sail heading north. Nelson hoped 'to close with them before they get to either Cadiz or Toulon.'[16] On the 20th, they sighted a British brig which had no news of the enemy, but carried newspapers that Lord Barham was now First Lord of the Admiralty, after impeachment had removed Lord Melville. This was a little confusing at first – Sir Charles Middleton had taken the new title on being appointed to the office. During the voyage Nelson told one of his officers, 'all the way out he was getting stronger and I was getting weaker. All the way home I am getting stronger and he is getting weaker. If we fell in with him now and fought him, I don't doubt we should beat him, and it would be a great thing for my personal glory; but I think I should be doing my country a great wrong, I know that in a week's time I shall get reinforcements, and he will get none, and then I must annihilate him.'[17]

On 1 July, the winds were so light that he wrote to Rear-Admiral Louis in the *Canopus*, 'I think you may, with great safety, venture to dine on board the *Victory* today, for I too much fear that we shall not have a wind to move us faster than boats can pass.'[18] On the 10th, Nelson sent a frigate ahead to Gibraltar to warn them to be ready to receive them. By the 13th, the fleet was 600 miles from Cape St Vincent and water was running low so the ration had to be reduced to five pints per man per day. Nelson calculated that the fleet had sailed 3,459 miles since leaving the West Indies. On the 19th, they anchored off the Rock, where Nelson landed for the first me since Malta. 'I went on shore for the first time since ne 16th of June 1803; and from having set foot outside f the *Victory*, two years, wanting ten days.'[19] Hardy ound it 'as hot and unpleasant as ever.'[20] Nelson issued rders to the parts of his fleet left behind, and he was leased to find that his old friend Collingwood had been n charge of the blockade of Cadiz since May, rather han Orde. But apart from that, Nelson was thoroughly niserable at having missed the French.

They sailed over to Tetuan in Morocco to pick up upplies of bullocks and water but they could find no nions and Nelson sent a brig out to find some, for signs f scurvy were beginning to appear. At 4am on the 25th, while off Cadiz, he received the first news that the *Curieux* had seen the enemy to the northwards from a newspaper carried by the *Termagant* brig. As yet he did not know of Calder's action three days earlier, but he headed northwards in unfavourable winds. Of his eleven ships of the line, the *Victory* was deemed to be 'fit for service' as were six more. The *Canopus* 'would be better docked before the winter', while the *Superb, Belleisle* and *Donegal* needed docking more urgently.[21] It was a tribute to the value of coppering that ships could stay at sea for more than two years and endure a double Atlantic crossing without the need of dockyard help.

On 3 August, Nelson wrote of 'this foul wind, but by the 15th the Squadron was in sight of Cornwallis's Channel Fleet off Ushant, which Calder had joined the day before. Captain Codrington of the *Orion* (which had just been commissioned after a refit) was impressed with the appearance of the ships after their long voyage. They seemed to be 'of a very high order indeed; and although their ships do not look so handsome as objects, they look so warlike, and show such high conditions, when once I think *Orion* fit to manoeuvre with them, I shall probably paint her in the same manner.'[22] This is the first sign of the 'Nelson chequer'. It had perhaps originated with Nelson's desire to

Calder's Action by William Anderson, showing the flagship *Prince of Wales* in the centre and other ships receding in the mist.

(© National Maritime Museum, Greenwich, London, BHC0540)

identify his ships. In the past, it had been common to varnish or paint the sides of the ship giving a yellow colour, with the lower wales and topsides painted black; Nelson's first innovation was to paint the middle and upper wales as well, which if done sparingly would identify a flagship through the smoke of battle, or if applied more generally would pick out ships of his own fleet – though there is no evidence that he issued any order to that effect. The next change was to paint the gunports black giving the 'chequered' appearance. It would not have much effect in battle when the ports would already be open, but it might help deter an enemy at a distance. In any case, Codrington's comments show how the paint scheme already carried prestige and an image of supreme competence.

Calder's action was reported in the newspapers, on which Nelson commented, '*John Bull* was not content, for which I am sorry for.'[23] Cornwallis was the senior officer and clearly the Channel Fleet took priority now that the French fleet was out of the Mediterranean. He ordered Nelson to go home in the *Victory,* along with the *Superb* which needed docking most urgently, plus a new foremast. They anchored at Spithead on the 18th and next day Nelson struck his flag.

Back at Home

Hardy went to Weymouth where he had a 'long conversation' with the King.[24] Nelson went home to Merton, which was conveniently close to the road between London and Portsmouth, to be reunited with his beloved Emma and his daughter Horatia. He was now accepted in society after being shunned because of his affair, and he was visited by the Duke of Clarence and others. But it was not uninterrupted leave, he journeyed to London several times to consult with ministers and the Admiralty. During one visit to the Admiralty, he made a note of officers he felt to be deserving of reward or promotion. Atkinson, he suggested, should become a master attendant in a dockyard, and Bunce the carpenter would be given a timepiece by Andrew Snape Hammond, who held his uncle's old job as Controller of the Navy. On the other side, he drew a diagram showing his possible tactics on meeting the enemy, so battle was never far from his mind.[25]

In Portsmouth, the *Victory* had what Midshipman Rivers called 'a slight refit.' Bunce and his crew were hard at work on various jobs such as making new hammock boards for the old decayed ones on the poop, whitewashing the compartments on the orlop deck, and blacking the wales outside the hull. By September they were 'fitting and completing the ship for sea, making and replacing ladders, gratings, half ports and bulkheads and the different apartments.'[26]

There was no chance for most of the crew to go home, or even to have shore leave. Benjamin Stevenson was no happier in August 1805, though he had been promoted to quarter gunner a year before, and to the responsible role of quartermaster, supervising the steering of the ship, in November.[27] After more than two years in the *Victory*, he wrote of 'this miserable situation'. He had seen several of his shipmates released after their friends found substitutes for them at a cost of forty shillings each and begged his brother to do the same – 'I would not begrudge the money to get clear of this prison'.[28]

New Officers

There were also changes at the top. George Murray decided to remain ashore to act as executor for his late father-in-law and Nelson did not have him replaced. Doctor Gillespie also left, but Beatty remained on board as the ship's surgeon. Several new officers joined at a junior level. Daniel Harrington was very old for a midshipman at 29. Phillip Thorez was twenty-one and a native of Naples, while Thomas Goble was also twenty-one and had been pressed into the navy from a merchant ship in 1804. With a good education, he became captain's clerk in the brig *Attack*. There was no vacancy in that post when he transferred to the *Victory,* so he became a master's mate. John Felton was twenty and had already seen battle under Nelson at Copenhagen. Eighteen-year-old John Pollard was transferred from the *Canopus* in which he had crossed the Atlantic with Nelson.

It was only by chance that Lewis Roteley found himself on board the *Victory*. As a boy, he seemed unpromising material, of 'a fretful peevish temper' and he was 'very fond of getting into brawls &c.' His schoolmaster suggested a counting house or a trade. His father made enquiries about the army but could not buy a commission for less than £340, so he became a second lieutenant in the Royal Marines instead. He aid £42.8s for his uniform plus 10/6 to the drill ergeant of the barracks so that he was 'perfect in my xercise.'[29] He hoped to be appointed to the new frigate *pollo* to make some prize money, but 'a young man ho had a little interest with the field officers, was ppointed over my head.' At the age of twenty, he was lready married with a daughter and constantly short f money. By 2 September, he had been 'ordered to mbark on board the *Victory* tomorrow morning, which s completely ready for sea, only waiting for Lord Jelson's return from town.' His father, an old seaman, old him, '...you will soon be in battle.... be sure to keep our head erect in battle, never bow to a Frenchman's hot, it's folly, for when you hear the balls whistle you re safe, the ball has passed harmless before you can ear it.' Once on board, there were more expenses, he ad to pay £40 as a contribution to stock for the ardroom mess, though he agreed they had 'capital inners on board'. He fretted about his trunk which ad not yet arrived from the family home in Swansea, nd it got worse when a draft on his agent was not ccepted – 'I am left without a guinea.'[30]

gainst the Combined Fleet

Ieanwhile, off Portugal, Captain Blackwood of the rigate *Euryalus*, who had gained Nelson's respect in he Mediterranean during the last war, heard a report f a great force of up to twenty-seven ships of the line ailing south – it could only be the combined Spanish nd French fleets heading towards the Mediterranean. Ie made contact with Admiral Collingwood, whose wn force was too weak to stop them entering Cadiz, hen he was sent home with word that a great force was ow assembled in the Spanish port. He left his ship in he Solent and on the way to London he called on at Ierton at 5am on 2 September. Nelson knew this would nean his recall and accompanied the captain to London, aying. 'Depend on it, Blackwood, I shall yet give Mr Villeneuve a drubbing.' He was indeed reappointed to he command by Barham and returned to Merton with en days to make preparations.

Nelson left for Portsmouth on 13 September and vrote in his diary, 'Friday night at half past ten drove rom dear, dear Merton, where I left all I hold dear in his world, to go and serve my King & Country.'[31] He rrived in Portsmouth next morning and took breakfast in the George Hotel. Benjamin Silliman of Yale University witnessed the scene as he left:

> Lord Nelson endeavoured to elude the populace, who were assembled, in great numbers, in the street... He went out through a back door and through a by-lane... But, by the time he had arrived on the beach, some hundreds of people had collected in his train, pressing all around, to get a little before him to obtain a sight of his face. I stood on one of the batteries near which he passed, and had a full view of his person. As the barge in which he embarked, pushed away from the shore, the people gave him three cheers, which his lordship returned by waving his hat.

He boarded the *Victory* again at 11.30am and she weighed anchor at 8am the next morning, in company with Blackwood in the *Euryalus*. On 30 September, Nelson wrote to his friend Thomas Acton in Naples, 'after only 25 days being in England I find myself again in command of the Mediterranean Fleet.'[32] But this was a different kind of fleet, more to Nelson's taste in many ways – there were fewer diplomatic negotiations to conduct, fewer allies or neutrals to appease and no convoys to organise. Instead, it was dedicated to the sole purpose of fighting a great fleet battle, a task at which Nelson excelled above all else. But, in terms of ships of the line, it grew into a much bigger fleet than he had commanded before, and he felt the lack of a chief of staff like Murray.

Captain George Duff joined the fleet in the 74-gun *Mars* at the end of September and dined with Nelson on 10 October, quickly identifying his leadership qualities. 'He is so good and pleasant a man, that we all wish to do what he likes, without any kind of orders.' He and the other captains soon ordered their ships to be painted 'a la Nelson, with the black and yellow chequer of the *Victory*.'[33] Nelson was keen that the French should not know their strength. He positioned the bulk of his fleet fifty miles off the coast so that they could not be observed from Spanish hilltops, with a line of frigates and ships of the line, including the *Mars*, to pass on the message of the enemy if he came out. Ships joining the fleet were ordered not to fire salutes, as these might give the numbers and position away.

Soon after his arrival, Nelson called his captains on

board the *Victory* and explained his tactics if the French and Spanish should come out. The old days of a single rigid line of battle were gone and almost forgotten. Nelson would form his force into three divisions, two under himself and Collingwood of sixteen ships each which would sail straight at the enemy carrying all possible sail, rather than reducing to topsails alone as was more conventional in going into battle. The third division would have the eight fastest ships and be under the command of an officer with the initiative to deploy them where they would be most effective. Nelson's division would cut the enemy line just ahead of its centre while Collingwood's would attack it about twelve ships from the rear. This would produce a melee battle which was what Nelson wanted, as he was sure his ships would prevail in the fierce fighting. But he recognised, 'nothing is sure in a sea fight... in case signals can neither be seen or perfectly understood, no captain can do very wrong if he places his ship alongside that of an enemy.'[34] Nelson was pleased with the reaction of his captains and wrote to Emma:

> When I came to explain to them the 'Nelson touch,' it was like an electric shock. Some shed tears, all approved – 'It was new, it was singular. It was simple!' – and from Admirals downwards, it was repeated – 'It must succeed, if ever they will allow you to get at them!'[35]

Despite the best possible tactics, the Combined Fleet might well have remained in port for years, frustrating Nelson and wearing the ships out with their hard service. But instead, Admiral Villeneuve was goaded by Napoleon and decided to come out. He was misled by reports of British ships under Rear-Admiral Louis which were replenishing at Gibraltar and he did not know that more ships had joined Nelson to make up the numbers. He knew that an order to dismiss him was on the way, and was determined to forestall it and perhaps gain some credit by taking his fleet into the Mediterranean to assist the French armies in Italy.

Ready for Battle

As a result, Nelson recorded in his diary for that morning, 'Saturday October 19th. Fine weather. Wind easterly. At ½ past 9 the *Mars*, being one of the look out ships made the signal that the enemy were coming out of port.'[36] The next day, the 20th, was spent preparing for battle as the Combined Fleet slowly made its way out of harbour. According to Hardy, the crew were 'employed on board the *Victory* getting up a thousand shot on each deck, stowing away chests, etc., etc., clearing for action.'[37] Nelson ordered a white cloth to be put over the hammock rails and saturated with water to help prevent fire, and for the decks to be wetted. When a marine officer rebuked a man who spilled water over him, Nelson turned to him and said, 'It was not the man's fault, you had no business to stand in his way.'[38] The carpenter and his crew broke up the hen and turkey coops and threw them overboard, they did not record what happened to the occupants. Many other items were '...thrown overboard with the bulkheads in clearing the ship...'[39] Nelson dined with some of the junior officers that evening and Masters Mate Thomas Goble reported him as saying, 'I will leave you such a victory tomorrow that you youngsters will think and talk about it for the rest of your lives.'[40]

At daylight on the 21st, John Brown, a twenty-three year old able seaman from Waterford, saw the French and Spanish fleets 'like a great wood on our lee bow which cheered the hearts of every British tar in the *Victory* like lions anxious to be at it.'[41] Lieutenant Pasco went into the cabin to talk to Nelson about his status as signal officer rather than first lieutenant. As it had been cleared of furniture, Nelson was on the deck writing his final prayer – 'May the great God whom I worship, grant my Country, and for the benefit of Europe in General, a great and glorious victory.' Pasco realised it would be inappropriate to raise a private grievance in the circumstances and withdrew.[42] Nelson called the captains of his four frigates on board to give them instructions. He addressed the crew at their quarters, 'admonishing them against firing a single shot without being sure of their object'.[43] After he appeared on deck, his officers noticed how his dress might reveal his status to enemy snipers. Though he was not wearing the full dress of an admiral with metal stars on his chest, even his 'undress' uniform carried cloth reproductions of his four orders, but no one was brave enough to mention it to him until Surgeon Beatty offered to approach him on the pretext of giving a report on the sick; but the chance never occurred.

It was wise to let the men eat before action as no one

The Nelson touch – a rather fictitious view of Nelson explaining his tactics to his captains, though in practice they were different from what he outlined. The plan below attempts to show the actual formation of both sides in the battle.

(© National Maritime Museum, Greenwich, London, PU4050)

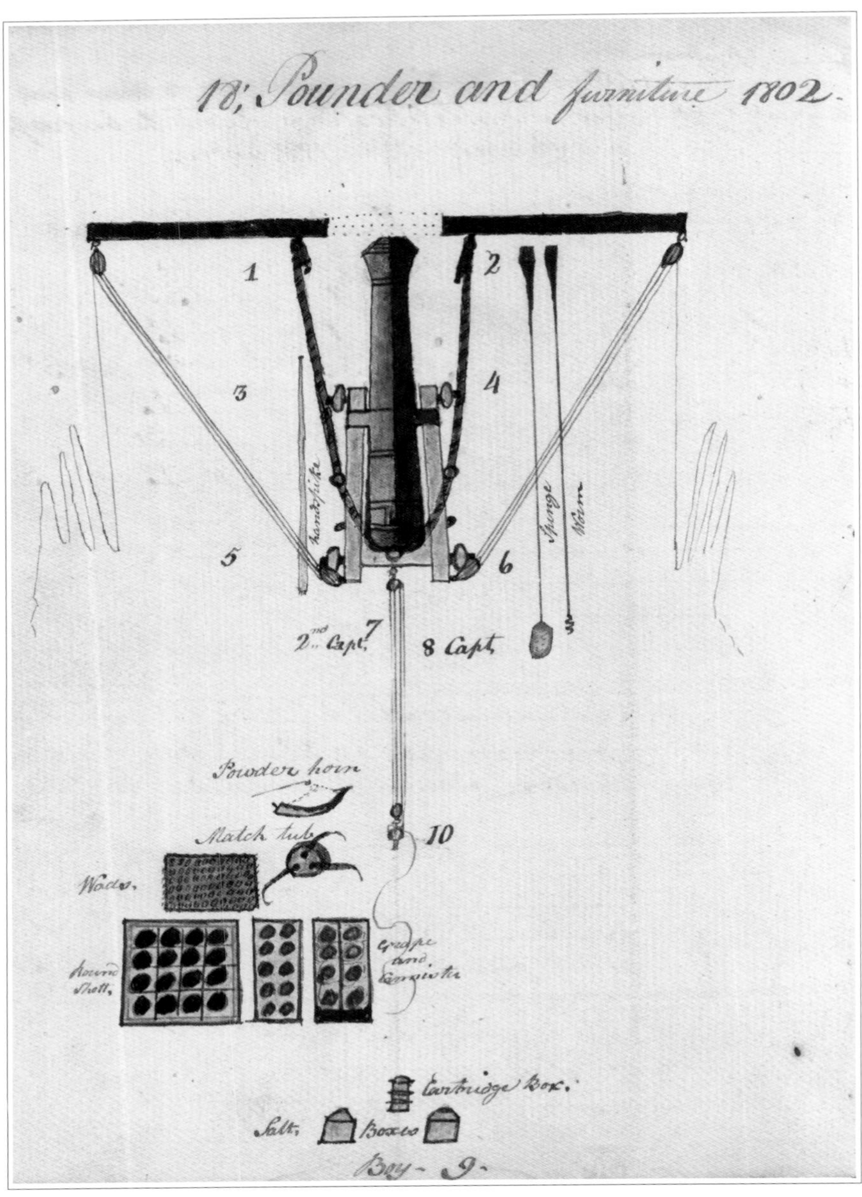

The crew of a 12-pounder gun, in this case on the frigate *Amazon* in 1799, but applicable to the upper deck guns of larger ships. Ten members are shown, with the position of each indicated by a number. The various implements are arranged round the gun.

(© National Maritime Museum, Greenwich, London, JOD/45)

knew how long it would last. Able Seaman John Brown reported, 'we piped to dinner and ate a bit of raw pork and half a pint of wine.'[44] The drums sounded and the men went to their stations. According to Brown, 'when coming close to the enemy [we] beat to quarters [and] got our guns double shotted to give them a dose and [we were] all ready for action standing at our quarters.'[45] There were perhaps a few men up in the tops to help handle the rigging, but they were not there to fire down as marksmen as their counterparts on the French ships were. About forty of the best marine marksmen were drawn up in ranks on the poop deck under the command of Captain Adair assisted by Lieutenants Peake and Reeves and Lewis Roteley. Also on the exposed deck were Lieutenant Pasco, Midshipman Pollard and Quartermaster King to observe and transmit signals. The main command of the ship was from the quarterdeck, around the steering wheel. The bulkheads of the captain's cabin had been thrown overboard and there was an open space under the poop, but the officers were expected to be in the area forward of the wheel, with no protection from above. They included, of course, Nelson and Hardy. Atkinson was the main adviser on seamanship. Both Scotts were there to take notes, along with Bulkeley, Hardy's aide, to carry messages. There were six 12-pounder guns on each side of this deck, three of them under the protection of the poop and three more in the open. Further forward, Boatswain Willmet took charge of the forecastle including the two 68-pounder carronades. According to the gunner, each was loaded with seven kegs filled with nearly 500 musket shot each, and a round shot 'to give it force'.[46]

Each deck was in the charge of the junior Lieutenants Williams, King and Brown, with John Yule on the lower deck. The great bulk of the crew was stationed at the guns of the upper, middle and lower decks. The captain of the gun – usually a petty officer or able seaman – would aim it and decide when to fire it by pulling a lanyard to set off a flintlock. Skilled and reliable men would worm and sponge out the barrel after each shot to remove any burning embers. Another man would insert the cartridge while a third rammed it home, to be followed by a wad, the ball or balls, and another wad to stop the ball rolling out. Heavier labour was needed to haul the gun out through the port, especially if it was against the heel of the ship. A single 32-pounder usually had a crew of seven which could be combined with the gun on the opposite side of the ship as it was not common to have both sides engaged at once. However, that did happen during the course of the battle on board the *Victory* and other ships, and one possibility was to adopt the plan suggested by John Davie in 1804, by which two crews of side-by-side guns assisted one another:

> ...Whilst one gun is in and the people are worming, sponging and loading it, the other should be run out

with the spare men from the gun which is in, in addition to those belonging to the gun which is run out, and so continue alternately to assist each other.[47]

Intensive training was needed to keep up a good rate of fire, and most of Nelson's ships were at their peak of efficiency. Aiming was largely disregarded, it was assumed that the enemy would be too close to miss for most of the action.

In the cockpit aft on the orlop deck, Surgeon Beatty and his mates and assistants prepared the midshipman's table for operations and laid out their instruments. Further forward, the carpenter and his mates stood by with tools and plugs in the 'wings' or 'carpenter's walks' on each side of the orlop and close to the waterline, ready to plug any holes 'between wind and water'. Below that were the magazines, each lit by a lamp in a separate compartment which shone through glass. The grand magazine aft in the hold contained the main store of powder, with men ready to make more of it into cartridges by ladling it into paper bags. But much of it was already in cartridges, and the grand magazine serviced the lower deck 32-pounder guns, while the middle hanging magazine, situated between the lower and orlop deck, supplied the middle deck and the forward hanging magazine was for the 12-pounder upper deck and quarterdeck guns. During a later commission (when the ship had a slightly reduced gun armament), Gunner Rivers had the gunner's mate in charge of the grand magazine, with a man to fill cartridges if the supply looked likely to run out, and two more to retrieve and open barrels. For more immediate needs, three men were to take the ready-use cartridges out of racks, put them in wooden cases for protection on the way to the gundecks, and pass them up the ladder to the lower deck. One man supervised the light-room which contained the lamp and was entered by a different route to reduce fire risk.

A quarterdeck gun crew in action showing casualties which were common in such an exposed position in close action. As with many pictures of the time, it shows a black seaman.

(© National Maritime Museum, Greenwich, London, PU8487)

Three more worked in the grand magazine passage, five in the light-room passage and one was stationed on the lower deck between the anchor bitts to pass them to the members of the guns crews (usually boys) who took them to the respective guns. The hanging magazines had a smaller crew, seven men each, for the cartridges were smaller, they were already made up and the entrances and exits were less tortuous.[48]

Victory in the Lead

The war had already tested the *Victory*'s stamina, with two years at sea with no docking. It had tested her long-distance sailing, as the first Royal Navy ship of her type to cross the Atlantic. Now it would test her in a different way, as a flagship leading the fleet into battle. It was far more normal for the commander-in-chief to station himself at the centre of the fleet to give orders by flag in either direction. In this case, the leading position was all the more dangerous in that the ship was approaching at almost right angles to the enemy, where she would be subjected to the full force of his broadsides while only making a feeble reply; and it was done in light winds so the ship would pass slowly through the danger zone.

As with many of Nelson's attacks, it does not seem to have been planned that way. Hardy and Blackwood tried to persuade Nelson to allow one of the other three-deckers to take the most dangerous position in the lead, and almost succeeded when he agreed to give the position to Captain Harvey's *Temeraire*. According to Blackwood's account, he went back to his frigate but failed to pass the message on. By another account, Lieutenant Yule happened to be forward when he ordered a studding sail to be taken down and reset. Nelson misunderstood and 'rated the lieutenant severely for having, as he supposed, begun to shorten sail without the captain's orders. The studding sail was quickly replaced; and the *Victory*, as the gallant chief intended, continued to lead the column.'[49]

There were three main options in the circumstances – to break the line about a third of the way from its head and cut off a portion to be dealt with by Collingwood, and Blackwood in the *Euryalus* had been told to pass on the message that 'It was the commander-in-chief's intention to cut through the enemy about their 13 or 14 ship...'[50] Or he could head for the enemy flagship, which would be in the centre of the line; or he could go for the head of the line to prevent them escaping back into Cadiz. The course of the *Victory* varied during the approach and Nelson may have considered all three options. According to Beatty, the *Royal Sovereign* passed on intelligence that 'the enemy's commander-in-chief was in a frigate'. This caused Nelson to head about forty-five degrees further north to cut off the retreat, but that may have been influenced by a fear that he was about to escape. But soon he headed for the centre of the line where he could see, among others, the great Spanish four-decker *Santissima Trinidad*, which had escaped him at St Vincent.

Nelson was on the poop when he turned to Blackwood and said, 'I'll now amuse the fleet with a signal.' Lieutenant Pasco was told, 'I wish to say to the fleet, 'England confides [ie is confident that] every man will do his duty', adding, 'You must be quick for I have one more to make, which is for close action.' Pasco pointed out that the word 'confides' would have to be spelled out in the new signal code, whereas 'expects' would be formed by the number 269. Nelson replied, 'That will do, Pasco, make it directly.'[51] The message was not fully understood in some ships at the time, but in the *Victory*, according to Beatty, 'confidence and resolution were strongly portrayed in the countenance of all.'

As they slowly approached a cluster of eight or nine enemy ships in light winds, they were in great danger from their broadsides while virtually unable to reply. As the first shots passed overhead, Nelson ordered Blackwood back to his frigate. According to Beatty, the enemy ships only fired one gun at a time until they found the range, which they did with a hole in the *Victory*'s main topgallant sail. This began 'an awesome and tremendous fire.' A shot damaged the steering wheel and the Master, Atkinson, had to go below to rig ropes to turn the rudder, being relieved occasionally by First-Lieutenant Quillam. Midshipman Pollard on the poop claimed to be the first officer hit, by a splinter from a cannon shot on the right arm, and he checked to see if it was broken.[52] Secretary Scott was in conversation with Hardy when he was cut in two by a ball, and Nelson asked, 'Is that poor Scott who is gone?' Another cannonball hit a party of marines on the poop deck and Nelson ordered Captain Adair to disperse them round the ship. Another passed between Hardy and Nelson, with a splinter bruising Hardy's foot. The two men looked at one another and Nelson observed, 'This is too warm work, Hardy, to last long.' By now the enemy ships were tightly packed and Nelson could not decide where to break through them. He told Hardy to take his pick.

Opening Fire

So far the *Victory* had not fired, but had lost about twenty men killed and thirty wounded.[53] Just after midday, the roles were reversed, she passed under the stern of *Santissima Trinidad* and across the bows of the *Bucentaure*, which had now identified herself as Villeneuve's flagship by raising his colours. According to Roteley, 'we might have thrown a biscuit on board.' Boatswain Willmet fired one carronade into the stern of the *Santissima,* doing great damage, and the other into the *Bucentaure*, to be followed by volleys of balls from the double-shotted guns of the main armament. According to John Brown, '...our ship went right under

The approach to battle showing the irregular Franco-Spanish line and the British in two divisions, led by Collingwood and Nelson.

(Taken from Julian S. Corbett, The Campaign of Trafalgar, *London, 1910)*

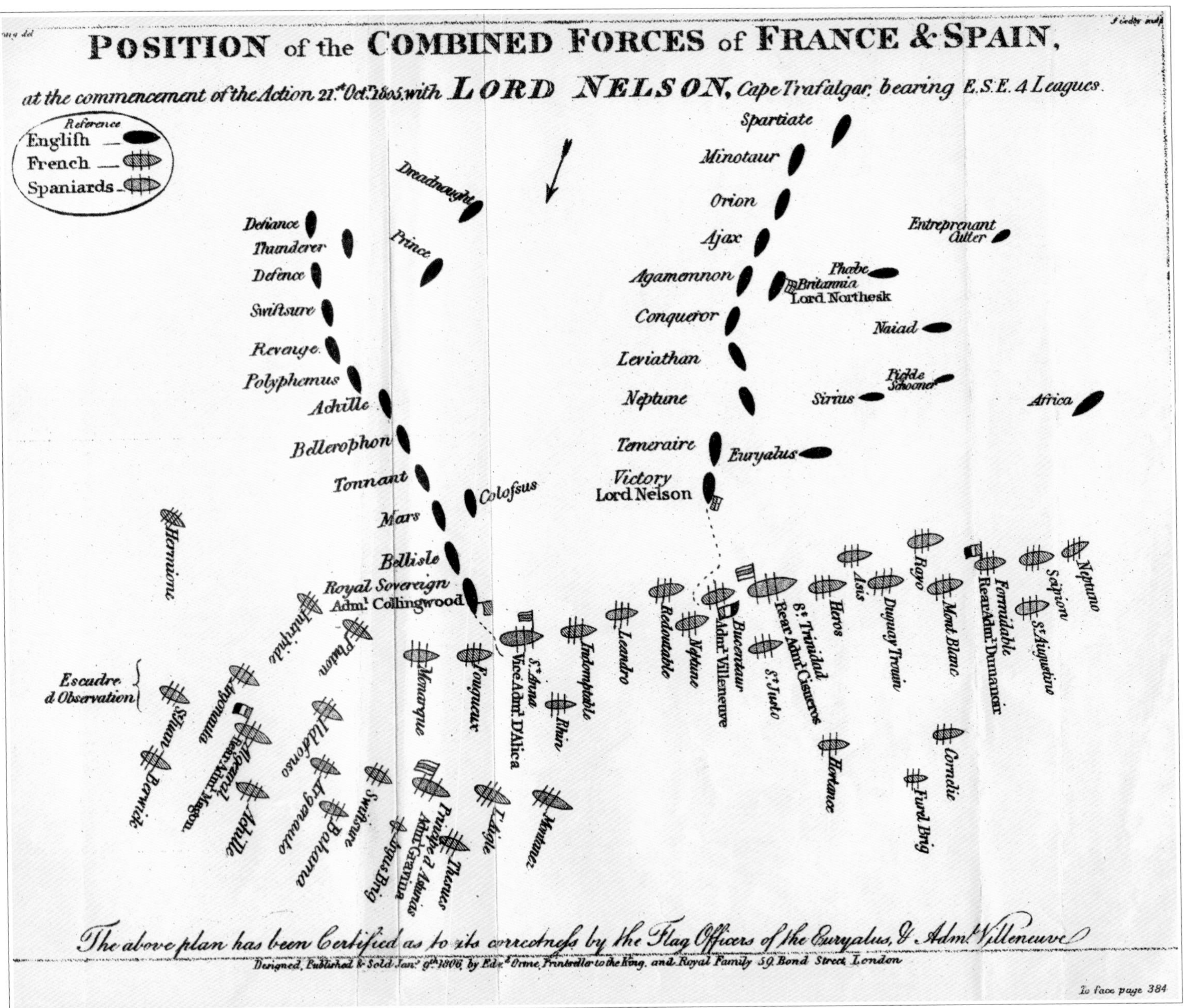

A ball which lodged in the *Victory*'s bow during the battle, still in its original timber.

(© National Maritime Museum, Greenwich, London, KTP1138)

the four-decker stern and we fired five broadsides into her, knocked all her counter in, her three masts went over the side.'[54] The *Bucentaure* was close on the other side and the starboard carronade also had devastating effect. The fifty other gun crews listened, with characteristic avidity, to the deafening crash made by their shot into the French ship's hull, while they themselves were almost overcome by smoke fumes.

As she turned to port to bring the wind on the beam, the *Victory* was confronted by the French 74s *Neptune* and *Redoutable* coming from behind the shattered *Bucentaure*. Captain Lucas of the *Redoutable* had planned to adopt unusual tactics. Realising that he could not beat the British at gunnery, he decided to use small arms fire instead, training his men in musketry and sharpshooting, mounting them around the upper decks and up in the tops to fire down. If that was successful, he planned to board the enemy. The *Neptune* struck first, damaging the *Victory*'s rigging and anchors. Then the *Redoutable* came alongside, closing her gunports to prevent boarding and the two ships were hooked together by damaged rigging. The *Victory* was in real danger from boarding by a ferocious and well-trained crew, but soon the *Temeraire* came along the other side of the *Redoutable* to give some

The beginning of the battle by Pocock. The Franco-Spanish fleet is running diagonally from left to right across the picture, interrupted by Nelson's division in the centre, and Collingwood's beyond that.

(© National Maritime Museum, Greenwich, London, BHC0548)

relief, while another shot from Willmet's great carronade helped clear the *Redoutable's* decks. Meanwhile, the French *Fougeaux* came on her other side, creating a raft of four ships all in violent conflict. Down below, the *Victory*'s starboard guns, some under the command of Lieutenant Yule, were loaded with three shots each and a reduced charge of powder, and depressed as far as possible to avoid passing through the *Redoutable* and hitting the *Temeraire* on the other side. Even so, the muzzles of the guns often touched the enemy side, causing a danger of fire. On the port side, the *Bucentaure* and *Sanitssima Trinidad* were still in range and fire was exchanged with them.

There were heavy casualties on the exposed decks and Second-Lieutenant Roteley was sent down to get marines from the gun crews to replace those lost in the small-arms parties and he saw the battle from below decks for the first time:

> A man should witness a battle in a three-decker from the middle deck, for it beggars all description. There was fire from above, fire from below, besides the fire from the deck I was upon, the guns recoiling with violent reports louder than thunder, the deck heaving and the side straining. I fancied myself in the infernal regions, where every man appeared a devil. Lips might move, but orders and hearing were out of the question, everything was done by signs.'[55]

It was, however, safer below, especially since the *Redoubtable* was not using her cannon which might have penetrated the sides. Beatty later observed that, 'the *Victory* did not lose a man on her lower deck; and had only two wounded on that deck, and these by musket balls.'[56] But it was not cowardice which made it difficult to get Roteley's marines up on deck, for they were totally absorbed in operating the guns. As Roteley observed later, 'I need not inform a seaman the difficulty of separating a man from his gun in the excitement of action. The marines had thrown off their red jackets and appeared in check shirts and blue trousers. There was no distinguishing seaman from marine, all were working like horses.' He got the help of two sergeants and two corporals to detach about thirty men from the guns, 'in some cases by main force'.

Back on the poop, there was carnage as the

Nelson lies wounded to the right of Denis Dighton's picture and is attended by Captain Adair and Sergeant Secker, while Hardy approaches. It also has many other incidents of the action on deck, including marines firing muskets to port and starboard, the captain of a gun lining it up to fire on the left, a midshipman and marine firing back at the *Redoutable*'s top and a seaman on the right using a handspike to manoeuvre a gun into position.

(© National Maritime Museum, Greenwich, London, BHC0552)

Redoutable's sharpshooters fired down and 'scarcely a person in the *Victory* escaped unhurt who was exposed to the enemy's musketry' according to Beatty.[57] Captain Adair ordered, 'Roteley, fire away as fast as you can', then a bullet struck him on the back of the neck and killed him instantly. Lower down on the quarterdeck, Nelson was talking to Hardy and in the act of turning when a shot from the *Redoutable*'s mizzen top struck him in the left shoulder and passed through his chest and lungs to break his spine lower down. He had no doubt about the seriousness of the wound. 'They have done for me at last, Hardy.' Sergeant Secker of the marines and two seamen carried him down four steep ladders to the cockpit, which must have been agonising and highly damaging to a man with a spinal injury.

Nelson Hit

Roteley now found himself in command of the marines on the poop and they were 'exasperated' and fired away at the enemy mizzen top. Midshipman Pollard also went into action:

> ...My attention was arrested by seeing on the tops of the *Redoutable* a number of soldiers in a crouching position, loading and directing their destructive fire on the poop and quarterdeck of the *Victory*. The Signal Quartermaster, called King, was standing by me at the time. I pointed them out to him and there being a number of spare muskets on the signal chest for the use of the marines, I took one of them... As often as I saw the French soldiers rise breast high in the tops to fire on the *Victory's* deck I continued to fire until there was not one to be seen. King, the Quartermaster, in the act of giving me the last parcel of ball cartridge was shot through the forehead and fell dead before me, this event gave me perhaps a great shock.[58]

Pollard gained a reputation as 'the person who shot the man who killed Nelson', but he never made that claim himself and he was not the only one to fire; Roteley's marines had 'every musket levelled at that top and in five minutes not a man was left alive in it.'

After that, the marines turned their fire on the decks of the *Redoutable,* taking care not to fire over them to the higher *Temeraire*. Gradually, she was defeated and parts of her began to burn. Roteley reported that Hardy sent him forward to try to get on board with a party of marines under Sergeant Secker, but the ships were beginning to drift apart and the gap was too big to jump. Therefore, he sent the sergeant aft to get a boat to take them over, but he found that Midshipmen Collingwood and Ogilvie had already gone across in the last undamaged boat to take possession of the ship. Roteley now had time to look out from the poop of the *Victory*. 'Never did I behold a thing so awfully grand. Straggling ships engaging ship to ship, one of the enemy's ships on fire and expecting to see her explode every moment. A number of ships laying like hulks upon the surface of the water totally dismasted.'[59] But *Victory*'s battle was not over.

Death in the Cockpit

While the great, noisy and world-changing affair was going on outside, a much more intimate and moving drama was taking place in the dim light of the *Victory*'s cockpit. Surgeon Beatty was first aware of Nelson's arrival when several of the wounded men called to him. He was laid against a knee in the cockpit with Purser Burke and Chaplain Scott supporting him, the former apparently forgiven for his lateness in arriving in the ship and now intimate with his chief. He was supported 'in nearly a semi-recumbent posture, the only one that was supportable to him.' According to Scott he was 'perfectly sensible the whole time, but compelled to speak in broken sentences, which pain and suffering prevented him always from connecting.'[60] The admiral rejected successive suggestions from Beatty, Scott, Burke and Hardy that he might recover. He told Beatty, 'he felt a gush of blood every minute within his breast: that he had no feeling in the lower part of his body; and that his breathing was difficult, and attended with very severe pain about the part of the spine where he was confident the ball had struck.'

He was anxious to speak to Hardy but at first he had to be satisfied with his aide Midshipman Bulkeley. Eventually, the captain was able to leave the deck and Nelson asked him about the battle. Hardy replied 'we have got twelve or fourteen of the enemy's ships in our possession, but five of their van have tacked, and shew [sic] an intention of bearing down upon the *Victory*.' Hardy went back on deck but came back again later. Nelson told him he had bargained for twenty captures and instructed him to get ready to anchor the fleet after the battle. He was reassured that his body would not be thrown overboard as battle casualties often were, and asked Hardy to kiss him, after which he said, 'Now I am satisfied. Thank God I have done my duty.' He apparently had doubts about his adultery and asked Scott, 'Doctor, I have *not* been a *great* sinner.' He left Emma Hamilton and his daughter Horatia as a 'legacy to my country', which was never likely to be honoured, and became speechless about fifteeen minutes after Hardy left. After another five minutes, Nelson's steward alerted the surgeon who felt his pulse and his cold forehead, but he was still alive and opened his eyes. After another five minutes, at about 4.30pm, the steward reported that 'he believed His Lordship had expired' and Beatty had to agree. He had spent two and three-quarter hours in agony while the battle was fought overhead.[61]

Around him in the cockpit the scene was even more horrific, for Nelson was not the only casualty. Beatty was disturbed to find that 'one of his dearest friends', the fretful amateur artist Lieutenant Ram, was dead.[62] Seaman John Smith, the second of that name in the ship's muster book, had a 'lacerated wound of the leg, gastroenervic muscle torn halfway down the leg', and was sent to the *Sussex* hospital ship after the battle. Able Seaman Richard Jeeves suffered 'Amputation of the thigh above the trachonter major. He had lost a great deal of blood before he was brought to the cockpit...' He '...died shortly after the operation, from the great violence as the habit pertained the removal of a large portion of the body...' In all, the *Victory* had 132 casualties, including fifty-seven killed and seventy-five wounded.

The End of the Battle

Up on deck, Lewis Roteley observed as Rear-Admiral Dumanoir, in command of five ships of the Franco-Spanish van which had not been engaged, began a belated counterattack. 'Captain Hardy therefore ordered some of our least damaged ships to our assistance, and everything was got ready to give them a warm reception.' Most of the quarterdeck guns and their tackle were badly damaged but he made one ready by shifting parts from others. 'When ready I had the honour of pointing and firing the first gun at Dumanoir's flagship, but he did not appear inclined to close with us but kept at long shot distance.' They kept up fire until 5pm when they made off, leaving one of their number behind, the Spanish *Neptuno,* damaged and soon to be captured. That was the end of the fighting, but the French *Achille* continued to burn and blew up an hour later. The log of the *Spartiate* recorded:

> At 5.20[pm] the firing ceased – observed fourteen ships of the enemy in our possession, including the *Santissima Trinidad*, and the *Santa Anna*, three-deckers, two admiral's ships, and the *Bucentaure*, Admiral Villeneuve... observed the *Belleisle* totally dismasted – the *Temeraire* between two enemy's ships lashed alongside one of their mainmasts, across the *Temeraire*'s booms – the *Victory* and *Colossus* had lost their mizzen masts – other ways much cut up – eight of the enemy's ships totally dismasted.[63]

The frigate *Polyphemus* took the *Victory* in tow, leading a hawser through her stern window, with the other end led through a middle deck bow port on the flagship to the riding bitts.[64] As Nelson may have predicted, a huge storm was building up in the Atlantic and before midday on the 22nd it began to hit the damaged ships with their exhausted crews, and dangerous position off a rocky lee shore. For many, the storm was worse than the battle – it lasted much longer, it was beyond human control and the men were already exhausted before it started. The *Victory* was not the worst damaged, the *Belleisle* was totally dismasted and needed a tow from the frigate *Naiad*. According to Lieutenant Nicolas:

> The hours dragged tediously on, and death appeared in every gust of the tempest. In battle the chances were equal, and it was possible for many to escape; but shipwreck in such a hurricane was certain destruction to all, and the doubtful situation of the ship kept the mind in a perpetual state of terror. In this horrible suspense each stroke of the bell, as it proclaimed the hour, sounded the knell of our approaching destiny, for none could expect to escape the impending danger...[65]

At last, at 7pm on 24 October, the *Victory* dropped anchor in Gibraltar Bay, a few hours after the *Belleisle*.

10 AFTER TRAFALGAR

Taking Stock

At Gibraltar there was time to assess the physical and mental damage to ships and men. Midshipman Rivers counted ninety-two 'most dangerous' shot holes on the starboard side, presumably close to the waterline so that they could cause leaks, and forty-two holes to port.[1] Midshipman R. F. Roberts reported:

> The hull is much damaged by shot in a number of different places, particularly in the wales, strings and spirketting, and some between wind and water, several beams, knees and riders, shot through and broke, the starboard cathead shot away; the rails and timbers of the head and stem cut by shot; several of the ports damaged and port timbers cut off; the channels and chain-plate damaged by shot and the falling of the mizzen mast; the principal part of the bulkheads, half-ports and portsashes thrown overboard in clearing ship for action.[2]

Rivers noted that the figurehead had a cherub on each side, the starboard one with a blue-painted ribbon representing the seamen and the other a red one for the marines. That one had lost an arm and the blue one a leg, and he noted that among the crew, sailors had mostly lost arms and the marines legs, perhaps because of their positions in the ship.[3]

Some of the crews were allowed ashore at Gibraltar, and those from ships in the thick of the action, such as William Robinson from the *Revenge,* regarded themselves as greatly superior to the others:

> Some of the crews belonging to the different ships in the fleet would occasionally meet on shore, and one would say to another tauntingly, on enquiring to what ship he belonged; 'Oh! you belong to one of the ships that did not come up till the battle was nearly over;' and others would be heard to say, 'Oh! you belong to one of the Boxing Twelves, come and have some black strap and Malaga wine,' at the same time giving them a

Clarkson Stanfield's painting shows the *Victory*, largely dismasted, being towed towards Gibraltar after the battle.

(© National Maritime Museum, Greenwich, London, PAH8042)

The ship had been superficially repaired by the time J.M.W Turner saw her in the Thames Estuary on the way to Chatham.

(© The Tate Gallery, London, Do8183)

hearty shake by the hand. This was signifying that the heat of the battle was borne by the twelve ships which had first engaged and broke the line.[4]

No doubt the *Victory*'s men were high among this elite band, but many of them were suffering from what we might call post-traumatic stress and Lieutenant Yule wrote to his wife:

> ...The horrors of an action during the time it lasts and or a short time afterwards makes everything around you appear in a different shape to what it did before...The action will be by the nation conceived as a glorious one but when the devastation is considered how can we glory in it? How many orphans and fatherless has it made?... the loss of our chief has thrown a gloom around that nothing but the society of family and friends can dispel. That quarter-deck which was formerly crowded is emptied. The happy scenes we formerly witness are now laid aside, the theatre, the music, the dancing which accompanied the dull part of our time is laid aside. We look to the seat of an old messmate and find he is gone – we ask for such and such a man – he was killed, sir, in the action, he lost a leg.[5]

Lewis Roteley described what happened to Nelson's corpse after the action:

> To preserve the body a large cask called a leaguer was procured and lashed on its end to the middle deck. The body was brought up from the cockpit by two men which I received from [them] and placed it head foremost in the cask. The head of the cask was then replaced and filled with brandy and a marine sentinel placed over it by night or day so that it was impossible for anyone to approach it unseen. It remained in this

This view of the quarterdeck is more finished than most of the sketches Turner made on board the *Victory*. It shows the decks largely deprived of guns, apart from a pair of very light ones on the poop. The captain's cabin in the stern is stripped out, as it would have been in action.

(© The Tate Gallery, London, D08725)

> state for several days when one of these sentinels came to me in great consternation and said there was something the matter with the cask. I went to the spot and found the head of the cask heaving and raised up ready to burst. A gimlet was procured and vent given and all was right. There had been an escape of air from the body which had caused this phenomenon, alarmed the sentinel and I suppose gave rise to the report of 'Tapping the Admiral'.[6]

Repairs were carried out, including a jury-fore topmast and a spare anchor was found in the dockyard. The *Victory* set sail on 4 November and entered the English Channel on 1 December, to be saluted by the naval ships she passed. She arrived in the Solent on the 4th and anchored at St Helens at 2pm, with Nelson's flag flying at half mast, while all the ships at Spithead lowered their flags in the same way. She was visited by the artist Arthur Devis who made sketches for a painting of the death of Nelson. Due to the damaged state of the ship, it was feared that the body might have to be unloaded and taken across country, but more emergency repairs were carried out and she proceeded on the 10th. She anchored off Dover and was seen by Thomas Pattenden, who observed, 'yesterday and today the *Victory* with the corps[e] of Lord Nelson on board came to anchor off the harbour. The wind was strong from the north and north-west which prevented her going round the North Foreland.'[7] Nelson's body was taken out of the cask and put into a plain elm coffin under a canopy of colours. The *Victory* arrived off the Nore on the 22nd, where the ships at anchor lowered their colours, but it was the 23rd before the weather moderated and the body could be transferred to the *Chatham* yacht for the voyage up river to Greenwich. The great artist JMW Turner arrived on board at this point and set about to fill several notebooks showing details of the ship and some of the crew, as well as a larger drawing of the quarterdeck. Having said her last farewell to Nelson, the *Victory* went to Chatham for much-needed repairs.[8]

The Funeral

Nelson's funeral was planned as a national event on 8 January 1806, perhaps the grandest non-Royal funeral ever staged in the country. The body was to lie in state in the Royal Naval Hospital at Greenwich, and Chaplain Scott, being 'stupid with grief', lodged nearby to watch over it. After that, it was taken up the Thames in a procession watched by vast crowds, in a barge which also carried Lieutenants Pasco and Yule and the Master Thomas Atkinson. Forty-three seaman and a dozen marines were to represent the *Victory* at the funeral, presumably chosen because they were least likely to desert or be seduced by the pleasures of the capital city after nearly three years at sea. Seventeen of them were petty officers, including Master-At-Arms Henry Ford, and the miserable Benjamin Stevenson. Eighteen more were experienced able seamen, with only five ordinary seamen and three landsmen. The marine party was headed by Sergeant James Secker who had carried Nelson's body below, and he was assisted by Corporal William Cogswell.[9]

The seamen marched as part of a great procession through London, 'two and two, in their ordinary dress,

Nelson's funeral. The scene inside St Paul's Cathedral with captured flags hung from the arches. The marines and seamen of the *Victory* are in the central area as the coffin is lowered into the grave.

(© National Maritime Museum, Greenwich, London, PAH7331)

with black silk handkerchiefs and stockings, and crape on their hats.' The body reached St Paul's Cathedral in the afternoon, with twelve of the *Victory*'s men carrying it on their shoulders while the others bore the battle-damaged colours from the flagship. Then, according to the official report in the *London Gazette*:

> The Comptroller, Treasurer and Steward of His Lordship's household then broke their staves, and gave the pieces to the Garter, who threw them into the grave, in which the flags of the *Victory* furled up by the sailors, were deposited. – These brave fellows, however, desirous of retaining some memorials of their great and favourite Commander, had torn off a considerable part of the largest flag, of which most of them retained a portion.[10]

Many portions of the flag can be found in museums today, and still appear occasionally at auction. And the selection of reliable seamen was not entirely successful – Able Seaman William Martin, Ordinary Seaman George Prescott and Landsman Thomas Matthews did indeed 'run' from the group.

Repaired Again

The Admiralty ordered Chatham Dockyard to survey the *Victory* as soon as she arrived, and on Boxing Day 1805 they reported optimistically that she would have to be docked and would require five or six weeks work. Able Seaman Brown wrote, 'we scarce[ly] have room to move the ship, so full of nobility coming down from London to see the ship so full of shot holes.'[11] The ship was given a certain amount of priority among all the other repairs, but by 11th January it was not clear whether she would be ready to dock by the next spring tide. Delays continued, but on 27 February the Chatham officers reported that she would at last be docked, while her crew would be distributed 'to greater advantage.' In fact, most of them went to the new second rate *Ocean,* including Benjamin Stevenson who was no happier when he wrote to his family from the ship on 4 July. But somehow he was reconciled to naval service, he was appointed boatswain of the brig *Halcyon* in 1809 and had made £273 in prize money by 1812.

The *Victory* finally re-entered her birthplace, Number Two Dock, on 6 March. It did not take long to discover that "the copper for the time it has been on is much worn' and needed to be replaced. It was no longer intended to put her back in service immediately and in April plans were made for airing and drying her in the ordinary. She was finally ready for undocking on 3 May. The dockyard officials continued to examine her and in October they reported that the drying and airing had proved beneficial and that she was now 'in a state to be brought forward for service.' By March 1807, it was

One of several existing fragments of the *Victory*'s flag, authenticated by its weave.

(© National Maritime Museum, Greenwich, London, AAA0924)

planned to dock her again, but on 11 April the tides were 'so very slack' that it had to be postponed for a fortnight and she entered Number Two Dock yet again on the 23rd to have her copper re-nailed during a short stay.[12]

The *Victory*'s headlong charge into battle highlighted one of the great weaknesses of the current form of construction – the structure of the bow was very weak above the level of the upper deck. Robert Seppings had already noticed this in his capacity as Master Shipwright at Chatham. When he cut down the *Namur* from a three to a two-decker in 1804, he got permission to leave the original bow structure intact. He wanted to build up the bows in other ships, but doubted if the conservative Navy Board would support him. He described his reaction when the *Victory* arrived for repair:

> ...It appeared that this ship had suffered very severely on the main deck, when in the act of bearing down on the enemy, in consequence of having only a flimsy beak-head, instead of continuing the regular built circular form to the upper part of the forecastle; for it was evident, that even the common grape shot had penetrated the birthing of the beak-head, when shot of the largest size had not made their way through the circular and regular built bow below.

He 'communicated to Captain Sir Thomas Hardy, who commanded her, what I had done in cutting down the *Namur*, and Sir Thomas was equally anxious for the change with myself; but all innovations are attended with difficulties and I could not get it generally adopted until the year 1811.'[13]

In November 1807, the Admiralty ordered the *Victory* to be made ready for sea 'with all possible dispatch', but the optimism about the state of her hull had dissipated. It was proposed to remove the internal structure of riders to air the planks and the Chatham officers wanted to put her into dock again to make it easier to move heavy materials. She was 'somewhat hogged' after long years of service. She was docked on the 18th and at the end of the month it was reported that, 'we find her to have received very considerable injury from the rapid progress of the dry-rot.' Although she had benefitted from the airing and the vegetation which caused the rot had been destroyed, it had 'made great progress' in the internal planking before the remedy was applied. The officers, including Master Shipwright Robert Seppings, were highly critical of the policy of sending the ship to sea so soon after her great repair – '...between four and five years since, the repair of this ship for the hull only cost the sum of £46,157 and many thousands expended since...' They were convinced that 'commissioning her immediately as she is launched or after receiving a great repair' was what did the damage. They recommended the ancient policy of 'snail creeping – defined by James Ballingal in 1832 as 'cutting small scores or channels on the faying [ie joining] surfaces of the timbers and planks'.[14] She was ready to undock by the end of December.[15]

On 11 November 1807, the ageing ship was reduced to the second-rate, which in practice meant a reduction in guns, rig and crew numbers. As early as April 1806 her gun armament had been under consideration, and the officials were not enthusiastic about the non-regulation 68-pounder carronades. Instead, they proposed a more conventional combination on the quarterdeck and forecastle – long 12-pounders 'in the wake of the rigging', where the blast of a carronade might set the shrouds on fire, and 32-pounder carronades in other places so that the forecastle would have one carronade and long-gun per side, and the quarterdeck would had two long-guns and eight carronades. The reduction to a second-rate also meant that the 24-pounders of the middle deck were replaced.[16] In March 1808 the *Victory* was listed as carrying twenty-eight 32-pounders on the lower deck, thirty 18-pounders on the middle deck and thirty 12-pounders on the upper deck. The quarterdeck and forecastle had six 12-pounders and ten 32-pounder carronades.[17]

New and smaller masts were made at Deptford, although there was much confusion over dimensions. It was found that the mainmast was too short and it was proposed to add twelve inches to its foot. At first, the foremast was thought to be ten inches too long, but it was soon discovered to be three feet short and Chatham recommended using a standard mast from a 74-gun ship rather than adding a piece to the bottom. The officers asked if new sails were to be made, or the old ones cut down, and eventually it was agreed that new ones would be made under contract as the yard sailmakers were busy.[18]

The Baltic

Many of Nelson's sailors believed that their victory at Trafalgar would end the war and allow them to go home, but they were severely disappointed. Yet again, Britain was victorious at sea while France was supreme on land, with Napoleon's destruction of the Austrian armies at Ulm and Austerlitz in October and December 1805. Prime Minister William Pitt reportedly said, 'roll up that map; it will not be wanted these ten years.'[19] Pitt died in January 1806 and there was no-one of sufficient stature to fill his place. But neither side in the war intended to give way, Napoleon instituted his Continental System to ruin the trade of what he called a 'nation of shopkeepers.' By the Berlin and Milan Decrees he forbade the ports of Europe to trade with

Map of the Baltic, showing the major powers in the region – Denmark-Norway, Sweden, Prussia and Russia, which included Finland.

(Taken from SR Gardiner, A School Altlas of English History, *London 1902)*

Britain, while the British retaliated by banning any port which enforced the decrees from trading at all, hopefully sending frigates and sloops to enforce this. The Royal Navy had to expand to cope with this, from 569 ships in 1805 to 673 in 1810.

British trade with the Baltic had increased tenfold since the wars began in 1793, largely because it was an entrance for manufactured goods and colonial produce to northern Europe, while most of the south was under French control or occupation. Furthermore, it was a vital source of naval stores. As well as iron ore from Sweden, the region supplied Russian mast timber, oak for planking and fir for decks of both naval and merchant ships. Most important of all, ninety percent of hemp used for rope-making came from Russia and attempts to grow it elsewhere had failed. It was essential to keep the sea open to trade despite Napoleon's attempts to seal it off.

Nelson's battle off Copenhagen in 1801 had been settled almost amicably by negotiation, but in 1807 the Royal Navy carried out a far more brutal and devastating attack on the city, though the Danes had done nothing more than maintain their independence and their fleet. This time, troops were landed and the city was shelled, causing much damage. The report of 2,000 civilian casualties was probably greatly exaggerated but it caused huge and lasting bitterness from the Danes, who now became a firm ally of France – though without their battlefleet which had been captured or destroyed by the British. Meanwhile, the Russians, forced into an unlikely alliance with the French, were conquering Finland from Britain's last remaining ally, Sweden. This was the complex and volatile situation which a commander-in-chief on the Baltic would be faced with. It has never been established whether the Admiralty's choice for the post was a product of great insight and prescience, or just fortuitous.

Vice-Admiral Sir James Saumarez was a Guernsey man whose uncle had served with distinction alongside Keppel in Anson's circumnavigation of 1740–44, but was killed in action three years later. Young James had a rapid rise and was captain of the 74-gun *Russell* at the Battle of the Saintes in 1782, when he showed great initiative, as he did at St Vincent fifteen years later. Two years older than Nelson, he served as senior captain under him in the Nile campaign of 1798 but was never under his spell. Nominally, he was second-in-command but Nelson never really recognised that and preferred to work through his friend Thomas Troubridge. Historians have made much of Saumarez's confession to his wife that, 'did the chief responsibility rest with me, I fear it would be more than my too irritable nerves would bear.' – but the Nile campaign was an exceptionally stressful one, which arguably damaged Nelson's mental health for some years afterwards. In the morning after the battle he had the temerity to criticise Nelson's organisation, to the admiral's annoyance. In July 1801 Saumarez was a rear-admiral and led an attack on a French squadron in Algeciras Bay near Gibraltar. HMS *Hannibal* was driven ashore and lost, but Saumarez retreated to Gibraltar and refitted his ships in record time. The French had now been reinforced by Spanish ships but Saumarez captured one French ship and destroyed three Spaniards.

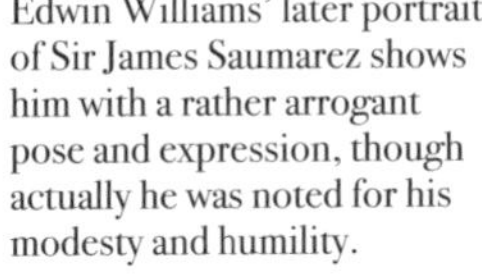

Edwin Williams' later portrait of Sir James Saumarez shows him with a rather arrogant pose and expression, though actually he was noted for his modesty and humility.

(© National Maritime Museum, Greenwich, London, BHC3010)

Saurarez was as religious as Nelson, but had a very happy marriage in which his wife Martha was his main confidante. He was deeply honest and highly sensitive about his honour, though largely indifferent to money, unlike many officers. He seemed aloof at first, but did not inflict his religion on others and was popular with officers and men. His bilingual upbringing in Guernsey perhaps gave him a flair for languages, and an understanding of other cultures which Nelson, for one, lacked. On 20 February 1808, Lord Mulgrave, First Lord of the Admiralty, wrote to him offering a fleet of twelve or thirteen ships of the line for 'the important service of attempting to destroy the Russian fleet and of affording protection to His Majesty's firm and faithful ally, the King of Sweden.' He was to have the assistance of two very able rear-admirals, Sir Samuel Hood, a cousin of his namesake who had flown his flag from the *Victory* fifteen years before, and Richard Keats, who knew the area well. Saumarez wrote back that he could not 'for a moment hesitate' to accept such a responsible role.[20]

Saumarez already knew the *Victory*, for he had been her seventh-lieutenant in 1780. By this time, she had long been overtaken by much larger ships, the 110-gun *Ville de Paris* and *Hibernia* were already in service, and the 120-gun *Caledonia* was about to be launched. *Victory* herself, though reduced to a second-rate, was still a three-decker and provided grandeur as well as space for a headquarters, for such ships were extremely rare in the Baltic. The large ships of the Danish Navy had been captured or destroyed, whilst the Swedes had nothing bigger than a 74. Under Catherine the Great (1762–1800), the Russians had built a class of eight first-rates of the *Ches'ma* class based on the *Victory*'s lines. They had fallen into decay by this time, but the 110-gun *Gavriil*, an expanded version of the class, had been launched in 1802 and was still in service. She was accompanied by the 130-gun *Blagodat*, built in reaction to the Spanish *Santissima Trinidad*. She had only once ventured beyond the Gulf of Finland to attack Swedish Pomerania in 1805.[21]

The *Victory* already had a certain amount of historical value after Trafalgar but she was not too valuable in what might be a risky situation, and suitable for a command which was regarded as less important than the North Sea, Channel and Mediterranean. The Captain of the Fleet was George Johnstone Hope, a member of a Scottish naval family who had commanded the *Defence* at Trafalgar. Though he was highly competent, relations could become strained with too much time together and Saumarez complained to his wife in 1811 of, 'passing so much of the day together, which often become[s] dull *et trés ennuyant*... we are too great for each other...'[22] The flag captain was another Guernsey man, Phillip Dumaresq, a cousin who had served under him for much of the wars and was his flag lieutenant at Algeciras. James Squire became master of the fleet with overall responsibility as adviser to the admiral, while Joseph Nelson was the master of the *Victory*. Saumarez was deeply religious and William Cooley was appointed chaplain. William Rivers stayed on as gunner, but the ship had two new standing officers – James Phillips became boatswain while John Barton the carpenter was superannuated and replaced by Edward Hogben in February.

After the death of Pitt in 1806, British politics tended to be fragmented and divided. The King was out of action, due to what was believed to be madness, from February 1811 and his son the Prince Regent was not respected. The period saw a duel between the cabinet ministers Castlereagh and Canning and the only assassination of a British prime minister, Spencer Perceval, in 1812. There were three different First Lords of the Admiralty in 1808–12, while public and parliamentary attention was focussed on the expanding war in Spain rather than on the Baltic, which provided far fewer dramatic events. All this gave Saumarez an unusually free hand in politics as well as naval affairs.

The *Victory* was ready for sea by 17 March, but Saumarez's arrival was delayed while a new scheme was set in place to provide a force of 10,000 troops in support of the Swedes, who faced a possible invasion across the narrow Oresund from Denmark. Saumarez finally arrived on board at the Nore on 22 April and hoisted his flag. He sailed on the 25th and anchored in Hawke Roads off Gothenburg on 9 May. The *Victory* became a centre for social life in a town which had expanded vastly to deal with British trade. Marianne Ehrenström, wife of the Swedish military commander, was one of those who visited. She wrote, 'it became a race to get hold of a skiff to look closer at this fine spectacle, this imposing picture formed by three ships of the line, frigates and more than two hundred sail.' She and her party hired a sloop and when they arrived alongside *Victory*, 'English officers showed themselves on deck to receive us, some embarking on our sloop to help the ladies to be hoisted on board in large barrels, formed as armchairs and dressed in different flags to bring them over the high sides.' Saumarez showed her the spot where Nelson had died, and she looked at the officers' cabins, which she considered very comfortable and with shelves containing the works of the latest British authors. She found the seamen's food was 'tasty soup, highly-flavoured and well-cooked meat and good white bread.' She visited the sick bay, 'a paragon of tidiness and functionality.' There were only two seamen in it, one of whom refused to take his medicine. She spoke to him in English, '"Do not refuse me this. Spare your life for your country and its friends". He sat up like a spring, smiled at me, took the cup and swallowed it in one gulp and said "God bless you, dear Lady."' A few days later there was a ball on board with the ships dressed overall, and the visits were returned with Saumarez and his officers spending time ashore.[23]

Sir John Moore, now a lieutenant-general and commander-in-chief of the proposed Swedish expeditionary force, arrived on board the *Victory* by ship's boat. He had been to Stockholm to discuss plans with the erratic King Gustav IV Adolf, but his tact had not improved since he had clashed with Hood and Nelson off Corsica in 1794. He dismissed the King's ideas out of hand and found himself under house arrest, from which he escaped. It soon became clear that there was no way in which the British troops could intervene effectively, while Saumarez found it a trial as his ship served as the headquarters for both the navy and the army. He endured 'a week of considerable anxiety and bustle, for exclusive of much official business... I have in addition had most of the general officers to dine with me and yesterday we were not less than twenty at dinner.' Saumarez was not sorry when the troops were sent home in transports, for a new front against Napoleon was developing.

The Spanish had revolted against French rule and that included 12,000 men in Denmark in the service of Napoleon who gathered on Langeland, Funen and other islands and wanted to go home. The *Victory* was needed to cover the transports which took them away, and delayed Saumarez's joining with the Swedish fleet in their base at Karlskrona. As a result, he missed an action off the entrance to the Gulf of Finland, when Hood and Captain Thomas Byam Martin (who had been so impressed with the stern of the *Royal George* as a boy) attacked a much larger Russian force and destroyed the *Sevelod*. It was the Russians' first experience of the ferocity of a British naval attack, and it made them extremely wary of it afterwards. It also showed that the Swedish fleet was poorly manned and trained. The Russians were now blockaded in Port Baltic or Paldisk near Reval, now Tallinn. Saumarez had to choose whether to risk all and attack them behind their defences, but decided against it and offered terms, which the Russians rejected. Hope went on leave and Byam Martin of the *Implacable* took over as captain of the fleet, but soon found he had to 'engage in a much more arduous duty than I expected.' He was not disappointed when Hope returned after a month.[24] Saumarez returned to Karlskrona at the end of September, then sailed for England in the *Victory* on 3 November, leaving Keats in charge for the Baltic winter when fleets were immobilised by ice over much of the sea. He was able to confer with ministers (who were not entirely satisfied with his lack of aggression) and visit his home in Guernsey.

To Spain

There was no such rest for the crew of the *Victory*. At the other end of Napoleon's empire, Sir John Moore had taken charge of the British army in Spain but, after a brilliant campaign, he was forced to retreat to the north-west by larger forces under the personal command of Napoleon. The *Victory*, now captained by John Searle, was one of the ships chosen to evacuate the army, along with a large fleet of transports. She was sent to Vigo with the even larger *Ville de Paris*, a 98 and three 74s but there was some doubt about where the army was to be found, compounded by a dragoon who got drunk and failed to deliver a vital message. Eventually, they were ordered to Corunna but the ships had to be towed out of harbour in light winds. The *Victory* was off the port by the evening of 14 January 1809, but was unable to enter 'from the great number of transports working in.' Eventually, she anchored at 11.30am the next morning and in the afternoon the crew observed, 'the British army on the heights near the town in action with the French army occupying the next heights.' Boat crews worked hard to embark troops and baggage, including thirty officers, 291 other ranks, twenty-one women and one child of the 81st Regiment of Foot. There was more heavy firing ashore in the afternoon of the 16th and next day the British troops retreated into the town, while the *Victory*'s carpenters fitted up berths for wounded men. The French set up a battery to fire into the harbour which caused many of the transport ships to 'cut and run' before they were fully loaded and even the *Victory* had to shift her berth half a mile further out. Sir John Moore was dead by this time and according to Thomas Wolfe's famous but inaccurate poem:

> We buried him darkly at the dead of night,
> The sods with our bayonets turning.

The embarkation of the army was completed early in the morning of the 18th and the boats were hauled in, though they had to be hoisted out again to help the *Barfleur* transfer some men. They set sail that afternoon, while the body of Lieutenant Hanwell of the 81st was committed to the deep. They headed for Plymouth but encountered strong gales on the way and had to reduce sail. They dropped anchor in Cawsand Bay near Plymouth on the morning of the 23rd, but it took several days to get the passengers ashore in bad weather.[25]

The evacuation of Corunna as seen from the hill above the town. The *Victory* is not to be seen in this picture, and there are very few ships offshore, but the harbour is very crowded, mostly with merchant shipping.

(© National Maritime Museum, Greenwich, London, PZ0007)

Turmoil in Sweden

Victory arrived back off Gothenburg on 8 May and anchored in Vinga Sound (known as Wingo to the British) fourteen miles out of Gothenburg, which was now her regular base. According to Masters Squire and Nelson, 'the best place to anchor in Wingo Sound is a line between Butto and Busker, in 12 or 14 fathoms water, good holding ground.'[26] During Saumarez's absence there was coup against the unstable King Gustav IV Adolf, witnessed by Lieutenant John Ross of the *Victory* who had been sent to liaise with the Swedes:

> ...The conspirators... entered and told the King he must leave Stockholm. Drawing his sword, His Majesty made a pass at one of the conspirators; in the mean time, the General seized the staff of power, and ordered the others to seize the King... [He] immediately escaped and .. called loudly for help. Some of the conspirators... called to the soldiers on duty, "The King is mad;" on which they secured him, and in the evening he was removed to Drottingen...[27]

His place was taken by his uncle as Charles XIII and he was accepted by the British, though not formally recognised by them.

An elaborate convoy system was needed to maintain the Baltic trade, organised by the Admiralty, the merchants William and Phillip Emes, Saumarez during his winter visits to London and by his secretary Samuel Champion on board the *Victory* in Vinga Sound. The trade was mostly carried in ships registered in neutral countries such as the United States, with carefully forged papers to show that they were trading with countries other than Britain – though they also carried permits from the British Privy Council, and their naval escorts would ensure that they did not head for French territory with valuable naval stores. Outgoing ships gathered in the Thames, Humber, Forth and Orkney and sailed in fortnightly convoys. They anchored in Vinga Sound under the protection of the *Victory* and her consorts, where they were split into groups for the dangerous passage into the Baltic proper. At the beginning they used the straight and narrow passage through the Oresund, or the 'Sound', as the British called it, but that proved too dangerous. They were obliged to use the intricate channels through the Storebaelt or 'Belt', often spending several days and anchoring at night under the protection of British ships of the line. Though the Danish Navy had lost all its large ships, they built up a fleet of more than 280 rowing gunboats which could harass trade and even overcome frigates in a calm on the narrow waters – in October 1808 they even attacked and damaged the 64-gun *Africa*.[28] Once out of the Belt, the next danger was the privateers stationed in the Danish island of Bornholm and the tiny Ertholms, which Saumarez declined to attack in 1808–9. Once clear, the convoys dispersed for they could not appear off their destinations under obvious British escort. The returning convoys, mostly loaded with naval stores, assembled at Karlskrona or Hano off the Swedish coast. They often built up to considerable size especially if delayed by bad weather, or towards the end of the season when ship owners tried to fit in a second voyage – 200 or 300 ships were not uncommon, and even convoys of 500 might be seen. The passage through the Belt was always hazardous, but by 1809 the system was well established and the trade was maintained.[29]

The Danish royal line was in danger of failing due to lack of issue and a crown prince had to be elected by the Rikstag of the Estates, who made a surprising choice in August 1810. Jean Bernadotte came from a middle-class French family and served as a private in the pre-revolutionary army before rising to the rank of marshal through his ability. He commanded French forces in the Baltic region and he impressed Swedish officers with his good treatment of prisoners. Other candidates as crown prince were too close to the enemies in Denmark and Russia, while the army felt the need for a soldier as national leader. At first, Saumarez was horrified at the choice and wrote, 'I very much apprehend that the election of a French general to the Heir Apparent to the Crown of Sweden must be with a view to detaching the country from all intercourse with England.'[30] But he later moderated this view and granted Bernadotte permission to cross the Belt from Denmark in the Swedish royal yacht. Two convoys totalling of 1,124 ships had gathered because of delays, and they formed a part of a demonstration of British sea power. According to Ross:

> The day was very fine; the fleet was anchored in a close, compact body, with the *Victory* in the centre, bearing the Admiral's red flag at the fore, surrounded by six ships of the line, and six frigates and sloops disposed for the complete protection of the convoy. The yacht, with a Swedish flag, containing the Crown Prince, passing within a mile of the *Victory*, was distinctly seen, and escorted by some barges from the men of war until past the whole of the ships; the convoy soon after weighed anchor, when the Royal stranger had the pleasure of seeing them all under sail and proceeding to their destination, regardless of the enemies who occupied the adjacent shores.

The sight was especially dramatic to a landsman like Bernadotte, who later told Ross that it made a deep impression and 'conveyed some idea of the wealth and power of the British nation'. It was 'the most wonderful and beautiful sight he had ever beheld, being one of which he had never formed an idea.'[31]

Bernadotte soon showed that he was not Napoleon's puppet and began to devote himself to Swedish national interests. This included relations with Britain, partly to maintain trade, but also to gain possession of Norway from Denmark in compensation for the loss of Finland to Russia. That could only be done with a British alliance, since the Danes were now staunch allies of France. Nevertheless, Bernadotte was under strong pressure from Napoleon to go in the opposite direction. On 17 November 1810, two days before Saumarez's main fleet left the area for the winter, Sweden declared war on Britain. To many, the situation looked bleak indeed, with no ally left in the Baltic, and some argued that only another devastating attack had any chance of remedying it. Saumarez knew better, his contacts with Sweden's rulers convinced him that the declaration was only formal and that the war would not be prosecuted.

Back in Portsmouth for the winter, the *Victory* was prepared for another trip to Iberia, this time to bring troops rather than evacuate them. By this time General Sir Arthur Wellesley had been raised to the peerage as Viscount Wellington and had adopted his strategy of conducting campaigns in Spain in the summer while retreating behind the lines of Torres Vedras around Lisbon for the winter. On 16 January 1811 the *Victory*'s lower deck guns were laboriously taken out and soldiers' beds and pillows were brought on board. The marines moved down to the lower deck leaving the middle deck for the soldiers – 717 officers and men including Generals Byrne and Long and their staffs, the 1st Battalion of the 36th Regiment of Foot under Lieutenant-Colonel Basil Cochrane, and various replacements and specialists. Most of them were brought on board at St Helens on the 28th.

The ship sailed on the 30th as part of a squadron under Rear-Admiral Sir Joseph Yorke in the 74-gun *Vengeur* but there was a bad start – Seaman John Atkinson fell from the booms and was killed. Out in the Channel, the winds were contrary and the ships moved out into the anchorage at Torbay. Over the next two weeks they tried three times to make progress but were driven back each time, until they finally got away on 15 February. Progress was still slow with 'fresh gales and squally' alternating with 'light breezes' recorded in the ship's log book. When land was sighted on the 23rd it was only a distant view of Cape Finisterre, some forty miles away. The fleet suffered further loss when William Fitzsimmons fell overboard and was drowned and there were disciplinary problems. Four men were flogged on the 27th and later Lieutenant Kentish was put under arrest for leaving the deck during his watch. The winds were better by 2 March and next day the Lisbon pilot was taken on board. The ship moved up the River Tagus in stages, and both services were probably relieved when five boats arrived alongside the *Victory* in the morning of the 5th to take the soldiers ashore. For the sailors, the voyage home was not much better, but they passed the Needles to enter the Solent on 26 March.[32]

A Phoney War

Saumarez arrived back at Vinga in the *Victory* on 2 May to face a new situation. Warships often served, in effect, as floating embassies in days when communications were slow and the man on the spot, whether diplomat or naval officer, had to make the decisions. It was the case even more so for the *Victory* now as, of course, Britain had no formal diplomatic relations with Sweden and contact was maintained largely through Saumarez and his flagship. The situation was clarified when Baron Tawast, the Swedish military commander at Gothenburg, came on board the *Victory* under a flag of truce ostensibly to discuss the exchange of prisoners; but informed Saumarez, '...that he was instructed to communicate with me, in the most confidential manner, that it was the earnest wish of the Swedish Government to keep on the most amicable terms with Great Britain; and it was not intended, under any circumstances, to commit any acts of hostility whatever.'[33] Saumarez acted with restraint over some merchant ships that had been seized at Carlsham and their cargoes sold. He also had to restrain his captains who did not share his indifference to prize money, and he even ignored an Admiralty order to stop Swedish trade, until it was rescinded a month later. He was in close contact with the Governor of Gothenburg, Count Axel von Rosen, who rowed himself out to the *Victory* in June 1811 to confer with the admiral in secret, spending eight hours in the boat because of unfavourable currents, covering his hands in blisters and ending up miles north of the city so that he had to walk back.[34]

Marshal Jean-Baptiste Bernadotte, crown prince of Sweden and founder of a dynasty.

(Musée de France)

A few of *Victory*'s crew had a taste of action in September. There was intelligence that two Danish gunboats were sixty miles to the south between Vinga and Anholt Island planning to attack a homeward bound convoy. The *Victory*'s pinnace and yawl were put under the command of Lieutenant David St Clair and Midshipman Edward Purcell and sent out to meet them. Despite strong fire and a defensive position among the rocks, they boarded the boats which had five times their own crew, and captured them. Purcell was promoted to lieutenant.[35]

As the year's convoy season drew to a close, bad weather and contrary winds delayed several sailings while the second-rate *St George* was dismasted and lost her rudder. Saumarez considered the possibility of leaving her behind off Gothenburg, but was persuaded to let her sail. He arranged the ships into three groups for the return to England. The first included the *Victory*, three 74s and two frigates, the second consisted of the *St George* being towed by the *Cressy*, the veteran 74-gun *Defence* and a frigate, while the third comprised a convoy of merchant ships plus an escort. They sailed on 17 December but the merchantmen failed to clear the Skaw at the head of the Jutland coast. Towards nightfall on the 19th, the *Victory* had a last glimpse of the lights of the *St George* group and by the 23rd, 'the storm increased with inconceivable violence: the *Victory* was scudding under close-reefed main topsail.'[36] By the 24th they were off the Suffolk coast. At Spithead two days later, Saumarez reported his arrival to the Admiralty but noted in the margin, 'I am uneasy about the *St George*.' He was right, she and the *Defence* had been driven onto the Danish coast with the loss of more than 1,300 men. The *Victory*'s sailing qualities had saved her from one of the greatest disasters in the navy's history.[37]

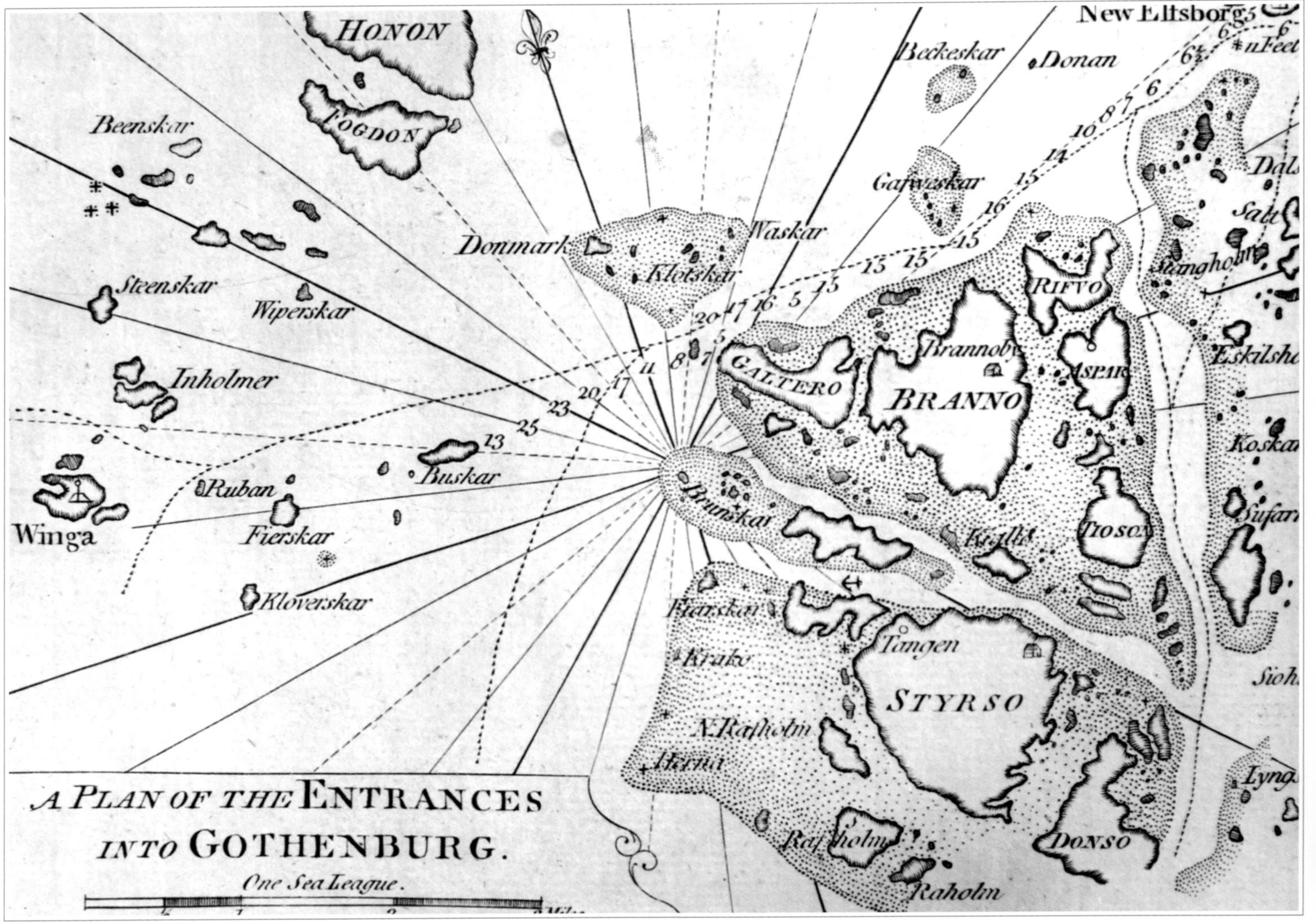

The approaches to Gothenburg, showing the main channel leading to the top right corner of the chartlet, with the anchorage off Winga Island on the far left.

(© National Maritime Museum, Greenwich, London, Coasting Pilot, 9931-2001)

1812

The fateful year of 1812 began with rapidly worsening relations between France and Russia, whose leaders had been as encouraged by Sweden's resistance as they had been chastened by Saumarez's ships. The admiral hoisted his flag in the *Victory* at the Downs on 14th April, sailed two weeks later and arrived at Gothenburg on 3 May. Peace negotiations with Sweden were already in progress and war between France and Russia was not far away. In August, Baron von Platen wrote the ultimate eulogy:

> You have been the guardian angel of my country; by your wise, temperate, and loyal conduct you have been the first cause of the plans which have formed against the demon of the Continent. He was on the point of succeeding... Two couriers have arrived this night from the head-quarters of the Emperor and the Prince. War was declared on the 24th of July... If providence have not decided something against all probability, Bonaparte will be defeated, humanity will breathe again, and Europe be once more raised up.[38]

Napoleon had begun his ill-fated invasion. The role of the British fleet was now largely passive, except that Byam Martin led a force which helped the Russians during the siege of Riga. Saumarez was honoured with a diamond hilted sword valued at £2,000 presented by Bernadotte, while the Admiralty sent their 'marked approbation' of his 'zeal, judgement and ability' during the last four years. They praised, 'your attention to the trade of his Majesty's subjects, and your conciliatory, yet firm conduct, towards the Northern Powers... [which] have been justly appreciated by the courts of Sweden and Russia'.[39] But Saumarez would have to wait for a peerage until 1832, after his friends in the Whig Party took power.

A large fleet was no longer needed in the Baltic, Saumarez retired and the *Victory* was laid up. However, she was still considered suitable for active service in the middle of 1813. John William Croker, the First Secretary to the Admiralty, produced a wide survey of the ships available for coming campaigns and noted, 'if the services of another line of battleship should be requisite, their Lordships may avail themselves of the *Victory* at Portsmouth, a ship that we did not expect to be paid off until the end of the year 1814, and which we apprehend may be brought forward in a very short time.'[40] She was part of the ordinary at Portsmouth, in mooring position number eleven with 22ft 8in of water at low tide, one of six ships under the charge of Superintending Master Thomas Edwards. She had a crew of five officers and five men.[41] By that time, Napoleon had been driven out of Russia with enormous losses, a new coalition had been formed against him including Russia, Sweden and Prussia, and they would soon defeat the French in the 'Battle of the Nations' at Leipzig, while Wellington's troops, some of them carried to the theatre in the *Victory*, crossed the Pyrenees to invade France from the south. On 11 April 1814, when the Emperor Napoleon abdicated and was exiled to Elba, the *Victory* could claim to have done more than any other ship to ensure his downfall.

Repair at Portsmouth

The *Victory* began yet another repair after a survey of 1813, though it expanded as more defects were revealed. On 15 October, the Portsmouth Dockyard officers thought she could be 'brought forward without entering a formal repair, by shifting the decks and such materials as are visibly defective, and by giving her additional strength where it can be with propriety be introduced.' The Navy Board agreed that this should be done, 'when a dock will be vacant, that may be appropriated without interfering with ships in commission.' The Board made it clear that they did not approve of 'stopping up so many large docks, and particularly the deeper ones', so one would not be ready for the *Victory* until February.[42]

In 1808 the damage to the *Victory* at Trafalgar had largely inspired Seppings' new round bow, and that became standard in 1811. 'In that year, when the Right Hon Charles Yorke was at the head of the Admiralty, I presented to him a model showing on one side the bow of a ship of the line with the then usual form, and the other with a circular one carried up as above mentioned; and so fully satisfied were Mr. Yorke and the naval members of the Board of its advantages, that orders were in consequence given for its general adoption in His Majesty's Navy'. But she was not fitted with Seppings' next and more important invention, the diagonal bracing, which would greatly strengthen the

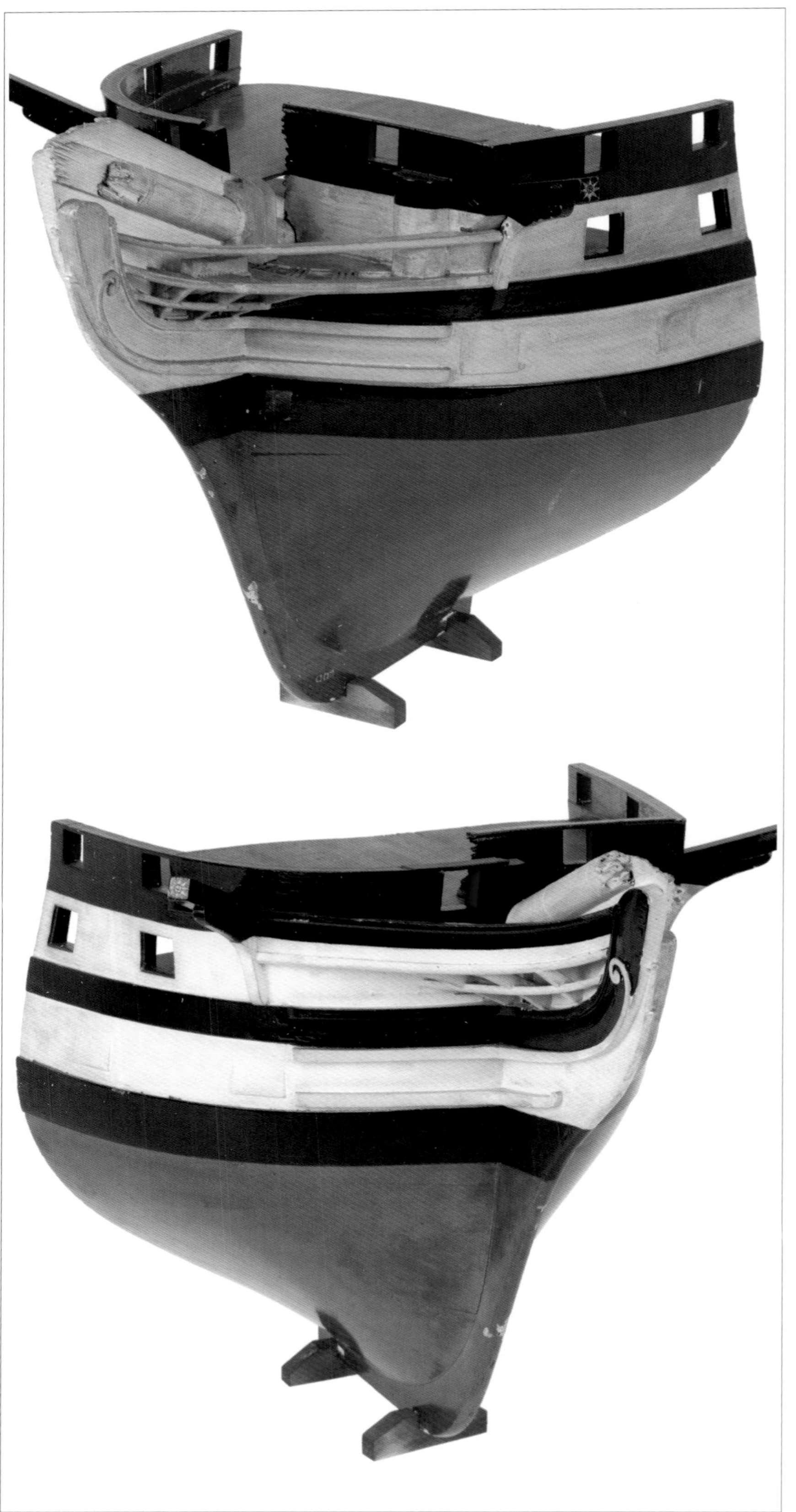

hull and make it possible to build much longer ships. It was probably just a matter of timing – *Victory* was under repair from March 1814 to January 1816, the Seppings system was not standard practice until 1817. But it soon became clear that ships fitted with diagonal bracing were much superior, and eventually they would be able to be fitted with engines, while much longer ships could be built for a given number of decks. Five 120-gun ships of the *Caledonia* class were begun in the ten years after 1815, 205 feet long on the gundeck, measured at 2,600 tonnes and twenty percent larger than the *Victory*.

The End of the War

Thus the *Victory* was not available when the Royal Navy was mobilised again after Napoleon escaped from Elba and took power in France. Designs for the head and stern were sent to London on 20 June, just two days after Wellington and Blücher defeated Napoleon at Waterloo. The actual plan is missing from the file, but the head would cost £65, plus banisters at the stern at £65 each. Napoleon surrendered to HMS *Bellerophon* which had fought in Collingwood's division at Trafalgar. He was taken to Plymouth Sound then put on board the *Northumberland* to take him to a far more distant exile on St Helena. In December the repairs to the *Victory* were only held up by a shortage of joiners who were mostly employed on internal work – they were overcome by 'the very great pressure of business…' though the *Victory* was 'in every other respect ready for them.' The Navy Board agreed that the ship should be taken out to free the dock, and the rest of the work should be done afloat. By January 1816 the ship was 'in a state to enable us to take in hand the store rooms and cabins on the orlop deck, and the Portsmouth officers asked how they were to be fitted. The Navy Board sent them a plan of the *Caledonia* as a guide.[43] Repairs were completed soon afterwards, at a final cost of £79,772, and the *Victory* was afloat and ready in a strangely peaceful world, after twenty-two years of almost continuous war.

The old square bow is shown on the top view of this model of a two-decker, still painted with the yellow of the Nelson chequer. The view below shows the round bow as fitted in 1814–16, with the black and white colour scheme which became common at that time.

(© National Maritime Museum, Greenwich, London, SLR2185)

11 VICTORY IN HARBOUR

Flagship at Portsmouth

The *Victory* now flew the flag of the commander-in-chief at Portsmouth, who was responsible for the ships afloat and in commission, while the dockyard dealt with repairs and the Navy Board commissioner was, in effect, a liaison officer. Portsmouth had a large number of service vessels, including old ships which would never go to sea again but were useful as store ships, receiving ships for pressed men, and sheer hulks which were used to fit masts to other ships. In addition, there were a dozen prison ships in the harbour, a fate which *Victory* had narrowly avoided in 1799 – though these were now used for civilian convicts rather than prisoners of war. *Victory* was never reduced to the status of a hulk, which would have altered her appearance greatly. Instead, as a flagship, she carried a full complement of masts and guns. In 1828, the middle deck was fitted with 'Sir William Congreve's short twenty-four pounders' and

E.W. Cooke's 1828 print shows the *Victory* still fully rigged and equipped for service and flying an admiral's flag at the mainmast. A small steamship can be seen to the right, a foretaste of things to come.

(© National Maritime Museum, Greenwich, London, PU5983)

the upper deck had 9ft long 12-pounders. Apart from men passing through, the ship had ninety-eight petty officers and seamen in June 1828. Twenty-eight of these were away manning the *Scorpion* tender which patrolled the Solent, four of them manned the captain's gig and twelve the admiral's barge. The ship's band had fifteen men and there were six wardroom and captain's servants – the admiral's servants were listed separately. There were six signalmen and yeomen of storerooms, a purser's steward and his mate, a cook and mate, an armourer and mate, a master-at-arms and two ship's corporals for police services, two men to attend the five who were 'sick on board', nine carpenter's crew for maintenance and two writers or clerks in the admiral's office.[1]

The C-in-C had no actual fleet to command, just ships fitting out for longer voyages. With the dockyard and other shore bases in charge of the material aspects, his responsibilities were mainly to do with personnel. He often took on midshipmen and cadets, perhaps giving them some preliminary training before sending them to seagoing ships. As to the lower deck, in 1828 the Duke of Clarence (Nelson's old friend) was Lord High Admiral and ordered that the flagship should take on 'any able seamen that may offer for general service'. Admiral Robert Stopford went further and asked if he could also take on 'in the same manner any good ordinary seamen, or shipwrights'[2]. Many captured smugglers were sent to the ship, having been offered the choice of prison or naval service – they were the only criminals that the navy accepted at this time, for their offences were not anti-social in the sense of robbery or murder, and they were often good seamen. In 1826, for example, forty-six-year-old Alexander Ferguson of Dumfries was taken – he was 5ft 5in tall with 'sallow complexion, woman [tattoo] on left arm' with hazel eyes.[3] In June 1825, Stephen Church found a scuttle or hole in the sick bay, where the bars had been set too far apart. He climbed through the starboard bow gunport, using a rope which had been left hanging there, and was not spotted by two marine sentries.[4]

Deserters and miscreants from other ships came on board the *Victory*, for example David Paine in 1828. Captain Elliot objected to his being transferred to another ship on the grounds that he might be reinstated in his rating as petty officer – his misconduct was 'of long-standing' and he had been repeatedly warned about it.[5] In 1829 the *Victory* had to cope with Boy John Davey who had already deserted from two ships. He was sent on board from the naval hospital and it was not felt necessary to guard him, but he stole clothes from some of the supernumeraries on board, then got ashore and was caught a few miles beyond Portsmouth. He was a 'worthless blackguard' who would 'never be of the least use to any ship.' Around the same time, James Manning, a returned deserter, was complained 'by some of the boys of his taking improper liberties with them' so he had to be confined on the upper deck.[6] The C-in-C also had responsibility for the naval defence of the area, and the coastal blockade which was maintained against smugglers. In 1827 Stopford departed on a tour of the local stations, leaving Captain Mingaye of the *Revenge* in charge at Portsmouth.[7]

There were considerable doubts about the navy's system of gunnery. The old system had worked well in 1805, when speed of fire was all-important and Nelson believed that 'no Captain can go very wrong if he places his ship alongside that of an enemy.' But in 1812 the navy came up against the well-trained crews of American frigates and suffered several defeats. At the same time it was increasingly involved in shore bombardment and, off the coast of Spain in 1812, Sir Howard Douglas of the army remarked that bad gunnery, 'made him tremble for the laurels of the navy.'[8] Trials of new systems of gunnery were sometimes carried out on board the *Victory*, for example in 1818, with 'a gun mounted upon a carriage constructed by Commander John Eole'. Gunnery training was still carried out on board the *Victory* and in 1824 one H. Hammerton kept a gunnery notebook of his training on board. Loaded guns could not be fired from the *Victory* herself where she was moored, but one of the ships in ordinary was fitted with a single gun for practice. However, in 1829 Commander George Smith suggested a specialist gunnery training ship in the harbour. He found that the old 74-gun *Excellent* of 1787 was moored in the best position for practice firing and in June 1830 Smith was appointed 'Supernumerary Commander of the Flag Ship at Portsmouth' to take charge of her. Two years later the *Excellent* ceased to be a tender to the *Victory* and became an independent ship in commission – a momentous step, the beginning of the first real training system in the Royal Navy.[9]

Reduced to the Ordinary

The commander-in-chief at Portsmouth often had a Nelson connection, and none was stronger than that of Thomas Foley. In 1798 he led the fleet into Battle of the Nile in the *Goliath,* almost certainly using his own initiative to attack the enemy on his unprepared side. In 1801, he was Nelson's flag captain at Copenhagen when Nelson famously put his telescope to his blind eye. Foley was also loyal to his old comrades and arranged a position for the grandson of a midshipman killed at the Nile. He arranged a passage back to Africa for John Duncan, 'a black man and a native of Sierra Leone', who had recently been paid off from the *Victory*.

Foley decided to have his headquarters ashore and arranged for the *Victory* to be paid off as a flagship, with the mates and midshipmen transferring to the 120-gun *St Vincent* under Captain Parker. The sixty-four-year-old carpenter of the ship, John Garbutt, applied for superannuation after thirty-seven years of service which had left him with defective vision. The schoolmaster, Mr Harkness, was 'a young man every way qualified for that situation' who had come down from Edinburgh in 1827, but missed the examination in the Royal Naval Academy and asked to be paid for the two months he had served unqualified, before passing with one of the best results that Dr Inman of the Academy had ever seen – but this, the Admiralty clerk noted tersely, 'cannot be complied with.'

It was reported that the Admiralty intended to cut the *Victory* down to a two-decker of 84 guns, which would perhaps have maintained her status as a fighting ship but would have destroyed much of her historical

The *Victory* is in the centre of this print by Fores in 1851, with the royal yacht *Fairy* under steam to the left, probably taking Queen Victoria to her home on the Isle of Wight. The hulk *Dryad,* formerly a 36-gun frigate, shows how drastically the *Victory*'s appearance might have changed if she had been reduced permanently to harbour service. The semaphore tower in the right background appears in many views of the *Victory* in harbour.

(© National Maritime Museum, Greenwich, London, PY9197)

value, including removing the deck where Nelson was wounded. This initiated a campaign led by the actor John Poole. He wrote, '...such a ship is [a] national heirloom, and ought to be preserved as a sacred relic... why do they not entreat that she may be preserved as she was at the day of Trafalgar?'[10]

When the *Victory* was not reduced, the press claimed a triumph and in July the *Standard* reported:

> In accordance with the feelings of the public, the Admiralty have abandoned the intention of cutting down the *Victory* (so endeared to us by many associations) to a 74 [sic]. Since it was understood that this step was contemplated, the public have been loud in their lamentations that such a national object of interest should not be suffered to remain unaltered. Consulting, therefore, with the general wish, the Admiralty have not only relinquished their first intention, but have decided that she shall be fitted to receive the pendant of the captain of the ordinary, thus rendering the *Victory* an object of double interest.[11]

Poole and his supporters claimed to have saved the *Victory*, though there is no evidence that the Admiralty actually had a plan to reduce her physically rather than merely in status. On 4 October 1831 the Admiralty allocated the ship a complement of 200, including a captain and two lieutenants, six warrant officers and fifty marines. They ordered her to be ready to hold a court martial on the 6th, and that was to be one of her new roles.[12]

Portsmouth Harbour now had a number of steam vessels, mostly used for carrying messages and towing ships in and out of harbour. The *Victory* encountered steam power in a rather different form, as a dredger owned by the firm of Joliffe and Banks cleared the waters around her mooring during 1830, while convicts were employed to remove the silt from barges. The dredger was so efficient that the Portsmouth officers wanted to buy one at a cost of £5,000 but the Navy Board discouraged them, as it would not find constant employment.[13]

The fourteen-year old Princess Victoria first visited the ship as part of a south coast tour on 18 July 1833. She was shown the spot where Nelson fell and where he died, misquoted his famous signal as the rather banal 'Every Englishman is expected to do his duty' and, rather like Marianne Ehrenström had done twenty-five years earlier, she sampled the sailors' food. 'The whole ship is remarkable for its neatness and order' she wrote, 'we tasted some of the men's beef and potatoes, which were excellent, and likewise some grog.'[14] Eleven years later she returned as Queen. On Trafalgar Day 1844 she and Prince Albert were returning from their new home at Osborne House on the Isle of Wight when they noticed flags flying from the *Victory* and a celebration taking place. The Queen demanded to go on board and was taken to the quarterdeck to view the plaque 'Here Nelson fell'. She then went down to the cockpit but there was confusion on the way. '...after descending the ladder, ...Her Majesty was run against by a powder monkey, who was bringing up a fresh supply to salute the Queen on her departure. Her Majesty was almost overthrown by the concussion, but bore it with the most gracious and condescending affability.' She continued down to see 'the figure of a funeral urn emblazoned on one of the knees of the ship, surmounted with the words, 'Here Nelson died.'' Her Majesty remarked that 'the orlop deck was not so high in the *Victory* as in other men-of-war which she had visited.'[15]

The *Victory*'s obsolescence as a warship was slow-burning. One factor was the changing armaments of ships of the line to make them more uniform, with 32-pounders on each deck. Thus in 1852 the naval architect John Fincham wrote:

> Whilst we regard the *Victory* and *Caledonia* as excellent ships during the last war, it is to be remembered that they carried a comparatively light armament, consisting of 18 or 24-pounders on the middle deck, 12 or 18-pounders on the upper deck, and 12-pounders and carronades on the quarter deck, forecastle and roundhouse. Their breadth, however, was too small to give enough stability with the modern system of armament which disposes a much greater amount of weights on the upper decks.[16]

Steam power continued to grow in importance, though the paddle wheel was not suitable for a ship of the line as it would block much of the gun armament and be highly vulnerable to enemy shot. The 1830s and 40s saw the development of the screw propeller, and in 1845–46 the *Ajax*, an old 74 of 1809, was partly converted in Portsmouth Dockyard then towed across the Solent to be fitted with a steam engine and propeller. She came back in 1846, to serve as a short-range steam blockship for the defence of the dockyard and three more ships were converted. In the next stage of the evolution, eight more ships were built or converted as seagoing steam ships of the line from 1851–54.[17] The *Victory* was not likely to undergo such a conversion, in view of her age and lack of diagonal bracing, but the sailing ship was still not considered obsolete. However, in 1848 Admiral Milne listed her among the 'non-effective ships' with a complement of twenty-two officers, fifteen petty officers, forty-nine able seamen, six first-class boys and twenty-four second-class, fifty marines and seven idlers or men who did not keep watch. They were employed 'embarking new[ly] raised men, marines, troops &c, hospital day boats, rowing guard &c.'[18]

A Midshipman on Board

Cecil Sloane-Stanley arrived in Portsmouth with his parents in 1850 to be tested for entry as a naval cadet. Appearing at Admiralty House in the dockyard, the family was directed to the *Victory* and rowed out by a boatman plying his trade from the Common Hard. 'The interminable chatter of this ancient mariner was happily brought to an end, 'ere many minutes had passed by our arrival alongside the flagship. After climbing the old three-decker's steep sides we found ourselves on the middle deck in the presence of a stern-looking official bearing a cane, who demanded our business.' They were led aft to 'a long room with a long table' to await the captain, who was Francis Price Blackwood, the son of Nelson's great frigate captain. The guard presented arms as 'a tall figure, wearing a boat cloak and glazed cocked hat' came on board and was eventually ready to receive the candidate in his cabin. Sloane-Stanley was taken for a 'very unpleasant ordeal' of a medical examination then tested in arithmetic by Mr Kerr the schoolmaster, who told him, in his Scottish accent, 'You've done verra weel, youngster'. It was largely a matter of chance or personal talent as nothing in his classical education prepared him for such a test – 'I could have translated a page of Virgil or Ovid with far greater ease than I could have worked a rule of three sum.' Eventually Captain Blackwood told him, 'Mr Sloane-Stanley, I have much pleasure in giving you your Certificate, and in welcoming you to a noble profession. May you prosper in it, and tread in the footsteps of that immortal hero who died, fighting for his country on board this same old *Victory*.'

The young man was given three weeks leave before returning to the *Victory*. His parents ordered a cadet's uniform and 'My school-boy clothes were cast off without a pang...' He was rowed on board by the same 'singularly persevering waterman' who had now attached himself to the family. On board the ship, he was greeted by the first lieutenant as a 'young Nelson' and he and his parents went to his future quarters on the gunroom, and his sleeping quarters further below. '"Here is your son's chest," said the lieutenant after we had proceeded a way into the gloom, "and his hammock will be hung up to a couple of those hooks overhead."' The prank of cutting down a boy in his hammock could not be eliminated, and Mrs Sloane-Stanley was not greatly reassured on being told that boys were never cut down 'by the head' nowadays. After his parents left, he was allocated a marine servant to tend his clothes and sling his hammock, and met the other members of the gun-room mess. The second master of the ship had been there for several years and was 'of a surly and unamiable disposition.' The mate was 'a capital fellow' but mostly lived on shore. There were three other cadets, soon joined by two more, and two clerks – the senior one made a 'Job's comforter' speech that Sloane-Stanley would repent his decision to join before long, but the others mocked him behind his back. The young man wolfed down his meal of tea, bread and butter and cold meat. At half past nine, the second master placed a fork in a beam overhead, a traditional way of warning the younger members of the mess that it was time to turn in. Sloane-Stanley had a traditionally farcical attempt to get into his hammock. He did not sleep well, though no one tried to cut him down.

The next day, he had his first experience aloft, going through the 'lubber's hole' in the maintop rather than the outer route via the futtock shrouds. 'It almost made my head turn to look down, the height at which I was perched seemed to my unaccustomed eyes so tremendous, and I involuntarily tightened my hold on the protecting rail as if to save myself from falling.' He was shocked when a petty officer demanded the customary half a crown (12 ½ p) for guiding them. He had some leave ashore when he and his colleague were tempted by local girls and next day he began to study navigation, starting with 'boxing the compass.' He learned how to keep a log, though in harbour that mainly consisted of recording the movements of other ships. He rebelled against a practical joke of being measured for a 'cocked hat and a regulation spoon' by the purser's steward in his 'little den of a cabin opening out of the store-room.' He practised rowing but found the heavy oars of a naval cutter very difficult for a boy, and he nearly drowned while learning to swim off Fort Blockhouse. After two and a half months, he was posted to HMS *Ajax* for sea service.[19]

In 1852 Captain Arthur Lowe argued strongly that boys should be trained separately. 'Flag-ships are the receptacle for all deserters, stragglers, thieves &c., in short, of men of the worst character from other ships; and the boys, with every precaution taken to prevent it, must be more or less thrown amongst them... and by degrees become familiar with their offences and language which, at their early age, must be injurious to them.' Indeed, two years later a lady visitor was rather shocked when she boarded the ship 'between a double row of miserable-looking handcuffed deserters'.

Even the life of the boy seamen was not easy, and in 1853 Surgeon William Guland reported:

> The transition from domestic to ship life is often so great and sudden as to produce an evident effect upon the general health of the newly raised men and boys. This appears principally to arise from the difference in diet, but also influenced by the air, exercise and clothing....[20]

In 1856 Chaplain Inskip suggested giving ten naval cadets six weeks training on board the *Victory,* in view of 'the early age & scant education of the majority of naval Cadets' and because of 'the difficulty of pursuing with proper regularity any course of studies on board a Sea-going ship in consequence of the many interruptions occasioned by unavoidable demands...'[21] The authorities were beginning to see that theoretical and practical training should be treated separately.

The Baltic Fleet Sails

War with Russia began in March 1854, leading to the first modern war fever, for the electric telegraph and newspapers made it possible to spread the news fast, while the railway system allowed people to move around. They began to congregate in Portsmouth in huge numbers in March, including an anonymous lady diarist who arrived with her family on the 6th. She was shocked by the tumultuous crowds in the city, including many women who had come to see their soldier and sailor husbands off on a war which might 'track with terror twenty rolling years', as the last one had done. The lady, possibly a Miss Rice, was the cousin of a naval lieutenant and found some relief when she visited the *Victory*:

> Captain [John C. D. Hay] received us... and took us over the ship.... We went down to the maindeck, the middle, the lower and the orlop deck or cockpit, where the midshipmen spend some years of their lives and to which the wounded are brought down during action.... Returning to the maindeck, we found the men just going to dinner and one produced a basin of soup which Captain [Hay] was very glad to taste by deputy. It was thick and well-flavoured.[22]

The party was invited back to the *Victory* later in the week, and Captain Scott of the *Odin* suggested they should not risk their lives in a hired boat, especially as the boatmen were charging outrageous prices. He offered the *Odin*'s launch, but first the party had to run the gauntlet of the crowds at the dockyard gate. They had to shout '*Odin*'s boat' several times through the keyhole, then the door was opened just wide enough to let in one at a time, while the disgruntled crowd shouted 'fair play's a jewel!' On the way out, the midshipman in charge of the boat collided with several wherries and the watermen, 'being deprived of their harvest, saluted us with volleys of oaths and curses.' But, again, all was different on the ship – 'On the poop of the *Victory* were Captain Hay and Captain Boyle in full uniform and a triple rank of marines'. They were getting ready to welcome Queen Victoria as she arrived in her train at the South Railway Jetty nearby, though it was feared that she would 'receive a damp welcome under the cotton umbrellas.' At noon the *Victory* fired a salute as the Queen arrived, but that was the old ship's only role in the ceremony – for the Baltic Fleet was anchored outside the harbour at Spithead and the Royal yacht *Fairy* took Her Majesty around them in the appalling weather. The *Victory* was not likely to see action in this war, for apart from her ageing timbers, the diarist observed 'our new line-of-battleships make her look like a pygmy, huge as she is.' But her past was not forgotten. Vice-Admiral James Dundas, in command of the Baltic Fleet, remembered that 'in former wars, when steam was not known, a squadron of British line-of-battle ships maintained a blockade in the Baltic till the end of November' and wrote that 'the journals of Sir James Saumarez are now before me.'[23]

There was another review in April 1856, when the ships returned to Portsmouth, and 240 of them anchored in two rows in the Solent for a mock attack on Southsea Castle and an inspection by the Queen. At last, nearly a century after she was ordered, the *Victory* was indisputably obsolete for the war had shown that ships without engines could not be expected to fight in modern conditions, and there was no question of fitting one to such an old hull.

The *Victory* was now in a limbo between a fighting ship and a much-valued relic. There were some who would have disposed of her in favour of more modern ships. R S Dundas, the Second Naval Lord at the Admiralty, wrote to the First Lord in September 1857, 'I am sorry to find that you are not disposed to find the *Victory* defective, & if she is once repaired you will not get rid of her for another term of years and I look upon her and the *Impregnable* as occupying the place of effective guardships & costing money without any countervailing advantage.'[24] However, the *Victory* was docked in October and it was found that a hundred of her frame timbers were defective, along with pieces of keelson, deadwood, riders and ceiling. Part of her planking had been worn out by the chain cables, but her caulking fitted in 1823 was 'remarkably good', as was much of the copper sheathing. She only needed a slight repair and caulking, and repair 'in a cheap manner by piecing with fir.' After that, the ship would last for several years, though only in 'still water'.[25] But even greater change was afoot and on 20 September 1860 the *Victory* was saluted by a strange new ship, black-hulled and nearly twice her length. This was the *Warrior*, built on the Thames as Britain's first ironclad warship, with the potential to make the wooden warship obsolete. Over the fifteen years of her seagoing life, she would return to Portsmouth many times for maintenance, passing the *Victory* each time.

Victory and the Law

As flagship, the *Victory* still had the job of firing gun salutes for visiting royalty and admirals, though there was some doubt about the effectiveness of her old guns. In 1859, there was a visit by a Russian squadron which fired a seventeen-gun salute at Spithead. The *Victory* duly replied from within the harbour, but in the fresh wind the Russian admiral only heard thirteen guns. The British admiral had to shift his flag to another ship and repeat the exercise to avoid an international incident, and he proposed to do so on future occasions, as 'the *Victory*'s guns are so small.'[26] Nevertheless, the *Victory* continued in the role and in August 1865, for example, she fired nineteen guns in honour of a visit by the French fleet.[27]

Portsmouth boatmen in 1852, ready to take well-wishers out to the fleet assembled at Spithead.

(Taken from Illustrated London News*)*

The *Victory* was relatively free from mutiny for all her career, despite some difficulties in the wake of the Keppel-Palliser affair. In November 1859, however, Captain Farquhar of the ship had to lead a party of 200 marines to restore order on the *Princess Royal* in Portsmouth Harbour – one of the last examples of the old-style mutiny.[28] By law, naval courts martial had to be held on board a naval ship – the main exception was

Keppel's trial in 1778, when a special act of Parliament was needed to hold it ashore, but that could not be seen as a good precedent in view of the disorder during and after the trial. To conform to the law, the *Victory* became the main centre for courts martial in the Portsmouth area. After the loss of the frigate *Thetis* in 1830, Midshipman William Mends was one of those subjected to the usual ordeal, as reported by his son:

> The court sat for three days, and my father being only nineteen years of age, and an unpassed midshipman, having been officer of the watch at the time she struck, was very stiffly catechized by the members. He came out of the ordeal, with flying colours.... This court martial gave him an immense start in the service by bringing him under the favourable notice of many of the most rising men of the day...[29]

One rather unusual case was the trial of Captain Arthur Wilmhurst, who was accused of seeking 'pecuniary

A watercolour by an unknown artist, dated October 1858. It shows the *Victory* in her mid-nineteenth-century black and white colour scheme, the flag of an admiral of the blue at the head of the mainmast. The Semaphore Tower and Round Tower are shown rather sketchily in the background.

(© National Maritime Museum, Greenwich, London, PAD5979)

advantage in respect of the wreck of the ship *Bremensis*.' The court was presided over by Admiral Pasley, the commander-in-chief at Portsmouth, and included a rear-admiral and six captains, including those of the *Duke of Wellington* and *Victory*. The prosecution was conducted by the paymaster of the *Victoria and Albert*, but he was clearly outclassed by the 'friend of the prisoner' or defending lawyer, Sir William Harcourt – Queen's Counsel, parliamentary orator and future cabinet minister. It was probably not a surprise when

Wilmhurst was found not guilty and there was 'an outburst of applause... and the hearty congratulations of a number of officers who heartily awaited the decision.'[30] These occasions were solemn but also 'a lively scene of brilliant uniforms', according to Hastings Harris.[31] They were not without rough humour according to 'Miss Rice', 'the captains would slyly fill each other's cocked hats with shavings of paper which descend in showers when the hats are put on during the passing of sentences...'

The *Victory* also served as the headquarters of the naval police for Portsmouth, though in 1861 Captain Byrne complained that he had only ten men to patrol the area.[32] The ship herself was apparently a target for crime in 1865. A convict in Dartmoor Prison overheard two of his fellow inmates planning to steal £2,000 of silver plate by approaching the *Victory* disguised as fishermen. They appeared to have some knowledge of the security systems on board. '...the Mess Room Steward locks up all about 11pm and nearly 12 O'Clock turns the hour glass and walks to chime the bells, from this he turns the glass mid-ships and walks to one forward and does the same, these operations with, it may be, some others occupy him nearly 20 Minutes.' The captain agreed that 'the attempt described, though difficult, might be successful' and decided to check procedures.[33]

The First Hundred Years

The ship was now 100 years in the water and the *Illustrated London News* reported, with an eye on Victorian etiquette:

> The centenary festival of the famous ship... was celebrated... with a ball... on the upper deck, to a party of some four hundred guests. The upper deck... was covered in with a sort of awning and tastefully decorated with the flags of all nations, and with festoons of evergreens around the masts, while pots of beautiful flowers were ranged on the poop. The ship had been brought alongside the dockyard for convenience of access. The dancing commenced at three o'clock in the afternoon and ended at seven in the evening. The company were therefore in morning costume; and some of the ladies wore their bonnets or hats all the time. The naval officers appeared in their

A ball to celebrate the 100th anniversary of *Victory*'s launch. Some of the women are indeed wearing daytime bonnets as described in the report. The width of the ship is greatly exaggerated.

(Taken from Illustrated London News, *15th July 1865)*

> blue frock coats with laced sleeves, or a scarf to denote their rank... Three wine glasses used by Nelson himself were among the furniture of this repast, and many of the guests were permitted to drink from them to the immortal memory of the great English hero.[34]

From the 1850s, the Royal Navy began to move towards 'continuous service', by which seamen signed on for ten, and later twelve, years, rather than being paid off after each commission of perhaps three years. By 1860, continuous-service men formed the majority, and by 1890 nearly nine-tenths of men were on such a scheme. This meant that the navy was responsible for its men between ships, but there was no shore barracks except at Sheerness, so larger depot ships were needed. Midshipman Louis Fleet came on board in August 1865, 'we found ourselves in a gunroom with many others who were waiting for a ship, thus being pitchforked into a gathering of youths with no duties to perform and not a soul who appeared to have any interest in them.'

The mess was dominated by the assistant paymasters, the successors to the clerks of Sloane-Stanley's day, who were permanently attached to the ship and 'endeavoured to make us uncomfortable with a certain amount of success.' One unpleasant custom was being made 'servants of the Queen' by having the government symbol of the 'broad arrow' cut on their noses:

> The subject was held down on a convenient table and the skin over the tip of his nose tautened. Then the point of a penknife was used to scratch the familiar token.... It did not hurt much but it was a bit of an eyesore [or shall we say nosesore?]for a few days until the disfiguring mark disappeared. In our case the indignity consisted in having the operation performed by the aforesaid Assistant-Paymasters.[35]

Reduced to a Tender

The *Victory* was no longer adequate for the role of depot ship, and at the same time there was pressure to cut expenditure, especially on non-seagoing services – 'Every man we can reduce in Ports is equivalent to a man added for sea service...' wrote the First Naval Lord late in 1868. The Admiralty wanted to replace the *Victory* with the *Duke of Wellington*, which was around fifty percent larger. Though only built in 1852, she was already in poor condition and the officers at Portsmouth objected to merging the two ships:

> Those who remember the different state of things that existed, when all disposable supernumeraries were sent to the Flag Ship, can appreciate the improvement in comfort and condition of the men, and their improved discipline and behaviour, and it would in my opinion be an undesirable and retrograde step to combine the duties of the two ships in one and to revert to what would be tantamount to the former state of things in the Flag Ship before any Reserve of Continuous Service Seamen existed.[36]

On 3 February 1869 the Admiralty made a decision which smacked of unsatisfactory compromise. The *Victory* was to be reduced to the status of 'tender to the *Duke of Wellington*' in which role, it was hoped, she might still be useful 'for the reception of Boys and for other purposes.' However, there was formal recognition, perhaps for the first time, of 'the historical interest attached to the *Victory*' which had 'determined my Lords to keep her in her present condition as regards her hull, rigging, and internal arrangements...' But the Admiralty was not sure of itself for once, and added, 'my Lords will be glad to receive any suggestions you may have to offer.'

There was outcry in sections of the press and the *Army and Navy Gazette* reported in February that, 'an order was received at Portsmouth on Thursday directing that the *Victory* is to be virtually removed from the books of the navy, and that she is to be at once removed from her present moorings and taken into that lumber of old used-up ships known as the 'ordinary'.' A 'host of county members, watermen and residents of Portsmouth... inundated the Admiralty with remonstrances [sic] since the rumours were set afloat' but a week later the journal was reassured, 'we are pleased to be able to remove the apprehension of some of our contemporaries, who are in a painful state of patriotic excitement in consequence of the wrong which it was supposed the Admiralty were about to do to the flagship of Nelson. My Lords never had the slightest intention of either removing or dismantling the *Victory*.' Instead, 'The *Victory* will be ranked as tender to the *Duke of Wellington*, and will be employed for the reception of boys and other purposes. For visitors she will continue to possess the same attractions as heretofore and will be as accessible as ever.'[37]

The Nelson Legend

All this reflected a growing enthusiasm for the memory and fame of Nelson. His reputation had largely declined after the wars, it took nearly forty years to erect the column in Trafalgar Square, and it was only completed with the lions in 1867. After that, it soared, with the increased interest in British naval power both past and present. Boy Sam Noble was delighted to be posted to the *Victory* after competing his training at nearby *St Vincent* in 1875, for it was his 'dearest wish' to be sent there. Officially, she was used for signal instruction, though Noble did not take to that. As a product of the Scottish education system, he was well schooled in history, and had read Southey's biography of Nelson, his 'pet, particular hero'. Despite the signalling, *Victory* was 'a cushie job – plenty to eat and not much to do.' He enjoyed the historical associations:

> All about the old ship was interesting, to me fascinating. Here, for instance, on the quarter-deck, was the spot where Nelson fell – on the yet wet blood of his poor secretary. Here, on the poop, the place where the two midshipmen stood while they plugged the fellow on *Redoubtable's* mizzen top who had shot him. Here, the point where, being carried below, the Admiral noticed that the tiller-ropes, which had been carried away, were still unrepaired, and ordered them to be seen to. Here, marked by another plate, the spot where, nestling in the loving arms of Captain Hardy, his friend, he died.

Even more, Noble enjoyed showing parties of visitors round – 'the Janes and Jarges from the country, or the 'Arrys and 'Arriets from London down for the Bank

Victory with the *Duke of Wellington* in the background, c. 1896. The larger ship has open galleries on a form of elliptical stern, but both ships are still rigged.

(© National Maritime Museum, Greenwich, London, Brass Foundry Album)

Holiday.' When a party arrived by boat, 'one of the boys would shout "Keb!" [meaning cabby, or conductor] and there would be a rush to see if the crowd was a likely one, i.e., good for a tip...' The boys learned tales and poems to impress the visitors and were not afraid to exaggerate – 'Didn't we make them gape! And the yarns we spun for their benefit!' They could earn substantial tips of up to half a sovereign or ten shillings – twenty times a boy seaman's weekly wage.[38]

During the nineteenth century, Portsmouth developed as the county's premier naval base. Unlike Chatham, it had direct and easy access to the open sea so it was good for experimental sailing, but it was also much closer to London than Plymouth. It was on the Queen's route to her favourite English home, Osborne on the Isle of Wight. Portsmouth Harbour had the leading gunnery school in HMS *Excellent* and the premier torpedo and electrical establishment in *Vernon*, though the Plymouth and Chatham commands also set up their own schools in due course. Portsmouth was well situated for ceremonial events such as royal visits and fleet reviews, with the sheltered water of the Solent and many viewpoints on the mainland and the Isle of Wight. The *Victory* would see most of these events and play a part in many of them.

For twenty-one years after 1869, the *Victory* remained afloat, but increasingly obsolete and in poor condition. On *The Navy List* she was only one of five tenders to the *Duke of Wellington*, appearing after the old gunboats *Ant* and *Medina,* the former yacht *Fire Queen* and the ex-Post Office steamer *Sprightly*, none of which was more than a quarter of her size. She was under the command of Chief Boatswain William Guard in 1884, with four more boatswains as his assistants. She was a fixed point in a rapidly changing world, as new ideas in warship design followed one another in bewildering confusion. The revolving gun turret, first used in the USS *Monitor* in 1862, presented the ship designer with a dilemma, how to combine the topweight of sails and rigging while mounting the turret well above the waterline. Captain Cowper Coles tried to solve this with his *Captain* of 1870. The ship left Portsmouth in the summer of 1870 and soon sank in the Bay of Biscay with heavy loss of life – though this time the court martial was held in the *Duke of Wellington* rather than the *Victory*. She was followed by the *Devastation*, which kept the turrets but abandoned sail and was launched at Portsmouth in 1871. For nearly two decades, there was confusion in warship design as improved engines were fitted to give a reasonable range without the aid of sail, and guns and armour both developed in competition with one another. Beatrix Potter commented in 1884, 'the *Glatton* is old for an ironclad, twelve years. It goes out for a few miles for target practice.'[39]

Victory at her moorings off Gosport, c.1895, again showing the semaphore tower in the dockyard.

(© National Maritime Museum, Greenwich, London, Brass Foundry Album)

The Navy and the Public

But, in some ways, the public image of the navy was still an old fashioned one. In 1878, while planning his light opera *HMS Pinafore*, W S Gilbert visited the *Victory* in Portsmouth Harbour to research the set design. Though the opera opens with the line 'We sail the ocean blue' there is no sign of the *Pinafore* leaving harbour during the action and she might as well be a depot ship like the *Victory*:

Sailors in the 1857 style naval uniform decorating the ship for Trafalgar Day, 1876.

(© Mary Evans, 10221390)

An original poster for *HMS Pinafore*, 1878. The uniforms are relatively modern but the ship is based on the *Victory* rather than any modern warship. Portsmouth can be seen in the background.

(Taken from East Norfolk Operatic Society, enosoc.co.uk)

Beatrix Potter with her father and brother.

(© The National Portrait Gallery, London, P1822)

When at anchor we ride
On the Portsmouth tide,
We have plenty of time for play.

The officers and sailors of the cast wore modern uniforms, which Gilbert had made in Portsmouth, and there is a satire on the current First Lord W H Smith:

Stick close to your desks and never go to sea,
And you all may be Rulers of the Queen's Navee.

But the plot was based on nautical ballads and plays dating back to the last century. There is no mention of steam power or turret guns and, judging by the posters, the set reflected Gilbert's research on the *Victory*. It was a breakthrough for the team of Gilbert and Sullivan, their first international hit.

Eighteen-year-old Beatrix Potter arrived in Portsmouth for a family visit in November 1884. It was many years before she would publish her famous children's books, but her coded diary already showed imagination and whimsy. On arriving, she noted the 'dirty old back streets, suggestive of the press gang.' She was impressed with the physique of the sailors, 'much sturdier and more sensibly dressed than the soldiers, except perhaps the Highlanders', so it seemed that the navy's recruitment policy was successful. She first saw the *Victory* from the shore through the mist, with the *Duke of Wellington* and *St Vincent*. She noted their high sides and thought, 'How easy they must have been to hit!' The next day, her father was approached by a 'seafaring gentleman' who persuaded them to take a boat tour and looked at his rivals 'with the contemptuous air of a man who has made a conquest.' They were taken down to the pier-head where 'a broad, yellow-whiskered man… had brought round a large old boat resembling a tub.' They were put in 'as prisoners, not without difficulty owing to the swell from two or three of the small steamers and tugs which seem positively to swarm here.' Her family showed some nervousness but young Beatrix 'didn't care tuppence for the water' – instead, she was nervous about how she would climb the steep side of an old ship.

The atmosphere changed as soon as they left the shore. 'When once we were fairly captured the naval gentleman suddenly relented and became very commuicative, and took us [on] a very pleasant row to the *Victory*. I think this ship one of the most picturesque sights imaginable, particularly from close under the stairs – looking up at the queer little port-holes, and he end like a quaint carved old house.' It was not hard o climb on board using a ladder, and soon they were on the 'extraordinary long' upper deck, 'very clean and roomy, with very few coils of rope or furniture of any kind to cumber them.' She saw the spot where Nelson fell and the boat which had borne his body during the funeral. She went below to see the original fore-topsail and the spot where it was believed that Nelson had died. She credited the well-known myth that 'There is hardly any of the old *Victory* left, she has been so patched' and her nautical terminology was not perfect – planks were 'floor boards' and at first she took the cabins down below for loose boxes – but she showed a good deal of insight when the tour continued to other ships in the harbour. The *Duke of Wellington* was now unseaworthy and the ironclad *Glatton*, out of date despite being only twelve years old, provided a total contrast. 'We examined the revolving turret, very strongly plated, and with two guns which looked immense.' Later, they visited the gunnery ship *Excellent*, which was 'a striking contrast to the two other ships, being full of sailors.' But she was most impressed with the troop transport *Poona* – 'I never saw such an immense ship, we seemed as if we should never get to the other end.'[40]

But, around this time, Admiral Sir Edward Seymour was less enthusiastic about the *Victory*:

> '...A more rotten ship than she had become never probably flew the pennant. I could literally run my walking stick through her sides in many places, and her upper works were mostly covered by a waterproof coat of painted canvas.'[41]

However by the next century the ship was receiving 18,000 visitors a year, an average of about sixty per day excluding Sundays, though, of course, that would peak during the summer.

The Royal Naval Exhibition

Nelson and the *Victory* were raised in the public consciousness as naval history was used in support of greatly-expanded sea power. By 1889, Britain was worried about the rise of various medium-sized navies including Russia, Italy and Austria-Hungary – though as yet the newly-unified Germany did not figure on the list. The Naval Defence Act (1899) decreed that the Royal Navy should be big enough to cope with any two existing navies combined, and a programme of warship construction began. Around the same time, an American naval officer, Alfred Thayer Mahan, published his *The Influence of Sea Power upon History* and it had a widespread effect by showing that large navies were essential to national trade and development. In Britain, the Navy Records Society was founded to publish historical texts, in the belief that they could provide guidance for the future. Nelson was at the centre of this, and in 1899 G Barnett Smith wrote in *Heroes*:

> In the Glory-roll of British heroes no name exercises such a strange fascination as that of Horatio Nelson. The record of his deeds stirs the most sluggish blood and makes the Anglo-Saxon proud of his name and race. He is the boy's hero and the man's hero, from the time when he first steps forth on the human stage to the sublime moment at the Battle of Trafalgar.

This was celebrated in a huge exhibition featuring 5,374 objects in 1891. Originally, it had been planned to hold it at Greenwich and tow the *Victory* there, but the site

Although the location has recently been challenged, the position of the knee against which Nelson died has been marked for some considerable time, as shown in this 1889 print by Barrett.

(© National Maritime Museum, Greenwich, London, PAD5973)

was changed to Chelsea and there was no question of taking the ship through the numerous bridges of London – in any case, there would be great risk in taking such an old ship to sea. Instead, a full-sized 'model' or replica was commissioned from the exhibition designers Campbell, Smith and Co. It was 'perfect as regards the outside, from the water-line to the bulwarks, with hammock nettings, &c., showing the bow with the old figure-head…' However, the local authority had refused permission to fit full masts and rigging. On entering through a port in the side, a visitor would arrive on the middle deck then go down to the lower deck, which was fitted with guns as at Trafalgar, run-out on the port side and stowed on the starboard, with mess tables and hammocks in place.

The exhibition was a great success, attracting more than 2.3 million visitors. Apart from the British Royal Family, the most distinguished visitor was Kaiser Wilhelm II, making a state visit three years after his accession to the German throne. He did not spend much time with the *Victory* replica, but his wife the Kaiserin did. It was perhaps on this occasion that he was presented with a desk made from the timbers of the *Victory*, produced by the high-class furniture makers Waring and Gillow. It is not known how much influence this had on his decision to build a great navy for Germany at the end of the decade. When the exhibition was over, the *Victory* replica was sold to the Isle of Man for £150 and set up there.

Signal School

Meanwhile, the *Victory* herself found a new role. With the advent of fast steamships and development of electric lamps, signalling became more important than ever to the navy and needed increased training. The flagship *Duke of Wellington* was considered unsuitable in view of 'the incessant and unavoidable noise…. Occasioned by the various drills being carried out.' As Signal Boatswain Henry Eason later recorded:

> At the latter end of the year 1889 HMS *Victory* was fitted up as a Naval School of Telegraphy. The instruments set up in the Admiral's after cabin were Sounders, Bells, Needles and Printers…. Manoeuvring signals were made and models worked, and everything such as turning flags etc.. carried out the same as it would be in a fleet at sea…. Fog-horns were also practised, men being posted round the deck each with a police whistle, and treated as a single ship, flagships and leaders being denoted, signals being made as in a fog, being answered or repeated according to instructions… Flashing signals were carried out on the orlop deck of the *Victory*, and two large Semaphores were in position for instructional purposes, one being set up in the [k]night-heads and the other on the poop.[42]

The next step was to develop wireless telegraphy and the Royal Navy was very advanced in this, with experiments by Captain Henry Jackson as well as close collaboration with Marconi. But in Portsmouth that work was carried out from HMS *Vernon*, the torpedo school, presumably because the torpedo branch provided the navy's electrical expertise, and because it was situated closer to the shore and electric power. In 1906 a signal school was set up in the naval barracks, and the *Victory* would have to find yet another role.

The navy had finally found money to build shore barracks, by means of the Naval Works Act of 1891. The Portsmouth buildings opened in 1903 and 'The hulks were vacated with no ceremony or regret as they were unpleasant and miserable quarters.' The men paraded into their new quarters to the sound of bugles and drums, watched by a large crowd, but the *Victory* was not forgotten. Men were only subject to naval discipline if they were attached to ships and vessels of the fleet, and those in Portsmouth were nominally part of the crew of the yacht *Fire Queen*, though in December the King directed that men in the barracks should wear the cap ribbon 'HMS *Victory*.' Early in 1905 the commander-in-chief reported that there was a 'strong local feeling' that they should be formally attached to the *Victory* – her name was world famous, that of the *Fire Queen* had 'little connection with the service'. This was agreed and the practice would continue until 1974, so many thousands of sailors wore the cap ribbon *Victory*, however briefly, and in most cases they never visited the ship herself. In 1905 the officers borne on her books included Admiral Sir Archibald Douglas and his staff, more than eighty officers of various branches to run the 'general depot' or barracks, twenty more 'for Portsmouth dockyard', four instructors and seven trainees of the School of

The full-size 'model' of the *Victory* in the grounds of the Royal Naval Exhibition at Chelsea.

(© *National Maritime Museum, Greenwich, London, P47508*)

Gymnasia, two dozen attached to the signal school (including one 'for training of homing pigeons'), five for fleet coaling duties, three for workshops, five for training boy artificers and thirty-nine for miscellaneous duties.[43]

Rammed

In October 1903, Christopher Arnold-Foster was a cadet in the new naval college at Osborne, just across the Solent on the Isle of Wight, doing sea time in the sloop *Racer* in the Solent. He was well connected as the son of a government minister, and 'played battle' with the Misses Fisher, daughters of the commander-in-chief at Portsmouth – though it was 'not a ferocious or violent game', he told his mother. He was on deck when the old battleship *Neptune* of 1874 was being towed to the breaker's yard by the German tug *Roland*. The tide was strong and when the tug turned the *Neptune* did not follow. She headed for the brig *Seaflower* but her ram went under her hull and did little damage. The *Neptune* drifted across the harbour, while the captain of the *Racer* ordered the cadets into boats. The hawser broke and she began to drift towards the *Victory*, where it was seen by another party.

> Amongst my class of Cadets... was an extremely pious parson's son who very properly objected to us using bad language. When it appeared certain that the *Neptune* would ram our old ship and probably sink her, he burst forth excitedly, 'We are all going to be drowned; Now is the time to swear. Damn the Devil!', which considerably relieved the tension and made us all laugh.[44]

As the *Neptune* struck, Arnold-Foster 'could easily hear the timbers of the *Victory* breaking, and for some minutes the captain thought she would sink.' All the ships sent collision mats to stop the leak and the old ship was towed into dry dock for emergency repair, after sinking several feet.

A Quiet Centenary

Two years later was the centenary of Trafalgar, though celebrations were restricted in order not to annoy the French, with whom the government had recently entered the Entente Cordiale. Royal Family and government officials were not involved, indeed the Prince of Wales had set off on an empire-voyage just two days earlier. But it was celebrated in many other ways, including the *Victory* which was decorated with evergreen at the mastheads and wreaths hanging between the masts and on the spot where Nelson fell. At night it was lit up with electric lights forming the outline of the hull, the rigging and the gunports, with Nelson's flag formed in lights at the masthead. To the *Illustrated London News*, it was 'the most picturesque of the Nelson celebrations.' At a dinner on board the ship, Admiral Sir Cyprian Bridge spoke on 'Trafalgar and its Effects on History.' He began, according to the *Times* correspondent 'The celebrations of the centenary were of a popular and spontaneous character; the government, wisely, as he thought, were leaving them to the people themselves.' He paid a subtle tribute to old enemies and new friends – '...one of the things that made Nelson great was the greatness of those with whom he had to contend.'[45]

Meanwhile, the father of Arnold-Foster's lady companions, Admiral Sir John Fisher, had become First Sea Lord. He abolished sail training and was unsentimental about the *Victory* – she was listed among forty vessels, '[as] utterly useless for fighting purposes – Depot Ships'.[46] One of his many reforms was to build a revolutionary new battleship on Number Five Slip at Portsmouth, less than a mile from the *Victory* on her moorings at Gosport. The *Dreadnought* was fitted with an all-big gun armament to outfight any ship on the oceans, and the new turbine engines to outrun them if needed. She heralded a new age in naval warfare and for the next decade or more the naval powers would measure their strength in Dreadnought battleships. She also opened up the arms race with the growing naval power of Germany, which increased tensions between the two countries. Her launch on 10 February 1906 was also slightly muted, if only because the Queen's father, the King of Denmark, had recently died. But it 'appealed to the popular imagination in a very exceptional degree' and extra police had to be drafted from London to control the crowd. *The Times* correspondent noted, 'the continuity of British naval history' to be seen around him. 'Here, first and foremost, always noted with loving recognition and affectionate solicitude, is Nelson's *Victory*. At a little distance is the *St. Vincent*, another example of the wooden wall of Old England.' There were several Royal and naval yachts of different ages, plus, 'the *Colossus*, the *Barfleur*, the *Drake*, and half-a-dozen other vessels of modern construction. And, finally, here is the

The old ironclad *Neptune* collides with the *Victory* in 1903.

(© IMDB, tt2824818)

)readnought ready to join them, the latest expression f thought and experience in the domain of naval rchitecture.'

:vents on Board

'rank Wiseman was a teenage Domestic 3rd-Class, t the very bottom of the naval hierarchy, perhaps ecause his short-sightedness prevented him becoming seaman. He was expected to bring breakfast into the varrant officers' mess at 8.30am on 5 March 1906 but id not appear. Instead, it seems, the 'inquisitive lad' ad climbed up in the pantry port, as was his custom, o see a passing ship. It seems that he fell out, and his ries might have been drowned by the noise of riveters vorking on the ship's boiler. As he could not swim, e was never seen again despite a search of the area y boat.

During her century in harbour, the *Victory* spent ime as a training ship for officers, seaman, boys and ignallers. She usually had Royal Marines as part of her omplement, as well as domestics and writers, or clerks. Vith no engines and very little modern machinery, she aw very little of the other great naval tribe, the stokers. Their numbers were expanding rapidly during the early 900s, as the new fleet of Dreadnoughts and battle-ruisers needed vast numbers of them to feed their ngines with coal. Physical strength was important and hey were recruited as adults rather than boys, but they lid not have the rigorous training and *esprit de corps* of the Royal Marines, so stokers often presented a lisciplinary problem. That was why eleven of them ame on board the *Victory* as prisoners in November 906. At the beginning of the month, Lieutenant Bernard Collard, an *Excellent*-trained gunnery officer, bjected to the ill-discipline of a group of stokers on he parade ground in the barracks. He gave the order 'on the knee', which he claimed was merely to allow he men in the rear ranks to look over the heads of the ront rank, but was seen as a deliberate humiliation by he stokers. It might have passed over but that night he seamen taunted the stokers with a cry of 'on the knee'. The canteen was smashed up and rioting spread to the townspeople over the next few days, with marines being called to restore order.

Eleven alleged ringleaders were tried on board *Victory* at the end of the month. Among them was Edward Allen Moody, twenty-three years old and eighteen months in the navy, with a poor disciplinary record, charged on three counts. There was no real evidence that he had taken part in the original incident, but it was testified that he had incited the men with the words, 'You call yourself men; directly an officer speaks to you, you salutes the fucker and then goes and turns in; stick together if you are going to.' He claimed he had tried to pacify the men but the court believed that 'he was a man of considerable influence with the rest

A programme of events commemorating the centenary of Trafalgar in 1905.

(© National Maritime Museum, Greenwich, London, SNR/7/2)

Witnesses arriving for a court martial in 1909 after HMS *Gladiator* was in collision with the American ship *St Paul*. Captain Lumsden of the Royal Navy was reprimanded over the affair, though most of the blame went to the *St Paul*.

(© National Maritime Museum, Greenwich, London, Brass Foundry Album)

The desk on which Kaiser Wilhelm II signed the order to mobilise the German Army in August 1914, setting off a chain of events which led to European war.

(Photo from Potsdam, Germany, Stiftung Preussische Schlosser und Garten)

of the men, pacifying or inflaming them as the fancy took him at the moment.' When he was sentenced to five years in Wormwood Scrubs, there was outrage, especially in the growing labour movement, for many stokers had links to the trade unions, and Moody himself was a former carter. Portsmouth United Trades and Labour Council claimed the sentence was 'out of all bounds of justice.' It was not helped when Collard was tried on board the *Victory*. He was cleared of two charges relating to the incident in November, but guilty of a previous incident when he had ordered Stoker Albert Acton 'on the knee', and reprimanded him. It was never established whether he used the phrase 'on the knee, you dirty dog', but popular legend believed he did and it represented the attitude of many officers to the lower deck. His career did not suffer however, he eventually reached the rank of rear-admiral where he fell foul of another highly-publicised court martial. Moody's sentence was reduced to three years, while several of the officers in charge of the barracks were removed from their posts for allowing the situation to get out of hand.

The Great War

The reserves of the Royal Navy happened to be mobilised for a test run in July 1914 as events in Europe began to move towards war. A great fleet of fifty-nine battleships, old and new, plus supporting vessels was already assembled off Portsmouth and Winston Churchill, as First Lord of the Admiralty, ordered them to be kept in service. The *Victory* had already played a key, if unrecognised, role in perhaps the most momentous event of the nineteenth century – Napoleon's campaign against Russia. Her timbers, if not the ship herself, were to have a passive and indirect part in perhaps the greatest turning point of the twentieth century. On 1 August 1914, according to the diary of Field Marshal Erich von Falkenhayn, Kaiser Wilhem II of Germany signed the order to mobilise his army, shaking the field marshal's hand with tears in his eyes. This was the trigger which set the German plan into motion, involving the invasion of Belgium and war with France, Russia and Great Britain and their respective empires. It was almost as devastating as the mythical 'button' which leaders were expected to push to start a nuclear war in the latter part of the century, as most of the nations of Europe were drawn into a war which would kill millions of them. He signed the order on a desk said to have been made from the timbers of the *Victory*, crafted by the firm of Waring & Gillow and presumably presented in the 1890s, when relations between the countries were much better.[47]

12 A NATIONAL SYMBOL

After a Long War

The *Victory* had a relatively quiet war in 1914–18. The great fleet of new Dreadnought battleships left Portsmouth to spend most of the war hundreds of miles away at Scapa Flow – although 1,200 refits were carried out in the dockyard and its workforce increased to 23,000. Almost everyone expected a short war, but a 'second Trafalgar' did not materialise. When the two fleets finally came into contact off Jutland in June 1916, the British lost more ships and men, though they claimed a strategic victory in that the German High Seas Fleet had retreated and hardly left port again. The spirit of Nelson was constantly evoked, but he would not have approved of the over-centralised system of command set up by Admiral Jellicoe for his Grand Fleet, or of his caution over risking his ships in battle. The public saw Sir David Beatty of the Battle Cruiser Fleet as being closer to the Nelson model, but he lacked the meticulous eye for detail that made Nelson successful. The navy was caught unprepared for the submarine campaign against merchant shipping and, by the end of the war in 1918, its prestige was greatly reduced as people asked whether the huge expenditure before the war was really justified. *Victory* remained at her mooring off Gosport through all of this, slowly rotting while thousands of sailors passing through Portsmouth

W. L. Wyllie's view of Portsmouth Harbour in 1916, probably painted from his house near the entrance, with a submarine entering and HMS *Victory* in the background.

(© National Maritime Museum, Greenwich, London, PW1782)

carried her name on their cap badges. On 25 September 1916, Zeppelin *L31* attacked the port instead of London but met a heavy barrage and dropped its bombs harmlessly in the harbour.

As the navy emerged from its long and disappointing war, £6,897 was set aside for repairs to the *Victory* in the 1919–20 budget. Thirty apprentices were employed under the normal workmen, but not all the money was spent that year. More defects were found under 'the accumulated thicknesses of paint' and £234 was added to the estimate to cover that, and ultimately just over £8,000 was spent. It was now believed that she was 'generally to be [considered] sound and fit for harbour service, with no leaks from the sea.'[1] Public attention was drawn to the ship by the press in June 1921, when a short report on the annual general meeting of the Society for Nautical Research in *The Times* carried the headline, 'Nelson's Flagship in Danger – The *Victory* likely to sink.'

Admiral Sir Doveton Sturdee, painted by Arthur Stockdale Cope in 1920, shortly before the 'Save the *Victory*' campaign began.

(© National Maritime Museum, Greenwich, London, BHC3042)

The Role of the SNR

The Society for Nautical Research had been founded in 1911 with the aim of publishing a journal (known as *Mariners Mirror* to this day) and to 'encourage research into Nautical Antiquities'; (a third aim, to publish the definitive nautical dictionary, was never achieved). The Society had always attracted leading figures in the naval and maritime world, besides its hard-working stalwarts, the prolific marine artist W. L. Wyllie, the historians R. C. Anderson and L. G. Carr Laughton, and 250 other members. Its president was the Marquis of Milford Haven, better known as Prince Louis of Battenburg, unfairly dismissed as First Sea Lord at the start of the war and father of Lord Louis Mountbatten – like the Royal Family, they changed their name because of its German associations. In June 1921 he approached the Admiralty on behalf of the Society, apologising for the premature leaking of the *Victory* story, and suggesting that they should 'endeavour to perhaps assist if necessary in the raising of any necessary sum by voluntary contributions...'.[2] It was possible that the hull might be strengthened by steel or concrete to remain afloat in Portsmouth Harbour, but already the Admiralty was looking at the possibility of installing the ship in one of the old docks, and perhaps filling it with sand. Milford Haven died in December 1921, and after six months interregnum he was replaced as Chairman of the SNR by Admiral Sir Doveton Sturdee, who had gained fame by beating a smaller German force off the Falkland Islands in 1914. The main reason for the delay was that Sturdee was reluctant to commit himself to the immense task needed on the *Victory*, but in the words of those who worked with him, 'it was entirely in keeping with Sir Doveton Sturdee's character that, when his reluctance was eventually overcome, he should have thrown himself heart and soul into the furtherance of the very object which had occasioned his hesitation.'[3] He devised the title 'Save the *Victory*' for the campaign.

Other ideas began to emerge – one, supported by one George W. Hershey – to mount her on a concrete plinth or dock and display her either at Portsmouth or Greenwich.[4] Sir Henry Grayson of Liverpool offered to repair her at his own expense in one of his docks on the Mersey, but it was considered too dangerous to tow her all that way. Another plan was to dredge a channel and install her in a berth at the unfortunately named Rat Island, but beaching her was dismissed as 'technically impractical'. The most obvious and simplest solution was to install her in a dry dock in Portsmouth, even though it was pointed out that 'the surrender of a dock would seriously interfere with efficiency of the yard.' Nevertheless, Number Two Dock was selected, as 'a small dock which has been utilised for E class submarines, tugs, drifters and other small craft', its loss 'will not be seriously felt as long as the fleet remains on its present reduced state.'[5]

In Dock

On 15 January 1922 the *Victory* was duly towed into the dock with a certain amount of ceremony, photographed for the press, filmed by Pathé News and painted by W L Wyllie, whose wife Marion wrote, 'Parade, Guards, and bands, *Victory* passes. A wonderful sight! The grand old ship had swung at her moorings, where she had fretted for so many years up and down with the tide, rugged and worn; now for the last time she was under way. The tugs had hold of her, and, slowly and majestically, she passed the grey Atlantic Fleet manned and lined up against the dockyard wall, the bands playing and flags flying.'[6] But the Admiralty did not accept that this was permanent and the admiral commanding the Reserve Fleet wrote, 'the question whether the *Victory* will return to her usual berth in the harbour, or remain permanently in dock, depends upon the survey of the hull which is being made.' That was completed by 10 February and showed that 'a large number of timbers and a considerable amount of planking, especially at the water line, are in an advanced state of decay... The structure of the vessels shows signs of excessive straining... The keel is hogged... The decks are generally distorted and drop appreciably from the foremast forward.' This was 'considered due to the strain put upon the vessel when swinging at her moorings in harbour.' In short, fifty percent of the test borings taken at random showed decay. It was agreed that she was 'beyond economic repair for maintenance afloat' and would be berthed permanently in Number Two Dock.[7]

This had already raised as many questions as it answered. Some officials worried about the livelihood of the boatmen who had taken visitors out to the ship, the descendants of the rapacious and greedy oarsmen of 1854 and Beatrix Potter's 'broad, yellow-whiskered man' of thirty years later. One suggestion was to employ them as guides, but that was finally dismissed as the work would require 'an intimate knowledge of the vessel, and considerable training', and 'the nature of the work' would be 'entirely foreign to their calling.' The policy in April 1922 was for dockyard guides to take the visitors to the ship's gangway, 'where Royal Marines of the ships complement are detailed to show them over the ship. These marines are non-commissioned officers and men of long-service and good conduct: they have acquainted themselves with the ship and her history, and are very suitable for the employment in question.'[8] This was not the experience of Sir Geoffrey Callender, Professor of History at the Royal Naval College and a strong supporter of the campaign. In September that year he described:

> ...How shocked I was at the flippancy of the young marine guides. "Yuss! This is where Nelson & Lady Hamilton sat canoodling.... (shrieks of laughter)... Go on, of course they did. Lady Hamilton was always on board when Nelson was. You bet. Not 'arf". It made me almost physically sick.

Undoubtedly, the move ashore had opened up the ship to less affluent and educated visitors and Callender was not entirely happy with the result. He complained about 'the irreverence of the crowds... Giggling girls flirting in Nelson's own cabin! Nauseating.'[9] He suggested a charge 'for the preservation of decency' but that was rejected by the Admiralty in 1923 and 1928. '...so long as the *Victory* is one of His Majesty's ships, and flies the flag of the commander-in-chief at Portsmouth, an admission fee is unsuitable, especially when the ship was Nelson's flagship, and had been restored by public subscription.'

Trafalgar Condition

The idea of restoring the ship to her condition at the time of Trafalgar had been around since the days of John Poole in 1830, and in 1909 Admiral Sir Arthur Fanshawe put it to the Admiralty again with no result.[10] However, not everyone agreed and the then Admiral Superintendent of the Dockyard, Alexander-Sinclair, wrote, while looking over the ship from his office, that 'to rebuild would be a pity as you would have a new ship and not the old *Victory*. I think all that is necessary to give her the general appearance of her Trafalgar days could be done comparatively inexpensively and would satisfy anyone but an extreme expert and there are not many of them left now a days.' An estimate showed that

Wylie's depiction of the *Victory* being towed into dock with ships of the Atlantic Fleet on the left-hand side.

(© National Maritime Museum, Greenwich, London, BHC3700)

essential repairs to the ship would cost £16,000 while restoration to her Trafalgar rig and appearance would cost ten times as much, £160,000. It was suggested that 'as *Victory* is essentially a national relic... the cost of her restoration, which is purely sentimental, should fall on the state or on the nation rather than the navy votes.'[11] This left the Society for Nautical Research to take up the challenge.

In June 1922 the Admiralty offered their co-operation in a letter to Sturdee. Only work essential to the safety of the ship could be done from the navy vote due to 'financial stringency' and anything else would have to be funded from elsewhere. 'Their Lordships would welcome any endeavour on the part of the Nautical Research Society [sic] to raise, in such a way as they think fit, the funds necessary for work in connection with the preservation and restoration of HMS *Victory*.'[12] The SNR set up two committees. The *Victory* Technical Committee had the aim of finding the evidence to restore her to her Trafalgar appearance. It was headed by Sir Phillip Watts, the former Director of Naval Construction who had designed the *Dreadnought* and had shown interest in the *Victory* since a lecture to the Royal Institution of Naval Architects in 1905. Wyllie and his son were members, along with L. G. Carr Laughton, an unstable character but sound nautical historian who would do much of the detailed research. Wyllie's daughter Aileen was also brought in. 'I wondered how I, a flapper, came to know that band of brother enthusiasts so well. Then I remembered – I drove the round-nosed Morris, and many were the journeyings between station and Dockyard and Tower House, often ending up at Monck's Oyster Bar in High Street.'[13] A meeting in June 1923 adjourned to the Royal United Services Institute to look at models of the *Victory* and *Caledonia* in their museum, followed by a visit to the Science Museum in South Kensington. Already, there was tension between the historians and the naval officers and Callender wrote that he was disturbed 'how completely the dockyard models its opinion re the *Victory* on what the Chief Constructor says; and how completely the chief constructor is AGAINST all that we come out for. Sir Philip Watts talked to him like a child.'[14] But Callender himself was later described as 'an outstanding personality and the one and only person whose opinion was decisive in all

Victory under heavy repair in 1926, with scaffolding round the hull and lower masts.

(© The Society for Nautical Research, Annual Report, 1937)

matters affecting the preservation of *Victory*, so at that time it made little or no difference how the business was arranged on paper.'[15] Carr Laughton resigned in July 1923, after he had already completed a substantial body of detailed research which would be published in *Mariners Mirror* in 1924. Watts agreed that 'in it we have made a thorough search through the Admiralty records' – which was far more difficult in those days when they were not well collected or catalogued.

The other body was the Victory Appeal Committee, chaired by Sturdee in person and including the official historian Sir Archibald Hurd and Professor Callender. They issued an appeal on Trafalgar Day 1922, but unfortunately it coincided with a general election campaign and '...invitations to contribute to the *Victory* fund were lost in a cataract of political placards.'[16] Sturdee and his committee issued emotional, if rather dated, appeals. 'The *Victory* represents, as nothing else can, the wooden walls of England. They existed before Britain. Without them there would have been no Greater Britain. The *Victory* ought to be safe – ought she not? – in the affection and gratitude of the people.' He hoped to get donations from poor as well as rich. 'It is because the *Victory* is a ship – the ship of memories that the friends of the Fund make their wide appeal. We want every boy and girl in the Empire to give something. If it is only a penny, it will be an education in patriotism....' But it was still slow going and in February 1923 *The Times* reported that the fund had still not raised enough money. A few days later Sturdee was delighted to receive a letter sent via the Admiralty:

> I regret to note in today's *Times* that the funds subscribed to save the old *Victory* are insufficient to start the work. I have already subscribed but it will afford me much pleasure to place at your disposal £50,000 (fifty-thousand) if it will enable the work to be proceeded with. Unless to encourage others you may not require to intimate that contribution. In any case only as from 'A Wellwisher of the Navy.'[17]

It was signed by Sir James Caird, a Dundee shipowner who had sold his interests in the Shire and Clan Lines in 1917, avoiding the post-war slump. Though the fund was still short of its target of £150,000, work on restoration could now proceed.

Repair Work

Work began in June 1923, with 'the removal of the figure head, preparatory to an entire reconstruction of the knee of the head and the rebuilding of the frame above it.' A film was made in time for Trafalgar Day that year, scripted by Callender and produced by F W Engholm, the main naval film-maker. Subscribers to *Kinematograph Weekly* were told it was 'a two-reel wonder film your patrons will insist on seeing.'[18] As to the ship itself, it was not long before the long-standing controversy over how much of it was original began to surface. Mr C.E. Kinder, a civil engineer, wrote to *The Times* that 'practically every part had been renewed before the present reconstruction, so that we now have only a vessel of the same shape as that which was in action when Nelson was killed.' Watts replied angrily, 'Kinder has been very much misinformed and has apparently taken little trouble to ascertain the real value of the information.' A reply was necessary or 'some people will think there is no good answer to his remarks and that contributions to the Restoration Fund might, in consequence, dry up.' Sturdee replied a few days later, referring him to Sir Phillip Watts' paper in the *Transactions of the Institution of Naval Architects* in which he stated rather vaguely, 'it is still true that much of the material of the old vessel still remains.'[19]

Every participant in the restoration had his own favourite project. Sir Phillip Watts was concerned that the ship did not sit well in its present position in the dock, and he convinced Sturdee, 'the restoration could scarcely be considered satisfactory unless the vessel in the dry dock presented such a trim and height of side in relation to the surrounding masonry as would give a proper reproduction of the appearance of the ship at Trafalgar.'

It was necessary to raise her three feet aft and seven feet in the bows. Watts produced a plan to float the ship and have divers place tanks under her hull to support her in the new position. This was rejected in favour of a dockyard scheme by which she was lifted in three stages, also by flooding the dock and employing divers. It was completed by April 1925.

The shape of the bow was more contentious. It had been reconstructed to the Seppings system in 1813–16, but clearly that was not how it had been at Trafalgar – indeed, its weakness in the battle was part of the story. W. L. Wyllie was of the opinion that 'it is much more

important to cut away the topgallant forecastle, Seppings bow and high bulwarks (added in 1820) than to attempt to re-rig the ship with the funds likely to be available.' Gregory Robinson, another SNR Council member, disagreed, 'if we were restoring the Abbey, we wouldn't start by pulling down King Henry VIII Chapel because it was later work.' The C-in-C seemed to rule it out on the grounds of cost, 'this impossibility of restoring the old 1805 bow really marks the limit of possible alterations for the present: as it would probably involve the expenditure of hundreds of thousands of pounds.' It had to be shelved for the moment.

The restoration was largely complete by the spring of 1928, though Callender noted pessimistically that it was 'only in a structural sense finished.' Nevertheless, it was marked by a Royal visit on 17 July when George V arrived on board:

> His Majesty chatted with those on the quarterdeck, and then proceeded to make the rounds of the ship.... He ascended the poop, viewed the quarters once occupied by Nelson and Hardy, and proceeded from deck to deck, displaying unflagging interest and asking questions of significance to those engaged in nautical research. At the conclusion of the tour, which lasted little short of an hour, his Majesty unveiled a simple tablet of oak an ivory to commemorate his visit.[20]

It was a great moment for James Caird who was presented to the King and created a Baronet in

The ship in its original position in the dry-dock, with the bow, in particular, too low to give a correct appearance.

(© National Maritime Museum, Greenwich, London, Brass Foundry Album)

The ship in the later stages of restoration, by W. L. Wyllie.

(© National Maritime Museum, Greenwich, London, BHC3701)

The Royal visit 1928. King George V talks to W. L. Wyllie while his son Harold, in RAF uniform, is to the right. The figures in the background near the break of the poop are Sir James Caird and Sir Geoffrey Callendar .

(© The Society for Nautical Reasearch)

recognition of his work.

The SNR had always intended that a museum should be set up alongside the *Victory* and in 1929 the Admiralty allowed the use of an old rigging house near the ship. An annexe was built to the rear, to house what was to be the museum's centrepiece for many years – a panorama of the Battle of Trafalgar painted by W.L. Wyllie. It showed the scene from the great cabin of the French *Neptune* with the *Victory* in the centre engaging the *Redoutable* and assisted by the *Temeraire*. Wyllie was assisted by his daughter Aileen who described the work. 'First we ruled in the horizon. W. L. had taught me how to enlarge with proportional compasses and so we were both off – a deck chair and a packet of sandwiches and the long day's work began; me pencilling in the detail for his sketches and he following with colour, making all well. When it came to the vast expense of sea and sky, we reversed the process.'[21]

But, by this time, the Save the *Victory* Fund was running out of money. Callender noted in December, 'our funds are practically exhausted'. There was a great deal of relief in April 1929, when the Admiralty agreed that the old question of the restoration of the bow to its Trafalgar condition was their responsibility as part of the ongoing maintenance programme.[22] The Technical Committee was no longer effective, meetings were now rare and, according to Callender, they usually involved 'fresh demands for expenditure' as members put forward their pet ideas, while he already had a 'long list of demands'.[23]

Nevertheless, the ship made steady progress in the next decade. Navy Days started in Portsmouth in 1928, largely as a counter to the RAF's highly successful and exciting annual displays at Hendon. The *Victory* was

Crowds of visitors queue to board the ship in 1937.

(© The Society for Nautical Research, Annual Report, 1937)

now able to receive visitors on a regular basis and became a centrepiece among modern warships. In 1932 the restoration of Nelson's sleeping cabin was complete and it was opened to the public. Some of the ship's boats – the barge, launch, pinnace and jolly-boat – were researched and constructed in teak for longevity, to be mounted on the booms in the waist of the ship. By 1937 the SNR was riding high. Visitors to the *Victory* reached nearly 105,000, with a cumulative total of 1.74 million since 1928.[24] Another of its long-term aims, the creation of a National Maritime Museum, was achieved largely due to the support of Sir James Caird, and Sir Geoffrey Callender became its first director. King George VI, accompanied by his wife and daughter Princess Elizabeth, opened it at Greenwich on 27 April 1937. But the next war was not long away, the museum would be closed for the duration and the *Victory* would find yet another role.

Victory in wartime with the yards and topmasts sent down for safety.

(© National Maritime Museum, Greenwich, London, Brass Foundry Album)

Victory at War

Victory and Nelson might have seemed irrelevant and outdated in the war which began in September 1939, for it was largely dominated by aircraft and submarines – except that it was the aircrews and the submarine, destroyer and escort commanders who were the true successors to Nelson in initiative and daring. The Commander-in-Chief at Portsmouth was Admiral Sir William James, known as 'Bubbles' because as a boy he had been painted by his grandfather Sir John Everett Millias, a picture which was turned into a poster for Pears soap. Two months after the start of the war, Alexander Grant was offered the command of the *Victory*.[25] He would be the eleventh captain since the ship was docked in 1922, for she had remained a commissioned ship of the Royal Navy for all that time. Grant was a rare example of an officer who had risen from the ranks, he was a gunner in Beatty's flagship *Lion* at Jutland and saved the ship from a magazine explosion. He was commissioned at the age of forty-six and commanded destroyers before taking up a position at the gunnery school HMS *Excellent* where he was known as 'Wormy'. He had retired as a commander before being recalled at the start of the war. Like the war itself, the *Victory* was quiet for the first few months. Her yards, jib-boom, topgallants and topmasts were lowered for safety. Many of the crew were recalled to active service while the dockyard was closed to visitors. Valuable relics were removed, though Grant feared that they would suffer more from the damp conditions in which they were stored than from enemy action. Life began to return to the ship as barrage balloon crews were accommodated on board, as well as soldiers for the dockyard guard. When British and French forces had to be evacuated from Dunkirk, James's own barge was one of those sent to carry out the rescue, under his coxswain.[26]

The historically-minded could not fail to notice that, with Britain alone against a continental enemy, the situation was similar to that of 1803–5, when the *Victory* had contained the French in Toulon and helped prevent an invasion. Carola Oman, who would publish a classic biography of Nelson shortly after the war, wrote *Britain Against Napoleon* and her publishers adorned the cover with comparisons – 'British volunteers drill to meet the invasion..., the evacuation of families to safe areas is planned... foreign royalties arrive in flight from the "protector"....' But the greatest single difference was that even if the Germans could not cross the English Channel in the face of the Royal Navy, they could still bomb the cities. After many raids on Portsmouth, Admiral James's house in the dockyard was hit. 'I had to find a new headquarters and, as all the buildings in the dockyard had been damaged, I installed myself in the *Victory*. It proved an excellent choice. Hardy's cabin under the poop provided me with a good office; my wife had Nelson's day cabin as a sitting-room, and there was room to entertain twenty guests in the dining-cabin.'[27]

Winston Churchill visited the *Victory* in January 1941 before going on to the heavily-bombed town of Portsmouth and delivering a typically uncompromising speech to the city councillors. He would invoke the spirit of Nelson many times during the conflict. According to General Auchinleck, 'time and again he would quote from Nelson's Trafalgar memorandum: 'No captain can do very wrong if he places his ship alongside that of an enemy.'[28] In Hollywood, the Hungarian/British director Alexander Korda commissioned a huge model of the *Victory* for use in his film *Lady Hamilton,* known as *That Hamilton Woman* in the USA. Some of its lines, including 'you cannot make peace with dictators. Wipe them out!' were so Churchillian that it was believed the great man had written them himself. Despite deep historical flaws, the film was Churchill's favourite and he saw it for the fifth time on board the *Prince of Wales* on the way to meet President Roosevelt in August 1941. Tears were seen in his eyes during the showing, and he addressed the wardroom officers; 'Gentlemen, I thought this film would interest you, showing great events similar to those in which you have been taking part.' The film was suspected of being British propaganda in some American quarters, but an appearance by the producers before a congressional committee was averted after the Japanese attack on Pearl Harbour catapulted the country into war

Meanwhile, in Portsmouth, Admiral James exploited the prestige of the *Victory* to the full:

> A continual stream of distinguished people – reigning Sovereigns, Dominion Prime Ministers, British Cabinet Ministers – came to Portsmouth to see what the Navy was doing and it gave them a thrill to be received and entertained on board the *Victory*. And as her noble and

An Air Raid on Portsmouth by Richard Eurich, with the *Victory* visible in the background.

(© The Tate Gallery, London, No5690)

unscarred lines dominated an area of rubble and twisted girders, she became a symbol of victory.[29]

Vera Laughton Matthews, director of the Women's Royal Naval Service, dined there several times, being amused by 'watching the Wren stewards in their white overalls officiating so quietly and capably in that historic place' – though as the sister of L. G. Carr, Laughton she was perhaps a little biased when she wrote, 'the restoration is so perfect that one seems to live in the shadow of the great Admiral.'[30]

If there was comfort and tradition in the cabin of the *Victory*, life was very different for the thousands of men who were formally attached to the ship – though in this war they did not wear the cap tally, for security reasons, junior ratings simply had the letters 'HMS' on their caps. The 1903 barracks had seemed progressive compared with the old hulks, but like many building of the age, they had descended into slums due to a combination of poor maintenance, changing standards and overcrowding, plus the threat of bombs and gas in wartime. '...In Portsmouth Naval Barracks in 1942 there were 120 men in messes meant for thirty, and sixteen knives and forks in the mess. Every other night ratings slept down cold, damp air-raid shelters. It could escape no intelligent person that the real reason why half the men slept down the shelters was that there was no room for them in the buildings. As a result of this many died of pneumonia.'[31] In addition, men and women were housed or worked in camps and barracks around the region, ranging from the accounting section at Newbury, *Victory II*, to the Portsmouth demobilisation centre which became known as *Victory X*.[32] Later, largely due to overcrowding in the barracks, young men who were candidates for temporary wartime commissions were housed on board the *Victory* herself, either before or after their minimum of three months as a rating at sea, and before going on to officer training in HMS *King Alfred* at Hove. These were the 'CWs', so called because they were administered by the Commission and Warrant Branch of the Admiralty. According to Grant, 'they were a fine type of men, and no better palace could have been found for them than on board this ship, steeped in tradition. They lived as Nelson's sailors lived, with their Mess between the guns and their hammocks slung to the beams at night.'[33]

The bomb damage to the bottom of the ship in 1941.

(© HMS Victory)

Grant wrote that 'the safety of the *Victory* during the recurring enemy air attacks was a source of anxiety. Incendiary bombs were the main trouble. The ship was built entirely of wood and that together with its tarred rigging meant never ceasing vigilance against the risk of fire.... Our air raid stations were simple to arrange. It was just a case of "all hands on the upper deck". It was no good taking shelter below decks whilst the ship might be burning furiously below.'[34] However, it was not an incendiary bomb that hit the *Victory*. In the morning of 10 March 1941 the dockyard was heavily blitzed, with eighty-seven service personnel killed, five ships damaged and almost all naval establishments hit, including the barracks. A 500 lb high-explosive bomb hit the masonry of the *Victory* dock between number two and three supporting cradles and exploded, damaging the cradles and shores which supported the ship. The *Victory's* keel was damaged, her back was broken and a hole 15ft by 8ft was blasted in the bottom, with minor damage on the orlop, lower and middle decks. However, the damaged area was soon shored up and the ship continued to function as a flagship.[35]

When Sir William James was relieved in September

1942, Grant organised events on board the *Victory*. 'I had arranged a small party of guests to bid them farewell. Arrangements had been made to give them a right Royal Naval send off when they left the ship. As they stepped on shore the band played the Admiral's salute followed by "All the nice girls love a sailor"'. The ship's company of *Victory* was drawn up to cheer them away, supplemented by a large crowd of men and women assembled in the vicinity. James was historically-minded and revived an old privilege of a retiring commander-in-chief to promote Grant to captain.

James was succeeded by Sir Charles Little, who was partly responsible for organising the forces for the Normandy invasion, especially those to transport Force J, the 3rd Canadian Infantry Division, which was based in the area and would land on Juno Beach. The *Victory* had been headquarters for amphibious forces before, off Toulon in 1793, Corsica in 1794 and briefly off Gothenburg in 1808. However, she was not truly a headquarters this time, for Little moved back to Admiralty House now that the threat of bombing had receded, and used the *Victory* for entertainment purposes. Admiral Sir Bertram Ramsay, naval commander of the invasion, dined on board several times, though at the end of April 1944 he commented, '...the Portsmouth command is weak in operational and administrative staff and the C-in-C does too much for himself rather than getting good and sufficient officers to do it for him.' Next day, he dined with Little on board the *Victory*, along with the First Sea Lord Andrew Cunningham and his wife, the commanders of the Eastern Task Force which would land on Gold, Juno and Sword beaches, and he 'met some generals.' At the end of May, just over a week before the invasion, he was back on the ship for lunch with the foreign secretary, Anthony Eden.[36]

The round of visitors continued and included exiled sovereigns. 'His Majesty the King honoured the ship by again lunching on board.' There were other Royal visitors, 'The Princess Royal; Duchess of Kent; the Queen of the Netherlands; the King of Norway; the prime minister; His Grace the Archbishop of Canterbury, Dr Temple; The Turkish Ambassador; Lord Chatfield; Field Marshals Smuts, Wavell and Montgomery; General Eisenhower...' When the motor magnate Lord Nuffield came on board Grant joked 'No mass production here' and thought it was well received. He was gratified when a Canadian group lingered longer than expected. 'We can see submarines any day but we may never see the *Victory* again.' A party from the youth movement of the USSR was incensed with the bomb damage, shaking their fists and saying 'We will let them have it when we get to the front.'[37]

Grant became the longest-serving commanding officer of the *Victory* after six years and, by the time he left in 1945, 'The public was again allowed to visit the ship and during the Whitsun weekend no less than fifteen- thousand came on board to look after the grand old ship. ...Before I left the dockyard riggers had made a start to replace masts and yards, and by Trafalgar Day of that year the topgallants were crossed and Nelson's famous signal was hoisted at the masthead and yardarms.'[38]

After the War

The Royal Navy had had a far more successful war than 1914–18 – it had evacuated the army from Dunkirk, played a largely unheralded role in preventing invasion in 1940–41, defeated the U-boat in the Battle of the Atlantic, fought successfully for control of the Mediterranean and provided the bulk of the naval forces for the Normandy landing in 1944. Yet, it had clearly lost it place as the world's greatest naval power. When the British Pacific Fleet was sent out towards the end of the war, it was found to be vastly inferior to American forces in numbers, technique and equipment. The Royal Navy had employed just over a million men and women during the war and the vast majority left the service with great loyalty and pride, but often mingled with regret. The left-wing journalist Hannan Swaffer used the great admiral's name negatively in the title of his book *What Would Nelson Do?,* exposing social conditions in the navy immediately after the war. 'For... the Royal Navy is ridden with a caste system that has been abolished in our civilian life; its lower deck is ruled with a discipline that is out of date; and its traditions belong to that age of Squiredom when the villagers bowed and curtsied when the landlord passed on his way.' Despite popular myth, the Navy was nearly always technologically advanced, but socially it was extremely conservative. In these circumstances, the *Victory* was an ambiguous symbol, of an old-fashioned order as well

Implacable being sunk in 1949, watched from the destroyer *Finisterre* by the French naval attaché and Admiral H.U.A Willis, drawn by his son-in-law Roderick Macdonald.

(© National Maritime Museum, Greenwich, ZBA1762)

as heroism and triumph.

The *Implacable* had fought on the French side at Trafalgar under the name of *Duguay-Trouin*. She was captured a few days later, renamed and fitted out in British style. In 1808, under Byam Martin, she attacked the Russian fleet off Port Baltic, after which they were blockaded by the *Victory*. She became a training ship at Plymouth and in 1908 she was saved from the scrapyard on the intervention of King Edward VII. She was afloat in Falmouth harbour before being towed to Portsmouth in 1932, and was taken up by the SNR as a training ship for boys during the school holidays. She was often mentioned alongside the *Victory*, but she was still afloat at the end of the war and in poor condition. In 1947 it was proposed that she might be taken to Greenwich and placed in a new berth near the pier; but it was estimated this would cost up to half a million pounds, which would be impossible to raise in the economic circumstances after the war. The Admiralty was extremely reluctant to help and would not offer a dry-dock for repair as 'it would be lost to the country for some considerable time.' The matter was debated in Parliament and Mr Emrys Hughes pointed out that there was 'a very serious shortage of firewood in France' before being suppressed by the Speaker. It was decided to sink her in deep water, but it proved impracticable to tow her far out, so she was taken to the Owers Light off the Isle of Wight. She was ballasted with 500 tonnes of iron to make her sink and fitted with charges inside her hull to blow holes in her bottom. Watched by two British admirals and the French naval attaché on board the destroyer *Finisterre*, the charges were exploded and the lower hull blown apart, but the upper works became detached and floated for three hours until they sank eventually.[39] The planned berth in Greenwich was allocated to the clipper *Cutty Sark*, which had better financial support and filled a different gap in the range of preserved ships.

The *Victory* herself was surveyed in 1949 and some major defects were found, but the dockyard was short of shipwrights and many active warships had to be repaired after wartime services and damage. It was only possible to put on small parties 'to keep pace with preserving those parts of the ship where visitors moved about – the gangways, ladders and so on.' Furthermore, timber was not available. A large quantity was ordered after the 1949 survey but was still seasoning in 1955.[40] The presence of death-watch beetle was becoming increasingly alarming. Nearly 6,000 were found in 1946, rising to more than 16,000 in the following year. Palliative measure were introduced, including 'application of insecticides and collection and destruction of all beetles found on the ship during the annual emergence period, April–June.' The number was brought down to 5,200 by 1953, but more had to be done. Fumigation began in April 1954. The ship, including the bomb-hole, was sealed from the upper deck downwards with plastic cocooning. On 1 April the London Fumigation Company began work in cool weather with a strong south-west wind on the starboard side of the ship. Gas was pumped in and tests showed that the great majority of the beetles had been killed. Numbers found alive were reduced from 5,200 to 933, but it was still necessary to carry out the process in 1955 and 1956. Eventually, by 1960, only forty-five death-watch beetles and fifteen blue beetles could be found.[41]

While looking at methods for preserving the ship in 1953, it was suggested that the waist might be covered over to prevent water reaching the upper deck and the rest of the ship. This soon incurred the wrath of Harold Wyllie, the artist's son, who considered it would be a departure from the plan to rebuild the ship as in 1805. R. C. Anderson suggested glass instead, but that would have been vulnerable in a gale. A removable cover was difficult because, as the commanding officer pointed out, 'insufficient hands were available at times for him to deal with an awning'. The controversy proved a catalyst for a reconsideration of how the ship was to be managed. It led to the revival of the *Victory* Advisory Technical Committee (VTAC) to reconcile the views of naval officers, conservators, historians, timber experts, naval architects and practical shipwrights.

A shipwright repairing the sternpost with an adze, c.1955. Some of the key features are marked on the photograph.

(© HMS Victory, Album D4)

More Work Needed

The ship had a major survey in 1955. Nine tiers of staging, each three planks wide, were erected round the ship, being braced to avoid resting on the vulnerable hull. More than 6,000 spots were selected for test boring, each carried out by two workmen with a 5/8 inch auger and a pneumatic drill. Beams and knees were drilled obliquely upwards to penetrate flat surfaces and deck planking. It was found that the lower structure from the keel to the turn of the bilge was in very poor condition, particularly near the sternpost. The hull was in real danger of collapse. The 'Save the *Victory*' fund raised £20,000 in support, but the work was very difficult, to be 'compared with the renewal of the foundations of a heavy building without disturbance to the building itself', according to constructor Arthur Bugler. Temporary supports were erected as each area was repaired in turn. Large quantities of teak were imported for the repairs, preferably from Burma, as English oak was no longer available in the shapes and qualities needed. Repairs continued until 1964, by which time British society had changed around the old ship.

The 150th anniversary of Trafalgar in October 1955 was celebrated by a dinner attended by the young Queen Elizabeth II, while the Duke of Edinburgh attended a service in Trafalgar Square. Events on board the *Victory* were rather constrained by the rebuild, but Nelson's signal was hoisted and the chaplain of Portsmouth Dockyard conducted a service. In the harbour, the ships fired 15-gun salutes and thirty naval fighters flew overhead. But, within a year, the optimism of a 'new Elizabethan age' was shattered, as the British and French had to withdraw from Suez after American intervention. The British Empire was largely wound up and the Royal Navy lost one of its main roles. It learned to live as part of an alliance, the North Atlantic Treaty Organisation (NATO), formed in 1949 against the Soviet threat. In 1960 the *Vanguard*, the last battleship and linear descendant of the *Sovereign of the Seas, Victory, Warrior, Devastation* and *Dreadnought*, was towed away for scrap and went aground at the entrance to Portsmouth Harbour. A new *Dreadnought* was launched that year, a nuclear submarine, but she was no longer in the forefront of technology – she needed an American reactor and her hull was slightly distorted to accommodate it. Britain's main nuclear deterrent in the 1960s, carried by nuclear-powered submarines, the new Polaris missile, was also American, and brought the navy into the anti-nuclear debate instigated by the Campaign for Nuclear Disarmament, while much of the submarine force moved to Faslane in Scotland. Symbolically, the all-powerful Admiralty was merged into the faceless Ministry of Defence in 1964. All this led to a crisis of national and naval identity, which was increased by popular culture. Elvis Presley was indisputably American and never performed outside that country, while even the native Beatles and Rolling Stones of the 60s were a long way from the disciplined, military culture of the 1950s.

The ship, however. remained the main attraction of Portsmouth Dockyard during the late 1950s, with around a quarter of a million visitors a year, naturally peaking in the summer months with a record of 78,385 in August 1958. The thirteenth meeting of the VATC was held on Trafalgar Day 1960 in the great cabin of the ship and the chairman asked the members to stand in memory of Nelson, remarking, 'how privileged they were to serve in the preservation of his "Symbol of Britain's greatness".' Visitor figures were good, and Rear-Admiral Unwin suggested that 'the poor summer weather of 1960 had probably driven some people off the beaches of Southsea into the ship' – for the British were just beginning to discover cheap flights and the beaches of Spain. Members were told of 'the best six months' progress which had ever been achieved in the ship', though now the emphasis was on furnishings and fittings as well as the structure. A few hammocks had been slung to show how overcrowded the decks were, and mess tables and utensils were put in position. A diorama was to be set up showing the cockpit in battle, and furniture including an Indian carpet was being found for Nelson's cabin.[42]

The navy always had a problem reconciling its long history with a modern image, as it competed with the RAF for the best recruits. In 1965 they produced *Your Navy – Past and Present* aimed at junior readers and the frontispiece showed a sailor from HMS *Excellent* carrying a kitbag in front of the *Victory*'s figurehead. However, apart from that, the navy produced little history for general consumption – the Naval Historical Branch was aimed at analysing recent campaigns for operational purposes and internal use. Soon the *Victory* would also have to compete with other attractions in the Portsmouth area, and with other preserved ships, both there and in other parts of the country.

200 Years

The 200th anniversary of her launch was celebrated in 1965. Chatham, still a working dockyard with no tourist infrastructure, staged a gundeck scene in Number Two Covered Building Slip, a dramatic setting, if a little anachronistic. Portsmouth had a ceremony onboard the ship attended by naval officers, local dignitaries, former commanders-in-chief including Sir Charles Little, and the First Sea Lord. In the evening there was a *son et lumière* with a cast headed by Sir Laurence Olivier reprising his role as Nelson in *Lady Hamilton* from twenty-four years earlier. It was scripted by Captain Jack Broome and other actors included Robert Morley as Chaplain Scott and David McCallum as 'Jock'. But, on the whole, society was increasingly anti-militaristic as the campaign against the American war in Vietnam gathered momentum and the hippy counter-

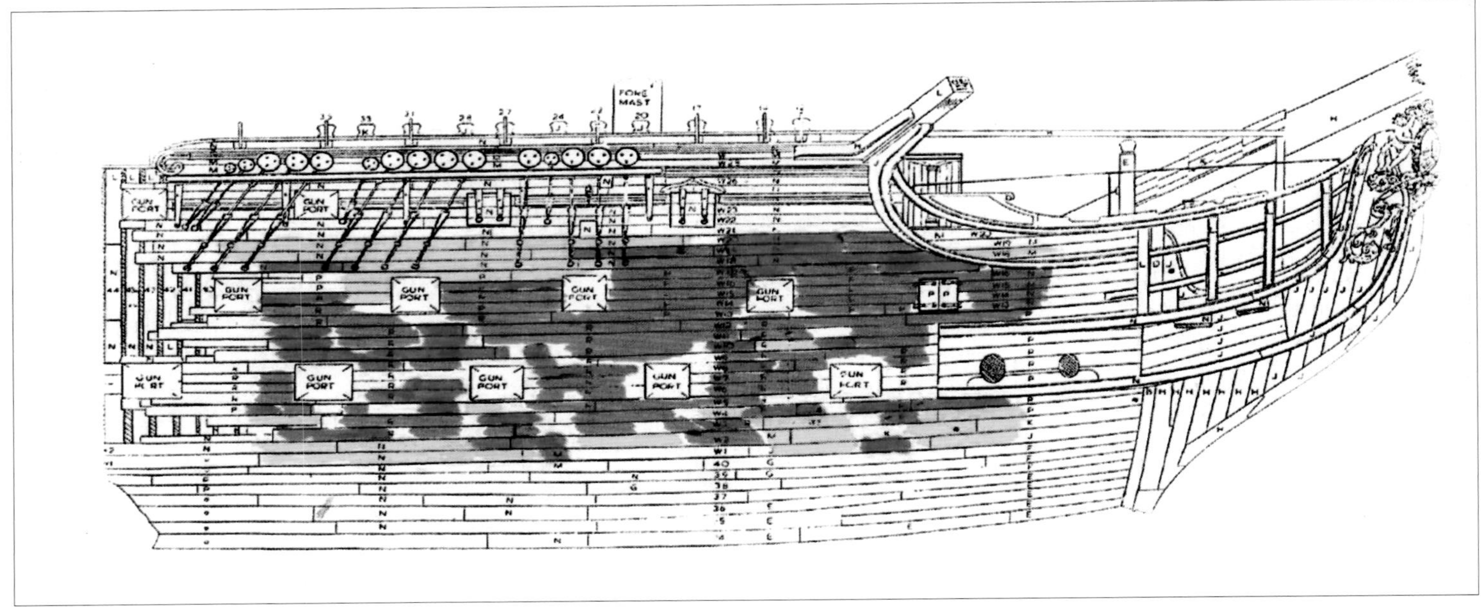

Some of the decay of the teak-iroko sandwich planking of the starboard bow in 2002. Timber marked in yellow is sound, that in blue has at least one laminate decayed and red shows two or more laminates decayed.

(© VATC Report)

culture was very far from the naval ethos. Meanwhile, in 1974, the naval base became known as HMS *Nelson*, and the only sailors wearing the cap tally *Victory* were those actually attached to the ship, mostly near the end of their service and employed as guides.

The *Victory* was far from complete after her major repair up to 1964. Arthur Bugler, the constructor in charge of the repairs, wrote in 1966, 'the major repairs in the hold were completed in 1964, but sandwiched between these repairs and those completed during the 1920s, there remains a belt extending round the ship that is in need of repair.'[43] Work was done in the area from the turn of the bilge to the lower deck gunports from 1964–73, the grand magazine and fore peak, 1968–73 and the stern structure in 1973–80. A modern chief petty officers' mess was set up at the stern of the middle deck, though historians have always argued that the area should really be the wardroom, and visitors might come away with the impression that the ship had an admiral, captain, crew, but no junior officers.

Work went on with the ship's bow in 1980–89. Portsmouth Dockyard was reduced to a Fleet Maintenance Base while its work was partly privatised, and cuts by the Defence Secretary John Nott threatened even further reductions. Sandwiched between anti-militarism and modernism which saw ships as outdated and the submarine as the only real threat from the sea, the navy was in danger of being erased from the public consciousness until the Argentineans invaded the Falkland Islands. A task force was sent to the South Atlantic in a great feat of organisation, and there was great emotion in Portsmouth as ships sailed out past the Round Tower, then returned victorious a few months later. But the city was having to change, and become less reliant on the navy. It moved increasingly into financial services, education and tourism. It always had Southsea beach for an older kind of holiday, but it began to exploit its very rich history with a series of publications sponsored partly by the city council. The city lives by the sea as much as any in Britain, with accessible views over the harbour and its warships, and the Solent with passing container ships, oil tankers, cruise liners and yachts. It came to public notice in 1982, the year of the Falklands, with the raising of Henry VIII's *Mary Rose* – though that proved a disappointment to many as the ancient timbers looked distinctly unimpressive. With the arrival of the ironclad *Warrior* in 1987, the dockyard acquired a unique ensemble of historic warships.

The sinking of the *Implacable* in 1949 provided a catalyst. The World Ship Trust was formed soon afterwards with the motto 'Never again.' Leaving aside that setback, England was one of the first countries to indulge in ship preservation, according to Norman J Brouwer in *The International Register of Historic Ships* of 1999, 'Great Britain was one of the first nations to become seriously involved in maritime historic preservation... When Sir Francis Drake returned from the first British circumnavigation of the globe with his ship *Golden Hind*... Queen Elizabeth decreed that the vessel should be permanently preserved in London....' Many factors – national pride, local initiative, and often the chance survival of individual hulls as hulks, training ships and depots – led to a collection of more than a thousand vessels which National Historic Ships regards as valuable. There are five major stars – the tea clipper *Cutty Sark* of 1869 at Greenwich, Brunel's *Great Britain* of 1843, rescued from the Falkland Islands and preserved in Bristol, and the three Portsmouth ships – the *Mary Rose, Victory* and *Warrior*.

The *Victory* Museum, founded by the SNR and opened in 1938, became the Portsmouth Royal Naval Museum in 1972 after gifts by Mrs J. G. McCarthy, an American admirer of Nelson, of memorabilia of the admiral. It expanded into the nearby Georgian storehouse and would eventually take over the whole range. Other exhibits included the state barge of Charles II, which had been kept intrusively on board the *Victory* for many years, and several figureheads from the Trafalgar period. Soon the museum expanded well beyond the Nelson and *Victory*, though to some it was still 'the regimental museum of the Royal Navy', appealing particularly to old sailors and their families.

Work continued on the *Victory* in the 1990s, and there was an increasing tendency for it to be seen as a demonstration of craft skills, rather than a nuisance. The policy, as described in 1992, was '"finish as we go", minimum areas of work at any one time' and attempting to give visitors value for money.'[44] However, the 1980s policy of using a 'teak-iroko sandwich' for much of the planking was proving unsuccessful as much of it began to decay quickly. Timber supply remained one of the greatest single problems; in 1998 it was reported that a supply of teak from Venezuela was delayed by more than two years, there was a ban on teak from India and Thailand while political problems in Burma meant that no orders could be placed there.

Changes

From 1990, civilian guides began to replace naval and marine personnel. They were retired chiefs and petty officers and senior NCOs and among them was Peter Goodwin, a former artificer on nuclear submarines who had already published a book on the structure of naval ships. In 1991 he was promoted to become the ship's first keeper and curator, though it took some time to have his appointment regularised. As well as providing an element of continuity among the ever-changing naval personnel, he brought a great deal of knowledge and enthusiasm to the job. He disputed the location of the site of Nelson's death on the orlop deck, and this led to a great deal of controversy. The Save the Victory Fund provided finance to build two cutters for the ship, in memory of the long-standing captain Peter Whitlock, who died on Trafalgar Day 1989. One, built by Jack Chippendale of Wrotham in Norfolk, was intended to be used at sea and proved highly successful, representing the ship at many events. For example, in 1997 she was transported to Santa Cruz by HMS *Grafton* to commemorate the loss of Nelson's arm at Tenerife. The Chatham cutter was not intended to sail but to hang from the quarter of the ship, but it decayed and was replaced by a yawl in 2008.

A sample of decayed planking, 2010.

(© *HMS Victory*)

There was frustration in 1993, when a planned sponsorship scheme of the dockyard sites by Sea Containers fell through after five years of negotiation. The ship had a good deal of media attention during 1994, with the Tour de France passing her, the D-Day commemoration and an episode of *The Generation Game*. The cutter and the ship herself were used in a

BBC production of Jane Austen's *Persuasion,* the beginning of an Austen boom which lasted several years. There was a revival of media interest in 2003–4 with the films *Master and Commander* and *Pirates of the Caribbean.* By 2003, the dockyard, successively managed by Flagship Portsmouth Trust and Portsmouth Historic Dockyard Ltd, had moved over to a single-ticket arrangement for each site with joint marketing. However, it remains true that the main attractions – the *Victory, Mary Rose, Warrior* – tended to tell their

Staging used to repair the planking of the port bow in 2011.

(© HMS Victory)

own stories and not the general story of British naval history and ship development. The *Victory's* fore topsail was the largest original object to survive from Trafalgar. Damaged by shot holes during the battle and by square holes cut by souvenir hunters afterwards, it was displayed at the Royal Naval Exhibition of 1891 but lost until rediscovered in the Portsmouth Naval Barracks in 1960. It was conserved and made ready for display during the great event of 2005.

Trafalgar 200

The Trafalgar bicentenary events are best described by its main organiser, the late Colin White, when he contrasted them with those of 1905:

Seven o'clock, on a fine sunny morning in late June 2005. The scene is the captain's cabin of the amphibious assault ship HMS *Ocean* – one of more than 150 vessels assembled at Spithead for the International Fleet Review, the first event of The Trafalgar Festival. Breakfasting with the ship's commanding officer, Commodore Tony Johnstone-Burt and the commander of the French contingent, Vice-Amiral Jean Mazar, I jokingly congratulate Amiral Mazar on his country's magnanimity in taking

part in an event celebrating a battle in which France had been defeated. "But of course we are here!" he exclaimed. "We are cousins. Sometimes we may not like each other very much – but we come to each other's weddings!"

...There were times during the summer of 2005 when all Britain seemed in the grip of what the *Daily Mail* (clearly somewhat surprised!) dubbed, 'Nelson Fever.' For four packed months, events were held all over the country, and indeed across the world. Over the Trafalgar Weekend itself (21–23 October) there were over 6,000 events, ranging from dinners in village halls to an international peal of church bells that began in New Zealand and winged its way westwards across the world to Honolulu....

It was 'a summer-long Festival' which included 'the National Maritime Museum's highly-acclaimed international exhibition *Nelson and Napoleon* [and] the moving national service at St Paul's Cathedral on

The figurehead and the starboard side if the *Victory* resplendent in Portsmouth, 2005.

(Jonathan Eastland/Ajax)

A service is held on the deck on the 21 October each year to commerate Nelson's sacrifrice at the Battle of Trafalgar.

(Jonathan Eastland/Ajax)

Sunday 23 October 2005, attended by almost all the Royal Family.'

> '...It is this more personal element that remains strongest in my memory. And one key moment stands out. Once again, the scene is a cabin in a ship at Portsmouth but this time it is Nelson's own cabin in HMS *Victory* on Trafalgar Night itself. Dinner is about to begin, and around the long, polished mahogany table sit all the most senior admirals in the Royal Navy. First, however, the Lord High Admiral – Her Majesty the Queen – rises to propose the traditional toast. But instead of using the simple words 'The Immortal Memory' with which Nelson was remembered in 1905, Her Majesty reverts to words used when the toast was first drunk on board the *Victory* in 1846: 'To the Immortal Memory of Lord Nelson and those who fell with him.'[45]

This naturally provided a peak in *Victory* visitors, and free-flow was used as an alternative to guided tours during Easter to October – though the appearance of the ship was marred by a huge escape tower.

In 2012 came the biggest single change in management in the ship's long history, when it was transferred to civilian hands as part of the National Museum of the Royal Navy. This had originated in the SNR's *Victory* Museum but had much expanded since then. It now included the Submarine Museum across the harbour at Gosport, the Royal Marines Museum in Eastney on the other side of Portsea Island and the Fleet Air Arm Museum much further away in Yeovilton. It also includes historic ships such as the World War I cruiser *Caroline* in Belfast. Reports of a change were treated with hostility by the press to start with, with headlines such as 'Skint Navy surrenders Nelson's HMS *Victory*.' There were fears that she might be used to host corporate events – though she had been doing so for many years – and it was implied that she might be taken over by foreigners. In fact, she was being transferred to an organisation with strong naval connections, still under the control of the Ministry of Defence, with headquarters 100 yards from the ship, and she would remain a naval flagship, now for the Second Sea Lord. The transfer allowed outside fundraising and immediately a £25 million donation from Sir Donald Gosling was announced, matched by a similar grant from the MOD – which may be enough to secure the ship for the future.

Victory Today

Today the Royal Navy plays a smaller role in the nation's consciousness than in the past. Apart from the Falklands, recent wars have been land-based and the other services have seemed subsidiary to the army – though there is no reason to believe that will always be the case. The *Victory*'s place in the national psyche seems secure. Among the other Portsmouth ships, the *Mary Rose* is, of course, much older but her hull is far less intact and it has taken considerable skill to display her attractively. The *Warrior* is more prominent at the entrance to the dockyard but her history is less glorious and she is unfamiliar to the public. Even the dispassionate tones of the National Register of Historic Vessels convey some of the excitement associated with the *Victory*:

> She is a national and international icon with special place in the affection of the British people... HMS *VICTORY* represents the embodiment of British Naval mastery at its absolute height, when Britain's supremacy over all of her actual or potential enemies was unchallenged and the Royal Navy enjoyed supreme command of the world's oceans... The ship is preserved and presented to a high standard and is the leading attraction in Portsmouth Historic Dockyard and a major landmark in the City of Portsmouth. She is held in great affection by the local residents.

BIBLIOGRAPHY

General and Local History

Kent in the Napoleonic Wars, ed Peter Bloomfield, place 1987
Linda Colley, *Britons*, London, 1994
Margaret J Hoad, *Portsmouth as others have seen it* Part 2, Portsmouth, 1973
Holger H Herwig, *The Origins of World War I*, Cambridge, 2003
Erasmus Phillipps, *Of the State of the Nation*, London, 1725

Naval History

William Bell Clark, ed, *Naval documents of the American Revolution*, Vol 1. Washington, 1964
Sir Julian Corbett, *The Campaign of Trafalgar*, London, 1910
Jan Glete, *Navies and Nations*, Stockholm, 1993
C I Hamilton, *Portsmouth Dockyard Papers*, 1852-1869, Winchester, 2005
Hoad and Patterson ed, *Portsmouth and the Crimean War, Portsmouth*, 1973
J Holland Rose, *Lord Hood and the Defence of Toulon*, Cambridge, 1922
William James, *The Naval History of Great Britain*, reprinted London, 2002
Barrie Kent, *Signal! A History of Signalling n the Royal Navy*, Clanfield, c 1993
Brian Lavery, *Nelson and the Nile*, London, 1997
— *Nelson's Fleet at Trafalgar*, Place date
— *Nelson's Navy*, London, 1989
J A Lowe, ed, Portsmouth Records Series, 1990, *Records of the Portsmouth Division of Marines, 1784-1800*
Janet Macdonald, *Feeding Nelson' Navy*, London, 2006
Bernard Pool , *Navy Board Contracts*, London, 1966
Nicholas Rodger, *The Wooden World*, London, 1986
--- *The Command of the Ocean*, London, 2004
A N Ryan, *The Defence of British Trade in the Baltic*, in *English Historical Review*, 1959
--- *The Melancholy Fate of the Baltic Ships in 1811*, in *Mariners Mirror*,
Tim Voelcker, *Admiral Saumarez versus Napoleon*, Woodbridge, 2008
Peter Warwick, ed, *Voices from the Battle of Trafalgar*, Cincinnati, 2003
John G Wells, *Whaley, the Story of HMS* Excellent, Portsmouth, 1980
Rif Winfield, *British Warships in the Age of Sail, 1793-1817*, Barnsley, 2005

Shipbuilding and Related Topics

D K Brown, *Before the Ironclad*, London, 1990
Burney, *New Universal Dictionary of the Marine*, 1815, reprinted New York, 1970
Edmund Bushnell, *The Compleat Ship-Wright*, London, 1664
Falconer's Marine Dictionary, 1769, reprinted London 2006
John Fincham, *An Outline of Shipbuilding*, 3rd edition, London, 1852
John Franklin. *Navy Board Ship Models*, London, 1989
Thomas Heywood, *His Majesty's Royal Ship*, reprinted New York, 1990
House of Commons, *Report on the Means of Supplying His Majesty's Navy with Timber*, 1771
R F Johnson, *The Royal George*, London, 1971
Brian Lavery, *The Ship of the Line*, 2 vols, London, 1983
--- *Arming and Fitting the English Man of War*, London, 1986
--- *Building the Wooden Walls*, London, 1990
— *Able seamen*, London, 2011
Sir Robert Seppings, A Letter Addressed to Rear-Admiral Sir Charles Ekins, London, 1824
David Steel, *Naval Architecture*, London, 1805, reprinted 1977
Tredrea and Sozaev, *Russian Warships in the Age of Sail, 1696-1860*, Barnsley, 2010

HMS *Victory*

Arthur Bugler, *HMS* Victory, *Building, Restoration and Repair*, London, 1966
Kenneth Fenwick, *HMS* Victory, London, 1959
C N Longridge, The *Anatomy of Nelson's Ships*, Hemel Hempstead, 1970
A P McGowan, *HMS* Victory, *Her Construction, Career and Restoration*, London, 1999
John McKay, *Anatomy of the Ship*, Victory, London, 1987

Biographies, Collective

Broadley and Bartelot, *Three Dorset Captains at Trafalgar*, London, 1906
John Charnock, *Biographia Navalis*, 6 vols, London, 1994-8
Dorothy Hood, *The Admirals Hood*, London, 1942
Nauticus [James Harris], *The Naval Atlantis*, 2 vols, London, 1788
John Marshall, Royal Naval Biography, 12 vols, London, 1823-35
Oxford Dictionary of National Biography, available online
William O'Byrne, *A Naval Biographical Dictionary*, 2 vols, reprinted Place 1990
James Ralfe, *The Naval Biography of Great Britain*, 4 vols, London, 1828

Biographies, Individual

Lady Jane Bourchier, *Memoir of Sir Edward Codrington*, London, 1873
Suffolk Records Society, *John Constable's Correspondence*, vol 2, 1964
Emma Minto, ed, *Life and Letters of Sir Gilbert Elliot*, London, 1874
Olaudah Equiano, *Interesting Narrative*, London, 2003
R H Harris, *From Naval Cadet to Admiral*, London, 1913
Frederick Hoffman, *A Sailor of King George*, 1901, reprinted London, 1999
A M W Stirling, *Pages and Portraits from the Past, being the Private Papers of Sir William Hotham*, London, 1919
Thomas Keppel, *Life of Augustus Viscount Keppel*, London, 1842
Mary Lacy, *The Female Shipwright*, 1773, reprinted Greenwich 2008
W R Mends, *The Life of Admiral Mends*, London, 1899
J F Maurice, ed, *The Diary of Sir John Moore*, London, 1904
Sam Noble, *Sam Noble AB*, London, 1925
G S Parsons, *Nelsonian Reminiscences*, reprinted London, 1998
Jeffrey Raigersfield, *The Life of a Sea Officer*, London, 1929
C G Sloane-Stanley, *Reminiscences of a Midshipman's life*, Remington, 1893
J S Tucker, *Memoirs of the Earl of St Vincent, London*, 1844
Sir John Ross, Memoirs and Correspondence of Admiral Lord de Saumarez, London, 1838
Alfred Gatty, *Nelson's Spy, the Life of Alexander John Scott*, Reprinted London, 2002
Sir Edward Seymour, *My Naval Career and Travels*, London, 1911
Viscount Esher, *The Girlhood of Queen Victoria*, London, 1912,
A Diary of Royal Movements in the Reign of Queen Victoria, London, 1883
The Adventures of John Wetherell, C S Forester, ed, London, 1954
The Wynne Diaries, Anne Fremantle, ed, Oxford, 1937

Nelson

William Beatty, *The Authentic Narrative of the Death of Lord Nelson*, London, 1807
Clarke and MacArthur, *Life of Nelson*, London, 1809
Roger Knight, *The Pursuit of Victory*, London, 2005
N H Nicolas, *Dispatches and Letters of Lord Nelson*, 7 vols, 1844, reprinted London 1997
Colin White, *Nelson, the New Letters*, London, 2005

Navy Records Society

Vol 14, *Blockade of Brest*, vol 1, 1898
Vol 16, *Logs of the Great Sea Fights*, vol 1, 1899
Vol 24, *Letters of Sir Thomas Byam Martin*, vol 1, 1903
Vol 32, *The Letters and Papers of Charles, Lord Barham*, vol 1, 1906
Vol 39, *The Letters and Papers of Lord Barham, vol 3, 1896*
Vol 48, *The Private Papers of George, 2nd Earl Spencer*, vol 2, 1914
Vol 63, *Naval Miscellany* vol 3, 1927
Vols 69, 71, 75, 78, *The Sandwich Papers*, 4 vols, 1932-8
Vol 83, *Russian War1854*, 1943
Vol 89, *The Sergison Papers*, 1949
Vol 91, *Five Naval Journals*, 1951
Vol 100, *Nelson's Letters to his Wife*, 1958,
Vol 102, *The Fisher Papers*, vol 1, 1960
Vol 110, *The Saumarez Papers*, 1968
Vol 112, *The Rupert-Monck Letter Book*, 1969
Vol 138, *Shipboard Life and Organisation*, 1998

Journals

Illustrated London News
Mariners Mirror from 1911
Naval Chronicle
The Nelson Dispatch
Trafalgar Chronicle, Year Book of the 1805 club
Society for Nautical Research, *Annual Reports* especially 1937

Other

John Chandler et al, *The Seaman's Guide and New Coaster's Companion*, 1788 edition
E T Cook and Alexander Wedderburn, ed, *The Works of John Ruskin*, London, 1899
Guido Hinterkeuser, *Das Berliner Schloss*, Regensburg, 2012

MANUSCRIPTS

National Archives

Admiralty in-letters, ADM 1, including letters from admirals and captains
Admirals' journals, ADM 50
Captains' logs, ADM 51
Masters' logs, ADM 52, more navigational detail than the above
Ships' muster books, ADM 36, 37, 38, giving lists of crew for various dates

Pay books, AM 34, similar information to the above, but often better organised
Medical papers, ADM 101
Navy Board papers, ADM 106, including minutes, letters etc. Many of the in-letters are now indexed, which makes it much easier to find relevant material
PROB for wills, which can occasionally be revealing

National Maritime Museum
ADM/B and BP Series, letters from the Navy Board to the Admiralty
Lieutenants' logs, ADL/L series, often duplicate the information in the captains logs
Chatham letters and reports in CHA series
Portsmouth Dockyard letters and reports in POR series
Sandwich papers, SAN series
Pakenham papers, PAK series
CRK series, Croker collection of Nelson manuscripts
BGY series contains many single documents of interest

British Library
Kings 44, map of the Medway and of Chatham and Portsmouth Dockyards, 1774
Nelson papers, Additional Manuscripts 34902-34992, 36604-12 – most of Nelson's own letters are to be found in Nicolas above, but not the replies

National Museum of the Royal Navy
Arnold-Foster letter, 2012/79.1
Gunners Accounts, 1792-3, 921/82
Pursers Accounts, 1796-8, 83/1051
Purser's Journal, 1796-7, 53/4
Roteley papers, Royal Marines Museum
Rivers Papers, 1998/41/1, 2
Slop book, 1983/49-50

Admiralty Library, Naval Historical Branch
Recueil des Plusiers Plans de Ports, Thomas Atkinson's copy
Baltic Seas – Directions and Remarks, London, 1810
Captain Arthur Wilmhurst's Court Martial, Portsea, 1869, 177/21

Chatham Historic Dockyard Trust
Allan Papers

NOTES

CHAPTER 1

1 National Archives, ADM 106/1069/3
2 See John Franklin, *Navy Board Ship Models,* (London, 1989), p 177
3 Erasmus Phillipps, *Of the State of the Nation,* (London, 1725), pp 1–2
4 Quoted in Linda Colley, *Britons*, (London, 1994), p 65
5 Francois –Marie Voltaire, *Candide*, chapter 23
6 Olaudah Equiano, *Interesting Narrative*, (1789; reprint London, 2003), p 58
7 National Archives, ADM 3/66
8 Brian Tunstall, *Naval Warfare in the Age of Sail,* (London, 1990), p 65
9 Ibid p 90
10 *Falconer's Marine Dictionary*, (1769, reprint 1970), p 177
11 Quoted in Franklin, op cit, p 179
12 Quoted in Thomas Heywood, *His Majesty's Royal Ship,* (reprint New York, 1990), p 76
13 *Falconer*, op cit, p 179
14 Brian Lavery, *The Ship of the Line*, vol I, (London, 1983), p 107
15 Ibid, p 106
16 Navy Records Society, vol CXII, *The Rupert-Monck Letter Book*, (1969), p 254
17 Navy Records Society, vol LXXXIX, *The Sergison Papers*, (1949), p 120
18 E. T. Cook and Alexander Wedderburn, (ed,) *The Works of John Ruskin*, vol XIII (London, 1899), p 28
19 Navy Records Society, vol XXIV, *Letters of Sir Thomas Byam Martin*, vol I, (1903), p 4

CHAPTER 2

1 Edmund Bushnell, *The Compleat Ship-Wright*, (London, 1664), introduction
2 National Archives, ADM 7/662
3 Bernard Pool, *Navy Board Contracts*, (London, 1966), p 85
4 British Library, Kings 44
5 David Steel, *Naval Architecture*, (1805; reprint London, 1977), p 143
6 National Maritime Museum ADM/B/162
7 National Maritime Museum BP I 303
8 Ibid p 16
9 National Maritime Museum SAN/F/13
10 British Library, Kings 44
11 National Maritime Museum, SAN/V/5
12 House of Commons, *Report on the Means of Supplying His Majesty's Navy with Timber*, (1771), p 19
13 Ibid, p 24
14 Ibid, p 85
15 Brian Lavery, *Building the Wooden Walls*, (London, 1990), pp 53–54
16 Chatham Historic Dockyard Trust, Allan Papers
17 Mary Lacy, *The Female Shipwright,* (1773; reprint Greenwich 2008), p 81
18 Ibid, p 151
19 *Report on the Means of Supplying*, op cit, p 79
20 National Archives, PROB 11/876
21 *Report on the Means of Supplying*, op cit, p 23
22 National Archives, ADM 106/1133
23 National Archives, ADM 106/1148
24 National Maritime Museum, ADM/B/179
25 National Archives, ADM 106/1156
26 National Maritime Museum, ADM/B/200
27 British Library, Kings 34
28 *Falconer*, op cit, p 223
29 National Archives, ADM 354/177/212
30 National Archives, ADM 106/1152
31 National Archives, ADM 106/1151
32 National Archives, ADM 106/1154
33 Ibid
34 National Archives, ADM 180/6
35 National Maritime Museum, SAN/V/5
36 National Archives, ADM 106/1198/113
37 National Archives, ADM 106/1195
38 National Archives, ADM 7/662
39 National Archives, ADM 106/1240

CHAPTER 3

1 Roger Knight, *The Pursuit of Victory: The Life and Achievement of Horatio Nelson,* (London, 2005), p 9
2 John Charnock, quoted in Lavery, *The Ship of the Line,* op cit, vol I, p 98
3 National Archives, ADM 106/1198
4 National Archives, ADM 7/662
5 N. H. Nicolas, *Dispatches and Letters of Lord Nelson*, vol I, (1844; reprint London, 1997), p 4
6 W. Burney, *New Universal Dictionary of the Marine*, (1815; reprint New York, 1970), p 47
7 National Archives, ADM 106/1205 f 6
8 John Chandler et al, *The Seaman's Guide and New Coaster's Companion,* (1788 edition), pp 64–67
9 Nicolas, vol I, op cit, p 4
10 Chandler, op cit
11 National Maritime Museum, ADM/L/T/253
12 Frederick Hoffman, *A Sailor of King George,* (1901; reprint London, 1999), pp 2–5
13 Nicolas, op cit, vol I, pp 4–5
14 Ibid, p 260
15 Ibid, p 70n

CHAPTER 4

1 *Naval Documents of the American Revolution*, vol I, (Washington, 1964), p 356
2 Navy Records Society, *The Sandwich Papers*, vol I, (1932), p 328
3 Thomas Keppel, *Life of Augustus Viscount Keppel*, vol II, (London, 1842), p 6; Navy Records Society, *The Sandwich Papers*, vol II, (1933), p 17
4 *Sandwich Papers*, op cit, vol I, p 341
5 National Archives, ADM 2/104
6 Nauticus, *The Naval Atlantis,* (London, 1788), p 128
7 Nicholas Rodger, *The Wooden World,* (London, 1986), p 260
8 *Sandwich Papers*, vol II, p 17
9 Brian Lavery, *Arming and Fitting the English Man of War*, (London, 1986), p 98
10 Keppel, op cit, p 21
11 National Archives, ADM 1/2504
12 Ibid
13 *Sandwich Papers,* op cit, vol II, p 24
14 National Archives, ADM 106/1244
15 National Archives, ADM 2/104
16 *Sandwich Papers,* op cit, vol II, p
17 National Archives, ADM 1/2504
18 Ibid
19 National Archives, ADM 106/1243
20 National Maritime Museum, SAN/F/14/115
21 Keppel, op cit, p 67
22 *Sandwich Papers,* op cit, vol II, p 243

CHAPTER 5

1 Navy Records Society *Naval Miscellany* vol III, (1928), p 136
2 Navy Records Society vol XXXII, *The Letters and Papers of Charles, Lord Barham*, vol I, (1906), p I 294
3 Ibid, p 305
4 Ibid
5 Ibid, p 294
6 *Naval Miscellany*, op cit, vol III, pp 129–30
7 National Maritime Museum, PAK/2
8 Ralfe, *Naval Biography*, vol XX (1828), p 218
9 National Maritime Museum, PAK/2
10 Ibid
11 Tunstall, op cit, vol I, pp 138-41
12 National Maritime Museum, PAK/6
13 Ibid
14 R. F. Johnson, *The Royal George*, (London, 1971), passim
15 Tunstall, op cit, vol I, p 153
16 National Maritime Museum, PAK/6
17 National Maritime Museum, POR/D/24
18 National Archives, ADM 106/1261/205
19 J. Tredrea and E. Sozaev, *Russian Warships in the Age of Sail, 1696–1860*, (Barnsley, 2010)
20 National Maritime Museum, POR/D/25
21 Jeffrey Raigersfield, *The Life of a Sea Officer,* (London, 1929), p 83
22 National Maritime Museum, POR/D/25

[23] Dorothy Hood, *The Admirals Hood*, (London, 1942), p 100
[24] National Maritime Museum, POR/D/25
[25] British Library, Add MS 34902

CHAPTER 6

[1] Nicolas, op cit, vol I, pp 297, 299
[2] National Archives, ADM 51/1028
[3] Royal Naval Museum, Rivers Papers, 1998/41 (1)
[4] Raigersfield, op cit, p 104
[5] A. M. W. Stirling, *Pages and Portraits from the Past*, vol II, pp 52–53
[6] J. Holland Rose, *Lord Hood and the Defence of Toulon*, (Cambridge, 1922), pp 96–99
[7] Raigersfield , op cit, p104
[8] Nicolas, op cit, vol I, p 309
[9] Ibid, p 308
[10] Holland Rose, op cit, p 126
[11] Ibid, pp 125–26
[12] Nicolas, op cit, vol I, p 324
[13] Raigersfield, op cit, p 110
[14] National Archives, ADM 36/11577
[15] J. F. Maurice (ed) *The Diary of Sir John Moore*, vol I, (London, 1904), p 41
[16] William James, *The Naval History of Great Britain*, vol I, (1826–37; reprint London, 2002), pp 82–3
[17] National Archives, HO28/15
[18] Stirling, op cit, pp 54-55
[19] Emma Minto (ed) *Life and Letters of Sir Gilbert Elliot*, vol II, (London, 1874), pp 235, 236
[20] Nicolas, op cit, vol I, pp 357, 359
[21] J.S. Clarke and J. MacArthur, *Life of Nelson*, vol I, (London, 1809), pp 166-68
[22] Maurice (ed), op cit, vol I, p 103
[23] Nicolas, op cit, vol I, p 412
[24] Ibid, p 415
[25] Maurice (ed), op cit, vol I, p 131

CHAPTER 7

[1] Nicolas, op cit, vol II, p 51
[2] *United Services Journal*, (1840), p 347
[3] James, op cit, vol I, p 270
[4] Nicolas, op cit, vol II, p 50
[5] Navy Records Society, *Nelson's Letters to his Wife*, vol C, (1958), pp 216, 221
[6] Knight, op cit, p 649
[7] J. S. Tucker, *Memoirs of the Earl of St Vincent*, vol I, (London, 1844), p 149
[8] National Archives, ADM 52/3526
[9] Tucker, op cit, vol I, p 189
[10] Navy Records Society vol CXXXVIII, *Shipboard Life and Organisation*, (1998), pp 210–11
[11] Tucker, op cit, vol I, pp 177–79
[12] Ibid, p 223
[13] Anne Fremantle (ed), *The Wynne Diaries*, vol II, (Oxford, 1937), pp 112–13
[14] Tucker, op cit, vol II, p 173
[15] Ibid, p 185
[16] Nicolas, op cit, vol II, p 298
[17] Tucker, op cit, vol I, p 236
[18] Ibid, p 201
[19] Nicolas, op cit, vol I, p 298
[20] Tucker, op cit, vol I, p 220
[21] *Shipboard Life and Organisation*, op cit, pp 211–12, 567, 577–84
[22] Nicolas, op cit, vol II, p 53
[23] Ibid, p 290
[24] Tucker, op cit, vol II, p 242
[25] *Shipboard Life and Organisation*, op cit, p 584
[26] Ibid, p 213
[27] Tucker, op cit, vol I, pp 255–26
[28] Nicolas, op cit, vol II, p 344
[29] Ibid, p 346
[30] Tucker, op cit, vol I, p 259
[31] Ibid, p 262n
[32] Nicolas, op cit, vol II, p 346
[33] Navy Records Society, vol XVI, *Logs of the Great Sea Fights*, vol I , (1899), p 205
[34] Tucker, op cit, p 231
[35] Navy Records Society, vol XLVIII, *The Private Papers of George, 2nd Earl Spencer*, vol II, (1914), pp 370, 379, 384, 387
[36] *Shipboard Life and Organisation*, op cit, p 587
[37] Ibid, p 215
[38] Nicolas, op cit, vol II, p 434
[39] Brian Lavery, *Nelson and the Nile*, (London, 1997), passim
[40] Dupin
[41] National Archives, ADM 36/14945
[42] National Maritime Museum, ADM/BP/17B
[43] National Archives, ADM 106/1819
[44] National Maritime Museum, CHA/B/3
[45] G. S. Parsons, *Nelsonian Reminiscences*, (London, 1844), p 73
[46] National Maritime Museum, CHA/B/6
[47] National Maritime Museum, CHA/B/3
[48] National Archives, ADM 106/1819
[49] Ibid
[50] National Maritime Museum, CHA/B/3
[51] Ibid

CHAPTER 8

[1] Colin White, *Nelson, the New Letters*, (London, 2005), p 309
[2] C. S. Forester (ed), *The Adventures of John Wetherell*, (London, 1954), pp 27–28
[3] Ibid, p 31
[4] Peter Bloomfield (ed), *Kent in the Napoleonic Wars*, (Kent Archives Office, 1987), p 121
[5] National Archives, ADM 1/408
[6] Nicolas, op cit, vol IV, p 507
[7] Suffolk Records Society, *John Constable's Correspondence*, vol II, (1964), pp 33–34
[8] National Archives, ADM
[9] White, op cit, p 344
[10] Knight, op cit, p 445
[11] Nicolas, op cit, vol V, p 51
[12] White, op cit, p 330
[13] Nicolas, op cit, vol V, p 50n
[14] Ibid, p 58
[15] Ibid, pp 65–67
[16] Ibid, p 69
[17] White, op cit, p 315
[18] Nicolas, op cit, vol V, p 71
[19] Ibid, pp 72–73
[20] Navy Records Society, vol XIV, *Blockade of Brest*, vol I, (1898), p 17
[21] National Archives, ADM 1/408
[22] National Archives, ADM 238/12
[23] National Archives, ADM 51/1647
[24] Nicolas, op cit, vol V, p 149
[25] National Archives, ADM 1/407
[26] Knight, op cit, pp 643-44
[27] *The Nelson Dispatch*, vol V, (July, 1996), p 398
[28] White, op cit, p 20
[29] Nicolas, op cit, vol V, p 461
[30] *Nelson Dispatch*, op cit, vol V, p 11; White, op cit, p 88
[31] Naval Historical Branch, *Recueil des Plusiers Plans de Ports*, op cit
[32] National Archives, ADM 1/407
[33] National Archives, ADM 1/408
[34] National Maritime Museum, CRK/8/152-154
[35] Knight, op cit, pp 652, 668
[36] White, op cit, p 113
[37] Monmouth letter book 18
[38] White, op cit, p 116
[39] Alfred and Margaret Gatty, *Nelson's Spy*, (n.d, reprint Shropshire, 2002), p 191
[40] Ibid, pp 191–92
[41] Portsmouth Records Series, *Records of the Portsmouth Division of Marines, 1784–1800*, (1990), p lii
[42] Navy Records Society, *Five Naval Journals*, (1951), p 11
[43] Stirling, op cit, p 120
[44] Nicolas, op cit, vol VI, p 361
[45] Ibid, p 279
[46] National Maritime Museum, CRK/8/43
[47] National Maritime Museum, CRK/2/8
[48] National Maritime Museum, CRK/2/18
[49] National Archives, ADM 36/15895
[50] National Maritime Museum, CRK/3/106
[51] National Museum of the Royal Navy, 1983/1049-1983/1050
[52] National Maritime Museum, BGY/T/1
[53] National Maritime Museum, CRK/12/58
[54] National Archives, ADM 35/1996
[55] National Archives, ADM 238/12
[56] National Maritime Museum, CRK/22/93
[57] Knight, op cit, p 477
[58] Nicolas, op cit, vol VI, p 236
[59] National Archives, ADM 1/408
[60] National Archives, ADM 1/407
[61] National Archives, ADM 1/5365
[62] National Archives, ADM 1/407
[63] National Maritime Museum, CRK/10/93
[64] National Archives, ADM 1/408
[65] *Nelson Dispatch*, op cit, vol VI, pp 184–87
[66] National Archives, ADM 1/408
[67] Knight, op cit, p 476
[68] White, op cit, p 81
[69] Ibid, p 295
[70] Ibid, p 302
[71] Ibid, p 336
[72] Ibid, pp 337–39
[73] National Archives, ADM 1/407
[74] Knight, op cit, p 464
[75] National Archives, ADM 1/407
[76] White, op cit, p 387
[77] National Archives, ADM 1/407
[78] National Archives, ADM 1/408
[79] Ibid
[80] Lavery, *Ship of the Line*, vol I, (London, 1983), p 211
[81] *Shipboard Life and Organisation*, op cit, p 518
[82] National Maritime Museum, CRK/6/115
[83] Gatty, op cit, pp 130–31
[84] National Maritime Museum, WEL/8
[85] Quoted in Lavery, *Nelson's Fleet at Trafalgar*, (Greenwich 2004), p 71
[86] National Maritime Museum, BGY/T/1
[87] National; Archives, ADM 1/408
[88] Gatty, op cit, pp 125–26
[89] National Archives, ADM 1/407
[90] National Archives, ADM 1/408
[91] White, op cit, p 364
[92] British Library, Additional MS 34953
[93] National Maritime Museum, CRK/2
[94] Nicolas, op cit, vol V, p 319
[95] Ibid, p 360; National Archives, ADM 1/408

CHAPTER 9

[1] Nicolas, op cit, vol I, p 309
[2] A. M. Broadley and R.G. Bartelot, *Three Dorset Captains at Trafalgar*, (London, 1906), p 125
[3] White, op cit, p 415
[4] Royal Naval Museum, Chevallier Papers
[5] National Maritime Museum, AUS/2
[6] Nicolas, op cit, vol VI, p 410
[7] Gatty, op cit, p 171
[8] Ibid, p 172
[9] National Maritime Museum, WEL/30
[10] *Naval Chronicle*, Vol XVIII, (1807), p 190
[11] Gatty, op cit, p 174

[12] Navy Records Society, vol XXXIX, *The Letters and Papers of Lord Barham*, vol III, (1896), p 398
[13] Nicolas, op cit, vol VI, pp 43–45
[14] Knight, op cit, p 496
[15] Ibid, p 493
[16] Nicolas, op cit, vol VI, p 462
[17] Sir Julian Corbett, *The Campaign of Trafalgar*, (London, 1910), p 170n
[18] Nicolas, op cit, vol VI, p 468
[19] British Library, Additional MS 34968
[20] Broadley and Bartelot, op cit, p 132
[21] Nicolas, op cit, vol VI, p 496
[22] Lady Jane Bourchier, *Memoir of Sir Edward Codrington*, vol I, (London, 1873) p 4
[23] Nicolas, op cit, vol VII, p 5
[24] Broadley and Bartelot, op cit, p 135
[25] National Maritime Museum, BRP/6
[26] National Museum of the Royal Navy, 1064/83
[27] National Archives, ADM 35/1996
[28] National Maritime Museum, BGY/T/1
[29] *Records of the Portsmouth Division*, op cit, pp lxvi, lvin
[30] Royal Marines Museum, Roteley Papers
[31] Nicolas, op cit, vol VII, pp 33
[32] National Maritime Museum, MON/3
[33] Nicolas, op cit, vol VI, pl 71
[34] Brian Tunstall, *Naval Tactics*, (n.p, n.d.) pp 249–50
[35] Nicolas, op cit, vol VII, p 60
[36] Ibid, p 133
[37] Broadley and Bartelot , op cit, p 140
[38] National Maritime Museum, WEL/30
[39] National Museum of the Royal Navy, 1064/83
[40] *Nelson Dispatch*, vol II, part II, (April, 2011), p 103
[41] *Five Naval Journals*, op cit, p 364
[42] Nicolas, op cit, vol VII, pp 139–40
[43] William Beatty, *The Authentic Narrative of the Death of Lord Nelson*, (London, 1807), p 18
[44] Peter Warwick (ed), *Voices from the Battle of Trafalgar*, (Cincinnati, 2003), p 127
[45] *Five Naval Journals*, op cit, p 364
[46] National Maritime Museum, WEL/30
[47] *Shipboard Life and Organisation*, op cit, p 274
[48] National Museum of the Royal Navy, Rivers Papers, 1998/41
[49] Nicolas, op cit, vol VII, pp 147–48
[50] Knight, op cit, p 515
[51] Nicolas, op cit, vol VII, p 150
[52] British Library, Additional MS 58050
[53] Beatty, op cit, pp 27–29
[54] *Five Naval Journals*, op cit, p 365
[55] Royal Marines Museum, Roteley Papers
[56] Beatty, op cit, p 29
[57] Ibid, p 31
[58] British Library, Additional MS 38050
[59] Royal Marines Museum, Roteley Papers
[60] Gatty, op cit, p 188
[61] Beatty, op cit, pp 36–53
[62] Ibid, p 35
[63] Nicolas, op cit, vol VII, pp 168–69
[64] National Maritime Museum, WEL/30
[65] Joseph Allen, *Memoirs of Sir William Hargood*, (Greenwich, 1841), p 289

CHAPTER 10

[1] National Maritime Museum, WEL/30
[2] Broadley and Bartelot, op cit, Appendix B, p 286
[3] National Maritime Museum, WEL/30
[4] Robinson p 64
[5] *Nelson Dispatch*, vol V, (July, 1996), p 398
[6] Royal Marines Museum, Roteley Papers
[7] Bloomfield (ed), op cit, p 64
[8] NC III 249-50
[9] National Archives, ADM 106/1156
[10] Nicolas, op cit, vol VII, pp 399–417
[11] *Five Naval Journals*, op cit, p 364
[12] National Maritime Museum, CHA/B/10, 11, 12
[13] Sir Robert Seppings, *A Letter Addressed to Rear-Admiral Sir Charles Ekins*, (London, 1824), pp 10-12
[14] James Ballingall, *The Mercantile Navy Improved*, (London, 1832), p 24
[15] National Maritime Museum, CHA/B/12
[16] Ibid
[17] National Archives, ADM 160/154
[18] National Maritime Museum, CHA/B/12
[19] *Oxford Dictionary of Quotations*, p 515
[20] Navy Records Society vol CX, *The Saumarez Papers*, (1968), pp 7–8
[21] Tredrea and Sozaev, op cit; *Russian Fleet*, pp 153 ff, 186 ff
[22] Tim Voelcker, *Admiral Saumarez versus Napoleon*, (Woodbridge, 2008), pp 186–87
[23] Ibid, p 43, translated by Captain Christer Hägg
[24] *Byam Martin*, op cit, p 57
[25] National Archives, ADM 52/3878
[26] Naval Historical Branch, *Baltic Seas – Directions and Remarks*, (London, 1810)
[27] Sir John Ross, *Memoirs and Correspondence of Admiral Lord de Saumarez*, vol II, (London, 1838), pp 131–32
[28] Jan Glete, *Navies and Nations*, (Stockholm, 1993), p 708
[29] A. N. Ryan, 'The Defence of British Trade in the Baltic', in *English Historical Review*, (1959), pp 443–56
[30] Voelcker, op cit, p 113
[31] Ross, op cit, vol II, p 215
[32] National Archives, ADM 37/2876
[33] Ross, op cit, vol II, p 233
[34] Voelcker, op cit, pp 151–52
[35] Marshall, *Naval Biography*, vol VI, p 54; vol VII, p 83
[36] Ross, op cit, vol II, p 268
[37] A. N. Ryan, 'The Melancholy Fate of the Baltic Ships in 1811', in *Mariners Mirror*, (1964), pp 123–34
[38] *The Saumarez Papers*, pp 293–94; see also Voelcker, op cit
[39] Ross, op cit, vol II, p 295
[40] National Maritime Museum, ADM BP/33C
[41] National Archives, ADM 106/3226
[42] National Archives, ADM 106/1887
[43] National Archives, ADM 106/1888

CHAPTER 11

[1] National Archives, ADM 1/1346
[2] Ibid
[3] National Archives, ADM 1/1333
[4] National Archives, ADM 1/1322
[5] National Archives, ADM 1/1346
[6] National Archives, ADM 1/1352
[7] National Archives, ADM 1/1339
[8] Quoted in Brian Lavery, *Nelson's Navy*, (London, 1989), p 172
[9] John G. Wells, *Whaley, the Story of HMS Excellent*, (Portsmouth, 1980), pp 201–03
[10] See Nelsonandhisworld.co.uk
[11] Ibid
[12] National Archives, ADM 106/235
[13] National Archives, ADM 106/1910
[14] Viscount Esher, *The Girlhood of Queen Victoria*, vol I, (London, 1912), p 83
[15] *A Diary of Royal Movements*, vol I, (London, 1883), pp 325–27
[16] John Fincham, *An Outline of Shipbuilding*, 3rd edition, (London, 1852), p 21
[17] D. K. Brown, *Before the Ironclad*, (London, 1999), pp 127–31
[18] Navy Records Society, vol CXLVII, *The Milne Papers*, (2004), pp 223–25
[19] C. G. Sloane-Stanley, *Reminiscences of a Midshipman's Life*, (Remington, 1893), pp 23-102; passim
[20] National Archives, ADM 101/125/2
[21] C. I. Hamilton, *Portsmouth Dockyard Papers, 1852–69*, (Winchester, 2005), p 133
[22] M. J. Hoad and A. T. Patterson (ed), *Portsmouth and the Crimean War*, (Portsmouth, 1973), pp 5-10
[23] Navy Records Society vol LXXXIII, *Russian War 1854*, (1943), p 141
[24] Hamilton, op cit, p 214
[25] Ibid
[26] Ibid, p 429
[27] Ibid, pp 325–26
[28] Ibid, p 320
[29] W. R. Mends, *The Life of Admiral Mends*, (London, 1899), p 26
[30] Naval Historical Branch, *Captain Arthur Wilmhurst's Court Martial*, 177/21 (Portsea, 1869)
[31] R. H. Harris, *From Naval Cadet to Admiral*, (London, 1913), p 3
[32] Brian Lavery, *Able Seamen*, (London, 2011), p 71
[33] Hamilton, op cit, p 90
[34] *Illustrated London News*, 15 July 1865, p 52
[35] H. L. Fleet, *My Life and a Few Yarns*, (London, 1922), pp 31–33
[36] National Archives, ADM 1/6062
[37] Tapprell Dorling, 'Officers on Board HMS *Victory*, Portsmouth, 1 March 1869' in *Mariners Mirror*, (1948), pp 120-21
[38] Sam Noble, *Sam Noble AB*, (London, 1925), pp 40–49
[39] Margaret J. Hoad, *Portsmouth As Others Have Seen It*, part II, (Portsmouth, 1973), p 19
[40] Ibid, pp 17–20
[41] Sir Edward Seymour, *My Naval Career and Travels*, (London, 1911), p 249
[42] Barrie Kent, *Signal! A History of Signalling in the Royal Navy*, (Clanfield, 1993), pp 20–21
[43] *The Royal Navy List and Naval Recorder*, (London, 1905), pp 272–74
[44] National Maritime Museum, SNR/6/1
[45] *The Times*, 23 October 1905
[46] Navy Records Society, vol CII, *The Fisher Papers*, vol I, (1960), p 14
[47] Quoted in Holger H Herwig, *The Origins of World War I*, (Cambridge, 2003), p 150

CHAPTER 12

[1] National Archives, ADM 116/2340
[2] National Archives, ADM 116/2340
[3] Society for Nautical Research, *Annual Report*, (1937), p 75
[4] National Maritime Museum, SNR/7/2
[5] National Archives, ADM 116/2340
[6] Nigel H. Grundy, *W. L. Wyllie R.A, the Portsmouth Years*, (Portsmouth, 1996), p 19
[7] National Archives, ADM 116/2340
[8] Ibid
[9] National Maritime Museum, SNR/7/2
[10] National Archives, ADM 116/2340
[11] National Maritime Museum, SNR/7/4
[12] National Archives, ADM 116/2340
[13] Grundy, op cit, p 18
[14] National Maritime Museum, MM SNR
[15] National Archives, ADM 1/27660
[16] *Annual Report*, op cit, p 76

17 Churchill College, Cambridge, Sturdee Papers, SDEE
18 National Maritime Museum, SNR/7/4
19 *The Times*, 14 September 1923
20 *Annual Report*, op cit, p 82
21 Grundy, op cit, p 22
22 *Annual Report,* op cit, p 84
23 National Maritime Museum, SNR/6/1
24 *Annual Report*, op cit, p 13
25 Alexander Grant, *Victory in Command; Through the Hawse Pipe; the Autobiography*, (n.d; reprint London, 2006)
26 Sir William James, *The Sky was Always Blue*, (London, 1951), p 210
27 Ibid, p 223
28 Martin Gilbert, (ed), *The Churchill War Papers Volume III: The Ever-Widening War*, (London, 2000), pp 162, 1028
29 William James, op cit, p 223
30 Vera Laughton Mathews, *Blue Tapestry*, (London, 1948), pp 241–42
31 Hannan Swaffer, *What Would Nelson Do?*, (London, 1946), p 26
32 B. Warlow, *Shore Establishments of the Royal Navy*, (Liskeard, 1992), pp 134–35
33 Grant, op cit, p 147
34 Ibid, p 143
35 Arthur Bugler, *HMS Victory: Building, Restoration and Repair*, (London, 1966), pp 169–70
36 R. W. Love and J. Major (ed), *Year of D-Day, the Diary of Admiral Sir Bertram Ramsay*, (Hull, 1994), pp 61, 76
37 Grant, op cit, pp 146, 144
38 Ibid, p 149
39 *The Times*, 3 December 1949
40 National Archives, ADM 1/27660
41 Ibid
42 Ibid
43 Bugler, op cit, p 99
44 VATC Minutes, 18 October 1992
45 Foreword to Richard Shannon, *Nelson Remembered: the Nelson Centenary, 1905*, (Karawara, WA, 2007).

INDEX

HN refers to Horatio Nelson,
ill to an illustration,
port to a portrait,
diag to a diagram